Performing the Iranian State

Anthem Middle East Studies

The **Anthem Middle East Studies** series is committed to offering to our global audience the finest scholarship on the Middle East across the spectrum of academic disciplines. The twin goals of our rigorous editorial and production standards will be to bring original scholarship to the shelves and digital collections of academic libraries worldwide, and, to cultivate accessible studies for university students and other sophisticated readers.

Performing the Iranian State

Visual Culture and Representations of Iranian Identity

Edited by
Staci Gem Scheiwiller

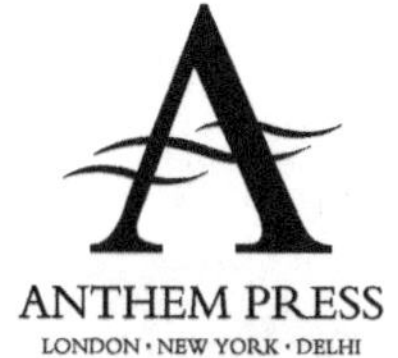

ANTHEM PRESS
LONDON · NEW YORK · DELHI

Anthem Press
An imprint of Wimbledon Publishing Company
www.anthempress.com

This edition first published in UK and USA 2014
by ANTHEM PRESS
75–76 Blackfriars Road, London SE1 8HA, UK
or PO Box 9779, London SW19 7ZG, UK
and
244 Madison Ave. #116, New York, NY 10016, USA

First published in hardback by Anthem Press in 2013

British Library Cataloguing-in-Publication Data
A catalogue record for this book is available from the British Library.

Library of Congress Cataloging-in-Publication Data
The Library of Congress has catalogued the hardcover edition as follows:
Performing the Iranian state : visual culture and representations of
Iranian identity / edited by Staci Gem Scheiwiller.
pages cm
Includes bibliographical references.
ISBN 978-0-85728-293-4 (hardcover : alk. paper)
1. Arts and society–Iran–History–20th century. 2. Arts and
society–Iran–History–21st century. 3. Arts, Iranian–Political
aspects. 4. Group identity in art. 5. Group identity in the
performing arts. I. Scheiwiller, Staci Gem, editor of compilation.
NX180.S6P444 2013
700.1'030955–dc23
2012047460

ISBN-13: 978 1 78308 328 2 (Pbk)
ISBN-10: 1 78308 328 X (Pbk)

This title is also available as an ebook.

CONTENTS

ACKNOWLEDGMENTS

I would like to express my deepest gratitude to all the contributors who made this anthology possible. They put in much time and hard work into producing the highest quality of essays. I am especially indebted to fellow contributor David Simonowitz who looked over preliminary drafts of the proposal and introduction and offered unending encouragement. Thank you so much. I am also grateful to those at Anthem Press for their support and patience, including Camron Michael Amin, Tej Sood, Janka Romero and Rob Reddick.

Finally, I appreciate the efforts of Michael Jerryson at Eckerd College. In 2008, our dissertation group had conceived of the idea "Performing the State," and later, he gave his blessing to pursue the idea on my own and in my own field. He has been a great inspiration and the truest, most loyal colleague. I am privileged to know him. Thank you.

A NOTE ON TRANSLITERATION

For the transliteration of Persian words in this volume, I have decided to Romanize them as closely to the spoken Western Persian in Iran as possible. I did consider the guidelines according to the *International Journal of Middle Eastern Studies*, as well as the Bahai system of transliteration developed by Shoghi Effendi, but opted for the simplest forms that match the vernacular.

1

INTRODUCTION: SETTING THE STAGE

Staci Gem Scheiwiller

What does it mean to "perform the State," and in particular, what does this action mean in relation to the country of Iran?[1] The concept of the "State" as a modern phenomenon has had a powerful impact on the formation of the individual and the collective, as well as on determining how political entities are perceived in their interactions with one another in the current global arena. In a time of mass globalization and hypercapitalism, State identities have become strengthened, as they demonstrate formidable presences in the globalized media, including satellite transmissions, the Internet and cellular phone communications. There has always been some sort of global contact, such as the silk roads that connected Asia, Africa and Europe, or the intricate infrastructure that led most of the ancient world back to Rome. Yet, increased daily contact between all geographic locations since the height of European imperialism during the nineteenth century has created a situation in which average persons are perpetually performing State identities for the world to see. The democratization of media has made us all international ambassadors, so to speak. Investigations of how these particular State identities may be formed, represented, disseminated, comprehended and maintained are crucial to discovering how structures of knowledge are constructed in relation to the world and to us individually.

In response to these continual rapid changes in defining and representing oneself and one's relationship to others through the dynamic mediation of State apparatuses and global media, this collection of essays is an attempt to understand the individual's and group's relationships to the State and how this bidirectional interaction is performed and depicted, particularly in relation to the State of Iran. Furthermore, this collection of essays features a variety of case studies focusing on persons or groups who perform the Iranian State or a State of Iran as outlined, manifested and confronted by Iranian society, those in exile and the world at large.

"Performing the State" refers to an individual or a group of persons reenacting rituals, ceremonies, customs, traditions and laws, or donning certain guises that either accomplish the State's goals or rebel against them as forms of critique. Performativity may occur through a process of citationality, in which persons are transformed and molded into perceived constructions of identity (i.e., through propaganda, modeled behavior, societal pressure or a religious norm), or through materialization, in which persons engage in material discursive practices (i.e., walking through the city) and apparatuses (i.e., contact with institutions). This anthology examines various approaches to determining the

Iranian State via the performativity of persons with the intention of illuminating how social practices, ideologies and identities are shaped, visualized, circulated and repeated – not only nationally, but also worldwide.

Two cartoons, produced by Iranians and published in Iran, comment on how the modern perception of Iran is performed and depicted at both home and abroad, presenting early examples of Iranian performativity. Both cartoons show "Iran" from the Constitutional Revolution (1906–11) and how the concept of world exhibitions in the colonial theater are mocked and later reconfigured (Figures 1.1, 1.2).[2] In the first cartoon, a typical exposition depicting life in the capital city of Tehran, as it would have been shown in a European or American world fair, illustrates an underdeveloped country in comparison to those in Europe and North America. Three booths, aligned from right to left, are entitled *kaleh-pazi* (literally, head-cooking shop), *dizi-pazi* (meat stew shop) and *haleem-pazi* (meat porridge shop) and are shown selling these inexpensive cooked dishes, usually to poorer segments of society. Peddlers, dogs, cats and one donkey traverse the dirty unpaved streets. The scene seems rather dismal and undeveloped, considering that it takes place in the nation's capital.

In another cartoon, the State of Iran is depicted differently by showing a State celebration. The portrait of the king, Mozaffar al-Din Shah Qajar (r. 1896–1906), rises above the architectural scene, centered with arms folded. His presence splits the composition into two parts. Flanking him are two flags that show the insignia of monarchial Iran, the lion and the sun. The slogan on the upper left-hand corner proclaims, "Became a constitutional monarchy; despotism was destroyed." This cartoon was published in the newspaper *Kashkul* (1907–1908) after the shah's death, as he had instated a constitutional monarchy on his deathbed in 1906. The then current shah Mohammad 'Ali (r. 1907–1909) is absent from the cartoon, perhaps because of his oppressive measures resulting in the Minor Tyranny of 1908. The words *jashn-e melli* (national celebration) flank Mozaffar al-Din Shah, indicating it is a gregarious event for the country. Historian Shiva Balaghi also confirms that the presence of lamps, mirrors and trays of sweets and flowers suggest that a festival is taking place.[3]

Beneath the looming presence of the king are several groups of well-dressed men who are discussing the affairs of Iran. They seem to stand in a compressed, metaphorical State of Iran. On the far left, a mulla shows his displeasure with the constitutional monarchy to another: "All the chaos, yelling of this group and child's play of constitutional monarchy are the conspiracy of these kids coming out of school [Dar al-Fanun, a State polytechnic]." The next European-garbed group, described by Balaghi as "educated technocrats,"[4] praises the students: "Wonder, everything [here] is from the schools and its students." The third pair is European, and one remarks with surprise, "To tell you the truth, Friend, never in Paris have I seen such a civilized, rational, impressive and splendid celebration! It appears that the Iranians are […] progressing." Finally, a government official exclaims, "[T]hese people run around like a four-horse carriage. God willing they do not fall onto the ground."

The first cartoon illustrates an Iranian cognizance of how Iran is portrayed abroad in the colonial theater as backward to justify European and American world dominance and superiority. This image was created when elaborate world fairs functioned as fabricated spaces of national performances through stages, props, booths and architectural façades with prosceniums, and actors and indigenous persons were hired to perform so-called traditional dances. Iran, in this case, is portrayed as bereft of the modern advancements that the king, Nasir al-Din Shah Qajar (r. 1848–96), had actually undertaken, while the neighboring exhibits of European and North American countries had shown mostly their great technological innovations. The first cartoon seems to address two issues: the racist depictions of Iranians abroad and the failures of the Qajar dynasty (1786–1925) to make Iran more competitive and pioneering in an international setting. Moreover, Iran as a political entity exists in relation to other States, and thus the modern State is inherently global by nature. Identities are continuously played out against one another as a way to differentiate one State from others, so that "Iranianness" (or any other national marker) is usually contingent on other national identities, which have all become actors in world politics. Sociologist Anthony Giddens has even remarked that the enormous scope and organization of modern States has transformed them into "players" or "agents" that possess anthropomorphic qualities.[5] They are all in a great chess game on the globe and negotiate relationships with one another.

The second cartoon, although not directly a response to the first one, shows a different Iran in front of another proscenium with persons who are all presumably powerful and educated (and not of the poorer segments of society). There is a conscious effort on the cartoonist's part to create a positive image of Iran by highlighting the significant roles of particular players: mullas, technocrats, Europeans and government officials. Most of their conversations speak highly of the Iranian State, promoting its semblance of progress that is indebted to the efforts of the students. The only dissenters are the mullas who question the students' abilities to know what constitutes a good government. Historically during the Constitutional Revolution, conservative religious elements were increasingly seen as hindrances to modernity and technological development,[6] so it is fitting that the cartoonist would frame the mullas as the antagonists in this period cartoon.

A more contemporary example of performativity in Iran proper takes place during the ancient Zoroastrian holiday Chaharshanbeh Suri, which always creates anxiety for the Islamic Republic, so much so that the government did not formally recognize it until 2004 under President Khatami (elected 1997–2005),[7] although it still strongly discourages the ritual as dangerous and un-Islamic. The occasion occurs on the evening of the last Tuesday of the Persian calendar year, and because *chaharshanbeh* means "Wednesday," the ritual theoretically lasts until early Wednesday morning. The event is celebrated by burning bonfires and leaping over them, fire being a revered and purifying agent in the Zoroastrian religion. Because of its pre-Islamic origin, the ritual is often used as a tactic to defy the Islamic Republic, which is fashioned after the tenets of Twelver Shi'i Islam. Considering that the Zoroastrian population in Iran is less than 2 percent,[8] and most of the celebrants are not Zoroastrian, the ritual becomes a subtle way of questioning State policies without outright political protest. The State understands this covert action of dissent, and so the event also provides an opportunity for the police to make arrests. In 2010 this holiday marked a particularly tense political moment in light of the contested 2009 presidential election victory of President Mahmoud Ahmadinejad (elected 2005–present) over former prime minister Mir-Hossein Mousavi (b. 1942), thus demonstrating a highly charged potential for protest through this celebration.

This non-Islamic ceremony is also a conduit to reaffirm a sense of Iranian identity in *différance* to an Arab or Islamic one, because many aspects of Iranian life had become Islamicized/Arabicized after the Iranian Revolution (1978–79).[9] Artist Shirin Neshat (b. 1957) has remarked that during her return to Iran in 1990 after an 11-year hiatus, Iranian identity in the public sphere had become more Islamicized and Arabicized: "Street names had changed from old Persian names to Arabic and Muslim names [...]. This whole shift of the Persian identity toward a more Islamic one created a kind of crisis."[10] The literal renaming of public space by the State was an effort to revolutionize even the physicality of the cityscape and to reinforce the State's message on the most mundane level. After the revolution, the new Islamic Republic had reclaimed the streets. Yet a ritual such as Chaharshanbeh Suri recovers not only the streets in the name of the people, but also affirms a pre-Islamic Persian identity of the streets themselves, which may have been mitigated by their Arabicized renaming.

One must be careful, though, not to demarcate which political stance is more compelling or to assume that the only competing ideologies in Iran are those influenced by Twelver Shi'i Islam or pre-Islamic history. The rhetoric of the Pahlavi dynasty (1925–79) constantly invoked a pre-Islamic identity, such as the 2,500-year celebration of the Iranian monarchy in 1971, an opulent occasion that incurred much ire, considering the vast divide between the wealthy and impoverished classes. In addition, one must not think that to protest the policies of the Islamic Republic one must proclaim a Persian, pre-Islamic identity. For example, in a photograph taken by Shirin Aliabadi (b. 1973), a woman assumed to be Iranian is called "Miss Hybrid IV" (2008), because she wears a *rosari* (headscarf), a denim jacket *manteau* (overcoat), blue eye contacts and a bandage on her nose, presumably from a plastic surgical procedure (Figure 1.3). She has dyed her hair blond and blows a bubblegum bubble defiantly into the viewer's face. On one hand, one could argue that this photograph demonstrates the nature of globalization or a colonial mentality that privileges blond-haired, blue-eyed women with smaller noses as ideals of beauty, to which women of color must aspire. Yet, it is possible to understand this photograph as one of rebellion against the State. The woman depicted has chosen an alternative Iranian identity to perform and in doing so, she visually shows her displeasure with the State, as she does not fit the ideal Muslim woman who behaves modestly and covers most of her hair. One may dismiss "Miss Hybrid" as seduced by the "West,"[11] but this condemnation is exactly what the ideology of the State wants one to think in order to devalue and denigrate this woman's attempt to express herself. In addition, it is misleading to think that each ideology is a closed system of beliefs and agendas, because they are actually porous and in dialogue with other ideologies. "Miss Hybrid" may be a Shi'a Muslim and celebrate Chaharshanbeh Suri, but she also adopts another veneer that communicates a different point of view from the other two, hence the name "Miss Hybrid."

What is Meant by the "State"?

In this project, the word "State" is used to distinguish a governing set of relations that set arbitrary borders that have been created though modern conflicts such as war and nationalism, whereas a "nation" is a group of people that claims an exclusive ethnic, cultural, linguistic, religious or blood relationship. Ultimately, all States and nations are constructed to accomplish political aims and are modern phenomena that enable surveillance, censorship, oppression and even ethnic cleansing. When discussing the materiality of bodies and matter (addressed below), States and nations themselves do not exist a priori, but are founded in reified objects or traces, such as in invented symbols and traditions,[12] through various ideological apparatuses that replicate power relations,[13] circulated printed matter in the vernacular that forms the consciousness of a nation,[14] or in material bodies (both human and nonhuman) that engage in material discursive acts.

The State's duty, in general, is to produce a sense of the nation that will unite its citizens, such as to create a common enemy for waging war,[15] but all States, regardless of how liberal and democratic they may seem, are oppressive, because they usually come into existence through some sort of violence. The State's social contract with its citizens is generally uneven, with people having to dispel most of their rights in order to obtain few liberties and protections. Frankfurt School intellectual Walter Benjamin describes in "Critique of Violence" (c. 1920–21) the inherently violent nature of this social contract, as the nature of a contract is inevitably brutal:

> All violence as a means is either lawmaking or law-preserving […]. [T]he origin of every contract […] points toward violence […]. [T]he power that guarantees a legal contract is […] of violent origin even if violence is not introduced into the contract itself. When the consciousness of the latent presence of violence in a legal institution disappears, the institution falls into decay.[16]

It is the threat of violence that compels parties to enter into agreements, and it is the threat of violence that holds the agreements together. Yet, the social contract can never be an equal relationship between the State and its people because of the State's immensity and power (i.e., military, police and infrastructure). As Benjamin states, only when the State is weakened can the other party (i.e., the people) rise in revolution, which in itself is another tumultuous event.

With this characterization of a generally violent, repressive State in mind, I follow anthropologist Michael Taussig in capitalizing the word "State" to connote a modern notion of the State that has become an entity unto itself.[17] He cites Shlomo Avineri's *Hegel's Theory of the Modern State* (1972), which explains that by capitalizing the word "State," one implies that the State is a foreboding and oppressive entity, much like the one described by Thomas Hobbes in the political treatise *Leviathan* (1651).[18] Capitalizing "State" also gives its signification a fictional character, because no "State" exists as a thing or machine except in material bodies (both human and nonhuman), interrelations and sign systems:

> [I]f precisely put as the cultural constitution of the modern State – with a big S – the fetish quality of whose holism can be nicely brought to our self-awareness by pointing not only to the […] way we […] entify "the State" as a being unto itself, animated with a will and mind of its own, but also by pointing to the not infrequent signs of exasperation provoked by the aura of the big S […]. For what the notion

> of State fetishism directs us to is [...] the existence and reality of the *political power* of this *fiction*.[19]

The State exists only as a fetish, because the State is not a living, breathing entity, although in the modern world it has become understood as such. Moreover, the State is not an actual thing, but an abstract concept. Its power structures then become instilled in people, things and signs, which creates an aura of omnipotence, even in one's own mind; hence, Taussig calls this relationship between a person and the State "the nervous system," because the body internalizes the concept of the State as a personal panopticon that continually surveys the subject.

One may think of the State as a monolithic being when the word is capitalized, but it exists, in part, as a set of co-opted relations that include the human body and its own material relationships with the world. A running theme in most of Taussig's work is the mimetic faculty (based on a 1933 essay by Walter Benjamin): when one coexists with the threat of the State on a daily basis, the body and the State become so entwined that they cannot any longer be separated. The image of the person and that of the State begin to mirror each other in the "nervous system." What exists as the "real" and what exists as an imaginary bogey become indistinguishable, thus magnifying the brutal persona of what is thought of as the State. Moreover, the interest of this collection is not the actual infrastructure of the State itself, but how it is interpreted, played out and represented by the human body and its relationships to its surroundings.

The concept of the "nation" in this project is defined as an "imagined one." In *Imagined Communities* (1983), Benedict Anderson traces the rise of national identity to the mass production of print capitalism (i.e., the printed word). When people began to read publications in their own vernacular, this act fostered a sense of shared experience and imaginary kinship with unknown persons in similar communities (as opposed to just one community, into which one was born). In 2001 Sandra Freitag expanded Anderson's creation of an imagined community in her essay on India, "Visions of the Nation," by including other popular media such as photography and not solely the printed word. Freitag's incorporation of other mass media into the production of a national consciousness moves away from Anderson's paradigm that privileges the European invention of print culture as one of the main components of establishing nationalism.

A major early work on Iranian nationhood as an imagined construct is *Iran as Imagined Nation* (1994), in which Mostafa Vaziri deconstructs both the political entity of Iran and the ethnic identities that exist there. He uses the historiography of European Orientalists to show how they reflected their own nationalist formations and struggles onto their understandings of Iran. The Orientalists created an idea of Iran, which in turn, the Iranians adopted. (In 2001 historian Mohamed Tavakoli-Targhi would later demonstrate the bilateral nature of Orientalism in *Refashioning Iran*, showing that both Orientalists and Iranians fashioned each other.) Orientalists became invested in Iran as an Aryan nation, because they viewed the cultural heritage of Egypt and Sumer as Semitic, and out of their anti-Semitic sentiments, sought another bastion of civilization with which to identify. Before Orientalist intervention, Iran's multiethnic, multilingual, diverse inhabitants did not fixate solely on an ancient Aryan heritage as the major or only basis of an Iranian identity.

Like the State, the concept of the "nation" is also violent. For a State of a particular nation to form, it must exclude those who do not fit the definitions of a nation or those whom the State deems defiant and rebellious. Yet, those excluded do not necessarily go away; they may still live within the State and remain part of its history and existence, despite their second-class or unwanted status. Edward Said explains this phenomenon in *Freud and the Non-European* (2003), in which he posits that psychoanalyst Sigmund Freud's *Moses and Monotheism* (1939) was a way for Freud to work out his identity of being both Jewish and European. In *Moses and Monotheism,* Freud describes how the escaped Jews from ancient Egypt kill Moses, a non-Jewish Egyptian, and Said views this act as the only way for those of the Exodus to create and sustain a monolithic sovereignty. Said sums up his main point: "[I]dentity cannot [...] constitute or even imagine itself without that radical originary break or flaw which will not be repressed, because Moses was Egyptian, and therefore always outside the identity inside [...] history either overrides or represses the flaw."[20] Said points out that a particular group identity forms at the expense of another, even if the groups share some striking similarities.

Contemporary discourses specifically on the theoretical nature of the Iranian State became particularly prominent in the years preceding the Iranian Revolution, as many intellectuals and revolutionaries sought to create alternative forms of government to the monarchy of Mohammad Reza Shah Pahlavi (r. 1941–79). One of the most influential publications that has, in part, shaped the current democratic theocracy of the Islamic Republic is *Velayat-e faqih* (Governance of the Jurisconsult) of 1970 by Ayatollah Ruhollah Khomeini (1902–89). In addition, events, such as the CIA-backed coup d'état of Mohammad Reza Shah over the democratically elected prime minister Mohammad Mosaddeq (r. 1951–53), the Iranian Revolution, the Iran–Iraq War (1980–88), diaspora, globalization and the Green Revolution (2009–10), have forever changed the modern Iranian State and have led to more scholarly revisions and reconsiderations of its porous, reflexive, malleable and mobile nature. This particular collection of essays highlights modern Iran, as it has developed during the long nineteenth century, when European colonization was at its height and the modern world was forming into the entity it has become today. Furthermore, the anthology creates dialogues with past discourses on the Iranian State and continues discussions that redefine it, in particular by featuring the performative, discursive acts of individuals, both living in Iran and in diaspora, and how that performativity through the presented human body either affirms the State's goals or becomes a tactic in rebelling against it.

The Body

If the State exists only in fetishized objects, symbols and signs, then its presence must emerge in material forms, and in this collection, the scholars focus particularly on the human body, its performativity and activity and how it is portrayed. Philosopher Tonja van den Ende mentions in "In Search of the Body in the Cave" that the image of the body is more than the photograph in one's passport,[21] but in relation to the State, that photograph actually says a lot about citizenship and representation, making the body a system of signs that potentially signifies national identity. It is difficult to imagine that not too long ago, in the early twentieth century, passports did not have photographs of the individuals carrying them. Inadvertently, through the contemporary passport, both its picture and the person holding it become representations of the State, whether the person carrying the passport wants to be or not. The material possession of the passport and its photograph, along with its signage, all work in tandem as one crosses international borders. Ironically though, while the passport may grant international freedom, it can also make one a prisoner within arbitrarily set boundaries.

The State has historically materialized through the human body as an important physical manifestation. Before modern types of government, sovereignty used to rest in the king's body. In modern States, however, sovereignty does not rest on a king-head and divine right, but on the body of the people who compose the State. According to Anderson in *Imagined Communities*, this shift occurred when print culture gave rise to a national consciousness that encouraged people to think of themselves as a united, special entity that excludes others, instead of as part of a conglomerate of tribes or cultural groups within a monarchy or empire.

In relation to the French Revolution (1789–99), philosopher Michel Foucault elaborates on this change of power from the king to the people based on prescriptions of the body:

> In a society like that of the seventeenth century, the King's body wasn't a metaphor, but a political reality. Its physical presence was necessary for the functioning of the monarchy [...]. On the contrary, it's the body of society which becomes the new principle in the nineteenth century [...] the great fantasy is the idea of a social body constituted by the universality of wills. Now the phenomenon of the social body is the effect not of a consensus but of the materiality of power operating on the very bodies of individuals.[22]

Therefore, before the modern State, the king's body was under constant observation, from what he ate to when he had sex, because he literally embodied the State. During the modern era, the body of each citizen has come under domination and scrutiny, molding them into proper citizens who will perform State agendas. In *Discipline and Punish* (1975), Foucault also details the rise of institutions, such as elaborate psychiatric asylums and prisons, along with daily controls, such as restrictions on masturbation and rigid timetables, which began a comprehensive project that would shape people's bodies into serving the State, thus making them into suitable representatives of a seemingly united society.

Although both Anderson's and Foucault's arguments center on European examples, I suggest that similar cases could be made in relation to Iran, especially during the Constitutional and Iranian Revolutions of the twentieth century. There has been a noticeable shift in modern Iranian history that, at first, focused on king figureheads such as Nasir al-Din Shah and Reza Shah Pahlavi (r. 1925–41), and now more on how social groups of people (i.e., women, religious groups, the youth and homosexuals) operate and function within the Islamic Republic. It is through these behaviors and actions of various social and political groups, as well as their codifications, that have helped defined the current Iranian State.

Perhaps, too, this shift from focusing on solely on the State to the performative actions of those living under the State is reflective of current trends in academia. For example, Cyrus Schayegh's "Seeing Like a State" (2010), whose title is a nod to James C. Scott's *Seeing Like a State* (1998), argues that the emphasis on formulating the history of the Pahlavi dynasty in terms of only the State has produced scholarship that fails to incorporate other aspects of life and local narratives into Pahlavi histories; hence, scholars of Iran have viewed histories of modern Iran like a State (a method that Schayegh calls "statism").[23] Scott's own book recounts how States reorganize society into forms that are "legible" to (only) itself – in ways that the State can see and govern clearly without respect to its subjects' needs and diversities. Afshin Marashi's *Nationalizing Iran* (2008), however, has demonstrated how the triad of State, society and culture have melded to conceive and to manipulate a modern Iranian national identity:

> Mohammad Reza Shah Pahlavi's claims of authority, as Shah *of Iran* and Light *of the Aryans*, thus were not tied to sources of power above or outside the nation but rather were grounded in the fabric of society itself. This transformation was based on the premise that state and society were tied together by a common culture [...]. [T]he notion of a social abstraction characterized by a congruence of state, society, and culture [...] presumed a novel set of institutional and cultural arrangements that became feasible only as a result of the changes that took place in the late nineteenth and early twentieth centuries.[24]

What both Schayegh's and Marashi's arguments shed light on is that scholars often take for granted both the power of the State on its subjects as well as its seemingly natural position between society and culture, when actually, that relationship is completely unnatural and not predetermined. There is a delicate balance between the modern State, society and culture, but State ideologies have become so pervasive and persuasive that those three have often been collapsed into one another or taken for granted. Furthermore, investigations of the State make one question whether the body cannot perform the State or its prescriptions in daily life. In a modern context, with the State controlling and dictating almost all aspects of society and culture, it is questionable if this triad of State, society and culture can be isolated or independent from one another in their current conditions. In a Foucaultian sense, perhaps everything "performed" directly or indirectly indexes the State (and by default, society and culture as well), even if the action is rebellious.

The human body is also important as a fetish and agent of the State, as a set of laws and regulations on paper mean nothing unless human beings carry them out and enforce them,[25] (either through their own bodies or human-made devices such as surveillance cameras). Both philosopher Louis Althusser and Taussig use the policeman as an example of an embodiment of the State. For Althusser, the policeman (among other people in society) interpellates a person of interest by calling out "Hey you!"[26]

By signaling out the other person, the policeman's interpellation reaffirms that person as a socially constituted being in a particular society. The person is metaphorically being called out by the State and is therefore not invisible or meaningless, but a very part of the system of signs and apparatuses controlling and monitoring other subjects. Althusser claims quite clearly, "[*A*]*ll ideology hails or interpellates concrete individuals as concrete subjects*."[27] The continuum of bodies in one social/political structure is interpellated as subjects who cannot escape this hailing. In a similar vein to Althusser, Taussig's example focuses on Jean-Paul Sartre's criminal figure Saint Genêt, who eroticizes the State by dreaming of seducing a policeman, because the policeman is a physical embodiment of the State itself. By fantasizing about groping the policeman, he would also grope the State and further find ways to penetrate a State that has always appeared elusive and unavailable to the average subject. If "[t]here is nothing outside of the text" or outside ideology,[28] then one always makes, breaks or obeys the law, but in the case of Saint Genêt, he longs to make love to it, as if it were another human body.

Although this collection is focused on the body performing the State and its visual representations thereof, I do want to note that the identity and legitimacy of the State may manifest in other forms, such as in the land or in public spaces, as demonstrated in Neshat's example of renamed streets. In another instance, historian Firoozeh Kashani-Sabet in *Frontier Fictions* (2000) examines discourses on nationhood in nineteenth-century Iran that have connected the land to the identity of Iran itself. The land, rather than the people or language, was used to construct a national identity, at least until Reza Shah's Persianization programs of the 1930s. The boundaries of Iran were fabricated, mainly according to Firdausi's national epic, the *Shahnameh* (Book of Kings, c. 1010). The preservation of Iran's ancient borders has created problems in the past, because the modern national borders had changed (for instance, Qajar forces had fought the British for the city of Herat in Afghanistan between 1856–57 and lost). Yet, since many scholars have also addressed the notion of Iranian Diaspora in their work, the cultural rhetoric of *Iran zamin* (the land of Iran) in defining the State and nationhood or performing them, proves difficult. For instance, many Iranians in diaspora are performing a Pahlavi State as opposed to an Islamic Republican one, even if they had been against the shah. Many customs, manners and vocabulary have changed since the revolution ended in 1979, so that the Iran remembered in diaspora is not the same one existing now. In addition, with the fluidity of persons traveling across the globe (whether in the material or virtual world), any State can be performed technically anywhere without regard to a physical border or land.

Finally, there has been much debate on materiality versus language in the formation of the world, ideology and understanding of how knowledge is produced. Some scholars suggest that material matter, and specifically the body, has been lost in framing the world as discourses, discursive statements and representations. These arguments, however, are not as oppositional as they may seem and go hand in hand in comprehending how societal and State formations operate. The State of Iran and its nation(s) are formed through discourses (predicated on the discourses of specific individuals and groups and on the power relations behind these collections of discursive statements), but these discourses find material ways of existing, such as through flags, money and land, as well as through actions, practices, rituals and laws performed by human bodies.

One must be wary however, as philosopher Judith Butler has argued in *Bodies That Matter* (1993), that the body is not simply a natural formation that has been inscribed by social and political discourses, meaning that the natural things of the world are not merely blank screens shaped by social constructions.[29] For example, philosopher Simone de Beauvoir's classic statement, "One is not born, but rather becomes, a woman," is certainly correct in that the notions of gender and how men and women should behave are social prescriptions that vary from culture to culture.[30] Yet, this statement may imply that sex is a natural condition, whereas gender is a construct, and this sort of worldview may dismiss the importance of the body in a material world and the physical body's own agency in both the discourses on power and discursive practices. In addition, a social constructionist or postmodernist view may privilege systems of language as the basis of building or dismantling society, but if everything is discourse and representation, then the bidirectional relationships between word and matter may be neglected.

Performativity

This collection of essays focuses on not only the human body and how it signifies the Iranian State, but also on the repeated discursive, material practices that various persons and groups act out in society that help define the State or subvert it. Furthermore, the human body can act as a representation and system of signs and indeed function as a cultural screen when it takes part in rituals, ceremonies, repetitions and performances. Yet, this collection also considers *how* human bodies come to signify the State or rebel against it, and in turn, how discursive practices may also bring about or reinforce particular materializations of the body.

"Performativity" is the course of repeated discursive practices that either delineate or reinforce societal agendas, expectations or norms: "Performativity is [...] not a singular 'act,' for it is always a reiteration of a norm or set of norms, and to the extent that it acquires an act-like status in the present, it conceals or dissimulates the conventions of which it is a repetition. Moreover, this act is not primarily theatrical; indeed its apparent theatricality is produced to the extent that its historicity remains dissimulated (and, conversely, its theatricality gains a certain inevitability given the impossibility of a full disclosure of its historicity)."[31] The repetitive performative act reinforces ideology continuously, but the theatrical nature of the performance also hides that the act is repeated and constructed. Yet that is how ideology works – it is incessantly embedded in the culture of one's society, so much so that one does not even realize it is there: "[T]hose who are in ideology believe themselves by definition outside ideology: one of the effects of ideology is the practical *denegation* of the ideological character of ideology by ideology: ideology never says, 'I am ideological.'"[32] The repetitious performative act is an ideological mask that becomes commonplace and thus taken for granted, to the extent that it may not be questioned or investigated, ensuring its longevity and ability to disseminate particular political aims. One may or may not have a choice or the wherewithal to choose particular performative acts, but when one does diverge from these models of rituals/actions, one may make it possible to contest stereotypes and expectations and therefore incite social change.

Although Butler does attempt to account for the materialization of the body through performative acts, the ontology of the body and the acts themselves are not thoroughly explained. Butler's theories rely mostly on citationality, such as gender performances based on significations whose "meanings [are] already socially established."[33] Yet, philosopher Karen Barad expands Butler's definition of performativity by including the intra-activities between human and nonhuman bodies within the discursive practices of materiality and not only citationality:[34] "[R]elational ontology is the basis for my posthumanist performative account of the production of material bodies [...] advocating [...] *a causal relationship between specific exclusionary practices embodied as specific material configurations of the world* (i.e. discursive practices/(con)figurations rather than 'words') *and specific material phenomena* (i.e. relations rather than 'things')."[35] Identities, such as those based on gender, nationality and so forth, may come about, not only by persons quoting an already-established sign system, but also through their interactions with the material world and with other material bodies, such as physical exchanges with the city or institutional shapings of the body through various apparatuses (i.e., the military or the hospital). For instance, one's physical body may actually change shape through contact in war or with medical practices, not solely by mimicking the surrounding sign system that demarcates a culture. Yet, whichever approach to performativity a scholar may take, this collection of essays does not seek to dispute Butler's notion of citational performativity over a more ontological one, but offers different studies on how the Iranian State may be performed and visually demonstrated, therefore keeping the notion of "performativity" in play and in flux.

Performativity in general occurs when persons engage in discursive practices that include participation in rituals, ceremonies, societal norms and laws. According to Louis Althusser in "Ideology and the State," discursive practices are indicative of State ideologies that continually oppress and reinforce the powers of the ruling elite: "[I]deology talks of actions: I shall talk of actions inserted into *practices*. And I shall point out that these practices are governed by the *rituals* in which these practices are inscribed, within the *material existence of an ideological apparatus* [...] a small mass [...] a funeral, a minor match at a sports' club, a school day, a political party meeting."[36] Therefore, one of the main conduits for the State to manifest in is the human body, which continually performs the State through various actions that seem commonplace and pervade everyday life. From the time of youth, when one recites certain affirmations in the classroom, to the time of death and the funerary rites that follow, one's life and death are continual performances of discursive practices that delimit one's society, culture and State.

Although Althusser defines discursive practices as replications of State ideology, philosopher Michel de Certeau in *The Practice of Everyday Life* (1984) adds the notion of "tactics," that is practices or actions that allow average people to empower themselves – to enunciate the "I" (which is itself composed of layers and not a monolithic Cartesian subject): "[A] tactic is a calculated action determined by the absence of a proper locus [...]. The space of the tactic is the space of the other [...] it must play on and with the terrain imposed on it and organized by the law of a foreign power [an outside power other than the self] [...] a tactic is an art of the weak."[37] These tactics include walking, reading and talking within a linguistic system dominated by power relations. Within de Certeau's definitions, one may able to find one's own individuality and agency in a situation, in which one typically does not. Returning to the case of the ritual Chaharshanbeh Suri, average people take to the streets – public venues – to light fires and leap over them, as a way to protest the Islamic Republic. For a small moment in time, the streets are reclaimed in the name of the people – until the police arrive. The ritual of Chaharshanbeh Suri creates a conversation with the streets (of the State), expressing the "I" for those who participate in the ceremony. As noted earlier in relation to competing ideologies, people within the State may perform activities that empower themselves but do not necessarily go against the State's interests. Another tactic that I would also include is voting. Voting can be a ritualized action that enables the voter to express one's "I" agency, and because the Islamic Republic is a democracy, voting is part of the ritual process of validating and re-creating the State (although the results of its voting process may be challenged, as seen in the Iranian elections of 2009).

Another specific Iranian example of performativity that gives both the State and the individual person a sense of agency is discussed in Azam Torab's *Performing Islam* (2007), namely the all-female *jalaseh* (religious meeting). The State actually encourages these meetings, but each jalaseh has a slightly different focus, and women may choose their own compatible female preacher and jalaseh within the neighborhood. In one particular jalaseh, the preacher, Mrs Omid, discourages all discussions of politics, as she believes that politics and religion should not mix.[38] If one wants to take part in a political religious meeting, one should attend a more suitable jalaseh. The contradiction in the rules of Mrs Omid's jalaseh is that the meetings take place within a theocratic democracy, in which the mixture of politics and religious is inevitable. Without making a direct comment on the State, Mrs Omid communicates her own politics, as well as those of the women, who choose to come to her jalaseh, even if she acts as an agent and patron of the Islamic Republic by reading texts published by the government itself and promoting Islamic piety. In addition, Mrs Omid's forum allows her to comment on social norms within the dictates of Islam. For instance, she indirectly tells her congregation that it is permissible for women to withhold sex from their husbands if their husbands do not perform *namaz* (daily prayers). She cites the example of Queen Anis al-Dowleh,[39] who refused to have sex with Nasir al-Din Shah during the Tobacco Protest (1890–92), because he ignored a *fatva* (religious ruling) against smoking tobacco.[40] Usually, a religious woman should not deny her husband's sexual requests unless she is menstruating or praying. Here in this particular forum of State-supported jalasehs, empowered women may negotiate ways to assert themselves in situations that are normally dominated by men.

The book begins with performing the Qajar State – a time of transitions, innovations, modernization programs and political uprisings, making it a pivotal and milestone era in relation to Iranian modernity and modern identities. In Chapter 2, Donna Stein's close study of "The Photographic Source for a Qajar Painting" reveals how the human body is performative, especially in relation to harem iconography. Her discovery of the exact photograph for the late Qajar watercolor *A Group of Prostitutes, "A Full House"* (c. 1880), the identification of the photographer through stylistic analysis, and comparative photographs and the recognition of the central character in the composition all successfully illustrate a new mediated Iranian identity performed in the then new medium of photography.

In Chapter 3, "Cartographic Desires: Some Reflections on the *Shahr-e Farang* (Peepshow) and Modern Iran," I examine the rise of modernity and national identity in Iran through the apparatus of the shahr-e farang (a peepshow box that displayed photographs of modern cities and pornography, among other subjects). The literal translation of shahr-e farang can be "French city," "European city," "Western city" or "foreign city." Vendors peddled the shahr-e farang, through which one may have gazed for a sum of one *shahi*, a coin of the smallest amount. In this essay, I discuss how Iranian subjects performed, what I call, "cartographic desires," using the shahr-e farang as a point of inquiry. The rise of modern Iran, such as reordering its cities, implementing State institutions and standardizing money, possessed a complicated, intertwined relationship with Europe and the rest of the world. The box of the shahr-e farang on the local level became a cartographic object that "world-ed" Iran and Europe into one mapped entity through the transmission of the space between the two, thus replicating or reinforcing political agendas on the State level.

In Babak Rahimi's Chapter 4, "Takkiyeh Dowlat: The Qajar Theater State," he looks at the symbolic-performative dimensions of political power of the Qajar State and considers how the Shi'i rituals are performed during the Islamic month Muharram when the martyrdom of the Prophet's grandson Imam Hossein is commemorated. In his study, Rahimi relies on the notion of a "theater state," a phrase coined by anthropologist Clifford Geertz in his study of Balinese rituals (1981), which he viewed as types of political actions that enact and represent power in the medium of ritual performances. The theater state exhibits visualized performances through ritual processes that rationalize power relations between authority and its subjects, therefore constructing a sociopolitical order that transcends ordinary time and space. Rahimi's focus on the Takkiyeh Dowlat, a large amphitheater where *ta'ziyeh* plays (passion plays) were staged, brings to light the central role of performance in the (re)invention of Qajar State power. Dramatic spectacles and representations of martyred imams, he argues, marked the ceremonial constitution of royal power, and under Nasir al-Din Shah, the Takkiyeh Dowlat became the most important performative site where the Qajar State was elaborately staged and theatrically visualized in public. Accordingly, the public staging of sacred performances in the Takkiyeh Dowlat marked an architectural site of temporal authority and a visual site of sovereignty, through which Qajar society could believe, desire, share, celebrate and participate in the rituality of State power.

The second division is dedicated to the performative representations of the Pahlavi State and the Iranian State's transition into the Islamic Republic. Chapter five features Donna Stein's private interview with HIM Shahbanou Farah Pahlavi from 1990, in which the queen opens a window into the thinking behind the arts programs initiated by the Pahlavi government, many of which have been retained by their successors in the Islamic Republic. Sophisticated and all encompassing, the queen's plans offered both educational enrichment for the people and a positive way for the State to engage globally through history, architecture and the arts.

In Chapter 6, "Shaping and Portraying Identity at the Tehran Museum of Contemporary Art (1977–2005)," Alisa Eimen explores the interrelationships between modern Iranian art and identity, as they are performed in Tehran's Museum of

Contemporary Art in the pre- and postrevolutionary eras. The museum, founded in 1977, developed on the heels of more than two decades of vibrant activity by a small avant-garde that included Parviz Tanavoli (b. 1937) and Kamran Diba (b. 1937) and was intended to be a center for this activity. Soon thereafter, the revolution halted this trajectory until the late 1990s when the museum reemerged as a cultural center, featuring a wide range of activities from biennials to international contemporary art exhibits. By 2000 the museum was again a site of active negotiation among artists and their enthusiasts, principally college-age youths. Eimen studies the museum's architecture, selected artworks and exhibitions to analyze the ways that various identities were marshaled and performed before and after the revolution. The museum and its activities became sites where the nation was redefined as modern during the Pahlavi period, and then after the revolution, this redefinition has continued by making art one of the major vehicles of performance by both citizens and the State.

Abbas Daneshvari, in Chapter 7, "Seismic Shifts across Political Zones in Contemporary Iranian Art: The Poetics of Knowledge, *Knowing* and Identity," presents his study of the poetics of knowledge and identity across the two political zones of the Pahlavi monarchy and the Islamic Republic that have defined Iran's cultural and historical conditions during the past seven decades. The changes in aesthetics and in the *weltanschauung* (worldview) across these zones are radical and at times surprising. The arc of change moves from a profound need to be identified with European and American modernisms to the grand spaces of wistful recognition of signs from Iran's glorious past (the Saqqa-khaneh) and later to the ontological perspectives of contemporary artists whose works undermine, deconstruct and question all instruments of knowledge from language to rationality and history.

The third section, The Islamic Republic: 1979–Present, contains chapters devoted to depictions of performativity in postrevolutionary Iran, primarily after the end of the devastating Iran–Iraq War in 1988 to the present. In Chapter 8, "Performativity and Ritual Space in Postrevolutionary Tehran," David Simonowitz examines the al-Ghadir Mosque and the Ibrahim Mosque, two ritual spaces completed in northern Tehran after the Iranian Revolution. The former is located in a semiresidential neighborhood and constitutes a noteworthy example of local patronage, whereas the latter sits at the center of the Tehran International Fairgrounds and is a State-sponsored building. Bearing no external resemblance, the mosques nevertheless merit comparison, for inside, the two structures articulate certain common Shi'i principles that are often cited as the foundations of the Islamic Republic. In its name, epigraphy and external structure, the al-Ghadir Mosque represents a clear, and to some, "communal," proclamation of Shi'i Islam. The Ibrahim Mosque appears to downplay communal tenets on the exterior, yet its internal spaces are in some ways more doctrinally and politically charged than those of the al-Ghadir Mosque. Outwardly, the Ibrahim Mosque may be understood to have reified a policy of conciliation and self-legitimation in a site of international commerce and ceremony at a time when the Islamic Republic had renewed efforts to normalize relations with other (Islamicate) States. Regardless of the religious and civic principles emphasized in their ornament, forms and respective locations, the mosques invite comparison for they both re-create other sacred spaces in distant lands through related strategies and techniques. Ultimately however, the Ibrahim Mosque informs a much larger space, in which different actors are both consciously and unconsciously led to interact within and ostensibly validate the discourses on the State by virtue of their participation in diplomatic, commercial and spiritual rituals, as they engage with the venues of the fairgrounds.

Chapter 9, "Reclaiming Cultural Space: The Artist's Performativity versus the State's Expectations in Contemporary Iran" by Hamid Keshmirshekan, examines the visual culture in postrevolutionary Iran and deals with discourses of identity politics, their associations with the State's cultural strategies and the artists' aesthetic rebellions versus the State's expectations. Keshmirshekan explores the ways in which the artists' focal beliefs about social relations and cultural essentialism find expressions in their work. The formulated interests of the State clearly promote particular values as resistance against the secular cultural norms of cultural globalization or so-called "Westernization." This general cultural attitude explains why in official cultural and artistic events, it has been perfectly clear that encouragement has been given to taking refuge in cultural authenticity, historical specificity, artistic identity and tradition, particularly in Islam or the so-called Iranian-Islamic Shi'i traditions as an integral part of Iranian "authentic" culture. There is, however, an artistic and intellectual reaction against these stereotypes and the idea of particularism in the sense of imposing a "monolithic" or "one view" formula. These artists variously create meaning, particularly through presentation of the human body as a cultural medium in their artistic practices, which make them ideological and political in the Iranian context. Hence, addressing critically the actual problems and issues in society becomes an approach for artists in rebelling against the State's ideological goals. This ironic, sometimes humorous, language has also become a common method to react metaphorically against united sacred values defined by the State. Artists have created negotiable identities and ideologies, which rise to the foreground, while hegemonic identities recede to the background.

"Female Trouble: Melancholia and Allegory in Contemporary Iranian Art" by Andrea D. Fitzpatrick (Chapter 10) analyzes artworks created by three female Iranian artists: Parastou Forouhar (b. 1962), Neda Razavipour (b. 1969) and Amitis Motevalli (b. 1969). Ambivalent, ironic or enigmatic messages are conveyed within all these artworks, by choice as well as by political necessity, due to the strict censorship to which all artworks publicly displayed in Iran are subjected to under Ershad (the Ministry of Culture and Islamic Guidance). Allegorical strategies in contemporary art have been theorized by Craig Owens as the presentation of one "story" (a visual-textual framework involving symbolic objects and icons) to narrate another that is historically different and distinct. What is perceived as an allegorical turn in recent Iranian art allows artists to "speak" about polemical issues in ways that are not only more safe, but also more poetic. Thus, the allegories of fabric, weaving and entanglement that are offered (seemingly to be unraveled) by Forouhar, Razavipour and Motevalli, present cross-cultural and trans-historical instances of mourning, reparation and – appropriate to the political violence that has been witnessed – glints of outrage.

Last, this anthology ends with the fourth section, performing the Iranian diaspora, thus complicating the notions of which State, whose State and how Iranian identity translate into other cultural environments. Furthermore, exiles are performing a State within a State, often engaging in several discursive acts that may be at odds with each other or that may be difficult to integrate. Frequently, the performative acts of an exile may not resonate within the new State of residence, or the exile might adopt certain practices incompatible with the former life in the homeland, creating a circumstance that mirrors Palestinian artist Mona Hatoum's insightful museum installation, *The Entire World as a Foreign Land* (2000). The title indicates that every place in the world, even the now mythic homeland, has been transformed by time, memory and politics, producing culture shock and hence, making alienation almost a universal global condition.

Chapter 11, "Performing Visual Strategies: Representational Concepts of Female Iranian Identity in Contemporary Photography and Video Art," addresses the theme of performing the individual in relation to the State, focused on images created by female Iranian photographers and video artists such as Shadafarin Ghadirian (b. 1974), Simin Keramati (b. 1970) and Parastou Forouhar, who express their different visions of the world and offer insights into private and public realms. Julia Allerstorfer explores these photographers and video artists' strategies, which dismantle traditional stereotypes, and specifically analyzes self-portraits, exploring issues such as artistic visualization strategies, identity, methods of representation, authorship, cultural codes, artistic autonomy and the social conditions of being a photographer or video artist in Iran and in the Iranian Diaspora. By deconstructing how identities are performed globally, she revisits the term "performativity" and its validity in contemporary Iran and explores the different visual strategies adopted by female artists to reveal the constructions and perceptions of specific feminine "Iranian identities" in ironic and parodic ways.

In Chapter 12, "Painted and Animated Metaphors: An Interview with Artist Alireza Darvish," Mina Zand Siegel and Carmen Pérez González speak with the painter and filmmaker Darvish (b. 1968) who explains the symbolic and recurrent elements, origins, meanings and implications of his symbolic imagery, tracing the ways in which this imagery has changed since his exile from Iran in 1994 to his present life as an artist in Europe. He shows how his linguistic and philosophical inquiries have developed throughout this doppelganger existence, with all its contradictions and tensions caused by his exposure to both Iranian forms of visual culture and poetry and a globalized world in which the borders between cultures have become increasingly indiscernible. Ultimately, he shares his view that identities are not performative but rather essential and unchanging, regardless of the State that one occupies.

Finally, Chapter 13, "In The House of Fatemeh: Revisiting Shirin Neshat's Photographic Series *Women of Allah*," returns to Neshat's much written-about series to explore further the series' relationship between text and image. I argue two major points: first, one must attempt to read the actual Persian texts inscribed on these photographs or find a translation, as understanding what these texts say result in a more nuanced exegesis of the images. Neshat's appearance becomes subversive only when one reads the texts, because the varied references in the writing and the images themselves index each other, thus dislodging prototypical representations of Iranian women during the postrevolutionary and post-Iran–Iraq War periods. Neshat's photographs offer more psychologically complex representations of Iranian women during this particular timeframe than the mass media in Iran and elsewhere have projected. Two, through the mixture of texts, both written and visual presented in Neshat's photographs, the representations of her body become metaphors for feminized spaces of sacred empowerment by reencoding signs that transform the female body into a House of Fatemeh. Hazrat-e (Her Holiness) Fatemeh Zahra' (c. 605–32 CE) was the daughter of the Prophet Muhammad (c. 570–632) and the mother of Imams Hassan (625–69) and Hossein (626–80), Hazrat-e Zaynab and Umm Kulthum, and Fatimeh's representation in Shi'a discourses has become a locus of feminine authority. Moreover, the writing inscribed on Neshat's images of women's voices, which in turn become visual images of the women themselves, follows a similar aesthetic form on literal Houses of Fatemeh – the mosque. This comparison between Neshat's photographs of the female body as a sacred site through texts with actual sacred sites with texts, such as the mosque, allots women a more privileged space in the theocratic State of the Islamic Republic of Iran and Shi'a Islam than politically or consciously accorded to them.

Overall, the contributors in *Performing the Iranian State* provide deeper insights on how the State, nationhood and identity work in complex networks to create meaning through the human body and its discursive practices and representations, particularly in relation to performing *an* Iranian State. By focusing on these types of performative acts and their visual codes described in historical discourses, one may discover more nuanced ways of piecing together what has become "Modern Iran" or what it may be seen as "Iranian" in the contemporary global arena, as Iranians interact with other world citizens. Furthermore, the conversations presented in this volume elucidate larger issues of defining various Iranian modernities and visual cultures in relation to the State, addressing how these concepts came to be and how these modes of modernity are currently being practiced, depicted and perceived worldwide.

Notes and References

1 Many thanks to David Simonowitz and Hope Werness for their comments and suggestions on this introduction.

2 I am indebted to Shiva Balaghi's discussion of this pair of images in "Political Culture in the Iranian Revolution of 1906 and the Cartoons of *Kashkul*," in *Political Cartoons in the Middle East*, ed. Fatma Müge Göçek (Princeton: Markus Wiener Publications, 1998), 64–8.

3 Ibid., 67.

4 Ibid., 68.

5 Anthony Giddens, *Modernity and Self-Identity: Self and Society in the Late Modern Age* (Stanford: Stanford University Press, 1991), 15–16.

6 For example, see discussions in Camron Michael Amin, *The Making of the Modern Iranian Woman: Gender, State Policy, and Popular Culture, 1865–1946* (Gainsville: University Press of Florida, 2002), 22, 25–6, 29.

7 "*'Chaharshanbesuri' sareinjam rasmiat yaft* [Chaharshanbesuri finally became official]," *BBC Persian*, March 16, 2004, accessed January 19, 2012, http://www.bbc.co.uk/persian/iran/story/2004/03/040316_si_chaharshanbesuri.shtml.

8 US Department of State, "Background Note: Iran," last modified February 17, 2011, http://www.state.gov/r/pa/ei/bgn/5314.htm.

9 I use the term "Iranian Revolution" and not "Islamic Revolution," as there were many diverse political groups driving the revolution and vying for power. For an account of the heterogeneous

nature of the Iranian Revolution, see John Foran, "The Iranian Revolution of 1977–79: A Challenge for Social Theory," in *A Century of Revolution: Social Movements in Iran*, ed. John Foran (Minneapolis: University of Minnesota Press, 1994), 160–88.

10 Susan Horsburgh, "No Place Like Home," *TIME Europe*, August 14, 2000, www.time.com/time/europe/webonly/mideast/2000/08/neshat.html. This article is no longer available online.

11 My "scare quotes" around "West" are meant to convey that the dichotomies of "East" and "West" are false, because in their totalities they do not mean anything. Furthermore, as blanket terms, they act as euphemisms for and reinforce the racist dialect of "Orient" and "Occident" as explicated by Edward Said in his landmark work *Orientalism* (1978). As loaded terms, they imply that the "East" is backward, feminized, irrational and Other, whereas the "West" is modern, masculine, rational, civilized and Self. In this particular reference, however, I am using the word "West" as an unwanted label, used much in the way that Jalal Al-e Ahmad did in *Occidentosis* (1962), in which he condemned the abrupt and undiscerning adaptation of foreign modern developments without considering Iranian cultural values and mores.

12 "'Invented tradition' is taken to mean a set of practices, normally governed by [...] accepted rules and of a ritual or symbolic nature, which seek to inculcate [...] values and norms of behaviour by repetition, which [...] implies continuity with the past [...] where possible, they normally attempt to establish continuity with a suitable historic past." Eric Hobsbawm, introduction to *The Invention of Tradition*, ed. Eric Hobsbawm and Terence Ranger (Cambridge: University of Cambridge, 1992), 1.

13 Louis Althusser, *Lenin and Philosophy and Other Essays*, trans. Ben Brewster (London: NLB, 1971), 136–7, 146.

14 According to Benedict Anderson, the rise of the imagined nation occurs in Europe after the dissemination of cheap printed materials in vernacular languages, a development indebted to the invention of the Gutenberg press during the fifteenth century. *Imagined Communities: Reflections on the Origin and Spread of Nationalism*, rev. ed. (1983; repr., London: Verso, 1991), 25.

15 Montserrat Guibernau, *The Identity of Nations* (Cambridge: Polity Press, 2007), 11, 25.

16 Walter Benjamin, *Walter Benjamin: Selected Writings, 1913–1926*, vol. 1, ed. Marcus Bullock and Michael W. Jennings (Cambridge, MA: The Belknap Press of Harvard University Press, 1996), 243–4.

17 Michael Taussig, *The Nervous System* (New York: Routledge, 1992), 112.

18 Shlomo Avineri, *Hegel's Theory of the Modern State* (Cambridge: Cambridge University Press, 1972), ix, quoted in Michael Taussig, *The Nervous System* (New York: Routledge, 1992), 112. Yet, Avineri himself does not capitalize "state" and actually does not agree with the practice of doing so, calling the State's capitalization "arbitrary and intellectually scandalous as any other willful misrepresentation," precisely because its capitalization evokes "enormous and oppressive" implications. As the capitalization of "State" pervades this anthology, I agree with Taussig's assessment. Avineri, *Hegel's Theory of the Modern State*, ix.

19 Taussig, *The Nervous System*, 112–13.

20 Edward W. Said, *Freud and the Non-European* (London: Verso, 2003), 54–5.

21 Tonja van den Ende, "In Search of the Body in the Cave: Luce Irigaray's Ethics of Embodiment," in *Belief, Bodies, and Being: Feminist Reflections on Embodiment*, ed. Deborah Orr et al. (Lanham: Rowman and Littlefield, 2006), 144.

22 Michel Foucault, *Power/Knowledge: Selected Interviews and Other Writings 1972–1977*, ed. and trans. Colin Gordon (New York: Pantheon Books, 1980), 55.

23 Cyrus Schayegh, "'Seeing Like a State': An Essay on the Historiography of Modern Iran," *International Journal of Middle East Studies* 42, no. 1 (February 2010): 38.

24 Afshin Marashi, *Nationalizing Iran: Culture, Power, and the State, 1870–1940* (Seattle: University of Washington Press, 2008), 6.

25 Judith Butler, *Gender Trouble: Feminism and the Subversion of Identity* (New York: Routledge, 1990), 135.

26 Althusser, *Lenin and Philosophy and Other Essays*, 158.

27 Ibid., 162.

28 Jacques Derrida, *Of Grammatology*, trans. Gayatri Chakravorty Spivak (Baltimore: Johns Hopkins University Press, 1997), 158.

29 Judith Butler, *Bodies That Matter: On the Discursive Limits of "Sex"* (New York: Routledge, 1993), 4–9.

30 Simone de Beauvoir, *The Second Sex*, trans. H. M. Parshley (New York: Alfred A. Knopf, 1957), 267.

31 Butler, *Bodies That Matter*, 12–13.

32 Althusser, *Lenin and Philosophy and Other Essays*, 163–64.

33 Butler, *Gender Trouble*, 140.

34 Karen Barad, "Posthumanist Performativity: Toward an Understanding of How Matter Comes to Matter," in *Belief, Bodies, and Being: Feminist Reflections on Embodiment*, ed. Deborah Orr et al. (Lanham: Rowman and Littlefield, 2006), 29.

35 Ibid., 20.

36 Althusser, *Lenin and Philosophy and Other Essays*, 128, 158.

37 Michel de Certeau, *The Practice of Everyday Life*, trans. Steven Rendall (Berkeley: University of California Press, 1984), 37.

38 Azam Torab, *Performing Islam: Gender and Ritual in Iran* (Boston: Brill, 2007), 53.

39 Anis al-Dowleh was actually a temporary wife but became head of the harem and held considerable political power over the shah and the other women of the Nasiri court.

40 Torab, *Performing Islam*, 35. The Tobacco Protest was against a British concession that would have given a British company access to all Iran's tobacco, including its production, sale and exportation, and was agreed on by Nasir al-Din Shah.

I

THE QAJAR DYNASTY: 1786–1925

2

THE PHOTOGRAPHIC SOURCE FOR A QAJAR PAINTING

Donna Stein

The gradual opening of foreign relations under the Safavid ruler Shah ʻAbbas II (1642–66) generated radical changes in Iranian court society, especially in the arts.[1] European diplomats, as well as the East India Companies, brought oil paintings to Iran as gifts, and visits by artists from abroad to the Iranian court strengthened the impact of foreign cultures on Iran. By the last quarter of the seventeenth century, naturalistic-style painting was popular, even though the rendition lacked a thorough understanding of the laws of perspective and modeling with light and shade. As they had done in previous eras, Iranian artists looked to foreign sources as points of departure, intentionally adopting those techniques that suited their own tastes and needs. The concept, subject matter and narrative style, however, remained unmistakably Persian.

The literature describing the life and times of the Qajar period (1786–1925) shows late nineteenth-century Iranian society in transition, adapting to modern and foreign ideas and technology. Nasir al-Din Shah Qajar (r. 1848–96), the ablest and most successful of the Qajar sovereigns, exploited the mutual distrust between Great Britain and tsarist Russia to preserve Iran's independence despite their economic penetration and cultural influence. During his reign, there was an accelerated importation of European prototypes, such as paintings, prints, clothes and artifacts – a process already begun by his two predecessors, his great grandfather Fath ʻAli Shah (r. 1798–1834) and his father Mohammad Shah (r. 1834–48).[2] His time in power coincided with a period of constant communication with European powers at home and abroad and a long procession of foreign travelers visiting what Europeans had perceived as the exotic "Orient."

Imported influences created a distinctive hybrid painting style that was an amalgam of photography and painting. The result was inevitably different than previous centuries when painting was not competing with photography. By the mid-nineteenth century, the most outstanding painter in Iran was Abu'l Hassan Khan Ghaffari (c. 1814–66) who was given the title Sani' al-Mulk (Craftsman or Painter of the Kingdom). He had studied painting, lithography and printing in Rome and Paris during c. 1842–47,[3] and was distinguished for his lifelike portraits of dignitaries, which convey a profound psychological intensity, such as *Prince Ardishir Mirza, Governor of Tehran* (1854; Figure 2.1). His rendering of expression is indicative of a modern character, unlike more stylized traditional Persian painting.

About 1861, Nasir al-Din Shah appointed Sani' al-Mulk as Director of Printing and Chief Illustrator and he was charged with the responsibility of editing the weekly court newspaper *Ruznameh-ye Dowlat-e 'Aliyeh-ye Iran* (The newspaper of the great government of Iran), printed by the lithographic process and illustrated with portraits of princes, statesmen and soldiers as well as representations of remarkable events.[4] According to the second issue of the newspaper, in which the new editor was introduced, it was Sani'al-Mulk's ability to work in the *basma tasvir* manner (painting after printed pictures) that he was given this new responsibility.[5] Sani' al-Mulk had opened a workshop on the Golestan Palace grounds in conjunction with the newspaper to train apprentices in the basma technique. Contemporaneous translations of basma suggest the use of photography, and there is no reason to exclude photographs from the repertoire of reproductions employed by Persian artists in the second half of the nineteenth century. We know from the literature that more than 105 native-born photographers were active during the second half of the nineteenth century, as well as about 30 European photographers.[6]

Twentieth-century art historians and critics such as B. W. Robinson and Karim Emami speak of late Qajar painting, and in particular, the work of the nephew of Sani' al-Mulk, Mohammad Ghaffari Kashani (1847–1940)[7] – who was given the title Kamal al-Mulk (Excellence or Perfection of the Kingdom) – and of other artists who followed his style, as painters of the "photographic style." These artists used relatively accurate perspective, chiaroscuro and gradations in the application of harmonious color. Emami suggests that at a time when photography was a novelty, Persian artists chose to compete with the camera in the recording of minute details, a stylistic characteristic that had always been an integral part of the Persian painting tradition since the Timurid period (c. 1320–1507).[8]

The first daguerreotype camera was brought to Iran during the reign of Mohammad Shah. Yet, it was under Nasir al-Din Shah that the exciting new art of photography was fully embraced, producing many calotypes, platinum prints, paper negatives and albumen prints. Nasir al-Din Shah, who began taking pictures when he was only 13 years old, was fascinated by this magical invention. In the late 1850s, he outfitted an area in his palace, known as the *'Akkaskhaneh-ye Mubarak-e Humayuni*, the first official photography studio in Iran.[9] As Lyle Rexer has commented on Nasir al-Din Shah and photography, "He studied it, practiced it, rewarded its practitioners and opened Persia to its influence."[10] Ultimately, the shah assembled more than 20,000 photographs on themes as diverse as the women of his harem, self-portraits, Persian antiquity, architecture, landscapes, hunting escapades and even political prisoners, which are archived in his annotated albums held in the Golestan Palace in Tehran.[11] This royal collection contains more than 43,000 images by Iranian photographers, European photographers and adventurous travelers. Inspired and encouraged by the shah, many of his courtiers, as well as students at the vocational college Dar al-Fanun,[12] tried their hands at photography.

Whereas the first European photographers based their work on the formal and aesthetic rules of painting, native photographers in Iran did not have the same naturalistic pictorial tradition to rely on for inspiration. Instead, they willingly explored European prototypes, borrowed from fictional Orientalist constructions of the Middle East by foreign travelers, painters and photographers and eventually developed a new mediated

Iranian identity performed in photographs. For instance, Nasir al-Din Shah's photograph of his concubine Marziyeh, who performs in front of his camera, illustrates the shah's own efforts to test the expressive limits of representation (Figure 2.2).

We know from the history of nineteenth-century European and American art and from isolated examples in Iran that photographs were sources for paintings, drawings and lithographs. Nevertheless, it is rare to fine the exact photograph used to create a late Qajar period opaque watercolor. This situation may change as more research is done in the field. Because so many European scholars and tourists had published commercially available photographs from Iran without identifying the photographers, it will take significant aesthetic analysis to establish a photographer's pedigree.

In the album *Views of Life in Persia* (n.d.),[13] now in the collection of Seikyo Press, Tokyo, there is a particular untitled albumen print that was the exact source for the opaque watercolor painting entitled *A Group of Prostitutes, "A Full House,"* (c. 1880; Figures 2.3, 2.4).[14] The unknown watercolorist faithfully copied every detail of the sepia-toned photograph except for the highly selective omission of the male figure in the center of the back plane. This aesthetic change transformed the originally pyramidal construction of the photograph into an open rectangle and, as a consequence, altered the intended interpretation of the photograph. There is little difference in size between the photograph and the watercolor (6 ½ × 11 15/16 in) and by comparing the two images, awkward aspects of the painted composition become apparent.

In both the photograph and the watercolor, the crowded arrangement of nine women is meticulously positioned in front of a backdrop that suggests a lavish interior setting. The symmetrical composition is typically Iranian. Like the theatrical staging of a performance, the women are carefully arranged on three parallel planes – reclining on the floor, sitting on a couch or bench and reclining on the back edge of the couch. The cadenced movement up the picture plane may also borrow from the orderliness and taut structure evidenced in classic Persian miniatures.

Photographic aesthetics and technical requirements imposed their own limitations. All the female portrayals are frontal, hieratic and static, illustrating a Victorian influence. Several women are posed with their heads firmly supported by a hand, suggesting the method early photographers used to steady their models during the long camera exposures necessary at that time and taught models to live inside rather than outside the moment.[15] A superstitious belief that staring directly into a camera lens steals part of one's life was implicit in American and European photographic portraiture, but nevertheless, here the women present powerful, modern pictures of themselves, with fixed gazes looking confidently into the lens, hence implying that they may have not had that belief. Each woman appears to be reacting differently to the camera or photographer. The photographer captures an accurate record of female clothing, documenting the sophisticated layering of the stylish components of Iranian dress at that time.[16] In Orientalist fashion, the women are elaborately adorned and available for male voyeuristic pleasure.[17] The artist depicts this harem scene as an erotic universe where there are no men.

The original albumen print is numbered on the lower left of the negative as 1381, a common practice that shows this work was created for European consumption and available for sale to tourists, which explains how it ended up in an album showing various aspects of life in Iran. Based on style, this photograph is most likely by the notable photographer Antoin Sevruguin (c. 1830s–1933), an Iranian Armenian who began his career as a painter, studying both traditional Persian and European art. He enjoyed royal patronage and lived and worked in Tehran as a pioneering commercial photographer from the 1870s until his death.[18] This striking group portrait emphasizes both depth of field and figural rhythm, suggesting a very skilled photographer. The subtle complexity of this intimate and highly ceremonial picture with its balanced composition and tonal contrasts conveys a specifically Persian character that transcends mere locale and costume.

The context and intention of an artwork are often implied by a title or caption. Here, despite the title *A Group of Prostitutes, "A Full House,"* it is doubtful this watercolor portrays prostitutes. Instead, the setting, attire, jewels and other details evoke a harem scene. These women are the epitome of Nasir al-Din Shah's taste – plump, with moustaches and dark, thick eyebrows that create a continuous line across the brow. The central figure, when compared with other photographs, appears to be Taj al-Saltaneh (1883–1936),[19] Nasir al-Din Shah's daughter by his wife Turan al-Dowleh (Figure 2.5). Therefore, the standing figure of the young man in the center of the photograph most likely represents a guard or a eunuch who serves the women and his master, completing the pyramid of the original composition. Clearly, the cultural frame of reference for this photograph serves different functions, from portrait to ethnographic "type."[20] Perhaps the elimination of the male figure makes the painting more acceptable in light of European criticisms of the Muslim practice of the harem.

The artist accurately copied the photograph, while taking liberties with applied color and the decorative enhancement of forms. The opaque watercolor technique used for centuries in Persian miniatures lends itself to the refined method and specificity that characterize this late Qajar watercolor. The painting is a study in contrasting patterns that cover every surface except for the back wall and window in the backdrop that defines the interior space.

As Iran opened up to foreign influences, it was subjected to new morals and ideas that are reflected in representations of sexuality. Prostitution, although forbidden by the Qur'an, was practiced freely. The woman pictured in *Prostitute* seductively looks at the camera as she reclines. A *poustin* (sheepskin coat), thrown aside by the naked odalisque, is in the center foreground (Figure 2.6). The erotic promise of this recumbent figure is a confrontational pose most nineteenth-century photographers would have avoided, posing their models modestly looking down or off into the distance, which they felt was more romantic.

Curiosity about the secrets of the harem created an excellent market for these types of cliché photographs. Such popular images of the Islamicate world both horrified and titillated foreign critics throughout the colonial period. The word "harem" derives from the Arabic *haram,* meaning "unlawful," "unprotected" or "forbidden." The sacred areas around Mecca and Medina are also *haram*, closed to all who are not Muslim. In its secular use, harem refers to the separate protected part of a household where women, children and servants live in maximum seclusion and privacy. In a noble and rich house, eunuch slaves guarded the harem. Women usually could not leave the harem precinct on their own, and with rare exceptions, such as tailors and doctors, who entered under the watchful eye of a chaperone, the only men permitted into the harem were blood relatives.

Several photographs demonstrate a similar repetition of motifs and arrangement of figures and postures. For example, the crossed-legged pose in *Girl*, from an album of Iranian photographs formerly in the collection of Stuart Cary Welch, is performative in its symbolic expressive action (Figure 2.7). The crossed legs suggest a masculine attitude and are also a provocative sign of easy virtue. Yet during the Qajar era, most Iranians sat on the floor and regularly did not use chairs, so the European sense of decorum may not apply. *A Persian Anderun (Harem)* and *A Woman of the Harem with Her Daughters* (c. 1870s) depict typical straightforward views of harem women (Figures 2.8, 2.9). As a kind of honorific portrait, the social hierarchy of the latter group is reflected in the physical positioning of the seven upper-class Iranian women and children within the frame, with the most important woman seated in the center and her daughters standing in the back or squatting in the left foreground. A servant is seated in the right foreground. In another albumen print by Sevruguin, two women from the harem, one seated and the other reclining, are posed with flower bouquets on a carpet in front of a painted backdrop, positioned exactly like the two figures in the frontal plane of the primary albumen source print (Figure 2.10). The artificiality of the backdrop is a reminder of the studio. In *Harem Women* or *Women and a Child in the Harem*, also by Sevruguin, two women and a young girl are seated around a low table covered in what appears to be a woven Kashmiri shawl (Figure 2.11). The older woman on the left, perhaps the mother, wears a chador and is smoking a hookah. The younger demure woman on the right, perhaps the older woman's daughter, is fashionably dressed in the *shaliteh* (short ballerina-style skirt), seated in a provocative manner with legs crossed and one raised to reveal her legs and thighs covered in white stockings. She is admiring herself in a mirror resting on the table in front of her. Although this photograph has been marketed commercially, as evidenced by the photographer's number on the lower left, it seems to have been a commissioned photograph because of the simple setting, without backdrops or other studio props.

These harem images both propagate and dispel some of the myths and stereotypes of the "Orient," a pervasive European tradition, both academic and artistic, of prejudiced outsider interpretations of the East, shaped by the attitudes of foreign imperialism in the eighteenth and nineteenth centuries. Sevruguin developed a way to satisfy his client's wishes for representation in the latest mode and effectively used the camera as a way to represent and critique Orientalist models of gender identity, challenging their paradigms.[21] His special access to the shah's harem allowed idealized studio scenes – outright fantasies of repressed desires based on European prototypes – as well as commonplace, straightforward depictions of Qajar court women, showing their familial relationships, modest dress and chic contemporaneous fashion in their palace quarters that reveal much about the period.

As a result of the newly established diplomatic relations between the Iranian court and various foreign powers, including the British, Russians, Italians, French and Austrians, these visits by European envoys and their retinues, merchants and wealthy travelers, which began at least by the time of Fath 'Ali Shah, encouraged the production of a superior type of "tourist" art by Persian miniature painters. Executed on paper, these album pictures illustrate Persian types, costumes, occupations and customs. As early as 1811, writing in *Travels into Various Countries of the East, More Particularly Persia*, Sir William Ouseley (1769–1842) records, "Of pictures very neatly executed in watercolors on leaves of paper either separate, or collected into books, many hundreds were brought for inspection to our tents and offered daily for sale in the shops of Ispahan. Among these I found several of interest as portraits of remarkable personages; and others as they illustrated manners and customs, representing scenes of frequent occurrence in domestic life [...] but of several offered for sale, those most highly finished were unfortunately of such description as precludes any further notice."[22] The subtle erotic allusion at the end of the quotation was enough to evoke pictorial images of Oriental sensuality by John Frederick Lewis (1804–76), Jean-Léon Gérôme (1824–1904) and others.

Many foreign travelers wrote about aspects of harem life after their special visits to this "forbidden" world to demystify and make public the private lives of women. Throughout Iranian history, clothing has always played an important role in defining a person's social, religious and gender affiliations. In 1894 Ella Sykes (d. 1939) took note of female attire and especially the progressive shortening of skirts by women of the harem:

> All the Persian ladies wore loose-sleeved jackets of the richest brocades and velvets, and had short, much-stiffened-out trousers, which did not reach to the knees, the costume being completed with coarse white stockings or socks. Before the Shah went to Europe the Persian ladies all kept to the old national costume of long, loose, embroidered trousers, but on the return of the monarch, this present ungraceful costume became the fashion in the royal *anderoon* [harem], and has spread throughout the whole country; it being, I believe, a fact that the dress of the Parisian ballet-girls so greatly fascinated the Oriental potentate that he commanded it to be adopted by his wives.[23]

A few years earlier in 1891 Dr Charles James Wills, a medical officer for the Persian Telegraph Department from 1866–81,[24] also took great delight recounting the finer details of female dress:

> The rest of the costume is composed of the "tumbun" or "shulwar"; these are simply short skirts of great width, held by a running string; the outer one usually of silk, velvet, or Cashmere shawl, often trimmed with gold lace, according to the purse of the wearer; or among the poor, of loud-patterned chintz or print. Beneath these are innumerable other garments of the same shape, and varying in texture from silk and satin to print. The whole is very short indeed; among the women of fashion merely extending to the thigh, and as the number of these garments is amazing, and they are much *bouffée*, the effect of a lady sitting down astonishes the beholder, and would scandalize the Lord Chamberlain. As the ladies are supposed however to be only seen by their lords in these indoor dresses, there is perhaps no harm done.[25]

These snapshots of harem life confirm not only its reality, but also the exposure of the hidden female world to foreign eyes – a fundamental premise of the harem picture.[26] The dramatic style of layered miniskirts typically worn with bare legs or white stockings by upper-class women during the second half of the nineteenth century was confirmed in Sevruguin's photographs of the harem. Nevertheless, it seems obvious that Persian women dressed as "ballerinas or ladies of easy virtue," with no understanding of the sexual social implications.[27]

Poor Iranian men could barely afford one wife, although they sometimes took two anyway – separating the women in their humble home simply by a curtain. Wealthier men often exceeded the four wives permitted by the Qur'an and made a display of them, groomed to the perfection of Persian taste as status symbols.[28] Nasir al-Din Shah made alliances through marriages with notables' and princes' daughters. He also married girls of modest background who appealed to him. He had a great passion for women, which found expression in the large number of his wives (85 of his wives survived him) and the extent of his harem, which had probably close to 1,600 people, including women, children, attendants, eunuchs and guards.[29]

Eunuchs were authorized to circulate freely in the harems and served as intermediaries between their master and his wives and concubines. Under Shah 'Abbas (1587–1629), it became common practice to enslave and castrate Georgian and other captives taken in war and to use them as palace servants, especially in the royal harem. Later, second-generation Georgians, whose parents had been enslaved in the 1790s, guarded the exterior gates of the harem and were permitted to enter only in the company of the shah. Black eunuchs, originally Abyssinian and Zanzibarian slaves, were imported despite the ban on the slave trade in the 1850s and were responsible for the internal security of the harem. Sir John Chardin (1634–1713), a Huguenot jeweler who had twice visited Iran in 1666–69 and 1672–77, placed the number of eunuchs at court in the late seventeenth century at about 3,000 and said they were mainly white people coming from the Malabar Coast.[30] By 1887 Etemad al-Saltaneh, Nasir al-Din Shah's Minister of Publication, reported that there were only 38 eunuchs in the royal harem;[31] 14 are pictured in a salt print by Luigi Pesce entitled *In the Mosque of the Damegan/The Eunuchs* (c. 1850s) in an album held by the Metropolitan Museum of Art (Figure 2.12).

Photographs provide an unrivalled testament to a traditional way of life and its architectural setting. Ethnographic imagery satisfied the fantasies of nineteenth-century armchair travelers, because as visual specimens of a passing era, photographs illustrate most aspects of everyday life, real and romantic, objectifying places, buildings, costumes, monuments, customs, landscapes and people. By the end of the nineteenth century, topographical photography by adventurous travelers in Iran was quite common. With the invention of the hand-held Kodak camera in 1888, the wife of a European building roads and bridges could also be an enthusiastic photographer.[32]

The camera created a new way of seeing and a new way of understanding the self. Photography added a three-dimensional and realistic quality to painting and a personal and candid point of view to Qajar imagery. Etemad al-Saltaneh recognized that photography had greatly served the art of portraiture and landscape painting by reinforcing the use of light and shade, accurate proportions and perspective. He wrote,

"Since photography was discovered, it has been of great service to the art of drawing (*san'at tasvir*), the art of rendering landscapes (*durnamasazi*) and portraits (*shabihkashi*), of light and shade (*vanamudan-i saya rushan*) and the utilization of the laws of proportion, as well as other aspects of this technique; all have found their originality and have been perfected."[33]

The photograph of a harem scene as the source for an opaque watercolor illustrates how photography provided pictorial imagery for artists that would have been impossible through direct experience of the women's quarters in the imperial seraglio. Artists welcomed the discovery of photography, recognizing its benefits for art.[34] It became an intermediary between firsthand observations and their work in the studio and augmented their vision. Iranian painters were able to render nature in a faithful manner, which may account for the rapid dissemination of the new invention. Artists could order photographs from the growing catalogues of commercial firms specializing in Near Eastern subjects. They learned to manipulate camera images the way sketches had traditionally been employed in earlier periods, either as notations when copying from nature or authenticating details. Much is revealed about an artist when we see what he keeps, what he omits and what he modifies. No study of the arts of the past 150 years can be made without taking into account the influence of the unique qualities of camera vision on artists and their patrons.[35]

Notes and References

1 An unpublished version of this article was written in 1990 as "A Persian Harem as It Really Was."

2 Fath 'Ali Shah's reign was marked by the resurgence of Persian arts, particularly portraiture and large-scale oil painting, which reached a height previously unknown under any other Islamic dynasty. His grandson Mohammad Shah, who fell under the influence of tsarist Russia and attempted to make reforms by modernizing and increasing contact with Europe, succeeded him. He was the first to bring photography to Iran and encouraged small-scale paintings on lacquer.

3 Eleanor Sims, *Peerless Images: Persian Painting and Its Sources* (New Haven: Yale University Press, 2002), 86.

4 Yahya Zoka, *Honar va Mardom*, no. 10 (August 1963): 14–19.

5 Yahya Zoka, *Honar va Mardom*, no. 11 (September 1963): 17–33.

6 For a list of Iranian photographers and biographies, see Yahya Zoka, *Tarikh-e 'Akasi va 'Akassan-e Pishgam dar Iran* [The history of photography and pioneer photographers in Iran] (Tehran: Elmi Farhangi Publishers, 1997), 47–57; and Iraj Afshar, *Ganjine-ye 'Aks-haye Iran: Hamrah-e Tarikhche-ye Vorud-e 'Akasi be Iran* [A treasury of early Iranian photography: Together with a concise history of how photography was first introduced in Iran] (Tehran: Nashr-e Farang-e Iran, 1992).

7 Mohammad Ghaffari Kashani visited Europe for the first time at age 47, after the death of Nasir al-Din Shah. He traveled widely for more than two years, visiting museums, copying works by artists such as Rembrandt, and generally improving his technique.

8 Karim Emami, *Modern Persian Painting* (New York: The Center for Iranian Studies, Columbia University, 1968), unpaginated.

9 Nasir al-Din Shah recorded in photographs the private daily life of his household, especially members of his family and personal harem. He used photography to document official aspects of court life.

10 Lyle Rexer, "A Persian Pioneer in a Western Art," *New York Times*, May 31, 2001, 27.

11 Iraj Afshar, "Some Remarks on the Early History of Photography in Iran," in *Qajar Iran: Political, Social and Cultural Change, 1800–1925*, ed. Edmund Bosworth and Carole Hillenbrand (Edinburgh: Edinburgh University Press, 1983), 276.

12 Iran's first polytechnic established by Nasir al-Din Shah in 1850 was based on European models to train officers, civil and military engineers, doctors and interpreters. Photography was introduced into the curriculum in 1860 under the aegis of the department of chemistry.

13 I first saw this album when Los Angeles photography dealer and collector Stephen White owned it. The album was eventually purchased by Seikyo Press, Tokyo.

14 The watercolor was recently sold at Sotheby's London on Wednesday, April 6, 2011 (Lot 61). Sotheby's, *The Stuart Cary Welch Collection, Part One: Arts of the Islamic World*, accessed November 25, 2011. http://www.sothebys.com/en/catalogues/ecatalogue.html/2011/c-welch-part-iil11227#/r=/en/ecat.fhtml.L11227.html+r.m=/en/ecat.grid.L11227.html/3/15/lotnum/asc/ In the catalogue, it was titled *A Group of Women and a Young Boy*, c. 1870–90, which is a misnomer, because the drawing includes only women.

15 Walter Benjamin, "A Short History of Photography," Screen (1972) 13, no. 1: 17, accessed November 7, 2011, http://screen.oxfordjournals.org/content/13/1/5.full.pdf

16 See *Encyclopaedia Iranica: Clothing IX – Coffee*, vol. 5, s.v. "Clothing X. in the Safavid and Qajar Periods."

17 Ali Behdad, "The Power-ful Art of Qajar Photography: Orientalism and (Self)-Orientalizing in Nineteenth-Century Iran," *Iranian Studies* 34, nos. 1–4 (2001): 146.

18 More than 5,000 glass plate negatives by Sevruguin were destroyed in 1908 by fire during the Constitutional Revolution. Julia Ballerini noted in her article "Passages: Studio to Archive to Exhibition," in *Sevruguin and the Persian Image; Photographs of Iran, 1870–1930*, ed. Frederick Bohrer (Washington: Arthur M. Sackler Gallery and University of Washington Press, 1999), 104, 117, that according to Sevruguin's grandson, Dr Emanuel Sevrugian, another 2,000 glass plates were destroyed by Reza Shah around 1937, because he did not want to show unfavorable aspects of Iranian life.

19 Taj al-Saltaneh's life epitomized the predicaments of a changing era. She chronicled her liberal lifestyle in *Crowning Anguish: Memoirs of a Persian Princess form the Harem to Modernity 1884–1914*, ed. Abbas Amanat, trans. Anna Vanzan and Amin Neshati (Washington: Mage Publishers, 1993).

20 Frederick N. Bohrer, "Looking Through Photographs: Sevruguin and the Persian Image," in *Sevruguin and the Persian Image: Photographs of Iran, 1870–1930*, ed. Frederick N. Bohrer (Washington: Arthur M. Sackler Gallery and University of Washington Press, 1999), 39.

21 Aphrodite Désirée Navab, "To Be or Not to Be an Orientalist? The Ambivalent Art of Antoin Sevruguin," *Iranian Studies* 35, nos. 1–3 (Winter/Spring/Summer 2002): 128.

22 Sir William Ouseley, *Travels into Various Countries of the East, More Particularly Persia*, vol. 2 (London: Rodwell and Martin, 1823), 224.

23 Ella Sykes, *Through Persia on a Sidesaddle* (London: J. Macqueen, 1898), 17, quoted in Jennifer M. Scarce, "Vesture and Dress: Fashion, Function, and Impact," in *Woven from the Soul, Spun from the Heart: Textile Arts of Safavid and Qajar Iran, 16th–19th Centuries*, ed. Carol Bier (Washington, The Textile Museum, 1987), 55–56; Nasir al-Din Shah traveled to Europe in 1873, 1878 and 1889.

24 Jennifer Scarce, "A Persian Brassiere," *AARP* 7 (1975): 20.

25 Charles James Wills, *In the Land of the Lion and Sun, 1866 to 1881* (London: Macmillan, 1891), 324, quoted in Jennifer M. Scarce, "Vesture and Dress: Fashion, Function, and Impact," in *Woven from the Soul, Spun from the Heart: Textile Arts of Safavid and Qajar Iran, 16th–19th Centuries*, ed. Carol Bier (Washington, The Textile Museum, 1987), 55.

26 Joan Del Plato, *Multiple Wives, Multiple Pleasures: Representing the Harem, 1800–1875* (Madison: Fairleigh Dickinson University Press, 2002), 14.

27 For a discussion of the questionable virtue of Parisian ballerinas, see Abigail Solomon-Godeau, "The Legs of the Countess," *October* 39 (1986): 65–108.

28 Alev Lytle Croutier, *Harem: The World behind the Veil* (New York: Abbeville Press, 1989), 21.

29 Ehsan Yarshater, "Observations on Nasir al-Din Shah," in *Qajar Iran, Political, Social and Cultural Change, 1800–1925*, ed. Edmund Bosworth and Carole Hillenbrand (Edinburgh: Edinburgh University Press, 1983), 8.

30 *Encyclopaedia of Islam*, vol. 4, s.v. "Khasi"; Jean Chardin, *Voyages de monsieur le chevalier Chardin en Perse et autres lieux de l'Orient* [The travels of Sir John Chardin in Persia and the Orient] (Amsterdam: Chez Jean Louis de Lorme, 1711), 283–85.

31 Chardin, *Voyages*, 283–85; Etemad al-Saltaneh, *Ruznameh-ye Khatirat-e Etemad al-Saltaneh* [The diaries of Etemad al-Saltaneh], ed. Iraj Afshar (Tehran: Amir Kabir, 1966), 644.

32 Ella Rebe Durand, *An Autumn Tour in Western Persia* (Westminster: Archibald Constable, 1902), 131.

33 Etemad al-Saltaneh, *Al-Ma'aser va al-Asar* [Contemporary impressions] (Tehran: Kitabhaneh-ye Sanai, 1970), 123, quoted in Chahryar Adle and Yahya Zoka, "Notes et documents sur la photographie Iranienne et son histoire [Notes and documents on Iranian photography and its history]," *Studia Iranica* 20 (1983): 274–75.

34 Maryam Ekhtiar, "Nasir Al-Din Shah Period (1848–96), Plate 88," in *Royal Persian Paintings: The Qajar Epoch 1785–1925*, ed. Layla S. Diba and Maryam Ekhtiar (Brooklyn: Brooklyn Museum of Art, 1998), 264; and Layla S. Diba, "The Qajar Court Painter Yahya Ghaffari: His Life and Times," in *Persian Painting From the Mongols to the Qajars: Studies in Honour of Basil W. Robinson*, ed. Robert Hillenbrand (London: I.B. Tauris, 2000), 85.

35 Van Deren Coke, *The Painter and the Photograph from Delacroix to Warhol* (Albuquerque: University of New Mexico Press, 1964), 1.

3

CARTOGRAPHIC DESIRES: SOME REFLECTIONS ON THE *SHAHR-E FARANG* (PEEPSHOW) AND MODERN IRAN

Staci Gem Scheiwiller

A late nineteenth-century photograph by the Iranian Armenian photographer Antoin Sevruguin (c. 1830s–1933) shows one Iranian man and two boys crouching under a floral curtain and watching a peepshow (Figure 3.1).[1] The vendor stands behind the box, spinning narratives that accompany the secret images the customers are enjoying. The curtain provides privacy, acting as both an enticement and a separation to potential customers; behind the barrier, only paying patrons can satisfy their curiosity and indulge in the hidden spectacle. Two framed pictures, which are difficult to decipher and sit atop the box, also elicit curiosity.

By the nineteenth century, during the height of European colonialism, one could find these types of mobile peepshow boxes worldwide – in Europe, Asia and the Middle East – showcasing pictures or photographs of foreign cities, pornography, wars and exotic images as spectacles to consume. The thorough distribution of these boxes worldwide situated them as sites of contact between colonial powers, political agendas, anthropological ventures and globalist designs, as one's understanding of the world was possibly framed, to some extent, through the moving pictures presented. In Iran, the traveling peepshow box was called the *shahr-e farang*. The literal translation of "shahr-e farang" can be "French city," "European city," "Western city" or "foreign city."[2] In any case, the name of the box implies that the images one paid to see were something of a more European nature that especially attracted spectators.

Many questions emerge in relation to this little-researched shahr-e farang. Was the viewer really gazing at images of European cities, as the name of the box suggests, and if so, what was it about these images that elicited the viewer's desires as he peered through the aperture? What was so fascinating about Europe and its cities that made the viewer spend the money in his pocket to see these shows? Furthermore, how did nineteenth-century Iranian men, within the boundaries of the State of Iran, possibly perform desires for Europe by viewing these peepshows? Did the shahr-e farang act as an interface between the desire of the viewer and images of European cities, therefore negotiating boundaries between two geopolitical entities?

In this essay, I explore how Iranian subjects performed cartographic desires, using the shahr-e farang as a point of inquiry. What I call a "cartographic desire" is a desire for a geopolitical entity that the subject has developed, thereby creating an attachment to a piece of land or State that is not necessarily the one that the subject currently occupies. According to psychoanalytic discourses, desires are the subject's attempt to reunite the Self with the Other, as the Other is the missing half that makes the Self whole and complete (again). In this particular case on the local level, the Iranian subject looking through the shahr-e farang was enacting desires vis-à-vis Europe and Europeans as his Other half, as well as assisting or fulfilling State agendas that were rethinking Iran's relationship to Europe. In the process, the spectator became cognizant of himself as his Iranian Self, and as a result, a type of mapping occurred when his body merged with the images through the act of viewing through the aperture.

Beginning in the eighteenth century and fully developed well into the nineteenth century on a State and global level, a historical heritage was devised, connecting Iranians and Europeans, particularly through studies of the Indo-European languages.[3] This linguistic relationship between Europe and Iran would then manifest itself as a racial one – the Aryan race – treasured by both Europeans and Iranians for various reasons, one of them being anti-Semitism toward Ashkenazi Jews and Arabs respectively. By uniting with Iranians racially, Europeans could claim an ancient cultural heritage that was not Semitic, and by drawing parallels to Europeans, Iranians could negotiate the overbearing forces of European colonialism in a strategic way that perhaps gave the Qajar monarchy (1786–1925) more tools to modernize Iran on their own terms as much as was possible. These conversations at the State were translated on the ground when the Iranian subject gazed through the shahr-e farang and was not simply viewing something completely "exotic" or radically different, but something constructed as strangely familiar.

I suggest, then, that the shahr-e farang was far more than simply a peepshow and an instrument of entertainment in Iran. I will show that this box could provide a glimpse into the complex political and cultural forces at work in Iran during the late nineteenth and early twentieth centuries. It also helped the State de facto to create and disseminate a local desire to possess Europe, when historically there had not really been one before Qajar Iran. The Safavids (1502–c. 1736) had assumed that Europe must have been a horrible place, forcing Europeans into their colonial excursions.[4] The Safavids also called their own capital at Isfahan *nesf-e jahan* (half the world), therefore creating a sense of superiority in Iran toward the rest of the world, including Europe, whose inhabitants were usually deemed as filthy.[5] Yet, those belated desires for Europe became fostered in popular culture during a moment when Qajar Iran was changing and modernizing, reconfiguring and shaping a modern Iranian identity that was special and different from the rest of the Middle East. By eliciting the average Iranian man's gaze, the shahr-e farang became a window, a bridge that connected Iran and Europe, joining them into one whole racial geopolitical entity within the corporeal body of the viewer through his actions of paying and peeping.

Vendors peddled the shahr-e farang, which comprised a 3 × 3 × 2 ft brass box with four legs that stood 4 ft tall and usually constructed with three holes containing magnifying lenses, through which one may have looked for a petty sum of one *shahi*, a coin of the smallest amount.[6] Artist Jinoos Taghizadeh has described the historical structure as "like a mosque, complete with minarets and colored glass."[7] Peering through the aperture, the viewer saw moving photographs or drawings, such as of London or Paris, and heard a story spun by the vendor.

There is no clear evidence regarding what kinds of images the vendors actually provided during the nineteenth and early twentieth centuries. Literature and scholarly work on these particular boxes are practically nonexistent. As a child, cultural critic Ali Behdad confirms that he did see images of European cities,[8] although he speaks from a later twentieth-century position, because he most likely saw these images during the 1960s, as the shahr-e farang was no longer in use by the 1970s. The advent of cinema, radio and television shifted the shahr-e farang's audience from adult entertainment to that of children and finally it went out of fashion altogether. Film scholar M. Ali Issari and theater historian Medjid Rezvani both agree that most of the images were indeed of "foreign towns."[9] Taghizadeh broadened the diversity of images to include foreign lands, buildings, persons, cars and animals.[10] Issari and Rezvani claim that one could have also viewed images of historical persons, the Russo-Japanese War (1904–1905), World War I (1914–18) and pornographic photographs of European women.[11] It is very plausible that the men were viewing pornographic peepshows, as imported pornographic photographs were common in Qajar Iran, and even the king Nasir al-Din Shah Qajar (r. 1848–96) had collected photographic pornography.[12]

Other possible images viewed were of popular tales, such as that of Amir Arsalan, "the young king of the Ottoman Empire," who had desired the daughter of a Christian monarch in Europe.[13] Not only did Arsalan take the woman by military force, but also introduced Islam throughout the European continent.[14] The court storyteller Naghib al-Mamalek told Nasir al-Din Shah fragments of this story every night until the shah fell asleep.[15] Perhaps through this narrative, the shah nurtured his own cartographic desires of Europe, which he had transcribed in his three published travelogues of his adventures in Europe, thereby creating his own personal shahr-e farang through word and text for both Iranian and foreign readership.[16] As David Motadel has described, travel literature in general creates "a self-other dichotomy," and the shah's own travelogues were no different by positioning Europe as an object to be gazed on "while simultaneously affirming Iran's cultural location."[17]

The name of the box, shahr-e farang, is complex, although the origin is unknown. The Arab counterpart was called *sunduq al-dunya* (box of the world),[18] and in different parts of the world, the peepshow had other various names. The name peepshow was used in the United States and Great Britain, as well as the magic lantern or Chinese lantern; in France, it was referred to as the *boite à vues d'optique* (box of optic views), the *Bilder-Guckkasten* (picture peep box) in Germany and *Il Mondo Nuovo* (the new world) in Italy.[19] Perhaps the label that each box carried in its respective country was only a coincidence, but nonetheless, the presentation of that particular box and what one was going to see may have been suggested by the box's name. For example, in China the peepshow was called *xiyangjing*, which translates to "Western mirror" or "Western scenes."[20] According to the Scottish photographer John Thomson (1837–1921), who had visited China in the 1860s and1870s and took a photograph of the xiyangjing, "[T]he eye of the spectator beholds the wonders of the world. Foreign pictures share the attractions with Chinese representations and moveable figures […]. Some of the subjects are of the most indecent character."[21] Although it was standard that one would see images of other countries in a peepshow, the Persian, Arabic, Italian and Chinese titles demonstrate this content most clearly. By the nineteenth century, capitalism and marketing were not new concepts, and in comparison to the names of the other peepshows, one has to consider why the Iranian version was specifically called the shahr-e farang. The name itself says that the vendors were selling a modern European content, specifically European cities and their modernization and technology.

The question of viewership is probably most difficult to assess, as primary sources ignore the shahr-e farang. The environment depicted in Sevruguin's photograph informs us of some of the types of persons viewing the shahr-e farang and its possible settings in which one could have found it (Figure 3.1). The males in Sevruguin's photograph seem to have been less than well-to-do, as their clothes appear simple and humble, yet a bit thick, indicating a rather cold climate. Their shoes, too, appear a bit worn. The man kneeling on the left wears an apron, indicating that he was an artisan or worker of some kind. Furthermore, the men look as though they were in an urban space, surrounded by brick buildings and an evenly laid out sidewalk.

The issue of social status has interesting implications here, especially when comparing the Sevruguin photograph to a later one of the 1940s, during the Pahlavi dynasty (1925–79), which shows a man peering through the shahr-e farang, wearing a smoothly tailored dark suit and intact shoes (Figure 3.2). The shahr-e farang through which he gazes has a shinier surface and more robust body than the dilapidated box in Sevruguin's photograph, although the environment he occupies seems to be going through some renovations or perhaps has been affected by the Allied invasion of 1941. Moreover, the quality and content of the images may have also corresponded to the quality of the shahr-e farang and the class level of its patrons.

The fact that Issari stresses the point that one could have enjoyed a peepshow for the smallest amount of currency suggests its accessibility to those of lower economic status. One could assume that initially during the Qajar dynasty, the peepshow was more or less popular entertainment for the lower classes, although that was not always the case in other countries. Sevruguin's photographic oeuvre carefully documented Qajar Iran, but his work had several motifs. These motifs included the Nasiri court, ethnography, architecture and daily life, usually of the mundane. The photograph of the shahr-e farang falls into the same group of photographs that illustrate average persons in the streets such as *The Ice Cream Vendor*, or less-than-noble scenes such as the corporal punishment of bastinado (Figures 3.3, 3.4).[22] The silence in the primary sources about the shahr-e farang may have also resulted from the idea that the earlier peepshow was oftentimes patronized by the lower classes and showed pornography and therefore was not worth mentioning.

The question that remains is what were those men thinking while they peered into the box? What drove them to pay to see what was inside? The men paid money to see the spectacles trapped within the box, a transmission definitely took place and a curiosity was aroused. What scholars do know about Qajar society includes the mass circulation of print matter from both within and without Iran, the modernization of institutions, such as the postal service and higher education, the arrival of Orientalist ethnographers and Europeans hired to assist modernization projects, the acceptance and incorporation of European inventions, such as the camera, the loss of territories to tsarist Russia and the British Empire, the increased presence of foreign diplomats and politicians and the departure of selected Iranian students to Europe. All those conditions (just to name a few) brought Iranians "closer" to the European cities at which they were gazing.[23]

Even more striking was the fact that major cities such as Tehran and Isfahan were being renovated to include paved streets, tramcars and commercial districts aside from the remaining old bazaars.[24] Many areas of the capital of Tehran were transformed into a style similar to the Haussmannization of Paris, which included the destruction of old city walls and buildings and the construction of long boulevards, sidewalks and commercial areas. Lord George Curzon (1859–1925) had even remarked in 1889, as he traveled the streets of Tehran, "Shops are seen with glass windows and European tiles [...]. Avenues, bordered with footpaths and planted with trees, recall faint memories of Europe [...]. [W]e are in a city which was born and nurtured in the East, but is beginning to clothe itself at a West-End tailor's. European Teheran has certainly become, or is becoming."[25] Eustache de Lorey, a member of the French legation at the Iranian court, wrote in 1907, "Of all his predecessors [...] it is [...] Nasr-ed-din who must be considered the Haussmann of Teheran. He constructed numerous edifices, and [...] built a quarter in the European fashion, with large avenues planted with trees."[26] Art historian Talinn Grigor also documents that several late Qajar buildings effectively incorporated Italianate, Christian and classical features.[27] With such striking similarities between Tehran and European cities, when the viewer looked through the shahr-e farang, the view virtually extended from the viewer's space into the space of the image. There were recognizable elements of his city in the views of the European cities, and his eyes were conduits that connected the two entities together. Although Lord Curzon also remarked, "[I]f the distinction can be made intelligible, it [Tehran] is being Europeanized upon Asiatic lines. No one could possibly mistake it for anything but an Eastern capital,"[28] there were also strange familiarities between European cities and (particularly) Tehran, so much so that even a colonialist such as Curzon could see them. Therefore, the shahr-e farang became more like Alberti's "open window,"[29] making the viewing experience seem more in touch with the viewer's own reality and creating surreal overlaps: had Europe and Iran really become two sides of the same coin?

As in any photograph, one looks through Sevruguin's eyes at the photograph presented, and it is through Sevruguin's lens that one sees the Iranian man and two boys watching a peepshow. One is shown Sevruguin's perspective as a way to understand this historical reality. Yet, perhaps as a way to make a "change in a sign system"[30] that creates a "site of displacement"[31] and somewhat dislodges the visual authority of Sevruguin, one could view Sevruguin's photograph from the male patrons' points of view, rather than understanding the transaction as simply an anthropological study.

The modern world has been framed through the primacy of vision,[32] privileging the "eye/I" positionality in the philosophies of positivism and Cartesianism to gather information about the world, and by looking through the shahr-e farang, a sense of agency and control over Europe had been acquired by these men.[33] Similar to the camera obscura, the shahr-e farang contained European cities between its suffocating walls for consumer pleasure. Communications theorist Suren Lalvani has described the camera obscura as a box that contains an exterior world as a private possession for a sovereign subject.[34] Professor of Critical Studies Anne Friedberg has also explained the effect of the camera obscura as "the outside is brought inside."[35] In the case of the shahr-e farang, men who had hardly any social or political power became sovereign subjects through the transaction, trapping the things of Europe inside the box. Unwieldy Europe was brought from without to within the peepshow, allowing for a certain metaphorical control and dominance.

In both photographs of the shahr-e farang, the shahr-e farang has two cylindrical, metal-like towers on either side, creating the semblance of a building. This structure becomes a theatrical setting, in which fantastic narratives come alive. The subject and the eye split, and the subject magically enters the space between his eye and the image. Through the aperture of the framed city, the subject acts out his cartographic desires, becoming a *flâneur*,[36] seeking to infiltrate the spaces of modernity – a voyeur who sees but is not seen – while experiencing new modern spectacles. The aperture connected Iran and Europe through the gaze of the patron, and when he looked through the shahr-e farang, while still standing in Iran, he saw Europe. He was transported through his gaze yet remained stationary in his own environment. This gaze connected the two geographical entities into one, uniting them into the materiality of his body. The cities of Europe connected with the changing cities of Iran, therefore making the melding of the patron's body and the box into a bridge that allowed the cities to run continuously together. While Nasir al-Din Shah was literally traveling in Europe and providing luminous detailed accounts of his journeys in his travelogues, these men performed repeatedly, through the act of looking into the shahr-e farang, visitations to Europe in their minds' eyes. Repetitively through each performance, through each show, they bent down, peered through the box and became one with Europe. Certainly, the shah's travels and his writings on them were performative acts that created a metaphorical shahr-e farang for his readers, but the average man, whose literacy was low or nonexistent,[37] could also become one with Europe almost whenever he pleased through the peepshow.

If the shahr-e farang did provide a similar type of intermediate space for one to consume the sights of modern Europe, then what could have this possession mean to its Iranian patron? I argue that through the gaze, the Iranian subject attempted to connect with Europe, creating a cartographic desire for Europe that was similar to the State's and that had to be repeated. Over time, Europe became the dialectical Other to the Self of the Iranian subject, and the reunion of the two could be completed and remapped through the shahr-e farang. The mobile and inexpensive nature of the shahr-e farang fostered a connection between Iran and Europe that became absorbed into the national narrative and memory, producing a longing for Europe as the Other half of the Self. In linguistic and other scholarly discourses during the height of European colonialism, both Orientalists and Iranians framed Europe as becoming more like Iran (as opposed to the other way around). The more that both Europeans and Iranians engaged and mimicked each other, the more connected they became as mirror images of each other.

In *States of Fantasy* (1996), literary critic Jacqueline Rose frames nationalism's goal of creating a State through Freudian theory. The fantasy, in general, is a psychic desire that has a historical memory in the mind of the human subject. The person who fantasizes has had a connection with the fantasized object or person at some point in the past but was separated from that object of desire through some traumatic event or dire circumstance. A desire for that object or person develops, and the person creates a fantasy that specifically attempts to reunite the Self with the Other, the object of desire. Rose frames a nation's desire for an exclusive State as a fantasy that exists within the minds of a group of people who share kinship ties.[38]

A desire for Europe, as created by the shahr-e farang for the general populace, is a fantasy about another State or geopolitical entity, separated by the framing of box itself. Yet, the "original" connection between Iran and Europe (that was supposedly severed in the distant past) meant that there was something familiar about Europe that had developed a desire in the Self (the viewer) for the Other (the European city). French psychoanalyst Jacques Lacan, particularly in his "mirror stage" argument, formulated this false self-recognition in desire. According to Lacan, the formation of the "I" occurs when the child looks in the mirror with the mother and realizes that he is a separate entity from his mother, thereby resulting in a fractured sense of Self. The mother, who was originally part of the Self, invariably becomes the Other, therefore making the Other something familiar and comforting.[39] Yet, because the notion of the Self is ultimately formed on fragmentation, desire for the Other is always based on lack – that the Self is never complete without the Other. Moreover, the search for the Self or its missing pieces is really the search for the Other and for reunification. Or in different terms, the desire for the Other is always the desire for the unfragmented Self.

The Self's desire for the Other is emphasized in the polarities between the two, which Lacan has defined as the "margin."[40] The margin, in this case, is the interface between the Iranian subject and the images of European cities, the box of the shahr-e farang. Every image has a border or frame, whether physical or implied, that cuts off the image and creates an unstable system with purportedly all the signs necessary to read it. In a larger context, this isolation created by borders of a city or State produces a traumatic split with the rest of the world. According to Jacques Derrida in *The Truth in Painting* (1987), the frame itself is violent and artificial, as it attempts to include and exclude, because the inside cannot be held within, nor can the outside be kept out.[41] Moreover, because of the artificiality and abnormality of these frames, those inside want out, and those outside want in. As those subjects penetrated the images within the shahr-e farang, they sought to enter the frames of the openings, placing them inside, from margin to center.

The shahr-e farang is a material, reified object that acted as a site of both latent State policy and the fetish of desire, through which patrons could physically perform desires after payment. Gender studies scholar Elizabeth Grosz, drawing on Deleuze and Guattari's concept of the machines of desire,[42] suggests that abstract desires are channeled into tangible sites by situating desire as "energies, excitations, impulses, actions, movements, practices, moments, pulses of feeling. The sites most intensely invested in desire always occur at a conjunction, an interruption, a point of machinic connection, always surface effects, between one thing and one another."[43] The site of the shahr-e farang is just such a machine of desire and site of contact, providing images of Europe to possess and consume, while at the same time making the patron quite aware of his

Self and position. The repeated discursive practices of paying the shahi, bending down and peering through the box were actions that enacted and completed the desire to see the things of Europe. Once the gaze and picture met through the box, that desire was temporarily fulfilled and satisfied.

Now, this desire to connect to a geographic location, which is repeatedly mapped by those who claim the land in one way or another, characterizes these desires as cartographic. Iran as a mapped entity is also an imagined one, because maps are only cartographic images that correspond to one's arbitrary ordering of the world. Literary critic Gayatri Chakravorty Spivak calls this concept of mapping "worlding": "The notion of texuality should be related to the notion of the worlding of a world on a supposedly uninscribed territory […] the imperialist project […] had to assume that the earth that it territorialised was in fact previously uninscribed. So then a world, on a simple level of cartography, inscribed what was presumed to be uninscribed. Now this worlding actually is also a texting, textualising, a making into art, a making into an object to be understood."[44] This textual "worlding" occurred when the Orientalists mapped themselves onto Iran as the designated area of European origins. Likewise, many Iranian scholars and politicians mapped Europe onto themselves as Orientalists basked in the glory of pre-Islamic Iran as their own. Both Europe and Iran were like *tabulae rasae*, waiting for (re)inscription at a moment of colonization and classification. Anthropologist Michael Taussig has claimed in *The Nervous System* (1992) that the State is a fetish, and so is the cartographic map that creates an image of a region that lives only in the imagination. Only earth exists. Moreover, as one performs this "worlding" through texts, as Spivak argues above, one then reifies these cartographic machinations into sensuous objects; hence, the box of the shahr-e farang becomes an object that enables a "worlding" of Iran and Europe into one mapped entity through the transmission of the space between the two, which takes place within the body of the viewing Iranian subject.

When Behdad discusses his perusal of Sevruguin's photographs in the Smithsonian archives, the photograph of the shahr-e farang re-created the most vivid memories of his childhood Iran.[45] The box posed as a door, through which he reentered the foreign Iran of his past. The fantasy of his Iran, which has traces in his childhood memories, reemerges when he remembers gazing into the box. Likewise, the men in the photographs opened their minds to foreign places that were not so foreign after all. The men looking through the shahr-e farang stood in Old Europe, looking at visions of New Iran, with its architecture and technology. As their gazes penetrated the holes, they united with the past and future visions of themselves; Iran cannot modernize, because it already has.

One must ask, "What are the roles of private, individual desires and the desires of the State?" Are the two different or intricately entwined? If one follows Rose's logic and believes that the State exists as a fantasy, feeding off one's own desires for belonging and oneness, then the private desires of the individual and that of the State always seem to find intersection. Even on a base level of mass consumption, which includes patronizing the shahr-e farang, Max Horkheimer and Theodor Adorno argue that mass or popular culture always comes from the structures of power, down to its populations.[46] By participating in mass consumption, one still, in some fashion, colludes with the State. Therefore, regardless of what kinds of images persons viewed in the shahr-e farang, they participated in popular culture together, and it was an act condoned, or at the very least ignored, by the State. Benedict Anderson describes the rise of the modern State through print capital; yet, Sandra Freitag and Eric Hobsbawm suggest that other media and material objects, such as films and flags, respectively, act as possible sites conducive to creating a sense of homogenized nationhood or Statehood.[47] In the case of the shahr-e farang, it confirmed to Behdad its "Iranianness," even though peepshow boxes have existed all over the world. There is nothing particularly "Iranian" about the shahr-e farang or the assumed images it highlighted. Yet, Behdad gazed at the nation, gazing at national desires, imagining Iran through the mutual consumption of Iranians of the past.

So, what were some of the conversations influencing the Iranian State during the Qajar period that may have promoted or encouraged, whether intentionally or inadvertently, a local desire for Europe, in addition to the visible modernization projects and cultural contacts taking place? It is clear that the travels and modernization projects of Nasir al-Din Shah and his son Mozaffar al-Din Shah (r. 1896–1906) were symbolically encouraged by and in harmony with the concept of the shahr-e farang, but another conversation taking place was by European scholars promoting a racial relationship between Europeans and Iranians. When the theory of Darwinism advocated that humans have a common ancestor, those claiming racial superiority had to reframe their positions, so that Europeans were not directly related to those outside who were already deemed inferior.[48]

Mostafa Vaziri has argued in *Iran as Imagined Nation* (1994) that most Orientalists latched onto Iran as an Aryan nation, because they had discovered through philology how Semitic the cultural roots of Egypt and Sumer were and therefore needed another bastion of ancient civilization with which to identify. One example of these Orientalist writers who constructed Iran as a pivotal Aryan civilization in Europe's cultural development was Joseph Arthur de Gobineau (1816–82) who worked for the French embassy in Tehran during the 1850s and 1860s. He wrote several texts on Iran that continuously bound Iranians, Aryans and Europeans, as well as enforcing the connections between Zoroastrianism and Christianity,[49] into one magnificent heritage: "[I]t is not uncommon to find the term 'Parsy,' or in the Arab transcription 'Farsy' for the more usual and correct 'Irany.' This name itself is nothing other than 'Ayrian' or 'Aryan,' which was the name common to all the white races at their origin."[50] He continued to explain that the white race emerged from Asia, splitting off into several groups, such as the Persians and "Hindus," while other groups migrated to Europe.[51] In his *The Inequality of Human Races* (1854), he claimed that out of the first seven civilizations in the world, six of them were created by Aryans (which included the Persians), and the last one owed its greatness to ancient Iran. He added, "There is no true civilization, among the European peoples, where the Aryan branch is not predominant."[52] His texts also repeatedly make cultural and temperament comparisons between Persians and other European groups, such as the Germans and Swedes, therefore creating a familiarity and sense of comfort for the European readers, as if the Persians were just one of them.[53] On a similar note, biologist T. H. Huxley (1825–95) had even argued that the home of the Aryans was actually Europe, and that the Iranians were originally descendents of migrating Scandinavians.[54]

The Persians, whom de Gobineau and others have constructed as white and related to Europeans, must also have been shown to be not Semitic (neither Jewish nor Arab), such as in their attitudes toward women. The treatment of women has long been a devised litmus test of a progressive civilization since the European Enlightenment of the eighteenth century, and in de Gobineau's texts, he showed Iranians to be superior to Semitic peoples: "In Iranian tradition there was no objection to women being seen out of doors, and the two sexes ate together at table; this followed from one of the oldest principles of the race, which gave great respect to wives and the mothers of soldiers. Semitic ideas were quite different; they considered women as merely love-objects, and therefore to be kept hidden on the assumption that any man who saw them would immediately desire them."[55] In de Gobineau's texts, including the quotation above, he accomplished several agendas. First, de Gobineau located European origins outside Europe by connecting them to Aryan civilizations. He was not the first to propose this concept, as linguists since the eighteenth century had made links between European languages and Sanskrit-based languages, such as Hindi and Persian, but certainly, his writings reinforced it, especially in relation to Iran.

Second, a Semitic origin would not have been deemed suitable for European heritage, because how could European imperialists have claimed global and racial superiority directly from ancient Semites, such as the Hebrews, Phoenicians, Egyptians and Assyrians? The legacy of attributing the death of Christ to the Jews, as well as the history of blood libel and sex with pigs (among other accusations of the Jews), could not have had a direct historical link to Christian Europeans.[56] So, as Orientalists lauded the successes of Aryan civilizations and Aryan-descended nations such as Iran, why not just say that Europeans came from the best stock? There is evidence of similar language patterns, so if anyone questions this relationship, just proclaim, "it's in the grammar."[57]

Even in relation to the arts, as European colonialism created an "Islamic Art" market, plundering and stealing artwork from Islamicate countries,[58] a discourse arose that differentiated Persian art from that created by Arabs. In a small handbook written in 1879 by Major R. Murdoch Smith, who participated in archeological expeditions in Iran and headed the Persian Telegraph Company,[59] he consistently argued that Persian "Aryan" art had remained more superior than that of the Arabs and what glory there was in Arab artistic contributions was actually made by Persians: "The successors and followers of Mahomed were after all but rude Bedouins, who gradually acquired culture from contact with the more refined countries which they overran […]. Persia, always an artistic country, could hardly have borrowed it [ornamentation] from her rude conquerors […]. The Arabs themselves were probably never an artistic people […]. It is far from improbable that even the Alhambra itself was chiefly the work of the Persians […]. Unlike the Arabs, the Persians have always been, and still are, artistic."[60] He continued to say that although there were Turkish elements in the Iranian population, the Aryan traits have remained strong and dominant. This ideology of Aryan superiority and dominance, as a discourse espoused by linguists and philologists, spread to the fields of art history, archeology and the European States, embodied in the governmental persons of both de Gobineau and Murdoch.

Yet, this legitimization of European heritage through Aryan peoples was not a one-sided project. Firoozeh Kashani-Sabet's *Frontier Fictions* (2000), Mohamad Tavakoli-Targhi's *Refashioning Iran* (2001) and Reza Zia-Ebrahimi's "Self-Orientalization and Dislocation" (2011) have demonstrated that the creation of "Iran" as Aryan and therefore racially superior and related to European blood was not only an Orientalist machination, but also one actively constructed by Iranians. Whereas European writers, such as de Gobineau, forged European origins onto Iran and participated in Orientalist discourses, scholars and politicians in Iran reciprocated and developed their own discourses about their relationship with Europe. Iranian scholar Mirza Aqa Khan Kermani (1853–96) mentioned that some *ulama-ye ishteqaq al-saneh* (historians) in Iran were attempting to make explicit connections between the French and Persian languages by saying that the root of the French word *histoire* (history) came from the Persian word *ostuvar* (firm, strong) and that for "the solidarity of the nation, we have no tool better than history."[61] Similar to Orientalist linguists, Iranian scholars had also attempted to connect the Indo-European languages as a basis to justify racial superiority and an intimate connection to Europe.

Yet, language was not only the proposed connection that Iran and Europe shared. Writer and critic Mirza Fath'ali Akhundzadeh (1812–78) believed that if the Qajar State could allow freedom of written expression, including simple prose and open critiques, Iran would be on equal footing with Europe within only 50 years.[62] Other writers, such as 'Abdu'l-Baha' (1844–1921), the son of Baha'u'llah (the founder of the Bahai Faith), promoted the advancement of Iranians as a given: "It should not be imagined that the people of Persia are inherently deficient in intelligence, or that for essential perceptiveness and understanding, inborn sagacity, intuition and wisdom, innate capacity, they are inferior to others [...]. On the contrary, they have always excelled all other peoples in endowments conferred by birth."[63]

Kermani had also assessed Iran and its accomplishments as already pivotal in the development of modernity: "[F]rom the darkness of history, it appears that things, such as the postal system and telegraph, were also invented in Iran, because the governments of wise need speedy correspondence and packages."[64] What has been considered "modern" or a sign of modernity in the rise of European political States, the postal system and telegraph were major components in connecting far-flung geographical regions into one homogenized national identity and conducive to creating a strong centralized State. In addition, the inventions of the many manifestations of the telegraph are usually credited to European and American inventors, but here, Kermani attempted to claim the telegraph for Iran. Signs of modernity and modern life did not disseminate from Europe (and North America) into the rest of the world for it to absorb; rather, Kermani provides the reader with an alternative site of modernity that competes with Europe's inventive prowess. In short, it was not Iran becoming more like Europe, but that Europe was *becoming* more like Iran.

In line with Orientalist anti-Semitism, Kermani had also made anti-Semitic remarks that suggested that whatever problems the Iranians had as a nation were as a result of Arabs and their forced influence on Iran. For example, in *Seh Maktub* ([Three letters], c. 1890s), he scolded in the third letter against religious Iranians who willingly endured abuses, while making the hajj (pilgrimage) to the city of Mecca in Saudi Arabia:

> You can imagine the degree of stupidity of Muslims, specifically Iranians, who, under no circumstances, intend to understand the main motive for the holy and

> clean religion and travel more or less for 1,200 farsakhs [leagues], for example, from the top of Tabriz to the Arabian Peninsula and bear all this hardship and struggle and spend a great amount of money into the Arab pockets, being belittled and insulted, beaten, half-dead, and they bring back with them as souvenirs the deadly and contagious cholera, bear buttocks, empty pockets, empty hands and many deaths.
>
> The wish that after all this hardship, they would learn their lesson and then not go back again. Oh, the wish that they would not go the second and third time and would not discuss and elaborate about the marshes of that hellhole Arabian Peninsula and the rat-eating, shameless Arabs. And also, they would not be satisfied with this and daily thirty-four times insistently face that burnt up land and would not worship this piece of rock covered in black cloth [Ka'ba].[65]

The passage reveals Kermani's negative sentiments toward Arabs and their perceived adverse effects on Iranian culture, differentiating Arabs from Iranians and blaming them for certain Iranian superstitious behaviors that Kermani certainly admonished. In addition to Kermani, Akhundzadeh held a low opinion of Arabs: "Illiteracy is throughout Arabia. Arabs are either begging and/or looting."[66] He also believed that the Arabic script was not efficient and useful for the Persian language and its expression, especially in contemporary literature; hence, another script should be implemented for Persian, such as Latin.[67]

The poet Yaghma Jandaqi wrote similar sarcastic sentiments about the Arabic language in his letters: "I don't know whether I have written *Salavatallah aleh* [the graces of God upon him] correctly, but it is a result of illiteracy,"[68] and "[A]las that I do not know Arabic, and since not knowing Arabic is considered illiteracy, claiming knowledge by illiterates, such as I am, is unethical."[69] Jandaqi was a great poet in the Persian language and was one of the first modern poets to privilege the Persian language: "[H]e [Jandaqi] has called them [his writings in Persian] himself '*parsi-e sareh*' or '*basit*' or '*parsinegar*' [Persian with little or no Arabic words]."[70] Jandaqi's comments show the overall predominance of Arabic and Arabic literature in intelligentsia circles,[71] in a country where Arabic was not the main language spoken; hence, he pointed out the irony, seeming bizarreness and contradiction in his letters, because he was devoted to writing Persian in Iran but was not socially considered educated or literate enough.

Finally, in 1866 Akhundzadeh wrote a letter to the editor of the *Ruznameh-ye Millat-e Iran* (Newspaper of the nation of Iran), complaining that the emblem of the newspaper was a mosque, which did not symbolize the nation of Iran at all, and that a more ancient symbol of Iran (i.e., before the Arab invasion) should be employed or one of Twelver Shi'a Islam, which is also definitive of (modern) Iran: "The symbols of the people of Iran before Islam are ancient Persian monuments, that is to say, Persepolis, the castle of Istakhr [...]. After Islam, one of the most famous monuments is that of the Safavid kings, who spread the Twelver religion throughout Iran and order its sentiments through the united realm – they were responsible for the separate, independent kingdom of Iran."[72] In *Maktubat* (Writings), Akhundzadeh blames Arabs directly for Iran's destruction, when Iran was defeated in 651 CE: "Where is the glory [in Iran], where is the power, where is the happiness – it has been 1,280 years that those naked and hungry Arabs destroyed you. Your land is destroyed, your nation ignorant […] and your kings are despots."[73]

These types of anti-Arab sentiments by nineteenth- and twentieth-century scholars and critics such as Kermani, Jandaqi and Akhundzadeh, were a strategy of *différance* that created an Iranian identity that excluded any semblance of an Arab one. These statements were not new to modern Iran, as the *shuubiyya*, a loose anti-Arab movement by non-Arab Muslims, can be traced back as early as the seventh century CE,[74] and scholar Rudi Matthee has shown that stereotypes of Arabs, such as being known as lizard eaters, hypocrites and robbers, were common cultural phenomena in Iran for centuries (but no less commonplace than prejudices toward Afghans, Turks and other Persian ethic groups, such as the Rashtis).[75] Yet, the sharp distinctions made between Iranians and Arabs and the framing of Arabs as illiterate, immoral people allowed for modern Iranian scholars to claim a more racially superior Aryan identity that was closer to Europe, and whatever problems Iran faced in its modernization process could be blamed on the supposed harmful Arab influences still circulating in Iranian culture(s). If Iran as a nation had trouble keeping up with Europe as a global power, it was the Arabs' fault, an anti-Semitic sentiment echoing that much like those in Europe toward Ashkenazi Jews. Historian Afshin Marashi has argued that this strategy was one of authenticity versus inauthenticity: because so-called Arab elements were "inauthentic" to indigenous Iranian culture, modernization in Iran was stymied. If Iranian culture could return to its "authentic" state, then Iran itself would realize its full modern potential (not so much different from the blood purity arguments in European nationalisms).[76]

The relationship, however, between Europe and Iran fashioning and mimicking each other for the benefit of the other was not always a reciprocal relationship. Whereas European scholars gladly accepted or posited a common heritage between Europe and Iran to escape any Semitic origin, some Iranian writers viewed this unity in more acrimonious terms. As European colonial empires were attempting to bring other geopolitical entities into submission through the proclaimed global and racial superiority of European imperialism, several Iranian intellectuals expressed resentment. This anger arose not solely due to the British, French and Russian empires' meddling in Iranian internal affairs, but also because if great European civilizations owed their white genes and languages to the Iranians, then why was Iran not also considered wholly modern by other global powers? Why did Iran lose major wars and territory to the European powers of tsarist Russia and Great Britain if Iran was racially part of Europe? If one follows the logic, global superiority originated in Iran, and powerful European countries stole or utilized that greatness at the expense of Iranians. Islamic intellectual Jamal al-Din Afghani (1838–97) argued:

> But what to do because many of you [in Iran] are so asleep, it seems that you are dead and the cotton of ignorance in your ear [referring to washed corpses that have cotton in the ears], you have no idea about anywhere. You people, your neighbors fooled you and you do not realize it, what science you know that they did not take from Iran and learned from it and completed it. Many of the industries were known by your scientists, that if you want, I can tell you and put forth the reasons: the

> lens – the camera [*dur bin*-binoculars?] – the telephone and the methods of when were they invented and who invented them. If the explanation were not long, I would tell you about them one by one that those [foreign neighbors] took those industries and completed them, and I am telling you why you were not able to complete them yourselves, as if they had six fingers […].You can answer that yes, the dictatorship [*hukomat-e istebdad* under the Qajars] has clasped our hands and feet that we could not pay attention or put our thought into these things. You people had had a strong government, but because of their [the Qajars'] negligence, it became weak.[77]

Jamal al-Din Afghani's words show that the reciprocation between Orientalists and Iranian scholars, although mimetic, is more problematic on the Iranian side of the equation. 'Abdu'l-Baha' also wrote similar sentiments: "Is it meet that a foreign people should receive from your own forebears its culture and its knowledge, and that you [Iranians], their blood, their rightful heirs, should go without? […] Is it commendable that you should waste away in apathy the brilliance that is your birthright, your native competence, your inborn understanding?"[78] At the expense of Iran, Europe became great, not the other way around, as the colonial model of modernization would have one think (i.e., that modernization disseminated from Europe to the rest of the world as a gift of civilization). European imperialism exploited natural resources, knowledge and labor for its wealth and did not give Iran its due credit or the share of the spoils, and the more Europe was becoming more like Iran, the more powerful it seemed.

Returning to the *Kashkul* image discussed in the introduction of this anthology, the Iranian artist was fully cognizant that Europeans looked down on Iran as a backward place and illustrated that contempt by depicting a deplorable Iranian booth at the world fair (Figure 1.1). What is even more important is that the second Iranian cartoon presented in the introduction shows two Frenchmen praising Iranian accomplishments: "To tell you the truth, Friend, never in Paris have I seen such a civilized, rational, impressive, and splendid celebration! It appears that the Iranians are […] progressing" (Figure 1.2). Although European scholars were willingly indebted to ancient Iran for part of Europe's modern grandeur, since they deemed the glory of ancient Iran now dissipated, some modern Iranians understood this condescension and felt robbed and insulted, expressing their disdain and restating the arguments in both writing and cartoons. Actually, there were many occasions when the European powers impeded the technological progress of Iran, such as the power play between Great Britain and tsarist Russia that had stymied a national railroad system in Iran until the 1930s.[79]

The second cartoon rectifies the situation with the Frenchmen praising the Iranians who even surpass the Parisians in their celebrations. In relation to the shahr-e farang, the momentary power of the box was in the possession of the men viewing the European cities. With these mixed feelings for Europe – attraction and repulsion – the shahr-e farang allowed for an Iranian dominance over Europe, for Europe to be consumed and penetrated, for Europe's identity to be shaped and codified within a box. Although the images themselves may have been taken by European photographers or drawn by European artists depicting a certain type of Europe, those images now belonged to an Iranian gaze, for Iranian pleasure and for Iranian interpretation.

The shahr-e farang could therefore provide a private world for the viewer, in which he could indulge in the pleasures of Europe without revealing that he was indeed gazing at European cities. Despite the government's support of innovations based on European advances, as well as sending Iranians from wealthier families abroad to receive European training, there was an overall societal ambivalence toward things European. Partly historical that Europeans were not as superior or clean as Iranians, there was also clerical and political opposition to things European, such as toward the losses of land to Russia and Great Britain, the Griboyedov Affair (1829) and the Tobacco Protest (1890–92). Furthermore, to be a flâneur, who had historical ties to the English male dandy, meandering in the European cities could elicit societal disdain in Iran. In *Women with Mustaches and Men without Beards* (2005), Afsaneh Najmabadi discusses the figure of *farangi'ma'ab*, a "Europeanized male dandy [...] who gravitates toward Europe."[80] This type of man could wear European clothes, perform European mannerisms and even mix his Persian with French.[81] Although this term could have been ambiguous or connote something positive, it could have also been used derogatorily.[82] Therefore, any delight in things European, although not discouraged by the State, was sometimes expressed discreetly, and the shahr-e farang provided the perfect outlet for viewing things forbidden or disliked, not only European cities, but pornographic images, as well.[83]

The Iranian male viewers had the desire to pay their precious money to see those European cities, but European war and sex were also possibly presented as narratives. Indeed, for these voyeurs the desire could be erotic as their eyes "penetrated" the cities of Europe. Their eyes became erect penises that entered the cities of Europe through the holes of the box and merged the two into one body.[84] This type of penetration could also apply to the many pornographic images also available for viewing in the shahr-e farang.

Yet, what does the pornographic image of a woman have in common with that of a European cityscape? Through the gaze, both are bodies – hollow vessels "awaiting" entry, possession, colonization and mapping. Postcolonial critic Anne McClintock writes, "The woman's body is the child's first space for knowledge and self-discovery, later the city, as the first space of modern self-knowledge, was mapped as a feminine space. Once feminized, the city was more easily represented and made docile for male knowledge, for such representations could depend on the prior fact of the social subordination of women."[85] From as early as the Safavid dynasty,[86] the motif of the city, where women, modernity, consumption and colonialism met, found its way into Iranian writings through the representations of European women who operated as sites of conquest, pleasure, modernity and progress: "The European woman (*zan-i Farangi*), was the locus of the gaze and erotic fantasy for many eighteenth- and nineteenth-century Persianate *voy(ag)eurs* of Europe [...]. The eroticized depiction of European women [...] engendered a desire for that 'heaven on earth' and its uninhabited and fairy-like residents [...]. The attraction of Europe and European women figured into political contestations and conditioned the formation of new political discourses and identities."[87] Bodies and borders reunited in both the images of the woman and the city. Inside the transformative space of the shahr-e farang, these cartographic desires found fulfillment through the penetrating eye of the viewing subject, who dreamed of bodies roaming European cities, merging the

Iranian body with the European one and creating one flesh in their copulation. In their viewing of the shahr-e farang, it was a modern tale of Amir Arsalan, in which the taking of Europe coincided with the taking of women.

The flâneur's "penetration" of the city in the shahr-e farang raises the question: "Was the gaze always male?" Did women also have access to the shahr-e farang during the nineteenth and early twentieth centuries? Certainly, girls viewed the shahr-e farang, but by the time television was available in Iran during the Pahlavi dynasty, the shahr-e farang had shifted to children's entertainment. Moreover, there is no documentation that women patronized the shahr-e farang when its primary pictures consisted of views of cities, war and pornography. Yet, possibly the head of a wealthy household could have invited a vendor inside the home, whereby women could have viewed the peepshow.

If Iranian women did view the shahr-e farang during the Qajar period, what were some of the implications of the female gaze? Did they "penetrate" the city as well? Yes, through the transmission between the orifice of the box and her eye, she, too, could have entered the cities of pleasure and consumption. Like her *flâneuse* counterparts in the department stores of Paris, for example, she was able to slip in and out of urban spaces, participating in the fluid crowds of the city.[88] While sporting the *shaliteh*, the ballet dress adopted by the shah's court after his trips to Europe, the Iranian woman of the court now possessed the modern mobile attire to roam these cities.[89] In the cities of Iran, she would have had to wear the *chador qalebi*, *chaqchur* and *roubandeh*. Yet inside the shahr-e farang, she was also not bound to the same restrictions as her female Parisian counterparts who were tied securely in their constricting corsets. The Iranian female eye could have moved and shifted through spaces that were otherwise forbidden to European middle- and upper-class women. She could have infiltrated these spaces without a chaperone, enjoying similar enticing spectacles as her male counterparts without defamation to her character.

Albeit, this reading of the viewer's relationship with the shahr-e farang and, by extension, Europe, may assume heteronormative interpretations, when sexuality in Qajar Iran was much more fluid,[90] and certainly, the viewing subjects could not be assumed to be monolithic stable ones (a problem in dealing with the subaltern, as it is not merely a positivist collective consciousness and a unified entity).[91] Finally, there is an assumption that European imperialism was a coherent institution, when it really varied from country to country, although in the case of Iran, the country itself did not undergo official colonization, but its sovereignty was still infringed on by the interests of primarily Great Britain, France and tsarist Russia. Yet, what I have attempted to show is that the repeated acts of patronizing the shahr-e farang during the Qajar dynasty created a desire to possess Europe on a local level, disseminating State agendas in relation to European colonialism and modernization and shaping modern Iranian identities.

Instead of Iran being simply a pawn in a colonial game (although it was at times), an alternative strategy emerged that framed Europeans as related to Iranians and even indebted to Iran for their greatness. By default in the discourses, Europeans were descended from Iranians, and their imperial prowess was owed to their Iranian heritage. Whatever successes the European powers had were due to their Aryan blood. In this way, Iran's constructed position in relation to European colonialism was special and more important than other non-European countries. Perhaps the encouragement of relating to

Europeans as lost Aryan brothers and sisters was itself a strategy, similar to Homi Bhabha's "Of Mimicry and Man,"[92] that Iranian officials and intellectuals utilized subversively to maintain Iran's uniqueness and sovereignty in the face of Europe's encroaching interests. Iranians became more cognizant of themselves as Self, as Iranian and different than the rest of the Middle East and Central Asia.

Even today, after the Iranian Revolution (1978–79) and the establishment of a democratic theocracy, Iran is still a unique, different entity in the Middle East. The many complex identities present in Iran, as well as having a classical past, claiming an Aryan heritage and executing modernization projects, while at the same time, being Muslim and Middle Eastern, still situate Iran as somewhere between Asia and Europe. Turkey has a similar hybrid identity, although part of Istanbul is actually in Europe. It comes as no surprise that Reza Shah Pahlavi (r. 1925–41) took many cues from Atatürk himself (r. 1923–38), and the earliest modernization reforms in Qajar Iran were inspired by the Tanzimat Reforms (1839–76) of the Ottoman Empire (1299–1923). Through their bodies and the desires of the humble men peeping into the shahr-e farang, political relationships between Iran and European powers were played out and ingested on a local level. Their small acts were indeed instrumental in creating a modern legacy by accomplishing State agendas and participating in new global identities.

Notes and References

1 I would like to thank Hope Werness, Michael Jerryson and Nuha Khoury for their comments in shaping this paper. Thank you to Farhad Tamadon for cross-checking my Persian translations. Finally, thank you to Julie Reuben and Betsy Kohut for helping me retrieve my research materials.

2 Although "farang" could possibly relate to the "foreign" in Persian, the word is mainly used for Europe and even the United States.

3 Talinn Grigor demonstrates how architecture and art history also accomplished these racial–political agendas in "'Orient oder Rom?' Qajar 'Aryan' Architecture and Strzygowski's Art History," *The Art Bulletin* 89, no. 3 (September 2007): 562–90.

4 Rudi Matthee, "Between Aloofness and Fascination: Safavid Views of the West," *Iranian Studies* 31, no. 2 (Spring 1998): 241.

5 Ibid., 227, 241.

6 Mohammad Ali Issari and Doris A. Paul, *A Picture of Persia* (New York: Exposition Press, 1977), 107–8; Mohammad Ali Issari, *Cinema in Iran, 1900–1979* (London: The Scarecrow Press, 1989), 42; and Farrokh Gaffary, "Evolution of Rituals and Theater in Iran," *Iranian Studies* 17, no. 4 (Autumn 1984): 364.

7 Jinoos Taghizadeh, Artist Statement, unpaginated.

8 Ali Behdad, "Sevruguin: Orientalist or Orienteur?" in Frederick N. Bohrer, ed., *Sevruguin and the Persian Image: Photographs of Iran, 1870–1930* (Washington, DC: Arthur M. Sackler Gallery, 1999), 79.

9 Issari, *Cinema in Iran, 1900–1979*, 42–3 ; and Medjid Rezvani, *Le Théâtre et la Danse en Iran* (Paris: G. P. Maisonneuve et Larose, 1962), 121–2. See also Sadek Asha, *The Evolution and Development of Iranian Cinema: From Film-Farsi to the Post-Revolutionary Cinema, with Particular Reference to Islam and Popular Entertainment Culture* (Dissertation: University of Sussex, 1998), 73.

10 Taghizadeh, ibid.

11 Rezvani, ibid. Perhaps the images these men paid to see were indeed of *farangi* [European] women, since mass production of *cartes-de-visite* and stereographs during the nineteenth century disseminated European pornography worldwide.

12 Nazila Fathi, "A Rare Glimpse of 19th-Century Iran," *The International Herald Tribune*, June 1, 2007, Feature, 22. Medjid Rezvani says that one could see pornographic depictions of European women in the shahr-e farang. Rezvani, *Le théâtre et la danse en Iran*, 121–2.

13 Issari, *Cinema in Iran, 1900–1979*, 43, and Issari and Paul, *A Picture of Persia*, 108.

14 Issari, *Cinema in Iran, 1900–1979*, 43.

15 Ibid.

16 Nasir al-Din Shah Qajar, *The Diary of H. M. the Shah of Persia during His Tour through Europe in A.D. 1873*, J.W. Redhouse, trans., and Carole Hillenbrand, introduction (Costa Mesa: Mazda Publishers, 1995); *A Diary Kept by His Majesty the Shah of Persia, during His Journey to Europe in 1878*, Albert Houtum Schindler and Baron Louis de Norman, trans. (London: Richard Bentley & Son, 1879); and *Ruznameh-ye Khaterat Nasir al-Din Shah dar Safar-e Sevvum Farang* (Tehran, 1370/1990).

17 David Motadel, "The German Other: Nasir al-Din Shah's Perceptions of Difference and Gender during his Visits to Germany, 1873–89," *Iranian Studies* 44, no. 4 (July 2011): 569.

18 Gaffary, "Evolution of Rituals and Theater in Iran," 364.

19 Laurent Mannoni, *The Great Art of Light and Shadow: Archaeology of the Cinema*, Richard Crangle, trans. and ed. (Exeter: University of Exeter Press, 2000), 71, 86.

20 I would like to thank Susanna Lam for this translation.

21 John Thomson, *China and Its People: An Unabridged Reprint of the Classic 1873/4 Work*, foreword by Janet Lehr (New York: Dover, 1982), unpaginated.

22 There are contemporaneous sources that mention the bastinado, partly because it was a punishment used at the court. For example, see Harry Gardner Cutler and Levi W. Yaggy, *Panorama of Nations; or, Journeys among the Families of Men: A Description of Their Homes, Customs, Habits, Employments and Beliefs, Their Cities, Temples, Monuments, Literature and Fine Arts* (Chicago: Star, 1892), 533–4; Reverend *Samuel Graham Wilson, Persian Life and Customs: With Scenes and Incidents of Residence and Travel in the Land of the Lion and the Sun*, 2nd ed. (London: Oliphant Anderson and Ferrier, 1896), 66, 86, 169, 184, 186; and Reverend Isaac Adams, *Persia by a Persian: Being Personal Experiences or Manners, Customs, Habits, Religious and Social Life in Persia* (London: Elliot Stock, 1906), 19, 117–22.

23 Department of Research Publication and Education, *Khoshunat va Farhang (Violence and Culture: Confidential Records about the Abolition of Hijab, 1313–1322 H.SH)* (Tehran: The Iran National Archives Organization, 1371/1992), x.

24 Afshin Marashi, *Nationalizing Iran: Culture, Power, and the State, 1870–1940* (Seattle: University of Washington Press, 2008), 32–4; Heidi Walcher, "Face of the Seven Spheres: Urban Morphology and Architecture in Nineteenth-Century Isfahan," *Iranian Studies* 33, nos. 3–4 (Summer/Fall 2000): 332, 346–7; and Jennifer M. Scarce, "Ancestral Themes in the Art of Qajar Iran, 1785–1925," in *Islamic Art in the 19th Century: Tradition, Innovation, and Eclecticism*, ed. Doris Behrens-Abouseif and Stephen Vernoit (Leiden: Brill, 2006), 233–5.

25 George N. Curzon, *Persia and the Persian Question*, vol. 1 (New York: Barnes and Noble, 1966), 306.

26 Eustache de Lorey and Douglas Sladen, *Queer Things about Persia* (London: Eveleigh Nash, 1907), 44–45.

27 Grigor, "'Orient oder Rom?,'" 573.

28 Curzon, *Persia and the Persian Question*, 306.

29 I am using the traditional understanding of Alberti's metaphor. For a more nuanced interpretation, see Anne Friedberg, *The Virtual Window: From Alberti to Microsoft* (Cambridge, MA: MIT Press, 2006).

30 Gayatri Chakravorty Spivak, "Subaltern Studies: Deconstructing Historiography," in *Selected Subaltern Studies*, ed. Ranajit Guha and Gayatri Chakravorty Spivak, foreword by Edward W. Said (Oxford: Oxford University Press, 1988), 3–4.

31 Ibid., 4.

32 Hal Foster, ed., *Vision and Visuality* (New York: The New Press, 1999) is a collection of papers by various scholars who challenge the supremacy of vision in modernity. These contestations range

from a phenomenological perspective of the world that includes the senses of the entire body to the psychological and mystical perceptions of the mind that do not depend on empiricism. These authors even challenge Cartesianism as a vision-centered philosophy. Although I agree with these scholars fundamentally, I still find that the gaze of the Iranian subject and the perspectival line it creates to the European city are what binds the two together into one entity. The shahr-e farang becomes the mediator, through which the gaze can connect to the image. Rosalind Krauss' essay in the collection, "The Im/Pulse to See," does bring up an interesting point in relation to the *Gestalt* of the image. Although one may attempt to order images or create a one-to-one relation between the gaze and the image, the perception of that image will vary depending on who views the image and one's psychological make-up. One's mind automatically reorders the image according to the a priori ordering of one's mind. Therefore, one could argue that with the shahr-e farang, it is not the primacy of vision that makes the box successful, but how each individual perceives the image psychically.

33 It should be noted that this positivist view of modernity is primarily European, but the power of the shahr-e farang depends, in part, on this positivist perspective and the primacy of vision. For a discussion on the European nature of positivism, see J. N. Pieterse, "Dilemmas of Development Discourse: The Crisis of Developmentalism and Comparative Method," *Development and Change* 22 (1991): 24.

34 Suren Lalvani, *Photography, Vision, and the Production of Modern Bodies* (Albany: State University of New York Press, 1996), 14.

35 Friedberg, *The Virtual Window*, 61.

36 I am basing the definition of the flâneur on Charles Baudelaire: "For the perfect *flâneur*, for the passionate spectator, it is an immense joy to set up house in the heart of the multitude, amid the ebb and flow of movement, in the midst of the fugitive and the infinite. To be away from home and yet to feel oneself everywhere at home; to see the world, to be at the centre of the world, and yet to remain hidden from the world." *The Painter of Modern Life and Other Essays*, ed. and trans. Jonathan Mayne (London: Phaidon, 1964), 9.

37 Juan Cole estimates that the literacy rate of Qajar Iran was around 2–3 percent. Juan R. I. Cole, "Marking Boundaries, Marking Time: The Iranian Past and the Construction of the Self by Qajar Thinkers," *Iranian Studies* 29, nos. 1–2 (Winter-Spring 1996): 37.

38 Jacqueline Rose, *States of Fantasy: The Clarendon Lectures in English Literature 1994* (Oxford: Clarendon Press, 1996), 5.

39 Jacques Lacan, *Écrits: A Selection*, trans. Bruce Fink (New York: W. W. Norton, 2002), 299.

40 Ibid.

41 Jacques Derrida, *The Truth in Painting*, trans. Geoff Bennington and Ian McLeod (Chicago: University of Chicago Press, 1987). See chapter "The Parergon," 37–147. Deborah Cherry, "Earth into World, Land into Landscape: The 'Worlding' of Algeria in Nineteenth Century British Feminism," in *Orientalism's Interlocutors: Painting, Architecture, Photography*, ed. Jill Beaulieu and Mary Roberts (Durham: Duke University Press, 2002), 103–30, pointed me to this reference.

42 See Gilles Deleuze and Félix Guattari, *Anti-Oedipus: Capitalism and Schizophrenia*, preface by Michel Foucault (New York: Penguin Group, 1977).

43 Elizabeth Grosz, *Space, Time, and Perversion: Essays on the Politics of Bodies* (New York: Routledge, 1995), 182.

44 Gayatri Chakravorty Spivak, *The Post-Colonial Critic: Interviews, Strategies, Dialogues*, ed. Sarah Harasym (New York: Routledge, 1990), 1. Deborah Cherry, "Earth into World, Land into Landscape," 103–30, pointed me to this reference. Art historian Svetlana Alpers has a similar term to Spivak's called "the art of describing," which implicates the perspectival lines of the gaze in art with the rise of cartography and correlates these lines of sight with the longitudinal and latitudinal lines of the map. Therefore, through the lines of the gaze penetrating through the shahr-e farang, one could colonize and re-map the image on the other side and even graft oneself onto it – a line is, after all, simply the distance between two points. See Svetlana Alpers,

The Art of Describing: Dutch Art in the Seventeenth Century (Chicago: Chicago University Press, 1983). Martin Jay, "Scopic Regimes of Modernity," in *Vision and Visuality*, ed. Hal Foster (New York: The New Press, 1999), 3–23, pointed me to this reference.

45 Behdad, "Sevruguin: Orientalist or Orienteur?," 79.

46 Max Horkheimer and Theodor W. Adorno, *The Dialectic of Enlightenment: Philosophical Fragments*, ed. Gunzelin Schmid Noerr, trans. Edmund Jephcott (Stanford: Stanford University Press, 2002), 115, 124–5. Culture becomes an industry, constructed and distributed by those who own the means of production to promote the goals and desires of those in power (i.e., CEOs of the film, music and print industries). We as consumers absorb the abundant advertising and propaganda and eventually "buy" into the standards set for us. In time, any deviation from these constructed standards elicits mostly disapproval from others.

47 Benedict Anderson, *Imagined Communities: Reflections on the Origin and Spread of Nationalism*, rev. ed. (1983; repr., London: Verso, 1991); Sandra Freitag, "Visions of the Nation: Theorizing the Nexus between Creation, Consumption, and Participation in the Public Sphere," in *Pleasure and the Nation: The History, Politics and Consumption of Public Culture in India*, ed. Rachel Dwyer and Christopher Pinney (New Delhi: Oxford University Press, 2001), 35–75; and *The Invention of Tradition*, ed. Eric Hobsbawm and Terence Ranger (Cambridge: Cambridge University Press, 1992).

48 Marashi, *Nationalizing Iran*, 73–4.

49 Although Christianity does have theological and historical relationships to Zoroastrianism, de Gobineau emphasizes them to enhance his racial arguments. J. A. de Gobineau, *The World of the Persians* (Geneva: Minerva S. A., 1971), 47, 81, 85.

50 De Gobineau, *The World of the Persians*, 6.

51 Ibid.

52 Arthur de Gobineau, *The Inequality of Human Races* (New York: Howard Fertig, 1999), 212.

53 De Gobineau, *The World of the Persians*, 115–16.

54 T. H. Huxley, *Man's Place in Nature and Other Anthropological Essays* (London: Macmillan, 1910), 305.

55 De Gobineau, *The World of the Persians*, 115–16.

56 See Henry Abramson, "A Ready Hatred: Depictions of the Jewish Woman in Medieval Antisemitic Art and Caricature," *Proceedings of the American Academy for Jewish Research* 62 (1996): 1–18.

57 For a short history of how Indo-European philology transformed into ethnology, see Reza Zia-Ebrahimi, "Self-Orientalization and Dislocation: The Uses and Abuses of the 'Aryan' Discourse in Iran," *Iranian Studies* 44, no. 4 (July 2011): 448–52; see also Marashi, *Nationalizing Iran*, 74–5.

58 Term coined by historian Marshall Hodgson: "Islamicate would refer not directly to the religion, Islam, itself, but to the social and cultural complex historically associated with Islam and the Muslims, both among Muslims themselves and even when found among non-Muslims." *The Venture of Islam: The Classical Age of Islam*, vol. 1 (Chicago: University of Chicago Press, 1977), 59.

59 Victoria and Albert Museum, accessed January 19, 2012, http://www.vam.ac.uk/content/people-pages/sir-robert-j-murdoch-smith/

60 Major R. Murdoch Smith, RE, *Persian Art* (London: Chapman and Hall, Limited, 1879), 3–4.

61 Mirza Aqa Khan Kermani, *Ayneh-ye Sikandari: Tarikh-e Iran* [The Alexandrian mirror: The history of Iran], vol. 1 (Tehran: s.n., 1324/1906), 14. See also Mohamad Tavakoli-Targhi, *Refashioning Iran: Orientalism, Occidentalism, and Historiography* (New York: Palgrave, 2001), 103.

62 Mirza Fath'ali Akhundzadeh, "The Art of Critica," in *Mirza Fath'ali Akhundzadeh: A Literary Critic*, trans. Iraj Parsinejad (Piedmont: Jahan Book Co., 1990), 70.

63 'Abdu'l-Baha', *The Secret of Divine Civilization*, trans. Marzieh Gail (Wilmette: Baha'i Publishing Trust, 1990), 9.

64 Kermani, *Ayneh-ye Sikandari*, 110.

65 Mirza Aga Khan Kermani, *Seh Maktub* [Three letters], ed. Bahram Choubine (Frankfurt/ Mein: Alborz Verlag, 2005), 205–6.

66 Mirza Fath'ali Akhundzadeh, *Maqalat* [Articles] (Tehran: Chapkhaneh-ye Ziba, 1351), 116.

67 Mirza Fath'ali Akhundzadeh, "The Methods of Writing," in *Mirza Fath'ali Akhundzadeh: A Literary Critic*, trans. Iraj Parsinejad (Piedmont: Jahan Book Co., 1990), 71. See also Marashi, *Nationalizing Iran*, 70–71.

68 Thank you to David Simonowitz for translating the Arabic phrase, which is indeed incorrect.

69 Yaghma Jandaqi, letter to Haji Ismael Tehrani, quoted in Seyyed 'Ali Al-e Davud, introduction to *Majmu'eh-ye Asar-e Yaghma-ye Jandaqi: Ghazalat, Masnaviha, Marasi, Sardarye* [Collection of writings by Yaghma Jandaqi: Ghazels, masnavis, tragedies, classics], ed. Seyyed 'Ali Al-e Davud, vol. 1 (Tehran: Entesharat-e Tus, 1357), 35.

70 Seyyed 'Ali Al-e Davud, introduction to *Majmu'eh-ye Asar-e Yaghma-ye Jandaqi: Ghazalat, Masnaviha, Marasi, Sardarye* [Collection of writings by Yaghma Jandaqi: Ghazels, masnavis, tragedies, classics], ed. Seyyed 'Ali Al-e Davud, vol. 1 (Tehran: Entesharat-e Tus, 1357), 35.

71 Seyyed Hossein Nasr, "The Significance of Persian Philosophical Works in the Tradition of Islamic Philosophy," in *Essays on Islamic Philosophy and Science*, ed. George Faldo Hourani (Albany: State University of New York Press, 1975), 72.

72 Mirza Fath'ali Akhundzadeh, "Qeritica," in *Mirza Fath'ali Akhundzadeh: A Literary Critic*, trans. Iraj Parsinejad (Piedmont: Jahan Book Co., 1990), 19.

73 Mirza Fath'ali Akhundzadeh, *Maktubat* [Writings] (Entesharat-e Mard-e Emruz, 1364), 20–21.

74 Roy P. Mottahedeh, "The Shu'ubiyah Controversy and the Social History of Early Islamic Iran," *International Journal of Middle East Studies* 7, no. 2 (April 1976): 161.

75 Matthee, "Between Aloofness and Fascination," 222–4.

76 Marashi, *Nationalizing Iran*, 72.

77 Jamal al-Din Afghani, "Tarikh-e Ijmali-e Iran [A brief history of Iran]," in Fursat Shirazi, *Divan Fursat*, ed 'Ali Zarrin Qalam (Tehran: Kitabfurushi-e Sirus, 1337/1958), 72.

78 'Abdu'l-Baha', *The Secret of Divine Civilization*, 91–2.

79 Staci Gem Scheiwiller, "Iran in the 1930s," review of *Exploring Iran: The Photography of Erich F. Schmidt, 1930–1940*, by Ayşe Gürsan-Salzmann, *History of Photography* 33, no. 1 (February 2009): 105.

80 Afsaneh Najmabadi, *Women with Mustaches and Men without Beards: Gender and Sexual Anxieties of Iranian Modernity* (Berkeley: University of California Press, 2005), 138.

81 Ibid., 139. Latent homosexuality was also tied to the figure of the *farangi'ma'ab*, much like the European dandy.

82 Ibid.

83 Negar Mottahedeh remarks that when aspects of modernization were disliked in Qajar Iran, the label "Babi" was applied to the innovations as a derogatory term, not "farangi." Her argument adds nuance to 'Abdu'l-Baha''s *The Secret of Divine Civilization*, which defends the modernization of Iran so pointedly. See Mottahedeh, *Representing the Unpresentable: Historical Images of National Reform from the Qajars to the Islamic Republic* (Syracuse: Syracuse University Press, 2008), 28; and 'Abdu'l-Baha', *The Secret of Divine Civilization*, 5, 13, 14.

84 Jean Clair describes the phallic power of the eye and the gaze in his article "La pointe à l'oeil [The gaze of the eye]," *Cahiers du Musée Nationale d'Art Moderne* 11 (1983): 73, 75.

85 Anne McClintock, *Imperial Leather: Race, Gender and Sexuality in the Colonial Contest* (New York: Routledge, 1995), 82.

86 Rudi Matthee, "Between Aloofness and Fascination," 242.

87 Tavakoli-Targhi, *Refashioning Iran*, 54.

88 The flâneur and the flâneuse, by default, are bourgeois or upper class. For one to roam the cities in search of modernity, one needs free time and economic freedom from harsh labor. In the case of women, they need generous incomes and credible chaperones to shop in department stores (shopping became one of the most dignified "avenues" that allowed women of good reputation

and high class to venture throughout the city). See Anne Friedberg, *Window Shopping: Cinema and the Postmodern* (Berkeley: University of California, 1993). Although I believe that we can contest and reframe these notions, my agenda here is not to argue who can be a flâneur or a flâneuse. The power structures behind modernity have intricate ties to capitalism and the bourgeoisie, shaping the modern experience for all of us in general, as cities, buildings and factories develop and expand, and obsessive consumption permeates all aspects of our lives. The flâneur and the flâneuse have played instrumental roles by having the agency to shape and define the modern experience for us. Positing the factory worker and prostitute as our subaltern flâneur and flâneuse opens up possibilities for further investigation. The case of the servant Hannah Cullwick in McClintock, *Imperial Leather* provides an excellent foundation for investigating the Other voices of modernity. See also Molly Nesbit, "In the absence of the parisienne […]," in *Sexuality and Space*, ed. Beatriz Colomina (New York: Princeton Architectural Press, 1992); and Janet Wolff, "The Invisible *Flâneuse*: Women and the Literature of Modernity," *Theory, Culture, and Society* 2, no. 3 (1985): 37–46.

89 Many have debated on the origin of the *zirjameh*. Most have agreed that this skirt is an appropriation of the ballet tutu that Nasir al-Din Shah saw in Europe, while attending many ballet performances. He did indeed record his fascination with ballerinas in his travelogues. For the ballet interpretation of the *zirjameh*, see Shireen Mahdavi, "Women, ideas and customs in Qajar Iran," in *Persian Studies in North America: Studies in Honor of Mohammad Ali Jazayery*, ed. Mehdi Marashi (Bethesda: Iranbooks, 1994). For contestation of this interpretation, R. Jackson Armstrong-Ingram, "The Shah, the Skirt, and the Ballet: A Menage à Trois, or Just Ill-Founded Gossip?" *Qajar Studies* 4 (2004): 91–107.

90 See Najmabadi, *Women with Mustaches and Men without Beards*; Kathyrn Babayan and Afsaneh Najmabadi, eds, *Islamicate Sexualities: Translations across Temporal Geographies of Desire* (Cambridge, MA: Harvard University, 2008); Willem Floor, *A Social History of Sexual Relations in Iran* (Washington, DC: Mage Publishers, 2008); and Janet Afary, *Sexual Politics in Modern Iran* (Cambridge: Cambridge University Press, 2009).

91 Spivak, "Subaltern Studies,"10–11.

92 Homi K. Bhabha, *The Location of Culture* (New York: Routledge, 1994), 85–92. Monica Ringer suggests that reform and modernization through Islam and technology were also strategies to counter or mitigate what would have been considered "Westernization," thus allowing the Qajar State to become modern without succumbing to imperialist influences. See "The Discourse on Modernization and the Problem of Cultural Integrity in Nineteenth-Century Iran," in *Iran and Beyond: Essays in Middle Eastern History in Honor of Nikki R. Keddie*, ed. Rudi Matthee and Beth Baron (Costa Mesa: Mazda Publishers, 2000), 60–61. Ringer also nuances how modernity did not necessarily equate Westernization in *Pious Citizens: Reforming Zoroastrianism in India and Iran* (Syracuse: Syracuse University Press, 2011), 10–13.

4

TAKKIYEH DOWLAT: THE QAJAR THEATER STATE

Babak Rahimi

Ta'ziyeh, the commemorative theatrical play that dramatically depicts the martyrdom of the grandson of the Prophet Muhammad (c. 570–632 CE) – Imam Hossein ibn 'Ali (c. 626–80) – at Karbala in 680 CE during the first ten days of the Islamic month of Muharram, appeared as the most significant public display in nineteenth-century Qajar Iran (1786–1925).[1] Under Nasir al-Din Shah Qajar (r. 1848–96), ta'ziyeh developed into elaborate theatrics of processional and stationary ceremonies, performed around a melodic eulogy and recitation of the Karbala event known as *rowzeh-khwani*, reaching its height in popularity with the construction of the royal theater, the Takkiyeh Dowlat, in 1868–69. Tied to the construction of city spaces such as boulevards and royal buildings, the Takkiyeh Dowlat represented a massive ceremonial site, the largest in the capital city, Tehran, where ta'ziyeh plays were organized and performed by actors with considerable elaborate preparation, performance sophistication and visual richness that underlined the splendor and dramatic effect of the plays.

Ta'ziyeh is a passion play of a sacred event, and yet it differs on many levels from the Christian commemorative rituals, with its roots in the medieval period, because its dramatic staging of mythical warfare between good and evil takes place in the course of a theatrical enactment of a military battlefield.[2] In broad theocosmological terms, the tragic martyrdom of Imam Hossein on the tenth day of Muharram, known as the 'Ashura', identifies an event of metahistorical importance. For Shi'i Muslims, Imam Hossein's drama of martyrdom represents not only a sinister episode in human history during which the rightful heir to the Islamic caliphate was unjustly murdered, but also a time to renew allegiance and fidelity to the celestial forces embodied in the Prophet and his family at an imagined battlefield of sacred importance, namely Karbala. Such devotion is less about expressions of a doctrine of suffering than the fostering of emotions, bonds and constructions of spatial and temporal forums of collective memory, through which a distinct worldview is established and reshaped in the course of ritual processes.

I would like to acknowledge Peter Chelkowski, Ali Gheissari and Afshin Marashi for their generous and thoughtful comments on an earlier version of this paper. Also, I would like to thank Peyman Eshaghi and Reza Kochak-zadeh, at the Majlis Library for providing me with valuable sources for this paper.

In a significant way, the cultural history of Karbala rituals marks the (re)formation of a community of remembrance, a collective of long-lasting moods as described by Clifford Geertz, that projects sacred meanings onto the here and now by symbolically allowing the ritual participants to partake in performances through embodied practices in the immortality of a transcendent entity, namely the prophets, imams and their devoted followers.

Throughout history, such community-building aspects of Muharram rituals have undergone many transformations. With the Safavid monarchy (1501–c. 1736) making Shi'i Islam the official religion of the State in Iran in the early seventeenth century, a politicization of Muharram took form that considerably transformed the commemorative ceremonies into State official rituals and hence spectacles of power, through which the Safavid shahs legitimized their authority and, more importantly, formed a Shi'i Iranian collectivity in contrast to a Sunni Ottoman identity. In the post-Safavid period, Muharram rituals had grown so popular and widespread throughout Iran that they had become an aspect of everyday life. With considerable economic and popular religious importance under the Qajars, ta'ziyeh emerged in civic theaters that shaped new sacred spaces, known as *takkiyeh*, closely tied to the social spaces of interaction in everyday places such as streets and public squares.

The construction of the Takkiyeh Dowlat in 1868–69 was a significant departure from earlier spatial practices of ta'ziyeh performances.[3] In symbolic political terms, the Takkiyeh Dowlat constitutes a type of performative space of mourning in making visible the permanency of monarchic claims of legitimacy based on the story of Karbala – a sacralization of the State through the performance of metanarrative(s) based on primeval myths of evil and good. The dramatic practices of rowzeh-khwani present a type of "social text" through which the State is rendered meaningful through spectacles of pomp and ceremony. Yet, more importantly, such political theater of mourning involves a collective space of embodied practices that inscribe a modality of citizenship that foster feelings of integration and evoke visions of awe and commitment with respect to a hierarchy of power relations – a site where both the monarchs and the people can feel and imagine being part of a community of mourners.[4] At the heart of the Takkiyeh Dowlat is the production of power as a performative site of its own visual production.

This chapter aims to elucidate the performativity of State power in its Qajar manifestation, not merely in terms of how elites use symbolic practices to legitimize power, but also how the State is essentially a performative process that is ultimately made meaningful (or recognized) through plots, scripts and ritual staging practices built around intense emotions of a collective force. Here, the key difference between what I call an "elite institutionalism" and a performative approach is that whereas the former focuses on the elites' abilities to use ideas, emotions or symbols effectively as means of propaganda to reinforce control over a population, the latter approach considers all the political actors, including the elites and the denizens, as performers situated in an unstable set of power relations and who creatively participate in fostering feelings of collective integration, thus making visible the State's power through dramatic practices.[5] In other words, elites, regardless of their cultural contexts, do not operate outside the performative processes by merely orchestrating or giving patronage to public events of commemoration; rather, their public identities are closely tied to various dramatic practices that *perform* a State into an entity of authorial importance. The notion of embodied practices, borrowed from Michel Foucault and elaborated by thinkers such as Talal Asad, underscores the Takkiyeh Dowlat as a major performative site in staging collective experiences to stabilize power and communicate the continuity of the institution of monarchy. [6]

This study is divided into two sections. The first will focus on the historical formation of takkiyeh as a performative space of political significance since the Safavid period. Tracing back the history of the Takkiyeh Dowlat to the Safavid period is critical, because the Qajar State had its roots in the Safavid project of State building between the sixteenth and seventeenth centuries, although the Qajar period maintained its own novel political ritual practices distinct to the nineteenth century. Inclusive of the Safavid State legacy was the formation of a distinct Perso-Shi'i collectivity identity that was shaped largely under the reign of Shah Abbas I (1587–1629), in close connection with the promotion of new State rituals and the construction of the new Isfahan.[7] The second section will examine the history of Takkiyeh Dowlat in the Qajar period, with a focus on its architectural and staging history. The study combines both cultural and social theories to frame an account of the Takkiyeh Dowlat as a theater State of a distinct Perso-Islamic nature.

Takkiyeh: The Formation of a Sociopolitical Space

Although its origins remain unknown, the term "takkiyeh" refers to Sufi lodges based in towns or cities where mystical ceremonies or devotional remembrances were performed by a medieval Anatolian network of mystical brotherhoods in the later Middle Period (1250–1500).[8] In the Persianate context, however, "takkiyeh" largely refers to a public site in which the Karbala story is theatrically staged and watched by an audience that closely interacts with the front stage where the mourning performances are put on display. Historically, the shift of meaning from devotional lodges, usually of a secretive nature, to public commemorative events, inclusive of denizens of a rural or urban local nature, derives from the transformation of Sufism, from a sectarian-mystical movement to a militant-political one during the fourteenth to sixteenth centuries. By the rise of the Ottoman and the Safavid-Sufi brotherhoods, mystical ceremonies of secretive orientation had merged with public devotional practices. In the case of Safavids, the fusion of Sufi practices and Shi'i commemorative ceremonies such as Muharram marked the development of unique cross-cultural practices grounded in mythical and symbolic references to the ethos of *javanmardi* (chivalry), camaraderie and mystical union with the divine and Shi'i ideals of martyrdom led by *futavvat* clubs or mystical fraternities.

By the nineteenth century, the idiom and imagery of takkiyeh had been fully inserted into the Muharram culture, specifically identified as a communal-ceremonial site in commemoration of the martyrdom of Imam Hossein. For the most part, the origins of takkiyeh can be traced back to the Safavid period when the commemorative rites were promoted as political rituals amid ambitious city and State building, especially in the early seventeenth century under Shah 'Abbas I (r. 1587–1629). Although the mourning ceremonies have been performed in Iran and Iraq since 963 during the reign of Mu'izz al-Dowleh of the Buyid dynasty (934–1055), by the rise of Shah Isma'il (1501–24) in 1501 and the declaration of Shi'i Islam as the official religion of the newly formed empire, Muharram saw a growth in popularity in major cities, such as Isfahan, Tabriz and Shiraz. In part, Safavid shahs gave patronage to Muharram ceremonies as a way to promote to Shi'i Islam and centralize their authority as the heads of the new imperial State founded on the ideology of Shi'i messianic monarchy.[9] Yet, the Safavids, by and large, also helped develop the rituals into new dramatic spectacles for shaping a coherent imperial identity as a distinct social space, wherein representations of Karbala generated emotional solidarity with the shah whose authority was identified with the holy imams on earth.[10] A major development in the rituals occurred under the reign of Shah 'Abbas when the Muharram festivals saw major developments in close connection with the building of new cosmopolitan spaces in Isfahan where the ceremonies were staged and shaped into public spectacles. With the building of Maydan-e Naqsh-e Jahan (1598–1629) and other public spaces, Muharram ceremonies developed into elaborate public performances, and their popularity grew dramatically with the introduction of new repertoires of pageantry and symbolic practices.[11] Under the reign of Shah Suleiman (1666–94) and Sultan Hossein (1694–1722) – the last Safavid shahs – the ceremonies developed into highly popular processions with distinct pageantry characteristics, which laid the grounds for the emergence of ta'ziyeh in dramaturgical terms of plot-driven plays and stage performances in the eighteenth century, as depicted by William Francklin (1786–87) in his travel account.[12]

It is not clear how extensively Muharram celebrations were performed in the earlier period of the Safavid rule under Shah Isma'il, because there are no indications of the ceremonies in any documents.[13] Even in the early years of Shah Tahmasb (1524–76), who gave patronage to various cultural and devotional Shi'i practices, Muharram celebrations were not mentioned in the works of either Persian historians or European travelers such as Giovanni Maria Angiolello in 1524 and the Venetian ambassador Vincentio d'Alessandri in 1527. The dearth of reports about the ceremonies in the early sixteenth century does not necessarily downplay the possible public performance of rituals under Shahs Isma'il and Tahmasb. The absence of accounts suggests that the rituals may have been performed by a limited number of Shi'i adherents to the Safavid shahs who were mostly minorities among a larger Sunni Iranian population.

The travel account of the Venetian diplomat Michele Membré marks the earliest recorded testimony of the ceremonies in the Safavid era under Shah Tahmasb in 1542. Membré described Muharram as follows:

> In the month of May they perform the passion of a son of 'Ali, wherefore they call him Imam Husain, who fought with a certain race which they call Yazid, and had his head cut off [...]. From evening to one hour of the night the companies go around through the city and through the mosques chanting in Persian the passion of the said Imam Husain. This they call 'Ashura, that is ακιουρ. And that began on 1 May, up to the tenth. I saw young men make their bodies black and go naked on the earth. I saw another thing on the square which they call after Begum, someone make a hole underground like a well, and put himself in it naked and leave only his head out, with all the rest in the hole, packed in with earth up to the throat; and that was to perform that passion. This I saw with my own eyes. In the evening all the

> ladies betake themselves to their mosques and a preacher preaches the passion of the said son of ʻAli, and the ladies weep bitterly.[14]

This illuminating description provides a rare glimpse into a new development in the history of Safavid Muharram rituals. First, there appears to have been a strong performative element of self-flagellation in the form of the "Begum" ritual, involving the burial of oneself as a way of mourning for the martyrdom of Imam Hossein. Various elaborate forms of physical and symbolic violent performances began to play a more important role in the ceremonies around this period under Tahmasb. Another element was the absence of the king from public displays of ceremonies. This feature later changed with the reign of Shah ʻAbbas and his successors, especially ʻAbbas II (r. 1642–66) who actively participated in the ceremonies. Under Tahmasb, Muharram rituals saw a major patron, whose absence from the ceremonies, at least according to Membré's account, would suggest bifurcated domains of symbolic authority that separated courtly from popular ritual cultures. Likewise, Tahmasb's support for Muharram should be viewed in the same light as his efforts to restore mosques, *awqaf* (endowment institutions) and shrines in Ardabil, Qom and Mashhad; moreover, his promotion of other ritual practices, such as eulogies and poetical elegies for the imams and ritual cursing known as *tabarra'iyan* of the first three Sunni caliphs, was as a policy of converting the Sunni population to Shiʻism.[15]

With the death of Tahmasb in 1576, the Safavid dynasty saw a period of turmoil that led to a major civil war. It is largely due to this political instability that there are no accounts of Muharram ceremonies from this period. Yet with the advent of Shah ʻAbbas to power in 1587, the understanding of Muharram underwent a considerable transformation. In 1602–1604, simultaneous with the first construction phase of the new Maydan-e Naqsh-e Jahan in Isfahan, Portuguese traveler António de Gouvea (1575–1628) provided the first description of the public mourning ceremonies in Shiraz. According to de Gouvea, the festival of "Achur" ('Ashura') was performed in the *maydan* (city square), where the governor, riding on a horse, accompanied the mourning procession amid a boisterous crowd and discordant music. With ten days of fasting and refraining from work, men and women came together in the maydan and marched toward the Grand Mosque. The procession included symbolic representations of the characters of Karbala, as children and women, seated on animals, cried and wailed. Along with realistic representations of wounds and injuries on the ritual participants' heads and faces, male penitents engaged in ritual battles with long painted sticks. In the course of these ritual combats, they fought to the point of death, and their corpses left on the square. Other dramatic performances, such as volley firing, fired by a number of male participants parading in front of the empty coffins, were also on display. In de Gouvea's account, self-burial rituals continued to be present in the course of the ceremonies.

The most important travel account after de Gouvea's is the report by Della Valle in Isfahan in 1618–19. He described in detail the ceremonies and what follows compromises a part of his account:

> [W]here people circulate in the square, towards noon every day one of their mullahs preaches about Hussein, recounting his praises and his death. This is usually carried

> out by one of those from the generation of Mohamet (who are neither called emirs, as in Constantinople, nor shereefs, as in Egypt, but, by the Persians in Arabic, seidi or lords), wearing a green turban on the head, such as I have never seen here at other times (contrary to Turkey, where those of the same breed wear one constantly). And he sits on a slightly raised seat, encircled by an audience of men and women, some standing, some on the ground or on lowstanding benches and from time to time he shows some painted figures illustrating what he is recounting; and, in brief, in every way he endeavours as much as he can to move the onlookers to tears. Such preaching are heard every day in the mosque, and also at night in the public streets, in certain recognized which they purposely adorn with many lights and with funeral displays; and the preaching is accompanied by the moans and groans of the hearers, and particularly the women, who beat their breast and make piteous gestures, often answering grief-stricken with these last words from some of their hymns: Vah Hussein! Sciah Hussein! Meaning "Ah Hussein! King Hussein!"[16]

Della Valle continued his account with a depiction of the final days of the ceremonies, leading up to day of the 'Ashura'. Similar to de Gouvea's report, Della Valle also wrote about various ritual fights between the participants. It is also worthy of mention that during the same period, according to Iskandar Beg Munshi, Safavid soldiers also observed Muharram before battle with the Ottomans. So, there seems to have been a connection between Muharram and military culture under Shah 'Abbas's reign, which may highlight features of the institutionalization of a new Ghulam military order in place of the Qizilbash tribal forces. In the context of State building and urbanization, by 1618–19, Muharram ceremonies appear to have become more dramatic in symbolic spectacles in the form of banners, ceremonial armory, pageantries of coffins and mock corpses of the martyred imam and his followers at Karbala.

The testimony of Spanish diplomat Garcia de Silva y Figueroa in Isfahan (1618–19), however, provides a slightly different account, which highlights a new development in Muharram rituals – that is, rituals of camel sacrifice. In his account of the ceremonies during the height of Shah 'Abbas' reign, Figueroa described a camel being ceremoniously taken outside the city and sacrificed on the day of 'Ashura'. First, the most beautiful and well-bred female camel, embellished with flowers, herbs, garlands of leaves, silk sheets, plates of gold, bells and carpets, was walked through the city. As the participants furiously beat themselves, the *darugheh* (chief of police) of Isfahan and other officials, accompanied by an armed crowd of noisy men, gathered on a large plain near the river outside the city. They made a circle around the animal, and as the camel lay on the ground with its legs tied, the darugheh struck a lance into the camel. Immediately, a boisterous crowd with sharp swords ripped the animal into pieces. Some were injured, and others are killed, as mourners continued to fight among themselves for the flesh of the animal. Once a piece of the slaughtered meat was obtained, some participants took it to the cemetery, while others ran through the city, beating themselves, shouting and crying. The aggressiveness and the fury of the people were so intense that the darugheh and his men failed to control the crowd. The city was then given license to chaos, as the ceremony led to great rage and unruliness. The ritual appeared to end at that stage.

For the most part, the growing importance of camel sacrifice rituals underscores an enhanced importance of symbolic performances in the mourning processions as emerging spaces of political theater where the State claims legitimacy through various spectacular performances of public violence.[17] Although there is little mention of camel sacrifice rituals during Muharram in travel reports that follow Figueroa's report, the accounts of travelers, such as Fedot Afanasievich Kotov (1624), Thomas Herbert (1628), Jean de Thevenot (1665) and Engelbert Kaempfer (1684–85), all spoke of a growing emphasis on dramatic performances and enhanced spectacles, mostly taking place at major public places, such as city squares.[18]

Under Shah Safi (r. 1629–42), Muharram became even more popular, mostly because of its various spectacular displays that attracted many people from both the cities and rural regions. However, as Adam Olearius and others have accounted, rowzeh-khwani also became a major feature of the mourning processions, highly popular among participants who participated in the ceremonies. Hossein Wa'iz Kashifi's *Rowzat al-shuhada* (908–1502) served as the main text for Safavid rowzeh-khwanis, providing a highly emotional commemorative account of the tragic events at Karbala for the devotees of the martyred imam, especially those in the futtuvat fraternal circles with mystical orientations and the Persianate ethos of javanmardi.[19] By the time of Shah 'Abbas II, early forms of *shabih-khwani*, according to the travel report of Jean Chardin (1643–1731), were put on stage at the royal court in the Talar Tavileh in Isfahan, serving as an occasional place for performing the rituals that would follow sumptuous feasts.[20] Later in the Qajar period, rowzeh-khwani developed into a more complex ritual known as *ta'izyeh-khwani*, sponsored not only by the king but also by a variety of social groups, such as the *bazaaris* (bazaar merchants) and guilds.

Later in the Safavid period, Muharram rituals had grown even more in sophistication under the patronage of Shah Suleiman and Sultan Hossein. The most intriguing description is by the Dutch traveler Cornelis De Bruyn (1704) who described the popular ceremonies performed in a dramatic fashion.[21] These later accounts also testify to the increase of pageantries and theatrical performances with participants acting out the tragic story of Karbala staged on shifting and stationary podiums. The dramatic performances were so elaborate that some of the actors had painted their bodies red and black as a way to exhibit injuries from battle. However, as Peter J. Chelkowski has argued, these dramatic displays were not ta'ziyeh performances in the way that we understand them today, because they excluded eulogies and textual lyrics so commonly associated with the theatrical passion plays.[22] The travel report of Jesuit Christian missionary Tadeusz Krusinski (1714) offers the final account of Muharram under the Safavid era, with a description that ultimately confirms the development of the processions into elaborate theatrical spectacles highly popular among the masses in all Iranian towns.[23] By the eighteenth century Muharram had become a major imperial festival deeply embedded in the seasonal religious life of Safavid Iranians. It was in the blending of auditory and visual practices, however, that ta'ziyeh emerged as a new theatrical genre in Muharram cultural practices.

Although sporadic references to Muharram are made in various sources after the collapse of the Safavids, the travel report of English traveler William Francklin in October 1787 in

Shiraz provides one of the first accounts of ta'ziyeh (or shabih-khwani) spectacles.[24] In this account, under the reign of Jafar Khan Zand (1785–89) and before the ascent of the Agha Muhammad Khan Qajar (1742–97) to power, Muharram had developed into a complex pageantry of stationary ritual performances, though temporary or shifting in ceremonial time, mainly inside the mosques where religious clerics exerted authority over devotional performances. In its later developments, the public street intersections and squares formed central forums in the staging of ta'ziyeh. Such public sites underlined the open-air, convivial aspect of ta'ziyeh theatrical performances, by which the boundaries that separate the audience and the actors were constantly disrupted by the street-carnivalesque tendencies of the dramatic ceremonies, or in what the English traveler Matthew Arnold had described as the place where "the public meets the actor halfway."[25] In light of the significance of the street and square as spaces of misrule and everyday interactions, it is highly likely that the Muharram ambulatory processions merged with the stationary practices after the collapse of the Safavid dynasty, as Chelkowski and others, such as Sadeq Humayuni, Farrokh Ghaffary and Bahram Bayzai, have suggested, sometime during the eighteenth century when the centralized State of Nader Shah (r. 1736–47) became weak, which led Muharram to distinct *civic* events of musical drama and poetic oratory ensemble.[26]

With the rise of Fath 'Ali Shah Qajar to power in 1797, ta'ziyeh, along with rowzeh-khwani, began to be organized in the houses of notables where the ceremonies had gained popularity among the elites.[27] By the middle of the nineteenth century, the popularity of ta'ziyeh had spread not only to private residences, but also to other civic spaces, especially neighborhoods where various social groups, later known as *heyat* or associations, would compete, interact and display their territorial markers in the course of the ceremonies.[28] The spread of ta'ziyeh also coincided with the proliferation of other Shi'i ritual practices in various art forms, including lithographic literature and the construction of *Hosseiniyeh*, where other Muharram rituals, mostly *sineh-zani* (chest-beating) processions and rowzeh-khwani, would be performed.[29] With the rise of Nasir al-Din Shah, the popularity of Muharram, especially in its ta'ziyeh form, had grown so expansively that Tehran included a number of major takkiyeh sites at the cross section of neighborhoods, the most famous being the Takkiyeh Nayib-e al-Saltaneh and Takkiyeh Sahib-e Divan.[30] This development served as a key indicator of the way that civic life had begun to revolve around spaces of sacred masquerade – sites of performances by devotee actors playing parts of the Karbala characters (or other prophetic or spiritual characters) in Qajar society that identified an integral fabric of daily and night life.

As a civic ritual, in the words of Afshin Marashi, ta'ziyeh "stood in sharp contrast to the insular ceremonies performed in the royal palaces."[31] But the formation of the first royal takkiyeh changed the disjointed zones between the courtly and civic ceremonial spaces. In the early nineteenth century, ta'ziyeh theatrics began to be performed opposite the king's Golestan Palace.[32] The movement from the public streets and squares to notable residences eventually appeared near the Golestan Palace at an old abandoned area known as the Argh (palace) where Nasir al-Din Shah had ordered the construction of the Takkiyeh Dowlat sometime between 1868/9 and 1873.[33]

The origins of the royal ta'ziyeh site can be traced back to vizier Mirza Aqa Khan Nuri (1851–58). The Qajar vizier promoted Muharram ceremonies, and specifically ta'ziyeh-khwani, in Tehran, naming the Haji Mirza Aqasi Takkiyeh as the first Takkiyeh Dowlat.[34] Yet the new State Takkiyeh, near the eastern side of the Golestan Palace, was most likely inspired by the Parisian Opera House and not, as it is commonly viewed, the Royal Albert Hall in London. This is so, since Nasir al-Din Shah returned from his first trip from England in 1873, nearly five years after the building of the takkiyeh, according to some accounts, had begun.[35] It is also likely that the takkiyeh was built under the supervision of the shah's advisor, Dust 'Ali Khan Muayyir al-Mamalik, though non-Iranian architects may have also helped in the design process.[36] While during his earlier years of rule, Nasir al-Din Shah was not entirely interested in promoting the ceremonies, hence giving authority to Mirza Aqa Khan Nuri to manage and organize State-sponsored Muharram events, in his later years, the shah offered remarkable patronage of the ceremonies.[37] With the construction of the State Takkiyeh, ta'ziyeh performance found its largest theatrical stage, thus transforming the dispersed civic ceremonies into singular official State rituals, mostly performed throughout the year, including the months of Muharram and Safar.[38]

The critical point of transformation here is not merely that the State transformed a civic ceremony into a political ritual, hence rationalizing a public ritual, but with the construction of the takkiyeh, the Qajar State became fused with the public ritual life as a way to constitute a civil religion of distinct Shi'i-Iranian character. In many ways, Nasir al-Din Shah's original intention for building the State Takkiyeh was not to stage a religious event, such as ta'ziyeh, but mostly to watch the performance of secular or comedy plays similar to those he had seen in Europe.[39] But with the opposition from the clerics and other social groups, the shah was forced into making the site into a mostly civic–religious site where ta'ziyeh would have been performed on a regular basis throughout the year for a larger audience made up of denizens. What the State Takkiyeh had to offer Nasir al-Din Shah was, in part, the possibility to legitimize power as, according to Abbas Amanat, "a logical, and inevitable, extension of these dramatic recitations that offered the shah and the Qajar State, rather than the 'ulama, the chance to display their dedication to Shi'ism and its martyred saints in full view of the multitudes."[40] However, what is missing in Amanat's account of the legitimizing process in the construction of the State Takkiyeh is the communicative aspect of the staged performances and their political significance. The key here, I suggest, is to understand how ceremonial space is shaped, not according to royal patronage (and its objectives), though certainly an aspect of the ceremonial space, but in connection with the visualization of power, or how power is staged in performative ways, through which the State can be communicated, felt, seen and remembered by both the audience and the performers. The critical point is to identify the performative processes, through which the monarchy (court) and denizens (civic sphere) shared a singular space of interaction, wherein a distinct Iranian national identity was affirmed through the symbols of mourning and public memory of martyrdom.

State Takkiyeh and the Staging of Power

In architectural terms, Takkiyeh Dowlat was unique from other takkiyehs in Qajar Iran. Unlike mostly square- or rectangular-shaped takkiyehs modeled after caravanserai (inns), Takkiyeh Dowlat compromised an ellipse-shaped arena, symmetrical in horizontal and vertical axes where auditory and visual practices intermingled in a fantastic circular space of dramatic sight.[41] American diplomat S. G. W. Benjamin famously likened the Royal Takkiyeh to the amphitheater of Verona, famous for its large-scale theatrical and operatic performances.[42] As a three-story building, with a removable tent suspended over six pieces of iron and wood ceiling arches, though at times like an open-air arena, the takkiyeh served as a public playhouse where audiences could see both the stage and other audiences in the hall.[43] Each floor was devoted to a segment of Qajar society according to social status, with the first reserved for the court, aristocrats and diplomats and, as the European traveler Lady Sheil has described, with the shah's box at a central position "facing the performers," the second floor for female court audiences and the third floor for the drummers (*nagharechiha*).[44] The tall brick structure, 24 meters in height and 2,824 meters in area, included three major doors, with each door functioning as a separate entryway for the male, female and royal audiences.[45] The walls of the amphitheater were covered with decorative tiles, creating a mosque-like atmosphere to the architecture's aesthetic ambience. In the middle of the hall, 40 lights hung over a circular stage where the ta'ziyeh performers would climb up from two of its sides. A circular pathway marked the space around the central stage, separating the audience from the space of performance, where actors on horses or camels would enact battle or travel scenes alongside the circular platform. Finally, on one side of the takkiyeh, an elevated *ayvan* (porch), where the shah would watch the ceremonies, formed a visible site from the view of the many who would attend the performances.

In his famous painting of the Takkiyeh Dowlat, court painter Kamal al-Mulk (1847–1940) provides a realistic pictorial depiction of a colossal circular space marked with geometric symmetry of a visual perspective from inside the building, a part hidden from the perspective of the painter (Figure 4.1). In a way, Kamal al-Mulk created a visual representation of the takkiyeh that has meaning only insofar as the observer participated in the visual order of what was presented as visible, emphasizing a visibility of a grand scale that entailed an illusion of depth in pictorial space. The paradigm of perspective in representing and participating in the takkiyeh's spatial order marked an enunciated strategy that not only underlined the interplay between space and visibility, but also performed as a way of participating in an enclosed, circular site where the audience and the actors merged into a single audience-performance stage.

Such an architectural practice of staging in the fusion of the spatial and visual, I argue, plays an integral role in the performative constitution of Takkiyeh Dowlat. In its circular structure, the Takkiyeh Dowlat had no "backstage." The doors, through which the performers and other theatrical objects or animals were brought into the building, were mostly transit spaces, walkways for entering the site, hence, part of the performative construction of the site. Unlike proscenium stages, which audiences sit in front of, the "theater-in-the-round" or arena stage of the Takkiyeh Dowlat did not have any singular or central platform where the actors could formally perform detached from the auditorium. The *sako* (middle platform stage) of the Takkiyeh Dowlat served only as one stage performance among many others, compromised by the audiences surrounding the stage in the amphitheater as an open space – perhaps an indication of ta'ziyeh's roots as a street-performance play. The "open space" stage identifies what Jamshid Malekpour has described as a communicative medium for the playful creation of characters, so the actors can "create the essence of their characters quickly, to demonstrate their essential characters quickly, and to distance themselves from their roles in a manner that allows them to participate in the performances not only as players, but also as spectators."[46] Yet, the intermingling between actor and audience domains in forming a "quick" play of characters enunciates the importance of symbolic performances, through which everyone can be at once both audience member and performer, thus demanding emotional empathy with the martyred characters and forming a public memory of shared grief.

The arena stage therefore inherently demanded participation from the audiences, as it brought the actors in the same staging site with the spectators. The audiences, in a performative way, became key actors in the theater process. In its minimalistic set design, audience and actors viewed one another in an open and interactive setting, hence making the *entire* Takkiyeh Dowlat into a massive, collective stage for performing ta'ziyeh. Such minimalist performative practice is also evident in the written *shabih-nameh* directorial plays, in which descriptions of plots and theatrical props are kept to a bare minimum by leading ta'ziyeh directors, such as Muhammad Baqir Moin al-Boka, and, at times, poetry is used for a guideline to the sequences of the play.[47]

Moreover, the spatial practice of designating the royal box, from which the shah watched the performances and received salutations from the actors at the beginning of the ceremonies, marked a unique elevated space *among* the audience. The ceremonial space highlighted a way of staging royal power, space from where the shah could have been viewed both in hierarchical distance and yet among the denizens in the auditorium. Such complex hierarchy-horizontal relations bespeak a spatial ordering of sovereignty that underscores legitimacy through an architectural practice of representing power amid a civic space crowded with the denizens. Given the proximity of the takkiyeh to the royal palace, the popular ritual life joined the domain of the monarchy in a "common ceremonial space."[48] Such a shared space partly served as an enunciation of kingship authority in the performance of the ceremonial presence of the king among the denizens of the city. Everyone, including the king, could have participated in the shared openness and in the recognition of a community of mourners, collectively participating in grief over the martyrdom of their imam at Karbala, though imagined from different perspectives and positions of sight.[49] Yet, in the takkiyeh staging of politics, royal representations were closely tied to the audience's field of vision in the organization of power in the theatrical space. The theatrical dynamics of power served not only a ceremonial function for enhancing royal authority, but also enabled the viewers to see the shah and his court as part and parcel of a greater performing process narrated, enacted and displayed within the building as a site of performing both societal and State relations.

In terms of performance, the ta'ziyeh served as an intertextual domain within the takkiyeh symbolic complex. As a ceremonial recitation of the Karbala story with performers depicting various scenes, ta'ziyeh at the takkiyeh could be viewed as a textual imperative, through which royal authority was musically or visually staged in a series of commemorative eulogies to the imam and his tale of martyrdom at Karbala. Here, the circularity of the Takkiyeh Dowlat conveyed the theatrics of sacred recitation in that all the denizens could have heard, seen, expressed and experienced during the course of narrative representations of Karbala in a contained, spherical space. The radical departure from earlier ta'ziyeh performances under earlier Qajar rulers lies in the visual practice of staging commemorative mourning practices as a way to experience the splendor of the performances on an immobile space that could have been viewed from all angles, experienced and therefore *internalized* from a circular-theatric perspective. Such an embodiment of sorrow, felt and shared by both audiences and actors though varied experiences and performances according to age and gender, reveals a cultivation of selfhood that revolves around a collective phenomenon, cemented in the experiences diffused among the denizens in an ensemble of operative staging of mourning.

Moreover, the circular platform, on which the ta'ziyeh performances would have been displayed, also marked a royal staging of power, because the actors and directors would have been sponsored by the monarch who would have paid them from the royal treasury. In both terms of organization and the theatrics of performance, power was visualized by making a performative domain wherein the physical and symbolic overlapped, thus endowing a shared space with an aura of mythical tales and signs of cosmic drama. The notion of mythical narrative here does not denote a discursive "paradigm" through which stories of Karbala merely attain a moral standard for action in diverse temporal and spatial settings.[50] In contrast, I consider mythical narratives as a set of disruptive performances – interruptive of ordinary time and everyday space – which can, in part, confirm the symbolic-mythical power of the State in cosmic-moral terms. In the commemorative stories of Karbala, both the shah and the people stepped outside ordinary time to participate in a mythical time of loss and triumph and in turn made the takkiyeh a social dramatic space of shared experiences, a site wherein Imam Hossein and his followers became the "we" inside the auditorium.[51]

Identity and theatrical textuality intertwine in a way that constructs a *performative boundary* of the inside-outside complex, wherein participants (both the shah and his subjects) felt integrated into a collectivity within the takkiyeh. Mournful eulogies as ritual performances play a key role here. The dramatic oral performance of rowzeh-khwani was sanctioned to transmit a metanarrative of the death of Imam Hossein to which the participants could have related and associated themselves so as to produce traditions and knowledge of a natural and eternally preexisting order. In this sense, State sacralization was achieved not because of the way the shah could effectively legitimize his political authority through religious rituals, but in the way power was constructed in spectacles and musicals of mourning that generated emotions among the civic audiences and foreign diplomats in the stalls and on the ground or the performers on the stage.[52]

The integration of civic and royal space is pivotal to the formation of what Geertz has famously called the "theater state," a reference to his famous study of Negara in nineteenth-century Balinese rituals that showed how States enact and represent power in the medium of ritual performances.[53] The "theater state" denotes textual/visual performances in the form of ritual processes that rationalize power relations between the symbolic center and the periphery, between authority and the subject, constructing a sociopolitical order that transcends ordinary time and space, in which death is always a spectacle of power. Ritual plays an integral role in the way performances can be displayed and reinvented. Dramatic spectacles and representations are more than merely legitimizing elite power; they are also about the ceremonial constitution of State power in an open space, visible and acknowledged by all. In other words, the power of the State is generated from performances of symbolic force, exemplifying royal power in the theatrics of stories, myths, tropes or metaphors of permanence and stability.

In its most theatric manifestation, the Qajar Takkiyeh Dowlat represented a type of political spectacle that recast already familiar myths and chivalric tales of heroism, mostly shared in everyday civic spaces, such as the open-space public squares or neighborhoods, within a contained, though (semi-)open, theater space. It is in such theatrical spaces that the royal institution is embodied among aesthetic practices, such as drumming, oration, colorful paraphernalia, art and symbolism closely associated with Imam Hossein and the tragedy at Karbala. This is precisely why after his assassination in 1896, the ta'ziyeh for Nasir Din Shah was also observed in the takkiyeh. The continuity of the monarchy after the death of a shah would have been staged in a visual site of shared, collective remembrance. The theatrics of takkiyeh primarily marked the effectiveness to memorialize and make permanent the authority of the monarch beyond his biological death. The shah's individuated death would therefore become collectively meaningful and attain a renewed vitality at the Takkiyeh Dowlat.

In this study, I have only focused on the formation of power in the performative processes of the spatial politics of sacred theatrics. I have been by and large concerned to show the complex relationship between emotion, narrative and visuality in ways that the State ultimately becomes a performative marker of creative force. In correlation with the visualization of memory, Takkiyeh Dowlat served as a political theater of emotions. In other words, for spectacles of mourning to have an impact, they first need to evoke passion in the audiences and actors who perform the State on a collective stage of mourning.

What I have not discussed here, however, is the role of transgressive practices that can simultaneously carve out new spaces of resistance within and counter to spectacles of power. This transgressive dimension raises the possibility of how politics can be both about power and contestation, an ambiguous process that defines politics as a contested theater of performative actions.

Notes and References

1 As a major Shi'a Islamic event, Muharram ceremonies traditionally take place over the span of the first ten days of the Islamic lunar month of Muharram when the ritual participants mourn the martyrdom of their saint Hossein.

2 Janet Afary and Kevin Anderson have argued that ta'ziyeh is a type of commemorative ceremony influenced by Christian passion plays, although the authors do not provide evidence to back up such a claim. Janet Afary and Kevin B. Anderson, *Foucault and the Iranian Revolution: Gender and the Seductions of Islamism* (Chicago: University of Chicago Press, 2005), 44. For a similar approach to ta'ziyeh and Christian rituals, see James A. Bill and John A. Williams, *Roman Catholics and Shi'i Muslims: Prayer, Passion, and Politics* (Chapel Hill: University of North Carolina Press, 2002), 63–74. For a critical study of such comparative approaches, see Babak Rahimi, *Theater State and the Formation of Early Modern Public Sphere in Iran: Studies on Safavid Muharram Rituals, 1590–1641 CE* (Leiden: Brill, 2011), 53, 212–14.

3 As elaborated in note 33, the exact construction date of the Takkiyeh Dowlat is unknown.

4 Here, my argument is somewhat similar to Afshin Marashi's claim that the Takkiyeh Dowlat served as a new socio-cultural site as to encourage public participation in court (ceremonial) spaces, hence affirming its legitimacy through religious performances. Marashi describes this as a new model of politics, part and parcel to a "nationalizing activity" that helped shape Iranian national identity in the nineteenth century. See Afshin Marashi, *Nationalizing Iran: Culture Power, and the State, 1870–1940* (Seattle: University of Washington Press, 2008), 39–48. This study, however, differs largely in its focus on various performative processes associated with the Takkiyeh Dowlat, in particular the staging and embodied practices.

5 "Elite-institutionalism" signifies a discursive way of depicting Muharram that tends to homogenize an understanding of power according to elite hegemony. See Rahimi, *Theater State and the Formation of Early Modern Public Sphere in Iran*, 36, 62–9.

6 For Foucault's famous study on embodiment and power, see Michel Foucault, *Discipline and Punish: The Birth of Prison*, trans. Alan Sheridan (New York: Vintage, 1995); and Talal Asad, *Genealogies of Religion: Disciplines and Reasons of Power in Christianity and Islam* (Baltimore: Johns Hopkins University Press, 1993). For a study of embodiment in the Shi'i cultural context, see David Thurfjell, *Living Shi'ism: Instances of Ritualisation among Islamist men in Contemporary Iran* (Leiden: Brill, 2009).

7 See Kathryn Babayan, *Mystics, Monarchs, and Messiahs: Cultural Landscapes of Early Modern Iran* (Cambridge, MA: Harvard University Press, 2002); Sussan Babaie, *Isfahan and Its Palaces: Statecraft, Shi'ism and the Architecture of Conviviality in Early Modern Iran* (Edinburgh: Edinburgh University Press, 2008); Babak Rahimi, *Theater State and the Formation of Early Modern Public Sphere in Iran* (Leiden; Boston: Brill, 2012)

8 *Encyclopedia Islamica*, 2nd ed., s.v. "Tekke, Tekiyye or Tekye(t.)."

9 Kathryn Babayan, *Mystics, Monarchs, and Messiahs: Cultural Landscapes of Early Modern Iran* (Cambridge, MA: Harvard University Press), 179; Rahimi, *Theater State and the Formation of Early Modern Public Sphere in Iran*, 199–234.

10 Rahimi, *Theater State and the Formation of Early Modern Public Sphere in Iran*, 235–72.

11 See Jean Calmard, "Shi'i Rituals and Power II: The Consolidation of Safavid Shi'ism: Folklore and Popular Religion," in *Safavid Persia: The History and Politics of an Islamic Society*, ed. Charles Melville (London: I.B. Tauris, 1996), 139–90.

12 Peter J. Chelkowski has famously argued that the vocal and dramatic performance of Muharram in a ta'ziyeh drama takes form with Francklin's description, though aspects of theatric practices can also be detected in Samuel Hmelin's 1770–72 account of Muharram in the city of Rasht. See Peter J. Chelkowski, "Bibliographical Spectrum," in *Ta'ziyeh: Ritual and Drama in Iran*, ed. Peter J. Chelkowski (New York: New York University Press, 1979), 257–8.

13 The available historical records on the Safavid Muharram performances, all from the Post-Shah Isma'il period, comprise European, Turkish and Persian sources. In Persian sources, short descriptions of the ceremonies can be found in the works of Iskandar Beg Munshi, *Tarikh-e Alam-ara-ye 'Abbasi* [The history of Shah 'Abbas the Great], and Mulla Jalal al-Din Munajjim, *Tarikh-e 'Abbasi ya Ruznameh-ye Mulla Jalal* [History of the Shah 'Abbas period, or the diary of Mulla Jalal al-Din] who refer to the ceremonies under the reign of Shah 'Abbas. Likewise, the account of Turkish traveler, Evliya Çelebi, serves as the only (Sunni) Muslim account of the mourning festivals in the Safavid period. It is, however, with the European travel reports that one has a more detailed sense of the ceremonies, as they developed into major public events of political significance under Shah 'Abbas when coincidentally, an increasing number of Europeans traveling through or residing in Iran witnessed the ceremonies in major public squares and palaces. In a total of 22 accounts, with the works of Pietro Dell Valle, Raphaël Du Mans and Jean Chardin as the most elaborate of all the reports, these travel journals offer the most intriguing ethnographic information on the Muharram ceremonies, although such accounts should be viewed in light of the cultural frameworks and ideological prisms through which the authors saw these ceremonies. See Calmard, "Shi'i Rituals and Power II,"139–90.

14 Michele Membré, *Mission to the Lord Sophy of Persia (1539–1542)*, trans. A. H. Morton (Warminster: Aris & Philips, 1999), 43.
15 See Rula Jurdi Abisaab, *Converting Persia: Religion and Power in the Safavid Empire* (New York: I.B. Tauris, 2004).
16 Pietro Della Valle, *The Pilgrim: The Travels of Pietro Della Valle*, trans., abridged and introduced by G. Bull (London: Hutchinson, 1990), 142–4.
17 Babak Rahimi, "The Rebound Theater State: The Politics of the Safavid Camel Sacrifice, 1598–1695 C.E.," *Iranian Studies* 37, no. 3 (2004): 451–78.
18 In his 1637 account of Muharram, the German traveler Adam Olearius also mentioned a final ceremony of fireworks and other spectacle events.
19 See Babayan, *Mystics, Monarchs, and Messiahs*, 17; and Abbas Amanat, "*Meadow of the Martyrs:* Kashifi's Persianization of Shi'i Martyrdom Narrative in the Late Tīmūrid Heart," in *Culture and Memory in Medieval in Islam: Essays in Honour of Wilfred Madelung*, ed. Farhad Daftary and Josef W. Meri (London: I.B. Tauris, 2003), 250–75.
20 See Babayan, *Mystics, Monarchs, and Messiahs*, 229; and Sussan Babaie, *Isfahan and Its Palaces: Statecraft, Shi'ism and the Architecture of Conviviality in Early Modern Iran* (Edinburgh: Edinburgh University Press, 2008), 233.
21 Cornelis de Bruin, *Reizen* [Travels] (Amsterdam, 1714), 167–71.
22 Chelkowski, "Bibliographical Spectrum," 257–8.
23 Father Judasz Tadeusz Krusinski, *The History of the late Revolution of Persia* (London, 1740), 90ff.
24 William Francklin, *Voyages au Bengale et à Chyraz* [Voyages to Bengal and to Shiraz] (Paris: 1801), 174–9. In two earlier accounts, Carsten Nibuhr and Samuel Hmelin also give testimony to a ta'ziyeh celebration in the northern city of Rasht (Nibuhr, 1775–76) and the southern Iranian city of Khark (Hmelin, 1770–72). In both accounts, ta'ziyeh mostly resembles the late Safavid processional performances, though in the Nibuhr account there appears to have been some kind of dialogue, which shows that the ceremonies had involved some level of poetic eulogies in recitation of the Karbala story. See Anayatullah Shahidi, *Pizhuhishi dar Ta'ziyeh va Ta'ziyeh-Khwani: az Aghaz ta Payan-i Dowreh-ye Qajar dar Tehran* [Research on the ta'ziyeh and ta'ziyeh-khwani: From the beginning to the end of the Qajar era] (Tehran: Iranian National Commission for UNESCO: Cultural Research Bureau, 2001), 76–9.
25 Matthew Arnold, "A Persian Passion Play," *Cornhill Magazine* (December 1871): 676.
26 Peter J. Chelkowski, "Time out of Memory: Ta'ziyeh the Total Drama," *Drama Review* 49, no. 4 (Winter 2005): 16. See also Sadeq Humayuni, *Ta'ziyeh va Ta'ziyeh-Khwani* (Shiraz: Navid, 1991), 19; Farrokh Ghaffary, *Theatre Irani* [Iranian theater] (Tehran: Shiraz Arts Festival, 1971), 2; and Bahram Bayzai, *Namayesh dar Iran* [Drama in Iran] rev. ed. (1965–66; repr., Tehran: Entesharat-e Roshangharan va Motaliat-e Zanan, 2001), 122. A bound collection of handwritten ta'ziyeh manuscripts from the Zand period (1750–94) suggests that the theatrical ceremonies had been widely practiced in Iran by the mid-eighteenth century. William O. Beeman, *Iranian Performance Traditions* (Costa Mesa: Mazda Publishers, 2011), 122n10.
27 Said Amir Arjomand, *The Shadow of God and the Hidden Imam: Religion, Political Order, and Societal Change in Shi'ite Iran from the Beginning to 1890* (Chicago: University of Chicago Press, 1984), 240.
28 M. le Comte de Gobineau, *Les Religions et les Philosophies dans l'Asie Centrale* [The religions and philosophies in Central Asia] (Paris: Ernest Leroux, 1900), 339–41.
29 For a study of lithographed literature under the Qajars, see Ulrich Marzolph, "The Pictorial Representation of Shi'i Themes in Lithographed Books of the Qajar Period," in *The Art and Material Culture of Iranian Shi'ism: Iconography and Religious Devotion in Shi'i Islam*, ed. Pedram Khosronejad (London: I.B. Tauris, 2012), 74–103.
30 Mahmoud Tavasoli, *Hosseiniyehha, Takkiyehha va Mosalha dar Memari-ye Iran, Dowreh-ye Islami* [Hosseiniyehs, takkiyehs and mosals in Iranian architecture of the Islamic period] (Tehran: Ershad-e Islami, 1366/1987), 81–3.

31 Marashi, *Nationalizing Iran*, 39.

32 J. M. Tancoigne, *A Narrative of a Journey into Persia and Residence at Teheran* (London: William Wright, 1820), 198. See also Jean Calmard, "Muharram Ceremonies and Diplomacy (A Preliminary Study)," in *Qajar Iran: Political, Social and Cultural Change: 1800–1925*, ed. Edmond Bosworth and Carole Hillenbrand (Costa Mesa: Mazda Publishers, 1983), 216.

33 The exact date of the construction and year of completion, along with the exact place where it was built, are still unclear. Various sources offer different dates of construction and completion, mostly 1849, 1868, 1869 and 1870. Lady Sheil offers an account of the Takkiyeh Dowlat in 1850s, hence undermining the theory that the year of construction of the building was after Nasir al-Din Shah returned from his trip to Europe in 1873. See Lady Sheil, *Glimpses of Life and Manners in Persia* (London: John Muray, 1856), 127–8. For a critical study on the construction date of the Takkiyeh Dowlat, see Anayatullah Shahidi, *Takkiyeh Dowlat va Barisiha-ye Naghes va Nadurust darbarye An* [Takkiyeh Dowlat and the incomplete and incorrect studies about it] (Markaz-e Tahghighat-e Computeri Ulum-i Islami).

34 Ibid. Both figures were considered among the most reactionary of the Qajar elite – perhaps a hint of a countermodernist attempt to develop new cultural sites of a distinctively traditional character.

35 It is interesting to note that the Royal Albert Hall was inaugurated on 1871, nearly around the time when the Takkiyeh Dowlat was apparently completed. The key question here is if, at all, the shah was solely inspired by European architecture during his travels abroad or to what extent did he know about operatic and theater architecture before his European trips in1873.

36 Abbas Amanat, *Pivot of the Universe: Nasir al-Din Shah and the Iranian Monarchy* (London: I.B. Tauris, 2008), 435; and Marashi, *Nationalizing Iran*, 41. It should be noted that there is a dearth of documents on who exactly was the architect of the building, though there is the possibility of several architects, according to the different stages of building the takkiyeh.

37 For an account of the Qajar patronage of the Takkiyeh Dowlat, especially under Nasir al-Din Shah, see Kamran Scot Aghaie, *The Martyrs of Karbala* (Seattle: University of Washington Press), 20–22.

38 Iraj Anvar, "Peripheral Ta'ziyeh: The Transformation of Ta'ziyeh from Muharram Mourning to Secular and Comical Theater," in *Eternal Performance: Ta'ziyeh and other Shiite Rituals*, ed. Peter J. Chelkowski (New York: Seagull Books, 2010), 111.

39 Humayuni, *Ta'ziyeh va Ta'ziyeh-Khwani*, 20.

40 Amanat, *Pivot of the Universe*, 435.

41 For an architectural account of takkiyeh, see Jamshid Malekpour, *The Islamic Drama* (London: Frankcass, 2004), 137–8.

42 Samuel Greene Wheeler Benjamin, *Persia and the Persians* (Boston: Ticknor, 1887), 382–3.

43 For a detailed description of the Takkiyeh Dowlat building, see Benjamin, *Persia and the Persians*, 382–6. See also James Bassett, *Persia and the Land of the Imams* (London: Blackie, 1887), 172–6; and George N. Curzon, *Persia and the Persian Question*, vol. 1 (New York: Barnes and Noble, 1966), 327–8. Originally, the Takkiyeh Dowlat had four floors, but due to faulty design, the story had to be demolished. See Malekpour, *The Islamic Drama*, 138–9.

44 Lady Sheil, *Glimpses of Life and Manners in Persia*, 127.

45 Mohammad Amin Riyahi, "Honarha-ye Ziba dar Iran Emruz [Fine arts in Iran today]," *Majaleh-ye Honar va Mardom*, no. 71 (1347): 17.

46 Malekpour, *The Islamic Drama*, 102–3.

47 See Reza Kochak-zadeh, ed., *Fehrest-e Tosifi Shabih-Namehha-ye Dowreh Qajari-ye: Shabih-Namehha-ye Ganjine-ye Khati-e Ketabkhaneh-ye Majlis Shora-ye Islami* [Explanatory index of the shabih-namehs of the Qajar period: Precious, handwritten shabih-namehs in the Islamic Majlis Library] (Tehran: Ketabkhaneh-ye Moseh va Markaz-e Asnad Majlis Shora-ye Islami, 2011).

48 Marashi, *Nationalizing Iran*, 41.

49 It is important to note that other non-Muharram plays were also performed at the Takkiyeh Dowlat, including the mystery plays of Imam Reza. See Kochak-zadeh, *Fehrest-e Tosifi Shabih-Namehha-ye Dowreh Qajari*-ye, 94–5.

50 See my critique of the "Karbala paradigm" in *Theater State and the Formation of Early Modern Public Sphere in Iran*, 50–53.

51 For an original study of ta'ziyeh in the Qajar period as a means in the production of national identity, see Negar Mottahedeh, "Karbala Drag Kings and Queens," *The Drama Review* 49, no.4 (Winter 2005): 73–85; and Negar Mottahedeh, *Representing the Unpresentable: Historical Images of National Reform from the Qajars to the Islamic Republic of Iran* (Syracuse: Syracuse University Press, 2008).

52 The audience in the takkiyeh also included European diplomats. Although as early as 1808 European diplomats, such as James Morier and J. M. Tancoigne, attended ta'ziyeh plays; by the mid-nineteenth century, European audiences played an important role in the ta'ziyeh performances at the takkiyeh. They were invited outsiders who would (voyeuristically) witness the ceremonies but not emotionally participate in the performances, though there were certain exceptions to this. As Kamran Scot Aghaie notes however, after 1855 Europeans were officially banned from attending the public ceremonies, though they continued to attend the private sessions of the rituals. Aghaie, *The Martyrs of Karbala*, 24. For an account of European diplomats' involvement in the Qajar Muharram culture, see Calmard, "Muharram Ceremonies and Diplomacy (A Preliminary Study)," 213–28; and see Aghaie, *The Martyrs of Karbala*, 22–4.

53 See Clifford Geertz, *Negara: The Theatre State in Nineteenth Century Bali* (Princeton: Princeton University Press, 1980).

II

THE PAHLAVI DYNASTY (1925–1979) AND TRANSITIONAL PERIOD AFTER THE IRANIAN REVOLUTION (1978–1979)

5

FOR THE LOVE OF HER PEOPLE: AN INTERVIEW WITH FARAH DIBA ABOUT THE PAHLAVI PROGRAMS FOR THE ARTS IN IRAN

Donna Stein

Since January 16, 1979, following 18 months of increasingly violent demonstrations against the shah's rule, HIM Shahbanou Farah Pahlavi has been exiled from Iran (Figure 5.1). Born in Tehran in 1938 to a family of diplomats, she was an only child raised by her mother who was widowed when Farah Diba was only 9 years old. She attended private Italian and French schools before moving to Paris to study architecture at the École Spéciale d'Architecture in 1957. She was introduced to Mohammad Reza Shah Pahlavi (r. 1941–79) at a reception held at the Iranian Embassy in Paris in the spring of 1959. That summer she returned to Tehran on break from her studies, and the shah began courting her seriously. Their marriage took place later that year on December 21, when Farah was 21 years old. They had four children: HIH Crown Prince Reza (b. 1960), HIH Princess Faranaz (b. 1963), HIH Prince Ali-Reza (1966–2011) and HIH Princess Leila (1970–2001).

Empress Farah was the first Iranian queen to be given the title of *shahbanou* (empress) and the first to be named regent in the event her husband died before their first child, Crown Prince Reza, turned 21. She was the patron of 24 educational, health and cultural organizations and instrumental in humanizing the Pahlavi dynasty by helping to modernize her country through land reform and the emancipation of women, such as women's suffrage, as part of the shah's White Revolution (1963). Today, she is devoted to her family and the Iranian people and divides her time between homes in Paris, France, and Potomac, Maryland.

On October 18, 1990, I spoke with HIM Shahbanou Farah Pahlavi. We had first met in 1976 when I was Advisor on Modern Art to her Secretariat in Tehran from February 1975 through May 1977. I had been employed to advise on all modern art purchases, including Iranian art, destined for the Tehran Museum of Contemporary Art. I also curated exhibitions at the Negarestan Palace Museum of Qajar Art from the personal collection of modern graphics held by Farah Pahlavi and for the inauguration of the Tehran Museum of Contemporary Art from the prints, drawings and photograph collections acquired during my tenure.

Donna Stein: What were your goals for Iranian culture?

Farah Pahlavi: I had such high hopes for the preservation of my country's heritage and Iran's emergence as a contemporary cultural force. I have loved art since my childhood and considered beauty life's principal pleasure. As a student, a queen and especially now, it adds a special dimension to my life. I really believe the old saying: "A thing of beauty is a joy forever." As a developing country, Iran had many economic and social problems. For a long period there was little attention paid to our art. I have an enormous respect, love, pride and belief in our thousands of years of history and civilization. I believe we have to learn from it. Although many programs started before I became Shahbanou, I hoped to make our heritage better known for all our people to be proud. Of course, there were many who cherished our past and culture, but to love it, you have to know it; to know it, you have to see it, to read and learn about it in books, to have museums and examine objects. Like other developing countries, we had an inferiority complex about the advanced world, and everything outside Iran was admired and considered more beautiful. But in the last years of the monarchy, we had passed through this period of emulation, and our identity was secure.

DS: Did the Iranian people need a point of comparison?

FP: Not really, because Iran is an ancient country, one of the cradles of civilization. Although we had been invaded by many cultures, like the Hellenes, the Arabs, the Mongols and had relations with the Chinese and Indians, we never lost our own authenticity. We learned from other cultures, and they learned from us. We have an unending treasury of beauty and inspiration – in poetry, science, philosophy, architecture, ceramic work, textiles, handicrafts, jewelry, metalwork, painting, miniatures and brickwork.

DS: Did you think it was important to distinguish what was unique about Iran?

FP: Absolutely. The architecture in our country, for example, is very special, because it was built for the region, climate and people. Even the material pisé was made from the earth, not to distract from a unity of form and color with the landscape. And simple uneducated people built these structures. They were artisans. They didn't have diplomas. Of course, our houses should have had better hygiene and more modern standards of living, but we had to make our builders understand and believe what they did was truly beautiful and should not be destroyed by development.

DS: Is the *badgir* [wind tower] a good example?

FP: Yes. When there was no air conditioning as we know it today, desert cities, like Yezd and Kashan for example, where it is very hot for most of the year, had *badgir*, which made living in such an inhospitable climate tolerable. The design of the *badgir*, while efficient and economical, was also pleasing to the eye.

DS: You have great passion for architecture.

FP: I really do. In preserving our old ways, we could not forget we are living in modern times. Henri Corbin [1903–78], a French scholar who wrote about mysticism in Iran, was a great lover of our culture. He said, and I have to paraphrase him, "Tradition is good as long as it is creative. If there is no creativity, tradition remains only a funerary cortege." We had to learn from our past, but at the same time, allow contemporary-inspired ideas to flourish. We wanted to encourage our creative people – painters, philosophers and architects. We could not always copy what we have had for thousands of years. From a national perspective, aesthetic considerations have a powerful impact on progress, invention, renewal of self-determination, social integration and quality of life. We had to improve our educational and cultural values, because physical and material developments proceed much faster than cultural advancement. Like so many other Third World societies, we had to break loose from the tyranny of resistance to change and the inertia of underdevelopment. My husband and I sincerely believed change required some cultural transformation. In this we were inspired and helped by many Iranians who believed in social change and had deep knowledge of our culture. It is not an accident that those, like some mullahs who were anti-development, are also virulently anti-art, anti-beauty and anti-happiness. Here again a comment by Avicenna [c. 980–1037], the great physician and philosopher who lived in Persia during the eleventh century seems appropriate: "The ultimate of life is love, love of beauty. And beauty is an ideal seekingness." We had to respect this fact and learn from it, not become depersonalized and lose our individuality in the course of rapid development. We could have succeeded because we had national wealth and human riches. What we had to instill was the desire and understanding, which, from my point of view, occurs with the growth of art and culture.

DS: Are you a collector?

FP: Not really. Of course, when I was in Iran I collected a few things, especially Persian art. I had some pre-Islamic objects and Safavid and Qajar lacquered papier-mâché *qalamdans* [pencil boxes] and Qur'ans and some enamel work. I bought some modern art, not many paintings and sculptures, but lithographs by artists, like [Joan] Miró [1893–1983], [Marc] Chagall [1887–1985], [Alexander] Calder [1898–1976], César [1921–98], Arman [1928–2005], [George] Segal [1924–2000], [Arnaldo] Pomodoro [b. 1926] and [Georges] Rouault [1871–1958], just for the sheer pleasure of looking at them. I wanted to have beautiful objects around me. I also bought artworks by contemporary Iranian artists because I like them and wanted to encourage and support our native artists by exposing their work in the palace. On the few occasions when government officials wanted to give us presents, I asked them to offer significant miniature paintings instead of a pretty box or object so our national patrimony would remain in the country. There were a few serious collectors in Iran. At first, most Iranians didn't have the money to collect, and later, some of those who had the money and the interest started some very beautiful collections of Persian art. I also received some presents, such as pre-Columbian sculptures from Latin America and masks from Africa. Ultimately, what I tried to collect were old books about Iran by travelers, published in previous centuries. So many of these books contain magnificent engravings of historic personages and monuments, many of which no longer exist. I wanted to study them. Of course, all of them remained in Tehran.

DS: Do you collect now?

FP: No. When I left Iran, times were so difficult and I was so upset mentally, thinking of all the efforts lost. It made me sick to go to an art gallery or museum. It took time to rehabilitate myself to a normal life. Unless one has been in exile, there is no way to comprehend that feeling. When I first came to America in 1982, I vowed I would never collect again. But life takes over. I needed to furnish a house, and empty walls are very depressing. So I bought some modern Persian paintings, because of their emotional, not just their artistic, value. I also have a few Persian objects people gave me or I acquired. Not many, just some symbols for my children to remember their heritage. If you have a carpet somewhere in the house, a Qajar period painted lacquer object, you begin to relate to your personal history and country. Now I am trying to find books about Iran, not just the old ones, but recent publications too, because so many of them are already out of print.

DS: Who were your cultural advisors?

FP: There were many, especially for Persian art history. Many Iranian scholars and artists would discuss their ideas, teach or advise me. In the field of modern art, I really didn't have an advisor. I visited galleries, cultural foundations, museums and artists studios when I traveled abroad and inside Iran. I didn't formally study art, but I love it and was in a position to make some dreams come true.

DS: Do you have any art advisors now?

FP: No.

DS: How do you think your architectural training and French cultural background affected your personal taste and approach to the arts?

FP: I finished high school in Tehran and then went to Paris where I was an architectural student for two years. During that time I visited galleries and museums regularly. I loved what I was doing. In my period, there was only one female architect in Iran. Later, there were many, and today, there are more still. After I married, I enjoyed meeting with architects, discussing what should be done in Iran. Many Iranian-born architects studied abroad. When they returned home, they copied whatever they had learned in America, England, France or Italy. Slowly, these architects realized they needed to find an individual style, not repeat the past or aspects of say, Los Angeles architecture. By using the old and ancient architecture as inspiration, they had to reconsider the lifestyle, climate and other factors, which was very hard, because the country was developing fast. By the time you took care of something, another building was destroyed, and something else was built in its place. We organized a committee to reward those who built beautiful buildings inspired by Iranian architecture. Architects would bring me their ideas about urban design and the development of our new society, and I would convey the information to the proper governmental authorities. Later, we created a High Council for Urban Design to help control the planning and rapid development of cities throughout Iran without destroying old sections of cities and monuments in a rush for the new. This was not easy.

One of my great joys was traveling many thousands of kilometers to the far corners of Iran by all means of transportation – car, jeep, one propeller, jet airplanes. I visited nearly every community from north to south, east to west. I planned these visits so members of government and concerned organizations would accompany me to speak with local residents and learn their problems firsthand. Sitting in Tehran, it was hard to appreciate the real needs and priorities of a distant community. People confided in me, and I reported back to my husband. Thank goodness I was young and had a lot of energy. I would go to different places, imagining I would be sad because of the poverty and underdevelopment, but people have such human spirit and integrity that I would return to Tehran filled with hope and resolve. I really loved village architecture in the desert. They needed repair and a healthier way of living, but they were beautiful, like sculptures made by hand. On one visit when I told the people of a village, "Why don't you let us repair your houses?" One of the village elders asked, "Why do you want us to live in these ugly ruins? Build us houses like Tehran." Whatever was in Tehran seemed better and more advanced. We preserved two of our beautiful towns as national monuments: one was the village of Massuleh near the Caspian Sea and the other was Tabas, which tragically was completely destroyed during an earthquake.

Architecture is not just one building; it is about the life of a family in society. City planning, urban design, housing for people have so much influence on society and politics. This was not just our experience but also the experience of most of the developing countries in the world. You cannot take a villager from his little hamlet and put him in a ten-story apartment house. He feels miserable and alienated and wouldn't know how to live in those conditions. There were so many social aspects of their lives we had to consider. Also, it was not always easy to implement our ideas, because there were people responsible who didn't believe in them.

DS: It was understandable that Iran wanted to buy back its national patrimony, building museums to represent the finest examples of indigenous art. What did you have in mind when you authorized the acquisition of international modern art and the building of more than one museum to house it?

FP: We created a number of museums to house our beautiful objects and treasures. We had to collect them from inside of Iran and buy back those collections that had fled the country. The Negarestan [Palace] Museum housed Qajar period paintings, jewelry and popular paintings called *Saqqa-khaneh.* The carpets of Iran are among the products that are most known to the world: there is Persian oil, Persian carpets and Persian caviar. It was unbelievable to me that we didn't have one museum for our carpets. Over many years we located the valuable carpets in Iran – sometimes in palaces and government offices. After identifying what was in our country, we purchased some special collections and brought them back to Iran for The Carpet Museum in Tehran. At the Reza Abbasi Cultural Center we housed pre-Islamic and Islamic objects and books that we had to buy and bring back to Iran. The Iran Bastan Museum was in the process of being restored and redecorated so we exhibited its collections at the Reza Abbasi Center as well. The Abgineh Museum, in an old Qajar house we managed to buy and restore, was designated for ceramics and glasswork. The building was restored, and vitrines were ready, but I did not have a chance to inaugurate it. I understand the objects were eventually installed, and the museum is open to the public. For the Museum of Luristan, which contained the bronzes from that region, we collected objects inside and outside Iran. I was intent that all the museums would not be in Tehran. Some people from Khorramabad, which was the center of Luristan, told me about a fortress-like building called Falaq Ophlak that in the olden days had been used as a prison. The governor of Luristan made this building available for the museum. In Kerman, a family interested in art and culture donated a beautiful old house and garden for another regional museum, which had its own board of trustees. The subject of their first exhibition was Persian painting and the design of carpets. We were happy to encourage private individuals to contribute to the nation's culture.

As for the museums of modern art, many Iranian painters came to me and complained that they needed a place to expose their work and wanted to see paintings from other countries in order to learn from them. Eventually, we decided to establish a museum of Western art for our people to see contemporary developments outside of Iran. After all, the Metropolitan Museum of Art exhibits Near Eastern art. We envisioned the museum as a lively center, a place where people would attend lectures, hear music and see films. The museum's placement in a park in Tehran helped to encourage visitors who happened to be walking nearby. I don't recall how we decided to create a Museum of Western and Iranian Contemporary Art in Shiraz, except that Shiraz was a developing city and becoming industrialized. We chose Alvar Aalto [1898–1976] as the architect, because he was such a famous international figure. We thought his building would be a work of art. He came to Iran and loved Shiraz where he chose a special site for the museum.

DS: The Shiraz Museum of Western and Iranian Contemporary Art was one project that was never realized. Were there others?

FP: There was a fortress in Shiraz from the Zand period [1750–94] – a huge building that at some point had been a prison. It had been empty for a long time, and we wanted to create a Museum for Handicrafts. The building was architecturally interesting and it had a huge garden. The underground cultural center for the

Marble Palace Park, the location of the Negarestan [Palace] Museum, was never completed. We also had plans for a Museum of Calligraphy.

DS: At what point in your life with the shah did you begin to become involved in Iran's cultural life?

FP: I was 21 years old when I married in 1959. I was young, didn't know my limitations and felt a person in my position could do so much. Nevertheless, it took me years to learn some of the problems of our country and people and also years to know where and how I could be of help.

DS: How involved was the shah in your projects? Was he interested in art?

FP: He was very interested in everything that was happening in Iran and was very proud each time we opened a new museum. He was promoting and encouraging many scientific, educational and cultural enterprises besides the government's official activities. He helped a lot with the preservation of monuments. His blessings and material support from the government permitted me to realize many projects and activities in organizations for which I was [a] patron. Personally, he was more involved with Iranian art and preferred classical art and music to modern.

DS: Were there conflicts between religious sentiments and cultural programs?

FP: I never sensed anything during the time I was shahbanou, because nothing was shocking, immoral, indecent or improper. In retrospect, the first signs of the subsequent Islamic Revolution occurred in 1977. During the 11 years of the Shiraz Festival, there had been hundreds of programs, mostly traditional but some avant-garde. Artists were free to express themselves. There was only one questionable incident.

DS: How did people react to the cultural advancement you proposed? Did you sense any dissatisfaction or lack of understanding?

FP: Not really. Iranian citizens respected their heritage and knew of my interest in saving historical monuments. I received numerous letters from private citizens, identifying interesting buildings for the government to protect, preserve and restore throughout Iran. What could people say against museums with the treasures of their country exhibited there? They were, on the contrary, very happy. For the modern art acquisitions, some people asked, "Why buy these paintings?" Even if everyone didn't consider them art, I was certain it was a good investment and would never be lost. Frankly, when the revolution occurred, I was afraid the Islamic fundamentalists might, out of anger and revolutionary frenzy, destroy the modern collections. But now they know the paintings and sculptures we purchased are worth ten or twenty times more than their original cost. Even if some Iranians don't like modern art, they know it's valuable. That's why it is still there.

DS: What do you miss most about being an empress?

FP: I don't miss being an empress. My life wasn't easy. I was there to serve. The privileges people saw from outside were so much a part of my life, I didn't consider them extraordinary. In retrospect, I appreciate some of the special opportunities I had. I especially miss my country – its nature, people, air, beauty. I would rather be back in Iran, if I could, as a simple citizen.

DS: How would you like to be remembered?

FP: I would like people to remember me as a caring individual, close to the people, not removed from them, trying to do my duty in the best way I knew how.

6

SHAPING AND PORTRAYING IDENTITY AT THE TEHRAN MUSEUM OF CONTEMPORARY ART (1977–2005)

Alisa Eimen

Setting the Stage[1]

In spring 2002 the Tehran Museum of Contemporary Art (TMOCA) hosted a five-day conference on postmodernism and contemporary art.[2] There were small panel discussions in the museum's library and public lectures in the auditorium, which comfortably accommodates 275 people. The auditorium is located at the base of the museum's main hallway, which is a three-story spiraling ramp. The afternoon of my first visit, the line to enter the auditorium queued to the top of the ramp and was peopled overwhelmingly by young adults. Their voices and laughter were restrained due to the codes of public behavior with which they have been raised. Yet, this restraint could not begin to mask their energy. As the doors opened, we poured in, quickly filling the seats. The standing-room-only crowd took up every inch of the side aisle and back wall. For four hours we remained, listening intently and rushing through the tea break to return to the increasingly stuffy space. Foreign presenters, among them art critic Edward Lucie-Smith and artist Joyce Kozloff, showed slides, spoke freely through interpreters and responded to a steady stream of enthusiastic questions posed by an insatiable audience that returned day after day.

I begin with this scene because of the impression it made – because of its vitality. There was a palpable sense of engagement and urgency to these gatherings that suggested more was at stake than just the latest trends in art. In Iran, public gatherings of any sort are generally religious and always monitored. Congregations of students resonate as riotous, even revolutionary; thus, they are stringently policed as summers of student protests have shown.[3] Considering the museum's proximity to the University of Tehran (the site of these protests) and the large number of students attending the conference, the museum gathering suggested a much broader significance than merely contemporary art. A series of uneasy dialectics were contained within the institutional walls of the State's museum: Iranian/foreigner, speaker/censor, female/male and citizen/guard. These oppositional pairings highlight the many challenges that continue to face the Islamic Republic – tensions revolving around belief, perspective and memory that resist containment and the official order. The aforementioned sketch of the conference scene thus seemed to be a microcosm of the ongoing struggles of day-to-day experiences, in which identity and self-determination remain central. In this context, the museum suggested itself to be a symbolic site – creative, consigned and even confrontational. As a space for gathering and interchange however, the museum is much more than a symbol. It is also an arm of the State that somewhat paradoxically provides a place for an international flow of ideas, a space of leisure and respite and a setting for debate and even defiance.

To aid the study of this power play in Iran and more specifically at TMOCA, it is useful to turn to social scientist James Scott's important analysis of the structure of power in *Domination and the Arts of Resistance* (1990).[4] To understand the constitutive elements of any power structure, he suggests a reading that assesses both the dominant discourse and that which occurs beyond the eyes and ears of those in power. Only through an investigation of what he calls "public transcripts" (the terms of power established by the dominant group and enacted by all) and "hidden transcripts" (all forms of response beyond the purview of the power holders) can the "infrapolitics" of power begin to be deconstructed.[5] The effects of hegemony in public discourse cannot be fully understood without considering not only the confines of power, but also the variety of ways in which those without power can confront and challenge them. It is important to note that there are countless forms of resistance, and many of these expressions are masked, indirect and even obfuscating. Resistance, in other words, can be disguised and intentionally hidden from the power holders.[6] TMOCA provides an opportunity for such an analysis, due to its role as a State institution that at times has fostered individual expression through exhibitions, conferences and informal community gatherings in its galleries and popular café. Although the museum has been tied to the State since its inception, the connection between the two has fluctuated over time and often in relation to the State's national identity and involvement in the international community. Analyzing these changes alongside a series of activities at TMOCA provides some insight into the ways in which museums, art and the State have been intertwined since the 1970s.

TMOCA, founded in 1977 with the support of queen Farah Diba Pahlavi (b. 1938), developed on the heels of more than two decades of vibrant activity by a small avant-garde, and the museum was intended to be a center for this activity, fostering ongoing engagement (Figure 6.1). However, the revolution had halted this trajectory until the late 1990s when the museum reemerged as a cultural center, featuring a wide range of activities, from Iranian biennials to international contemporary art exhibits. By 2000 the museum was again a site of active negotiation among artists and their enthusiasts, principally college-age youths. By examining the museum's architecture and select exhibition history, I analyze the ways in which various identities were marshaled and performed, both before and after the Iranian Revolution (1978–79). To this end, some discussion of twentieth-century nation building is necessary, for it will help clarify how the nation was redefined as modern during the Pahlavi dynastic period (1925–79). After the revolution, this redefinition continued, and art became one of the vehicles, both for identity's performance (by citizens) and its regulation (by the State).

The timing of the TMOCA's opening could have easily suggested its death knell. The museum opened in October 1977, the very same month during which protests against the government began to accelerate. These protests were the forerunners of the Iranian Revolution and the eventual overthrow of the Pahlavi monarchy, resulting in the demolition of various cultural organizations associated with both the former ruler and what the revolutionaries saw as evidence of Western imperialism. It is not only the timing of the museum's inauguration, however, that could have threatened its existence, but also a number of other factors, including, most significantly, the queen's support and direct involvement with it. The museum's architect and first director, Kamran Diba (b. 1937), is her cousin, and the museum's most valuable artworks were created by notable non-Iranian artists, such as Francis Bacon (1909–92), Vasily Kandinsky (1866–1944) and Pablo Picasso (1881–1973), collected by the Daftar-e Makhsus-e Shahbanu (Office of the Empress). The juxtaposition of the museum's opening with the swelling mass of protestors in the nearby streets is a telling portrait, depicting the growing cultural divide that still haunts Iranian politics today.

Surprisingly, the museum was not a direct target of the revolutionaries and since the revolution, it has been a center for contemporary art, exhibiting revolutionary artworks in the early years of the Islamic Republic of Iran and developing into the vibrant center for contemporary art that I had sketched at the essay's outset. As a contemporary center operated by Ershad (the Ministry of Culture and Islamic Guidance Network), the museum has been shaped and reshaped, often in response to changes in the political climate. These transformations resulted from events precipitated by the Iranian Revolution, which in turn was a response to a century's worth of dramatic changes.

Developments in Modern Art and Its Exhibition

From the late nineteenth century through the Pahlavi monarchy, Iran's political and intellectual leaders were focused on modernizing the State. During these decades, every aspect of life was affected, from public school education to legislation regarding one's dress, as the government attempted to forge a homogenous and unified Iran. Various policies created changes that fundamentally restructured society, including settling nomadic groups, eliminating tribal authority and shifting to a single national language, all in the service of a centralized State.[7] Since the early twentieth-century emergence of the modern State of Iran under monarch Reza Shah Pahlavi (r. 1921–41),[8] there has been a hierarchic governmental structure in place, maintaining varying degrees of control over the apparatuses that help foster a particular national identity. Iran's leaders recognized the paradox of absolute power and attempted to craft a particular national narrative that sought to galvanize the majority in their favor, and cultural policies were an important part of this program. By mid-twentieth century, Tehran boasted a secular government center, modern hospitals and an international airport, alongside a national archaeological museum and art schools.[9] Yet, there was no institutional art center that addressed the contemporary era. It would be more than another two decades before TMOCA would open its doors to the Iranian public.

During these intervening decades, many artists were coordinating their efforts, forming collectives and galleries in the nation's capital city. Throughout the 1940s and 1950s, increasing numbers of students were being sent abroad for training, and among them were artists. Emboldened by their experiences abroad, some of these returning artists began to challenge the institutionalization of artistic training, experimenting with both style and art space. By the late 1940s, several artists had opened galleries where they exhibited their work and hosted group exhibitions. Until this point, there had been predominantly two general categories of painting in Iran. One category was grounded in an academic formalism informed by a European-style arts education, and the other was largely untrained and rooted in a vernacular tradition of narrative works, illustrating popular, religious and legendary stories. This latter category functioned as visual aids as the stories were recounted to crowds at coffee houses. Coffeehouse paintings, as they became known, were not viewed as valuable artworks until recent decades, largely because of their naïve style and connections to non-elite classes.[10] Midcentury art being made by artists in Tehran did not conform to either of these categories and often blurred the boundaries between them. By the 1950s signs and symbols traditionally associated with Iran's Shi'i folk art or pre-Islamic traditions became increasingly part of the visual vocabulary that modern artists were marshaling.[11] A dedicated space for modern art's exhibition was a shared and increasing concern among many artists, including Parviz Tanavoli (b. 1937), Charles Hossein Zenderoudi (b. 1937), Siah Armajani (b. 1939) and Jalil Ziapour (1920–99).

While Iranian artists were forging a place for contemporary art in Tehran's cultural sphere, connections to the international arts community remained couched in a teacher–student relationship that was uncomfortably close to the State's moves toward modernization. The Pahlavi government was often criticized for being too reliant on European and American governments and today, tensions still remain around modernity and its accouterments as foreign imports which directly bear on questions of identity, authenticity and place. Not only did these concerns preoccupy government and religious officials, but they also weighed on the minds of intellectuals and artists. Modernization was transforming society and as time progressed, some were beginning to see that unguided "progress" would systematically destroy what distinguished Iran from elsewhere.[12] The work of many of midcentury artists merged formalist aesthetics and regional elements to create a "modern" art capable of responding to both local and international audiences.

This goal demanded a venue as a means to enter the international stage, and in 1958 the first of five Tehran biennials laid the foundation. The inaugural biennial was funded through a foundation established by Mehrdad Pahlbod ('Ezzatollah Minbashian, b. 1917), an important member of court and the director of the University of Tehran's Department of Fine Arts,[13] and was held at the Abyaz Palace, which was part of the Golestan Palace complex in Tehran's city center, located in southern Tehran.[14] The biennials were quite successful at fostering connections with the international art world. They served as meeting grounds for Iranian artists and international aficionados.[15] Additionally, works were selected from the biennials for inclusion in the prestigious Venice Biennale. As Iranian artists continued to study and exhibit abroad, this increasing exposure to European and American art centers emphasized the infrastructure still necessary in Iran to foster the Iranian community of artists.

Although the biennials had succeeded in creating an initial foray into the international scene, their infrequency failed both to sustain these connections and to incorporate their activities into city and State. Without a dedicated space, art would remain a product of the past, the imperial and the periphery. Frustration with what was quickly becoming the status quo led a network of artists functioning as the Contemporary Artists Group to write an open letter to Pahlbod in 1961. The artists called for reform. Criticizing an inexpert administration for its parochial approach to exhibitions, they stated, "Nowhere in the world does a governmental office hold official exhibitions for beginners [...]. Measures should be taken so that artists' affairs are run by artists, so artists are not transformed into administrative officers and administrative officers are not transformed into critics and semi-artists."[16] This letter was both a political rebuke and personal affront to Pahlbod and resulted in the elimination of government funding for Tanavoli's studio, Atelier Kaboud, a gathering space of the group.[17] Real reform and, in particular, a dedicated art space remained more than a decade away.

The sentiment expressed by the Contemporary Artists Group, however, was not extinguished and as student exchanges continued, the absence of a contemporary arts center became ever more conspicuous. A museum invested in the collection and display of modern and contemporary art would be necessary to maintain associations with curators and collectors on a consistent basis. Moreover, if inroads were going to be made toward creating an Iranian market and audience, this sustained presence was a necessary investment. Kamran Diba, principally known for his work as an architect, during the early 1960s was a painter who had written of his interest in promoting precisely this project.[18] He conceived of the project as a museum that collected and exhibited the finest examples of modern and contemporary art, with particular attention focused on Europe and the United States. His rationale was that in order to participate in the international art world, the State had to make an investment of spaces and funds that would amass capital, both in terms of artworks by famous artists, such as Vincent van Gogh (1853–90), Picasso and Jackson Pollock (1912–56), as well as in knowledge of this art world through an educational component.[19] By the mid-1960s, Diba had joined forces with Nader Ardalan (b. 1939); both had received their architectural training in the United States and set to work on a design for such a space. For years the plans they had drafted lay idle on various desks at the culture ministry until the queen and her Foundation for the Arts and Sciences intervened. By 1975 the museum was becoming a reality; Kamran Diba and his firm, DAZ Architects, Planners, and Engineers returned to the decade-old plans to begin the project. Nearly 20 years after the First Tehran Biennial, this dedicated center of contemporary art was inaugurated with opening fanfare and international press.

The Architectural Setting

By the 1970s the transformation of Tehran had expanded well beyond the capital city's boundaries. The government's policies of the early 1960s had brought land reform to the provinces, the privatization of State industries and nationwide increases in literacy and women's rights.[20] However, these were inconsistently applied and at times detrimental to local socioeconomic structures. By the mid-1970s the focus of reform had shifted away from domestic affairs, favoring larger geopolitical machinations. Despite the shah's strategic negotiation of higher oil revenues during that period,[21] inflation was an ever-growing concern for the masses, visible in the widening disparity between the haves and the have-nots on the cities' streets. With this backdrop unfurled, the fashionable gala opening of TMOCA suggested to many the government's continued corruption, nepotism and "Western" predilections. Therefore, the activities of Iran's contemporary artists – however inspired by local traditions – were displayed within the bounds of elite culture.

The perennial problem of the art market and its attendant risk of elitism and institutionalization presented itself at the ceremonial opening of the museum. Contemporary artists were dependent on their elite patrons and government stipends and sponsorships. The realization of the dream of a dedicated art space seemed to quicken the loss of running counter to culture. The contemporary museum was designed to be the Iranian node of the international art scene, but the exorbitant cost of the project ($7.2 million for the building construction alone) and the queen's unflagging support indebted the museum to the government.[22] The social realities of the mid-1970s impeded the museum's neutrality, as the culture of dissent and censorship grew in Iran. Therefore, the museum's opening celebration highlights an incongruity between artistic freedom and State patronage, which continues today.

Upon its opening, the museum was inaugurated by the royal couple, attended by Tehran's high society and written about in some of the top architecture journals.[23] The exhibitions organized in conjunction with the opening bridged Iran's modern and contemporary art scene with an international one, illustrating both the State's modernity and its locality. To this end, the museum's nine galleries were brimming with canvases, from an exhibition of Iranian contemporary painters to an installation of a valuable collection of impressionists, fauves and cubists. The opening exhibition also included an outdoor sculpture garden and newly commissioned works by Dennis Oppenheim (1938–2011).[24] In addition to the installations, there were performances throughout the opening event. In the galleries there were musicians, in the interior courtyard there were living sculptures and throughout the galleries there were dancers, including a modern dance troupe that performed alternately with Iranian folk dancers dressed in colorful regional costumes. At every turn, one may have imagined that "East met West": American curators worked alongside an Iranian staff, artists traversed national borders and the exhibitions suggested the harmony of this union; similarities existed even in difference.

Following this line of interpretation, it is useful to think about *why* this museum and this investment at this particular moment. Considering the State's internal turmoil, what may have been the intention behind approving the museum's plan and its exorbitant costs? What may be suggested in terms of the relationship between cultural and political capital at TMOCA? Since Iranian oil revenues were at their zenith circa 1975, it is easy to see that cost was not likely to be a principal concern. Because Iran's cultural history had been written to demonstrate that the Pahlavi dynasty emerged from a long line of past monarchies, the government's continued investment in culture, alongside the geopolitical, would further bolster the king's re-creation of Iran as the Tamaddon-e Bozorg (the Great Civilization), a program that was intended to elevate Iran's status among other nations.[25] Although the aim of this program fostered economic and military growth, the development of the State's cultural centers was an important component in the shaping of Iran's national identity, its modernity, political stability and international viability.

The site of the museum further supports this reading of international pretensions alongside State interest. The museum on Kargar Avenue (originally Amir Abad) shares its city block with the high-end Laleh International Hotel (formerly the InterContinental), the Carpet Museum and a large sprawling park named after the queen, Park-e Farah (Farah Park, today called Park-e Laleh, or Tulip Park).[26] The block's organization provides a useful metaphor for thinking about Iran under Mohammad Reza Shah Pahlavi (r. 1941–79). Its features represent two key elements of modern society: leisure and high culture – the warp and weft of a cosmopolitan city. Moreover, the Carpet Museum, modern in design, exhibits Iran's history through a collection of its most luxurious export-cum-fine art. In effect, the museum enshrines one of the culture's most valued traditional arts. Just around the corner, standing as a testament to Iran's modernity, is TMOCA. Taken as a whole, the block's design reflects official preoccupations with the State's presentation. The proximity of the hotel to these museums, where past and present intersect, reinforces the extent to which national designs were intended for an international audience. Framed by a verdant field, the park's structures stand as both museums and monuments; they are narrative in function, symbolic in form and iconic in design. Their garden setting presents to an international public a space to pause and perhaps to contemplate this meeting of past and present.

TMOCA contributes additional places of gathering and repose through its meandering design and garden spaces. The museum's architect, interested in the social implications of the built environment, has written about his own practice: "One of my obsessions," Diba states, "was to influence and intensify human interaction and activity."[27] The museum's layout illustrates this preoccupation. It is composed of a series of adjoining gallery spaces that wind around a central courtyard, conceived of as an interior sculpture court (Figure 6.2). As the museum visitor moves through the galleries, ample views of the exterior spaces and interior galleries invite the viewer to explore and discover. The design, through an interplay of corridor and chamber, encourages intervals of movement and rest, engagement and contemplation.

The museum's public entrance is crowned with four salient skylights that face the four cardinal directions. Beckoning the visitor, they draw attention to the museum's main entryway. Upon entering the building at street level, one walks through the lobby and into the top level of the structure's largest interior space, which takes the form of a three-story spiral. This spiraling space anchors the museum both in form and concept. The museum's overall design is based on a series of relationships between inside and out, private and public and intimate and communal. The nine interior galleries wind around exterior gardens that provide daylight, vistas and oases. The movement of persons activates these spatial connections, which begin and end at the museum's central corridor. It is as if from centrifugal force that the museum's galleries are pushed to the structure's perimeter, winding down around a long hallway that culminates at the spiral's base. Persons moving through the constructed space are the museum's lifeblood. Diba has addressed his design goal as creating "sociable" architecture. Indeed, staff and visitor alike contemplate, interpret and give meaning to the representations on display, thus animating the body of the museum.

The nine galleries that comprise the structure radiate out around the site, beginning and ending at the museum's central corridor. Housed within this main core on the two lower levels are the museum's administration, the curatorial division and library. It is at the base of this spine that the auditorium is located, the public gathering space that holds the metaphor of the body firmly in place. On the first page of the postrevolution museum catalogue, one is told of the building's "excellent" architectural example. Considering the pride with which employees address the building's design, the absence of the architect's name in the catalogue is indeed conspicuous.

This absence of the architect will be all the more revealing as the subsequent history of the museum is considered. For all the emphasis that Diba placed on human interaction with the structure, his own disappearance is indicative of the ensuing political situation and shifting of the body politic. As revolutionary fervor boiled over, Iran's national identity was violently contested and ultimately reconstituted. This shift in identity was nurtured by a refashioning of every sphere – from the educational to the political and certainly the cultural. The politics of identity at the time of the formation of the Islamic Republic were literally enacted on the Iranian body. Public discipline moved to the forefront of policy concerns and was made manifest in morality squads brutally policing the streets, executions as public spectacle and perhaps most visibly a nationwide dress code, for which the long, all-encompassing woman's chador became the symbol. Such policies, codes and symbols comprised a clear public transcript, to recall Scott's terminology, of the State's assertion of authority. The individual body as a representative of the State was disciplined in opposition to American and Pahlavi influences, both of which were increasingly identified as synonymous. Considering the pervasive reforms instituted soon after the founding of the republic, no cultural institution would be left untouched. Museums as bastions of national heritage and mores would comprise an important arm of the government's realignment of values, aesthetics and identities. Their production, maintenance and exhibition in the State's museums would remain an integral vehicle of nation- and identity building, however refashioned by the ascendant authorities.

What, then, would become of TMOCA under the new republic? Built to create space for and relationship to an international art scene at the center of the Iranian nation, the contemporary museum in its very concept must have posed a decided challenge to the leading clerics and their traditionalist and retrogressive ideology. The national archaeological museum's collection, for example, could be reinstalled to uphold a particular historical reading, because its permanent collection comprised ancient objects. Yet, how could the same strategy work in a museum whose most valuable collection consisted of European masterworks? What would become of Picasso and Willem de Kooning (1904–97) and their disrobed, disfigured women? Would these bodies also be erased from the record and denied their existence, just like those Iranians who had challenged the rising ruling order?[28]

Revolution and Transformation

The months leading up to the revolution were tumultuous and unpredictable. As employees of TMOCA unpacked crates and installed artworks, Iran's foreign nationals were simultaneously packing their bags and preparing for departure. By the time of the museum's autumn opening in 1977, insecurity about Iran's future was palpable. Many families had already departed, and countless others were planning exit strategies. By the early months of 1978 the museum, too, was beginning to suffer under increasing pressure. Its chief curator, American David Galloway, had arrived in Tehran via Düsseldorf only four or five months before his resignation in early 1978. And by October Diba also had announced to the staff that he, too, would be leaving Iran due to illness.[29] The subtext of this message was corroborated on January 16, 1979, when the shah and his family fled the country.

The succeeding months of revolution wrought immense changes to the very fabric of the Iranian landscape. Statues were among the first to suffer, as likenesses of the king and his allies were quickly destroyed along with cinemas, nightclubs, casinos and all other signs that could be taken as symbols of Pahlavi decadence and American imperialism. After the revolution, the new government took great steps toward annihilating any lingering memories of the past order, including an immense renaming campaign. Names of streets and landmarks were systematically altered to better align with the State's new trajectory, while others, such as the museum's architect, were erased from the record altogether. Despite several noteworthy prerevolutionary commissions, Diba is rarely mentioned in the Islamic Republic due to his familial affiliation with the Pahlavi monarchy. Although his name has appeared in many journal and newspaper articles over the years, the leaders of the newly founded republic relied on the vagaries of memory and the powers of suggestion until they could overhaul both the educational system and museum.

For nearly two years, universities, most museums and even international travel were regularly closed to Iranian citizens.[30] Recognizing the significance and size of the restructuring they would need, not to mention the added complications brought on by an eight-year war with Iraq (1980–88), the government divided its work into segments. Various Pahlavi arts and culture organizations, including Sazeman-e Ettela'at-e Jahangardi (Tourist Information Organization), Daftar-e Makhsus-e Shahbanu and the Ministry of Culture and Art, would eventually be collapsed into Ershad. Yet, this was less of a priority than restructuring the educational system, for example. Therefore, beyond securing valuable objects, museums were not a top priority, and they only slowly reopened throughout the mid-1980s. The history of TMOCA, however, is a telling exception.

By the time of the revolution, the institution had acquired an important collection of approximately 1,500 European and American artworks in a range of media, as well as several hundred pieces by prominent Iranian artists. Works from Picasso to Andy Warhol (1928–87) were among hundreds of valuable objects that went into storage upon the formation of the Islamic Republic. The original permanent collection was acquired by Daftar-e Makhsus-e Shahbanu, principally under the guidance of American curator Donna Stein. Knowledgeable and endowed with a large budget, Stein guided the acquisition of numerous important works, including those by Picasso, Georges Braque (1882–1963), Paul Gauguin (1848–1903), de Kooning and Jackson Pollock. She also oversaw the purchase of sculptures by luminaries, including Max Ernst (1891–1976), Alberto Giacometti, Henry Moore and Marino Marini (1901–80), a number of which remain in the museum's sculpture garden. Stein and her colleagues' charge was largely without a directive other than to build a collection that began with impressionism.[31] There are today approximately 4,000 paintings in the collection of both Iranian and foreign origin, 400 of which are likely the most significant. At the time of the revolution, protecting these artworks was a shared goal of a group employed by the museum.

It is nonetheless surprising that unlike other museums in Tehran, TMOCA was closed for only two weeks at the height of the revolution. Then, for approximately six or seven months, a skeletal museum staff continued to work, while the museum remained closed to visitors until it was reorganized under new directorship. With a governmental mandate, TMOCA publicly reopened to all citizens with a new and very specific directive: to support the ideals of the revolution. During the following 15 years – and roughly 15 directors – the museum, in effect, served as a gallery space, exhibiting works that paid homage to the revolution, revolutionary posters and images of Iranian martyrs from the Iran–Iraq war, as well as exhibitions of revolutionary works by Mexican and Palestinian artists.[32] Clearly, the tone of the exhibition schedule was intended to support the State and memorialize the revolution and martyrs for the country, as well as link the struggles against the United States and Israeli imperialism with similar struggles around the world. The museum was a transparent arm of the State and, like its previous Pahlavi incarnation, principally attracted partisans of the State.

According to the leaders of the young republic, contemporary art was that which would support the revolution and reinforce State ideology. TMOCA was indeed the best and most malleable place to start. Because the museum had previously been an imperial and elite institution, opening it up to a wider public was a way to subvert its original meaning. Additionally, when Ershad had created the regulatory Visual Arts Center in 1982, its directorship was officially linked to that of TMOCA; each new director of the museum would then become the director of the Visual Arts Center, whose responsibility would be to maintain the moral currency of contemporary art through the licensing of private gallery spaces and operating several studios, including some in Paris.[33] Therefore, by co-opting the new and lauded exhibition space for international art and the Pahlavi elite, the museum emerged as an ideological arena, visibly juxtaposing Islamic values and principled character to the memory of Pahlavi Westernization and decadence.

A Cultural Revolution at TMOCA

How then did this center for revolutionary art and State propaganda become a forward-thinking, risk-taking establishment that has been highly popular among the capital city's youth, as noted at the chapter's outset? While there are many sociopolitical factors at play in the museum's transformation, an important turning point is certainly the 1997 election of President Mohammad Khatami (elected 1997–2005). A former Minister of Culture himself, Khatami's first presidential term ushered in a period of increasing tolerance that gave way to what was occasionally referred to as a cultural revolution.[34] A new director was then appointed to head the museum and therefore the Visual Arts Center, Dr Ali-Reza Sami-Azar (1999–2005).[35] Like Khatami, this new director similarly pushed conventional boundaries.

Sami-Azar was knowledgeable about contemporary art and the international scene, unlike his predecessors. A British-trained architect, he not only appreciated the museum's physical architecture, but also valued its collection and unique cultural role in the Islamic Republic. In a discussion we had in December 2003 at the museum, the director, suddenly donning his Visual Arts Center hat, summarized the center's mission as he viewed it, which was to create spaces for artists to learn, discuss and exhibit what they chose to create.[36] A former colleague of his corroborated this position, when she stated that the director was truly the artists' biggest advocate, placing their exposure and concerns at the forefront of his responsibilities.[37] Sami-Azar did not intend to police artists and their work as his predecessors did; rather, he viewed the center as a supporting institution. The work of the museum, by extension, was to provide a forum for education, exhibition and connection to the international scene, thereby signaling a radical departure from the previous 20 years of ideological programming.

Picking up where his immediate predecessor left off, Sami-Azar continued a series of biennials that included graphic design, painting, drawing and sculpture, among others. These were significant means to broaden the museum's base of participation and audience. Public calls for entries resulted in thousands of submissions by established and young artists alike. Internationally renowned filmmaker and photographer Abbas Kiarostami (b. 1940) and painters Aydin Aghdashlou (b. 1940) and Farah Ossouli (b. 1953) were among a series of well-known figures who exhibited alongside the nation's young and emerging artists. Until Sami-Azar's directorship, the museum had offered little to contemporary artists who were interested in creating work beyond the party line. So biennials, such as the Sixth Biennial of Contemporary Iranian Painting (2002), served as an important invitation to the disenfranchised arts community.

Work selected for this biennial illustrates the museum's range – and risk – in curatorial choices. Since the founding of the republic, the debate regarding the veracity of the Islamic proscription of figural representation has been revived. The international debut of this debate may have well been the widely televised destruction of the ancient rock-cut sculptures of the Buddha at Bamiyan by the Afghan Taliban (March 2001).[38] Far less extreme than the Taliban's action, the debate in Iran has nonetheless continued, and many works in the exhibition were nonrepresentational, abstract or symbolic. Alongside these paintings, however, hung images that deviate from and even subvert Iranian traditions and expectations – an impossibility in the pre-Khatami era. From paintings of unveiled women returning the viewer's gaze to an adaptation of an icon of European art, *Mona Lisa* (c. 1504), the range of paintings on exhibit clearly illustrated the increasing latitude allowed artists, because "Western" art and references to "Western" culture were publicly banned by the Islamic Republic in its first decade. Together, the biennial's paintings challenged the boundaries that have been constructed over the years between genders, societies and religions, as well as artistic media. Their place on the galleries' walls in 2002, among some 150 other works, illustrated a noteworthy shift – one that contributed to the museum's increasing popularity among the Iran's young people.

By 2003 the museum's major demographic was university-age youths. On a daily basis, student tickets outsold adult tickets by at least three to one, and these figures did not include student tours arranged by teachers.[39] It is by now commonplace that 65 percent of Iran's population is under age 25 – that is to say, born since the revolution. They were born into a system that was designed to educate new ranks of revolutionaries and principled Muslims who are ideologically opposed to "Western" ideas, precepts and entertainments. Yet, this did not happen, as summers of student protests suggest. The religious conservatives knew all too well that if they approved reform-minded candidates to run for parliament in the 2004 election,[40] they would have been approving their own defeat. This actually had been the case in the two previous presidential elections, when the nation's youth came out in droves to elect and reelect President Khatami, representing as much as 70 percent of his vote. Despite his presidency, the economy continued to degenerate, job opportunities declined and the government remained dominated by a harsh and unpredictable conservatism. Young unmarried men and women dared to meet at trendy fast-food restaurants or more intimate pizzerias and coffee shops – meetings that could result in them being fined, jailed and lashed. Shopping malls were also popular meeting places which offered a bit more anonymity and safety due to the constant bustle of shoppers. For budding artists, critics and bohemians, there was also TMOCA.

The youth visited the museum for many reasons. Most came to see art, meet artists, attend conferences and use the art library. The museum's café and cinema were also enticing, as were the nine galleries that punctuate the main thoroughfare. Each of these rooms provided intimate space where the youth could gather for critique, debate and laughter – quite paradoxically – under the mantle of the State. At a time when Tehran's young people had few social outlets and dwindling hope for their future with a rising unemployment rate around 30 percent,[41] the contemporary museum offered miles of terrain for imagination, dialogue and possibility – a fact that was missed neither by the director nor the curators and artists.

To consider the activities at TMOCA through Scott's method of examining the hidden transcripts, one is able to see an elaborate choreography of power and the points at which it may begin to break down. As Scott maintains, "[A] partly sanitized, ambiguous, and coded version of the hidden transcript is always present in the public discourse of subordinate groups," which can be discerned in many aspects of the museum's programming.[42] While the State wields a great degree of power over the museum and modes of representation more broadly, avenues of expression persist that can, at least momentarily, circumvent hegemonic constructs. There is a space for artists and curators to create work that engages what Scott aptly calls the "dialectic of disguise and surveillance."[43] Additionally, these works and exhibits converge with other discourses beyond the museum's walls; the content is made and transported elsewhere by students, visitors and media personnel, expanding the discourse and its fissures in innumerable ways.

Soon after Sami-Azar's appointment as director, he began expanding the museum's exhibition repertoire beyond the biennial. Aware of official prejudices against all things "Western," the museum's curators had to walk a tightrope of sorts. To be relevant, the museum needed to function as other contemporary centers, exhibiting international artworks and a broad range of styles, providing related programming and educational resources for the community. The international aspirations of the museum can be noted in the museum's many well-produced exhibition catalogues for sale in its book kiosk and its extensive website, all of which were presented in English and Persian. The timing of these activities coincided not only with Sami-Azar's tenure, but also a bit of political détente with US and European governments. Still, if the museum were viewed by hard-liner critics as exhibiting too much "Western" art or Iranian art unduly influenced by "Western" culture, jobs would be lost, and the museum could potentially be shut down. On the part of Ershad, it was quite strategic to marry the directorship of the museum to that of the Visual Arts Center, for it placed the censorial eye at the head of the museum. Sami-Azar wielded his authority just as strategically.

Interspersed among the various biennials, there have been many exhibitions of modern art movements, solo shows and series exploring *Pioneers of Iranian Modern Art*.[44] The museum also organized the first retrospective of the work of Tanavoli, which was presented as part of the "Pioneers" series in winter 2003. The exhibition covered his extensive career, including a range of works and media, and was inaugurated by a conference at the museum. Although Tanavoli remained in Iran for years after the revolution and is one of Iran's better-known artists, the exhibition received criticism from the hard right. Conservative critics focused on the favor the artist held among the Pahlavi court and cited the anthropomorphically suggestive and therefore "un-Islamic" nature of the artist's work. Their campaign was successful enough that they managed to close down his house that had later become a museum of his work.[45] The artist's significance among international circles of artists, collectors and intellectuals has made him a particularly potent symbol on both sides of the party line. The conservative hard-liners learned that despite their revamping of society's institutions, they were not successful in capturing the imagination, in particular, of Tehran's youth. They persist in their attempts to restrict expression through legislation, including the prohibition of certain artworks, books, songs, plays, movies, satellite dishes, clothes and hairstyles. The infrapolitics of this power play – its delicate choreography – merits a full-length study of its own, for the nuances, ambiguities and subtleties to severe opposition suggest a great deal about the structures of power in Iran and its fragility. What all too often is a black-and-white reading of overt oppression would reveal, I suspect, a very tenuous situation.

Whether it was fairness in programming or clever strategy on the part of the former director and his curators, the museum continued to pepper its exhibition schedule with shows that explored Islamic and traditional themes, such as *A Spiritual Vision* (2003) and *Gardens of Iran: Ancient Wisdom, New Vision* (2004), which explored the influence of spirituality on contemporary Iranian art. While exhibitions like these were not big draws in terms of attendance, they were politically savvy.[46] The government remained unpredictable, and despite his growing international renown, Sami-Azar remained a State-appointed servant.[47] Since his 2005 resignation, the museum has continued to remain a vital institution. Although a look at its exhibition schedule suggests that culture has shifted since Mahmoud Ahmadinejad's initial 2005 election. In 2008, for example, programming included events in support of Palestine and the Gaza Strip and various exhibitions of Iranian art. Biennials and the "Pioneers" series continue, too, as do exhibitions of international art, but not nearly at the rate that they did in the early 2000s. Nonetheless, the museum's significance remains evident as soon as one enters the building. The galleries, art library and café reverberate with youthful energy. The youth's thirst is palpable and their imagination unbridled.

In conclusion, through a historical analysis of Iran's contemporary art museum TMOCA, this study has demonstrated that the museum is not only an important locus of identity struggles, but also a paradoxical microcosm of the State, bearing significant relation to the political struggles that continue to destabilize the government from within. An important pillar of Iran's national identity is its cultural heritage, and its resilience has been measured in terms of its archaeological record and institutions that collect, preserve and display this past to the public. Therefore, throughout the course of Iran's twentieth-century development as a State, its modern identity is one that has roots in an historical past. TMOCA is a particularly useful case study, because its permanent collection and function illustrate ambivalence with regard to the State's identity that has been catalogued, exhibited, editorialized and even engaged by the public in a surprisingly unmediated fashion. As artists and citizens interact at the museum, the private is made public in a manner that reveals the daily negotiations of the people, while officials attempt to harness identity through rhetoric. The last visits I made to the museum presented an unprecedented glimpse of hope as hundreds of Tehran's young people visited and openly addressed the impossible.

Notes and References

1 This chapter would not exist without support from a number of institutions and persons during the past decade, including generous interlocutors at TMOCA, Catherine B. Asher and the Department of Art History at the University of Minnesota, the Social Science Research Council's International Dissertation Research Fellowship and a Faculty Research Grant from Minnesota State University, Mankato. I also am grateful to Staci Gem Scheiwiller for her expert editorial counsel and dedication to this volume.

2 The official conference title was Contemporary Art & New Horizons: International Conference on Post-Modernism & Contemporary Art (April 2–May 1, 2002), which also included European and American presenters.

3 The 2003 protests resulted in over 4,000 arrests from Tehran to Shiraz, Ahwaz to Mashhad. These uprisings have continued, most visibly during the 2009–10 election cycle, prompting what is now called the Green Revolution, and again during 2011's Arab Spring.

4 James C. Scott, *Domination and the Arts of Resistance: Hidden Transcripts* (New Haven: Yale University, 1990).

5 Scott derives the term "infrapolitics" from the idea of infrastructure – that which constitutes and undergirds the power structure. Building on the idea of a dialectic between disguise and surveillance, Scott reads power as a dialectic built of formal politics (the perquisite of elites, bureaucracy and public courses of action) and infrapolitics (the discussions and unofficial actions of non-elites). Ibid., 183–201. For a detailed discussion of public and hidden transcripts, see ibid., 2–4.

6 Ibid., 184.

7 There have been a number of historical analyses of these changes published in the last decade, including Mohammad Tavakoli-Targhi, *Refashioning Iran: Orientalism, Occidentalism and Historiography* (New York: Palgrave, 2001); Farzin Vahdat, *God and Juggernaut: Iran's Intellectual Encounter with Modernity* (Syracuse: Syracuse University Press, 2002); Ali Ansari, *Modern Iran Since 1921: The Pahlavis and After* (New York: Longman, 2003); and Afshin Marashi, *Nationalizing Iran: Culture, Power, and the State, 1870–1940* (Seattle: University of Washington Press, 2008).

8 Reza Pahlavi initially came to power in 1921 through a coup d'état; he became king in 1925 and held his coronation ceremony in 1926.

9 For an extensive study of Iran's modernization vis-à-vis architecture, see Talinn Grigor, *Building Iran: Modernism, Architecture, and National Heritage under the Pahlavi Monarchs* (New York: Periscope, 2009).

10 For a succinct overview of this body of work, see Peter Chelkowski, “Narrative Painting and Painting Recitation in Qajar Iran,” *Muqarnas* 6 (1989): 98–111. Additionally, contemporary artist Monir Shahroudy Farmanfarmanaian writes about her quest to rescue these works in the late 1960s in her memoir in Monir Shahroudy Farmanfarmaian and Zara Houshmand, *A Mirror Garden: A Memoir* (New York: Knopf, 2007), 175.

11 For a discussion of these developments in the visual arts, see Hamid Keshmirshekan, “Neotraditional Painting and Modern Iranian Art: The Saqqa-khaneh School in the 1960s,” *Iranian Studies* 38, no. 4 (2005): 607–30.

12 During the 1940s, *gharbzadegi* (Westoxification or Occidentosis) had been coined to denote this anxiety, which resulted in the 1962 publication of the same title. See Jalal Al-e Ahmad, *Occidentosis: A Plague from the West*, ed. Hamid Algar (Berkeley: Mizan, 1984).

13 The brother-in-law of Mohammad Reza Shah, Mehrdad Pahlbod, was an influential advocate and patron of Iran’s artist community who was Minister of Culture and Art (1964–78).

14 The Fifth Biennial (1966) differed from the previous four in that it was held at the Ethnography Museum at Golestan and invited artist participation from Turkey and Pakistan. There would not be another biennial for nearly 30 years. Wijdan Ali, *Modern Islamic Art: Development and Continuity* (Gainesville: University Press of Florida, 1997), 80; Kamran Diba, “Iran,” in *Contemporary Art from the Islamic World*, ed. Wijdan Ali (Essex: Scorpion, 1989), 151.

15 This is precisely how Abby Weed Grey, a prominent American collector of contemporary international art, first encountered several Iranian artists she continued to patronize until the end of her life. See Abby Weed Grey, *The Picture is the Window, The Window is the Picture: An Autobiographical Journey* (New York: New York University Press, 1983).

16 The group consisted of Manuchehr Shaybani, Sohrab Sepehri (1928–80), Sirak Melkonian (b. 1931), Bijan Saffari, Marcos Grigorian (1925–2007) and Tanavoli, and the statement they issued coincided with an exhibition held from mid-June to mid-July at Saderat Bank in 1961. “Chronology,” in *Pioneers of Iranian Modern Art: Parviz Tanavoli*, ed. Ruyin Pakbaz and Yaghoub Emdadian (Tehran: Iranian Institute for Promotion of Visual Arts, 2003), 28.

17 Ibid. Details regarding the elimination of funding are taken from Tanavoli’s memoir, made available to the author by Tanavoli. Parviz Tanavoli, “Atelier Kaboud” (unpublished manuscript), MS Word document.

18 Kamran Diba, *Buildings and Projects* (Stuttgart-Bad Cannstatt: Hatje, 1981), 32–3.

19 Diba addresses this mission from a different vantage point than he did thirty years previous. See Saher Samedi, “Art Collection: A Chain of Meaning (Conversation with Kamran Diba),” *Art Tomorrow* 4, accessed June 29, 2012, http://www.artomorrow.com/eng/index.asp?page=49&id=334

20 These reforms of 1963 were a part of the shah’s White Revolution, which originally had been conceived by Prime Minister ‘Ali ‘Amin who resigned in July 1962, after about a year of holding the post.

21 In 1973, an initiative by Organization of Petroleum Exporting Countries (OPEC) was spearheaded by Mohammad Reza Shah to increase the barrel price of oil from less than $2 a barrel in 1971 to nearly $12. By Iran’s 1975 peak, the nation’s annual oil revenues had increased from $200 million to $20 billion. Elton Daniel, *The History of Iran* (Westport: Greenwood Press, 2001), 160–61.

22 John Morris Dixon, “Cultural Hybrid,” *Progressive Architecture* 59 (1978): 70.

23 In addition to *Progressive Architecture*, the museum appeared in the following journals: Yvette Pontoizeau and Nasrine Faghih, “Musée d’art contemporain, Téhéran” [Museum of Contemporary Art, Tehran], *L’Architecture aujourd’hui* [Architecture today] (February 1978): 5–8; and “Museo Imperiale” [Imperial museum], *Domus* 579 (1978): 14–17. For a more recent recollection, see Ali-Reza Sami-Azar, “Le Musée d’art contemporain de Teheran,” *Art Press* 2, no. 17 (2010), accessed January 25, 2012, http://www.artpress.com/Alireza-Samiazar--le-musee-d39art-contemporain-de-Teheran,8904.media?a=23568

24 Sculptural works by Henry Moore (1898–1986), René Magritte (1898–1967) and Alberto Giacometti (1901–1966), among others, were included. "Museo Imperiale,"17.

25 Daniel, *The History of Iran*, 158.

26 The park was built on a plot of land that had belonged to the military for parades and troop reviews. Its republican renaming bears evocations of martyrs through their major symbol of the red tulip, in an attempt to imbue the park with Post-Pahlavi meaning.

27 Diba, *Buildings and Projects*, 8.

28 Indeed it is noteworthy that TMOCA's painting by de Kooning, *Woman III* (1952–53), was de-accessioned in 1994, when it was exchanged for what has been referred to as "the greatest surviving Persian manuscript," a sixteenth-century copy of Firdausi's national epic *Shahnameh* [The Book of Kings] (c. 1010), part of a manuscript once known as the Houghton Shahnameh. For more information, see Martin Bailey, "The Book of Kings for a de Kooning," *Art Newspaper* 5 (1994): 1.

29 My principal sources on museum-related information are persons affiliated with the museum in one way or another, because few to no documents were made available to me, if they exist at all. Because of political uncertainties, my sources shall remain anonymous.

30 Former Tehran University professor Azar Nafisi addresses the strictures that were increasingly put in place during the formation of the republic in *Reading Lolita in Tehran: A Memoir in Books* (New York: Random House, 2003).

31 Donna Stein, formerly of the Museum of Modern Art, was hired to participate in this effort; she worked for the Daftar-e Makhsus-e Shahbanu from December 1974–77. Due to her previous experience and expertise in the field, Stein was hired to guide the majority of acquisitions during her tenure. Donna Stein, email to the author, January 20, 2012.

32 During this period, museum directors were selected by Ershad and were primarily unlettered in the arts. Museum professional, interview with the author, December 4, 2003.

33 Ali-Reza Sami-Azar, in discussion with the author, December 10, 2003.

34 Khatami served two terms as Minister of Ershad, from 1982–86 and then from 1989 to 24 May 1992, when he resigned.

35 Sami-Azar resigned from his post in fall 2005, soon after President Mahmoud Ahmadinejad (elected 2005–present) took office. It is likely that his resignation had to do with the varying reception of his work from the hard right and the election of a president aligned with their political views.

36 Sami-Azar, in discussion with the author, December 10, 2003.

37 Museum professional, interview with the author, December 3, 2003.

38 For an interesting analysis of this act and its relation to the place of images in Islamic art, see Finbarr Barry Flood, "Between Cult and Culture: Bamiyan, Islamic Iconoclasm, and the Museum," *The Art Bulletin* 84 (2002): 641–59.

39 This information was given to me by the museum's Public Relations Department in December 2003. Statistics posted on the museum's website for the *10th Iranian Poster Biennial* (2009) remain similar, for they show that 20-year-olds comprised 66 percent of the attendees. Tehran Museum of Contemporary Art, accessed December 15, 2011, http://www.tmoca.com/userfiles/Amar%20namayeshgahha/Amar%20poster.pdf

40 The Council of Guardians (the governing body that oversees all legislation, ensuring it conforms to Islamic law) disqualified thousands of reformist candidates in that controversial election that sealed the conservative's control of parliament in February 2004.

41 According to 2004 statistics reported by the Management and Planning Organization (MPO) and Iran Youth Organization (IYO), over 31 percent of Iran's 15–29-year-olds are unemployed, and these numbers are expected to rise. "Iran's Unemployment Rate to Hit 50% for 15–29 Age Group in Two Years," *Payvand Iran News*, September 5, 2004, accessed August 13, 2010, http://www.payvand.com/news/04/sep/1035.html. These statistics vary from source to source but seem to stay within the range of 25 to 30 percent. More recent official statistics list this number

at 20 percent, as noted by Thierry Coville, "An Economic Crisis after a Political Crisis in Iran?," *Affaires Strategiques*, July 27, 2009, accessed August 13, 2010, http://www.affaires-strategiques.info/spip.php?article1735

42 Scott, *Domination and the Arts of Resistance*, 19.

43 Ibid., 4.

44 Examples of these exhibitions include *From Cubism to Minimalism* (May–October 2000), *Impressionism & Post-Impressionism* (December–May 2002), and *Abstract Expressionism* (January–September 2003); two notable one-person exhibitions are *Arman* (May–July 2003) and *Gerhard Richter* (June–July 2004); artists in the "Pioneers" series include Zenderoudi, Massoud Arabshahi (b. 1935), Tanavoli, Mohsen Vaziri-Moghaddam (b. 1924), Behjat Sadr (1924–2009) and Mansoureh Hosseini (1926–2012). In recent years, these exhibitions have continued, as the museum's website states, but more sporadically, including exhibitions of Iranian conceptual art and "Pioneers" exhibitions in 2009 and 2011, as well as an occasional exhibition of non-Iranian art from the museum's permanent collection, such as an exhibition of "Great World Artists" in 2009.

45 Tanavoli's museum was closed within its first year because of a discrepancy in the financial agreement between Tanavoli and the municipality.

46 This decline in attendance was suggested by my sources and verified by the TMOCA PR Department, December 2003. Museum professional, in discussion with the author, December 10, 2003.

47 Sami-Azar was honored by the US National Art Club in spring 2003 for his leadership of the museum and its promotion of the arts community.

7

SEISMIC SHIFTS ACROSS POLITICAL ZONES IN CONTEMPORARY IRANIAN ART: THE POETICS OF KNOWLEDGE, *KNOWING* AND IDENTITY

Abbas Daneshvari

This article is a study of the poetics of knowledge and identity across the two political zones that have defined Iran's cultural and historical conditions during the past seven decades. The changes in aesthetics and in the *weltanschauung* across these zones are so radical that one is often surprised by the styles and contents of the emerging arts that have also manifestly reflected the rapid transformations in Iran's political and cultural life. The arc of change moves from a profound need to be identified with European and American modernisms to the grand spaces of wistful recognition of signs from Iran's glorious past, and later, to an ontological perspective that undermines, deconstructs and questions all instruments of knowledge from language to rationality and history. In this regard, Iranian contemporary artists are more in line with the attributes of Western postmodernism. Yet, these attributes are often expressed through non-Western morphological structures. Looking back on this short span of cultural history one has to admit that no reasoning could have possibly foreseen such dramatic transformations. Clearly, the so-called logical forecasts of the early 1970s regarding the fate of contemporary Iranian art turned out to be radically different from what is presently at hand.[1] However, whatever the dialectics of this process may have been, the seismic shift in the arts of Iran by the late 1980s is undeniable.

To understand the issues of knowledge and identity in Iran's contemporary arts one must first acknowledge that Iranian art since the mid-1940s has undergone three important transformations: The first radical change took place in the 1940s with the birth of Iranian modernism,[2] exemplified by the works of artists such as Manuchehr Yektai (b. 1922), Behjat Sadr (1924–2009), Hossein Kazemi (1924–93), Jalil Ziapour (1920–99), Ahmad Esfandiari (b. 1922), Jazeh (Zhazeh) Tabatabai (1931–2008), Nasser Oveisi (b. 1934), Houshang Pezeshknia (1917–72) and Marcos (Marco) Grigorian (1925–2007).[3] The second transformation, which is to some degree indebted to the Iranian modernists, took place with the founding of the school of the Saqqa-khaneh in (1961–62).[4] The works of some artists, such as Oveisi and Grigorian, straddled both the modernists and the Saqqa-khaneh. Likewise, Monir Farmanfarmaian (b. 1924) was also modern before her neotraditionalist mirror panels, rather nebulously, relating both the content and the style of her art to the Saqqa-khaneh. Most of the leading members of this group – Charles Hossein Zenderoudi (b. 1937), Parviz Tanavoli (b. 1937), Massoud Arabshahi (b. 1935) and Mohammad Ehsai (b. 1939) – are still active today, except Faramarz Pilaram (1937–82), and represent the classical phase of Iran's contemporary art. The Saqqa-khaneh (whose name is derived from public fountains set up for the thirsty,[5] recalling the memory of Shi'i martyrs who had died of thirst) represents the classical phase of contemporary arts. These classical–contemporary artists, similar to the Iranian modernists, experienced their creative genesis and achieved their stylistic maturity during the Pahlavi reign (1925–79). As the modernists were mostly concerned with European and American styles, the members and the followers of the Saqqa-khaneh displayed a profound proclivity for Perso-Islamic iconographical subject matter communicated, of course, in modern European styles.[6] The themes of the artists of the Saqqa-khaneh were *often culled or were based on the earlier revered or the assumed magniloquent signs of Iranian culture and history* (i.e., Qur'anic calligraphy or pre-Islamic kingship).

However, one should also keep in mind that not all the artists of the older generation practiced art in the vein of the Saqqa-khaneh. A second branch, exemplified by artists such as Sohrab Sepehri (1928–80), Abbas Kiarostami (b. 1940), Parvaneh Etemadi (b. 1947), Akbar Behkalam (b. 1944),[7] Siah Armajani (b. 1939)[8] and Koorosh Shishegaran (b. 1945),[9] followed, for the most part, the more nihilistic and ontological paths of expression. This branch of classical–contemporary artists is, on one hand, less dependent on any specific European style and, on the other hand, may be, rather obliquely, viewed as a precursor of the contemporary generation's artwork. Their art may to a great extent be defined by their willingness to abandon themes that allude to national identity and signs of Iran's civilization.

By contrast, the new generation of contemporary Iranian artists, most of whom were born in the 1960s–1970s, and several as late as the late 1980s, have artistically matured during the Islamic Republic period (1979–present). The shift of perspectives across these two political zones – from the Pahlavis to the Islamic Republic – is phenomenal, and the stylistic and iconographic changes are varied and various. Whereas the artists of the classical generation imply absolutes, the art of the new generation deconstructs these absolutes and undermines the notion of a center, from which values and identities may emanate. The new generation, unlike the classical generation, gives rise to doubt and at times even anxiety regarding the veracity of historical narratives and cultural identities assigned to individuals. The critique of (one) Truth is implied in practically every work of the new generation and this critique is brought forth through the opalescence and mystification of metaphysical principles. As an example, in the works of the new generation, issues such as the deconstruction of textuality and language and the rise of an ontological hermeneutics regarding identity and gender are wholly new and unprecedented in Iranian art. These artists, such as Sadegh Tirafkan (b. 1965), Neda Razavipour (b. 1969), Samira Alikhanzadeh (b. 1967), Peyman Houshmandzadeh (b. 1969), Shadafarin Ghadirian (b. 1974), Shirin Neshat (b. 1957), Mandana Moghaddam (b. 1962), Parastou Forouhar (b. 1962) and Shirin Aliabadi (b. 1973), among many others, exemplify, through their styles and contents, the disintegration of the past and the birth of a new vision. Thus, as a theoretical preamble to better understand these three dominant styles of Iranian art since the 1940s, one may state *that the Iranian modernists were principally concerned with European styles, whereas the artists of the Saqqa-khaneh, through a juxtaposition of European styles and Perso-Islamic iconography, were almost wholly concerned with the metaphysical signs and symbols of civilization (often Eastern and occasionally Western). The art of the new generation, however, has shown itself preoccupied, either directly or obliquely, with the semiotics of society.*

Iranian modernism was complicated. All branches of Iranian modernism, be it the visual arts, literature or music, addressed many cultural, political and social deficiencies that had haunted the psyches of intellectuals since the Qajar dynasty (1786–1925).[10] Iranian modernism also sought to structure a new identity for a nation that was at best culturally, politically and militarily marginal. Thus, at times, Iranian art signals escape from its own historical identity and seeks a reformulation of the artist's personal and also the national identity within certain accessible frames of the so-called advanced civilizations. This is not to say that the Iranian modernists did not find the authenticity, liberation from tradition and purity of the Western art attractive.[11] These points cannot be ignored as they return in various guises, most important of which was the Saqqa-khaneh that attempted to remedy the conflicts at play in Iran's cultural psyche.

Among the modernists who identified themselves with European and American styles were Yektai and Sadr. Yektai had a sophisticated and mature understanding of both European and American styles. He was one of the Honarkadeh's first students and left Iran in 1945.[12, 13] His education in Paris and New York provided him with a fundamental understanding of the emerging abstract expressionist techniques, compositional schemes and above all, the metaphysical principles of heroic self-expression.[14] In New York, he was so immersed in the abstract expressionist style that he was soon viewed as a member of the group and thus made friends with American artists Mark Tobey (1890–1976), Mark Rothko (1903–70), Milton Avery (1885–1965) and Philip Guston (1913–80), as well as the art dealer Leo Castelli (1907–99) and the influential American poet John Ashbery (b. 1927). Ashbery even composed admiring essays on Yektai's art.[15] However, his style never became as conceptual and intellectual as those of the New York artists, perhaps because he painted with a romantic heart, and resultantly, he created heart-warming paintings that belonged as much to the external world as they did to his own internal sensations. Often as his influences, from Paul Cézanne (1839–1906) to Alfred Leslie (b. 1927) and possibly Norman Bluhm (1921–99), shine through his works, so does his ability to interpret these styles in an individuated and personalized manner. Whereas he was viewed, for all intents and purposes, as an American artist and one who often painted in the vein of the second generation of the New York school of abstract expressionism, he himself remained unsure of his stylistic affiliation. Later in the 1960s, clearly under the influence of pop art despite his claims of profound disdain for pop, his art turned figurative and revealed influences from artists, such as Wayne Thiebaud (b. 1920) and Alex Katz (b. 1927). Among his best works are *Open Window* (1951) and *Fruit on a Table* (1953).[16] Similar to Yektai, the prerevolution works of Sadr are also wholly American-European in taste and style.[17] The early abstractions were controlled gestural acts and remain indistinguishable from American-European artworks (Figure 7.1). After the Iranian Revolution (1978–79) however, she moved to Paris, and her style changed to a combination of realism (appearing at the center of the canvas) surrounded by her earlier abstract architectonic forms.[18]

Among these modern artists, Houshang Pezeshknia (1917–72),[19] who is often ignored by the art historians, was influenced by fauvism and cubism and, at times, even surrealism. His *Crucifixion* is an excellent example of his stylistic proclivities. Unlike Pezeshknia, Kazemi (1924–96) thought in flat spaces, and his works were often abstract fields of color, mostly blue (Figure 7.2). He was among the avant-garde Iranian artists who exhibited at the first modern art show held at the Iran–Soviet Cultural Society in 1945. It is, however, Grigorian, an artist of many styles, who influenced his students by teaching them Iranian folk art and may be viewed as a harbinger of the Saqqa-khaneh.[20] He was born in Kropotkin, Russia, and was brought to Iran by his parents at the age of five from Kars. He studied in Tehran and later at the Accademia di Belle Arti di Roma, from which he graduated in 1954. On his return to Iran he opened the Galerie Esthétique and exhibited the works of two Coffeehouse painters, Hossein Ghollar Aghassi and Mohammad Modabber. He also organized the first Iranian Painting Biennial in 1958,[21] which introduced Farmanfarmaian to the art world. Grigorian had many different styles, some figurative and some abstract, but his figurative art was often political in content and addressed the Armenian genocide (1915–23) in the Ottoman Empire (1299–1922). Grigorian's abstractions were quite novel, especially for Iranian audiences, as he incorporated bread, baskets, straw and earth into his paintings. Similar technical issues were at play in the works of Arte Povera of Italy and, of course, much later in the German postmodernist paintings of Anselm Kiefer (b. 1945). Grigorian was also a theoretical force in Iranian art of the 1970s as he, along with a number of other Iranian artists (Arabshahi, Morteza Momayez (1935–2005), Pilaram), established the group of free painters and sculptors in 1975.[22]

The question remains: What did the Iranian modernists seek and promote? At face value, it seems to have been cubism, impressionism and postimpressionism, not excluding a number of the abstract works made by Armajani and Grigorian. But, as Fereshteh Daftari has asked, "Why in the late 1940s would an Iranian artist militantly espouse cubism, a style that had been invented nearly forty years earlier?"[23] She offers a number of explanations, among them the popularity of the cubist style in the Paris of the 1940s as a nationalistic expression against the Nazi occupation of Paris (1940–44). A second interpretation she offers is that that figuration would have appeared regressive and may have signaled a return to the likes of Kamal ol-Mulk (1847–1940).[24] One must of course ask: Did they not know of the neoclassical style revived by Pablo Picasso (1881–1973), of German New Objectivity and of American Social Realism exemplified by the works of Ben Shahn (1898–1969) and Thomas Hart Benton (1889–1975), to name a few? I am sure that they knew of some, if not all. However, the distorted figurative arts of Europe and the United States in the "Age of Anxiety" would have most likely made their works appear similar, solely, of course, in the language of art criticism and not in style, to the distorted works of Qajar artists.

Regarding the fascination with cubism, an apt example is Ziapour and his Persianized cubism.[25] In 1948 he, along with a number of Iranian writers and composers, established the Khorous-e Jangi (Fighting Cock) association and issued a magazine by the same name dedicated to the promotion of modern dance, literature and music.[26] In the visual arts, Khorous-e Jangi placed a high premium on cubism.[27] However, its loosely expressed manifesto, culled from the various articles written for the magazine, was rather Nietzschean-nihilistic as it sought individuation and authentic self-expression rather than the traditional and consensual modes of aesthetic communication. Khorous-e Jangi was an apt metaphor for resistance against the shopworn art of Iran, platitudinous expressions of Truth-centered worlds and meretricious creativity. Therefore, cubism was, to use Robert Hughes, Ziapour and many other Iranian modernists' term, *Shock of the New*.[28]

Ziapour himself had a signature style of colored grids, which he placed as backgrounds for his geometrically rendered figures, often with Iranian titles and figures in Iranian-type costumes (Figure 7.3). His paintings, like the works of Ahmad Esfandiari, Tabatabai and Oveisi were unmistakably Iranian. Esfandiari, though, wavered across various styles from cubism to plein air California paintings. He had a way of transforming Iranian imagery, whether miniatures or textiles (Safavid to Qajar), into cubist and abstract imagery. His subject matter is almost always Iranian, but his style shows affinities with impressionist, postimpressionist and cubist paintings.[29] Esfandiari's paintings are, however, often linearly designed, softly modeled, stylistically uniform and morphologically consistent (Figure 7.4). It should be mentioned that among the Iranian modernists, Esfandiari's love of horror vacui (fear of leaving empty space) equals the early works of Zenderoudi.

Tabatabai, a poet, writer of short stories, plays and novels and the owner of the Iran Art Gallery in the 1960s, made sculptures out of discarded metal parts. Karim Emami mentions that his sculptures were satirical reinterpretations of Qajar types.[30] Tabatabai's sculptures, whether satirical or not,[31] were, despite their novel style of construction, wholly Iranian in appearance as exemplified by works, such as *Khorshid Khanum* and *Dragon Birds*, which adorned the hallway of the last two Tehran Biennials. The impact on Tabatabai's methodology was clearly European, as his methods of sculptural construction were practiced in the 1920s by Julio González (1876–1942) and later by Picasso. His paintings however, sometimes similar to Oveisi's, did not have the same sense of originality and emotional impact because they appeared as versions of earlier decorative Qajar imagery. The success of his sculptures may have been because he had less control over his metal material or that the metal would not yield to certain habitual and traditional manipulations as did paint on canvas.

It is worth noting that most of these artists were criticized in some circles for being European imitators and lacking connection to their own local, national and historical conditions.[32] Cyrus Zoka's criticism of the abstract artists at the Third Tehran Biennial can be summarized by finding them inauthentic.[33] Akbar Tadjvidi, however, in his catalogue essay of 1962 for the *Exhibition of Iranian Contemporary Paintings* justified abstraction and European modernism by viewing Iran's experiences and travails in the age of technology and atom, somewhat similar to those of Europe and North America. He wrote, "If some of the works show an inclination toward the 'informal' or abstract style, they should not be considered as an imitation of western art, but rather, it should be borne in mind that we, too, are living in the Twentieth Century."[34]

The seeds of Saqqa-khaneh were present in most of the modern works and may be palpably experienced in the works of Farmanfarmaian, Grigorian, Tabatabai and, to a lesser extent, in Oveisi. These artists were not of course proper Saqqa-khaneh artists, as were Zenderoudi, Tanavoli and Pilaram. Yet, they present that magical combination of Eastern iconography and Western styles. Farmanfarmaian and Grigorian, for example, were attracted to Coffeehouse paintings and saw these works as authentic and genuine expressions of the Iranian experience.[35] The works of the Saqqa-khaneh often conflated Eastern passion and Western stylistic disciplines as, for example, Ehsai, Nasrollah Afjei (b. 1933) and Pilaram exemplify. In this sense, so much of the Saqqa-khaneh is imbued with the religious and nationalistic fervor represented through Western styles.

Farmanfarmaian is a fascinating figure on many levels in Iran's modern art movement. She resurrected passionately the interest in Iranian handicrafts and created works of profound beauty, which provided a new sense of identity by taking pride in what had been viewed as marginal and even unworthy. Her account of hunting for daily and quotidian Iranian artifacts is recounted in her *A Mirror Garden: A Memoir* (2007).[36] Her journey of collecting and salvaging old Safavid and Qajar doors, windows and *orsi* (sash window frames) began in Qazvin, her hometown, in the late 1950s. Like Tanavoli, who also collected quotidian artifacts and crafts,[37] she was a pioneering force to put a premium on her native land's artistic accomplishments. Her comment, "If I don't buy it […] a piece of our culture will be lost, and that would be a shame,"[38] exemplifies a new vision, having reversed the westward gaze sought by most for artistic and cultural acculturation. In 1958 she was taken by the beauty of Coffeehouse paintings that often depict scenes from the *Shahnameh* (The Book of Kings, c. 1010) of Ferdowsi or the Shi'i stories of martyrdom, especially of Imam Hossein's death at Karbala in 680 CE. Even when Farmanfarmaian experienced the scorn of her family and friends for collecting such "trash," she passionately persevered and continued to purchase and even to restore them.[39] She found the works primitive and powerful.[40] Coffeehouse painters Modabber and Aghassi, whose works were the subject of many lectures by Grigorian to his students and were also exhibited at his Galerie Esthétique, became the focus of her collection. An exhibition of Coffeehouse paintings in the Iran–America Society in 1967 and a catalogue of the works with a preface by Emami brought the collection to the attention of Queen Farah (b. 1938) who later arranged for their exhibition at the Maison de l'Iran of Paris,[41] and a collection of such works were placed in the Negarestan Museum.[42]

Farmanfarmaian's visit to the Shah Cheraq Mosque in Shiraz (with Marcia Hafif (b. 1929) and Robert Morris (b. 1931)) mesmerized and inspired her to make her mirror panels.[43] She spoke of the experience in her memoir: "Splashes of color rippled like jagged lightning across the walls and domed ceiling. It was a universe unto itself, architecture transformed into performance, all movement and fluid light, all solids fractured and dissolved in brilliance, in space, in prayer. I was overwhelmed."[44] Later, her hiring of a mirror cutter, Hajji Ostad Mohamad Navid,[45] set her on a course to make impressive works that were reminiscent of minimalist art on one hand and a reminder of Iranian traditional crafts on the other (Figure 7.5).

In retrospect, the Saqqa-khaneh fulfilled many roles for its proponents. At one end of the spectrum, many saw the Saqqa-khaneh as a sign of a new national identity and as an avant-garde movement. Though rightly so, it was also a portent of the conservative and traditional changes to come. Like Jacques-Louis David's *Oath of the Horatii* (1784), the Saqqa-khaneh was admired by State agencies and the class whose destruction the art signaled. At the other end of the spectrum, Kamran Diba compared the Saqqa-khaneh artists to the American pop artists,[46] ignoring, of course, that American pop was all about semiotics and Saqqa-khaneh was almost all religious symbolism. Actually, if Karim Emami had not coined the term Saqqa-khaneh (which has a quotidian and mundane reference), none of the material displayed in its paintings would ever have been viewed as cultural–quotidian signs. In other words, pop's interest in the quotidian was without prejudice as it included the mundane, the daily and the apparently insignificant objects of the American life. The Saqqa-khaneh, however, was interested in the religious–metaphysical signs of Iranian history. Actually, so much of the Saqqa-khaneh was inspired, directly or indirectly, by religious art that its name was derived from it.[47] The name was ascribed by Emami whose review of a show at Gilgamesh Gallery in 1963 compared Zenderoudi's "raw materials to objects found in a Saqqa-khaneh in old Tehran."[48]

Zenderoudi stands at the forefront of the art and spirit of the Saqqa-khaneh. The association of Zenderoudi's art with the Saqqa-khaneh often bespeaks of how religious his art must have appeared. The signs of Saqqa-khaneh were often a hand, a padlock, a bowl and other religious items which appeared regularly in Zenderoudi's art.[49] Zenderoudi's *K+L+32+H+4* from 1962 (bought by Alfred Barr (1902–81) for the Museum of Modern Art, New York) is more of a mystery because of its title (as are many other of his early paintings) than its morphology. The cubic shape on the right with luminous bodies hovering over it is perhaps in reference to a religious altar as the raised hands on the left are possible references to a genealogical map of the martyred Shi'i imams. One may wonder if Zenderoudi in his cryptic approach to art placed L for light, H for Hossein and K for Karbala. If so, why would they appear in English letters and numbers? Perhaps because despite his religious and nationalistic tendencies, he was addressing a non-Iranian audience and this meretricious tendency does reveal a trait of the Saqqa-khaneh.[50] As the styles of Ehsai, Pilaram, Arabshahi and Afjei bear the syntax of Western art, they also express the presence of a Western audience. To continue with Zenderoudi, Shiva Balaghi has written, "Zenderoudi established a fully developed syntax brewing a private mythology out of religion, superstition, augury, numerology, divination and coded signs. *K+L+32+H+4* is his cryptic confession."[51] The works of Zenderoudi and especially the early ones are designed with such horror vacui that the viewer is overwhelmed, if not with religious fervor, then visually (Figure 7.6). His collage *Hand* (1960) is a juxtaposition of various religious depictions (a bowl, a star and a hand) on a page of divination surrounded by a handwritten inscription framing the image. The inscription reads, "The tree died because of the lack of water and the fierce fire (?), and not because of the gardener's care of it, the moon is not connected to Mars." I assume he is connecting the death of the Shi i martyrs (the trees) to the lack of drinking water rather than to God's (the gardener's) failing. As the moon is not connected to Mars, neither is God responsible for these events. Of course, as the Saqqa-khaneh provides water, then an important issue of suffering is remedied. And yet, who has remedied this ailment, God, the martyrs or the believers? In time, Zenderoudi moved toward a stylized calligraphy that so many of his Saqqa-khaneh contemporaries were practicing.

A survey of the works of Aydin Aghdashloo (b. 1940), Arabshahi, Pilaram, Afjei, Sadegh Tabrizi (b. 1939), Reza Mafi (1943–82), Sedaghat Jabbari (b. 1961), Ehsai, Tanavoli and Zenderoudi, to mention a few, point to a unity of iconographic purpose, though Arabshahi, Tanavoli and Aghdashloo are different because of their pre-Islamic and non-Islamic subject matter. What binds all these artists, with few minor exceptions, is that their art is made up of signs that identify the golden traits and the golden ages of the Iranian civilization, be they pre-Islamic or Islamic. At times, as in some of the works of Aghdashloo, the appropriations of European art help promote the cultural European signs of the Italian Renaissance or other European periods.

I will now discuss the works of calligraphy-inspired artists often described as the artists of *Naqqashi-Khatt* (calligraphic painting).[52] Despite their often abstract appearances, the works allude to various facets of Iran's so-called spiritual (i.e., Qur'anic, mystical, calligraphic and poetic) artistic heritage. Naqqashi-khatt, also referred to as "neo-traditionalism,"[53] "neo-calligraphy,"[54] the "modern-classical,"[55] and the "neo-classical" style,[56] among a few others, is a style of painting and, at times, sculpture, in which the meanings of the words are subservient to their modernist style of rendition. This feature distinguishes these works from calligraphy and the products of artists such as, to cite one example, the members of the Society of Iranian Calligraphers. For these artists, the concept of calligraphy served and still serves as a reference to civilization and cultural signs.

The Qur'anic and the calligraphic paintings of, for example, Ehsai, Afjei, Pilaram, Tabrizi and Zenderoudi, are epistemologically centered,[57] and their meanings are inextricably linked to the historical stream of ideas that have defined the Islamic-Iranian world. Actually, a majority of these works imply that these artists have access to a deep Truth (*aletheia)*. With few exceptions, the subject matters are transcendental, address metaphysical structures and values and are never concerned with issues of the physical quotidian life and, above all, society. These works transcend their contemporaneous context and refer to assumed metaphysical golden plateaus. Tanavoli's observation that these paintings use calligraphy as their central theme complements Hengameh Fouladvand's comment on Ehsai's paintings (Figure 7.7).[58] She wrote, "In Ehsai's works a deep and intimate process of art making happens, by which he approaches the divine love of the Qur'anic word and relays this message according to each person's capacity."[59] To apply Jacques Derrida's critique of Heidegger's "Metaphysics of Presence," these expressions refer to and infer the presence of signs, which allow us to view the past and the present as one. They do so by their opposition to movement and becoming and by their deep metaphysical need to deny flux and the surprising Kafkaesque turn of the events and telos.[60] Of course, there are subjective and ontological facets to all these works, and they are almost exclusively communicated through European-inspired styles.

Another important example here is the series of *Heech* (Nothingness) sculptures by Parviz Tanavoli, which evokes esoteric notions of Islamic Iran's mysticism.[61] One could compare these works to Zenderoudi's and Ehsai's, because they are part of the historical and religious and cultural narratives of Iran. The meanings within them shine through because they stand on well-known cultural and artistic edifices. Martin Heidegger's comment, "Meaning is that wherein the understandability of something maintains itself, even that of something that does not come into view explicitly and thematically,"[62] is most apt here. Of course, Tanavoli is an artist with "complexity of direction,"[63] as he creates transcendental imagery by employing the quotidian and mundane vocabulary of culture. Whereas his contemporaries began and ended with the metaphysical (religious and national signs), Tanavoli's gods and heroes are dragged from the soil of Iran's daily life and experiences.[64] However, regardless of their thematic orientations, most of these paintings and sculptures evoke a sense of the immeasurable either by denoting God and religion or by connoting national symbolic signs. *Actually, it is reasonable to assert that the members of the first generation sought their identities by projecting the Self onto cultural narratives and historical signs. Thus the issues of personal identity in their works have many facets of Iran's national identity and European modernism.* This tendency continues into their present works, such as the 2007 painting *The Divine Names* by Jabbari.

Returning to Aghdashloo, as different as his paintings appear to be from the expressions of his contemporaries, he, too, evokes a sense of the lost civilizations. As an example, his *Memories of Destruction* series,[65] which date back to the Pahlavi period, are, on the whole, a series of wistful expressions and backward glances at selected icons of Iranian and European civilizations. His art is a swan song of lost glories and of time's power to efface beauty. Actually, most of his paintings are either appropriations or reinterpretations of earlier works. For example, his *Lovers* (1980), reproduces one of the miniatures of Mohammad Yusuf, a Safavid miniaturist of the seventeenth century. It is almost a faithful reproduction, except for the fact that he has effaced the faces of the lovers. Sami-Azar has rightly pointed out that in Aghdashloo's works, "miniatures are burnt, crumpled and torn, to show his ongoing resentment of the time in which old values and qualities are neglected."[66] Although his effacements (i.e., placing a bag over the head, cutting out or effacing facial features) may appear to have certain affinities with mystifications and opalescence of identity in the works of the new generation, it must be noted that in his case, the signs are all cultural rather than personal.

The second branch of the first generation is best represented by artists, such as Kiarostami, Etemadi, Sepehri, Behkalam, Armajani and Shishegaran. Kiarostami is a well-known filmmaker and photographer. At the outset I should point out that the laconic style of the Persian poet and painter Sepehri displays a few affinities with those of Kiarostami. Unlike the artists of the Saqqa-khaneh, Kiarostami's photographs lack references to Iran's past cultural heritage. He often photographs trees placed apart and against a pure snow-covered ground. If not trees, then solitary figures in deserted or snow-purified landscapes. The simplicity and austerity of his designs are striking. His trees stand as controlled and ordered edifices in a cold and barren environment whose shadows cast a burdened presence on the land. Though he considers his photographs a reflection of nature[67] and has stated that he is "searching for simple realities hidden behind appearances,"[68] his photographs remain less about nature and more about a heroic stance against it. A sense of stoic drama pervades his scenes as if an imperious, orderly and disciplined will perseveres against the void.

One of the fascinating members of this category is Etemadi. Her paintings of beautiful clothes, shoes and other vestmentary features may be thought of as attractive designs, but they are far more than decorative. They are deep statements about the truth of human nature. The clothing in her paintings is arranged around absent bodies, and within them are the breathing ghosts of the humanity that she often depicts as monstrous and uncaring. Her designs are reminiscent of several scenes in Luis Buñuel and Salvador Dali's surrealist film *Un Chien Andalou* (An Andalusian Dog, 1929), wherein the clothes are to hide the animal *id*. Her message is often that clothing dissembles the truth of human nature; humans are all about appearances and about hiding their monstrosity through elegant and beautiful coverings.

Yet, the poetics of the new generation of contemporary Iranian art is fundamentally ontological. That is, unlike the older generation of contemporary Iranian artists, their works express doubt, uncertainty and ambiguity regarding structures of knowledge, knowing and the veracity of historical narratives. To be sure, this feature, while subtle, is nevertheless a dominant device of the new generation's iconography. The corollaries of this ambiguity extend from a crisis of knowledge and knowing to a crisis of identity, both personal and cultural. This is a phenomenal and revolutionary stance in contemporary Iranian art. Behind these works is a psychology that both directly and obliquely scrutinizes and resists conventional narratives. The works of a majority of these artists question the Platonic ideals by which the Iranian and the Middle Eastern worlds have defined themselves. Among the contemporary artists, the traits of mystery and inscrutability are central themes. At the heart of their expressions is an intersubjective, tacit and yet potent vision of doubt regarding Truth centers and metanarratives. Often, they point out that the source of light by which they are guided has been dead a long while. It would not be an exaggeration to say that the viewer encounters (infinite) worlds in the works of the new generation of contemporary artists, whereas one is the occupant of a homogenous environment among the older generation of contemporary (modern) artists.

The central trope of contemporary art of the new generation is opalescence. This art is guided by a desire to undermine the known epistemological structures, the grammar of reality and the imposed historical glue by which the events and objects of a time are strung together and fit into schemes of understanding. Often, the art fits into ontological zones, through which a fresh but definitely ambiguous view of art and life emerges.

The works of Ghadirian, Tirafkan, Alikhanzadeh, Mehrdad Afsari (b. 1970), Barbad Golshiri (b. 1982), Neshat, Mohammad Ghazali (b. 1980), Houra Yaqubi, Saba Alizadeh (b. 1983) and Houshmandzadeh, among many more, prominently feature masks of all sorts. These masks not only conceal identity, but also question the structures of knowledge as they have been known and as they have defined personal and cultural identity. Some of Ghadirian's photographs, for example, utilize the everyday banal items (cups, irons, brooms) as devices of concealment that foreground in an intuitive manner that cast doubts about identity, history and cultural purity (Figure 7.8). In these works, the forces that assert themselves are wholly quotidian commercial and serve in one manner to successfully erase the identity of the individual. Actually, the only assertion of an identity is, in many of these works, through historical models, such as the Qajars (and rarely the earlier Safavids). The Qajars appear in the works of many of the new generation, not so much as a clarifying structure but also as a device to further the complexity of artistic expression.

The choice of referring to the Qajars in many of the contemporary works such as those of Ghadirian, Tirafkan, Ardeshir Mohasses (b. 1938), Afshan Ketabchi (b. 1966),

Bahman Jalali (1945–2011) and Yaqubi, is understandable, as in one sense the Qajars have a dual significance in Iranian history.[69] They are a symbol of both modernity and regression.[70] Qajar art expresses this historical and cultural crossroad effectively by alluding to Iran's need for *taraqi* (progress), a euphemism for Westernization, and also asserting the myopic intransigence of Iran's religious and cultural practices. The Qajars, in succinct terms, are both the gateway to Iran's modernism and also a sign of Iran as a failed modern State. These two qualities are today, in many respects, the defining force of the conflicts that emerge regarding Iran's identity and life. But the past also returns in the artworks of artists such as Yaqubi and Ghadirian as displaced sentiments, like cartoons or parodies, of Iran's distorted values.[71] This fact is readily seen in some of Ghadirian's earlier works, which juxtapose gestural painting and imagery. The result evokes a kind of uncertainty about essence and values of objects. However, in most of Ghadirian's works, as in Jalali's, the world of the Qajars is colliding with the modern world. The juxtapositions evoke incongruity and glaring cultural disparity.[72]

Tirafkan's works are another potent expression of Iran's contemporary sense of identity. He creates and addresses existential dilemmas. Like Golshiri, his works directly and indirectly allude to the question of *Being* and the place of beings within it. His humanity lives out its life on theatrical stages. They are hidden either by having their backs turned to the viewer (often holding a dagger or tattooed) or by being masked by loin cloths (which also extend to some of his architectural photographs). He further mystifies through horror vacui in multitude series which portrays stereotypical imagery, and frames humanity by various carpet designs (Figure 7.9).[73] However, the most mystifying device is the theatricality of the persona in his photographs. They communicate as symbols of a deeper reality, one that is hidden from the eye but is felt strongly. Clearly these actors bring a quality of opalescence and ambiguity to all his compositions. The work of Tirafkan, as in those of Yaqubi, Ghazali, Alikhanzadeh and Ghadirian, foregrounds the problem of origin, and by extension, that of truth. His characters are all, to use a term by Baudrillard, "hyperreal."[74] The world, rightly so, has no substantial essence, for our histories, our characters and personal makeups, concomitant with our present conditions, which serve as scripts, from which our roles and our destinies are forged.

In Golshiri's works the strategy of irresolution pervades. One recurring theme is the deconstruction of identity – mostly the reality of his own character and pursuits. In a strain similar to the French poet Stéphane Mallarmé (1842–98), who undermined both the person of the poet and poetry, Golshiri also erases the presumed foundations of meaning and asserts the absence of essence. Jean-Paul Sartre's descriptive term for Mallarmé was the poet of nothingness,[75] and in this sense the works of Golshiri qualify him for a similar designation. In his *Aporia* (2007), as he sits among fragments of Greece's cultural edifices, what is evoked is not only man's ruined world but also his ruinous recognition of nothingness and the absence of any fundamental structures of meaning. Golshiri also erases identity by rejecting the conventions that impose identity (State, religion and cultural and familial perspectives). He clearly views them as intertwined and intertexted games. Regarding his own identity and ego he once said, "I replace this kind of I with a schizophrenic one lost in intertextuality."[76]

The issue of intertextuality and identity need to be discussed, especially in regard to Golshiri, who has often raised it. Most of Iran's younger generation of contemporary artists juxtapose earlier Iranian imagery (i.e., the Qajars) with the present. Intertextuality is, of course, about contamination and the absence of purity and originary causes. No doubt that globalization has hastened intertextuality as entities often wholly alien to one another interpenetrate and render new realities. It presents identities as a patchwork of various forces and without accessible causations. As Derrida has said, "Every thesis has a prosthesis."[77] And he wrote in *Positions*, "The motif of homogeneity, the theological motif *par excellence*, is what must be destroyed."[78] All presences, therefore, show the infinite grafts of other entities. However, the grafts admitted provide clues to the conditions within which identities are formed and defined. Most contemporary artists of the new generation are conscious of intertextuality as they cross-reference and juxtapose cultural and temporal zones. But Golshiri attaches a negative value to its presence as he defines it schizophrenic (schizoid?). This may be partly due to his pursuit of an originality that is impossible to find, and partly because his passions and cognitions are strictly about himself. His masks and his use of French and English languages assert a unique identity for him. Moreover, given that his logic is often textual and derived from readings of European sources, he appears ill at ease with his native narratives and yet, unavoidably, he cannot escape them. Golshiri's *Portrait of the Artist as a One year Old Child* (2005), whose title recalls James Joyce's *Portrait of the Artist as a Young Man* (1916), treats identity as a transtemporal phenomenon without a locus or nexus.

The questions of identity and knowledge are inextricably linked in the works of the younger emerging Iranian artists. Alikhanzadeh's works move from reproduction to reevaluation. Each photograph is an image, a sound, a dialogue stretched across time and mystified by time. When one should be wistful one becomes doubtful. Her mirrors make for infinite reflections through infinite readers when there is no absolute reader but only the ineluctable ontologies of self-reflections (Figure 7.10). Houshmandzadeh's *Belt* and *Moustache* (2008) series or even his *Razor-Blades* (2003) are fragmentary signs by which identities may be established. Houshmandzadeh's works reveal that every minute facet of human fashion, vestmentary or other, is a key (sign) to identity within a culture. At first a mustache or a belt buckle gives one the impression that one knows the type and the identity of these characters. But soon, however, the evoked identities come across as too abstract and only define groups rather than the uniqueness of the characters portrayed. Thus, the semiosis of his works are ultimately symbolic and bespeak sectors.

Whereas Houshmandzadeh's above-discussed works are inductive in nature, the photographs of Nima Alizadeh (b. 1983) are often deductive. Alizadeh, a young, talented and rising photographer, identifies the individual through natural sites. The series *You Were Here and Did Not Know It* (2008) establishes identities through the more mysterious and inscrutable natural environments. In another series, *Kurdistan* (2008), Alizadeh presents a more traditional view of identity befitting of both cultural and individual referencing.

A young and highly promising photographer, Saba Alizadeh (Nima Alizadeh's brother), confronts the conundrum of identity through his *Eyes Shut* series (2010). He explores the psychological identity of his subjects by avoiding the stain of self-consciousness and the specious theatrics of cultural consensus inherent in the acts of self-presentation.

He clearly disorients the subject's relation with the context and does so by deconstructing the concept of identity as an externally recognizable phenomenon. He actually mystifies identity by severing the one device (eyes) that gives rise to the illusion of mental connection and understanding among us. In a Nietzschean and Freudian scheme, he returns to the subconscious and communicates more emotionally through the eyes shut than if they were open. Identity becomes in his works a matter of subconscious and hidden forces that neither language nor knowledge may ascertain. What Saba foregrounds is the inaccessibility of the interior through any exterior agency. His works, as in the works of Ghazali and less so with Tirafkan's, erase most traces of cultural identity and map grief, ennui, enchantment and fear through visions draped.

Ghazali's photographs are on one plane, depictions of constellations of daily Iranian life and yet, on another and more critical plane, the mystification of the same experiences. His zips create zones where the obvious is made enigmatic and inscrutable. Another phenomenal photographer, Afsari, defines knowledge in terms of intermediaries. One knows things because of one's instrumentation (language, methodology, level of knowledge, context and mood at a particular time). His pixels, the science of digital photography, create new boundaries of vision, so radically different from the so-called original stance that one is impelled to be mystified by how any meaning may possibly exist.

The genius of these works is that they communicate far more through mystification and opalescence than any work has managed to convey through knowledge. What one calls knowledge is, after all, either a bias or a stage of discovery soon to be outdated. Knowledge is at the mercy of change and the reader's perspective. The early generation viewed knowledge as immutable and iconic and, above all, referred to it as truth. The works of the younger generation treat it as a state of emotional unfolding. Moreover, the works of the younger generation are discursive and open ended. They contain because of their opalescence, myriad bits of information and render the complexity of the setting. In all these works there is a constant shift from the particular to the abstract and universal. The individual identities are masked but the broader conceptual visions are emphasized. Almost, as in Razavipour's *Alice in the City* (2010), one only knows the frame; the interior pieces are too quantum to understand and pin down. In Yaqubi's artwork, the concept of veiled women, Qajar history and the theater of life are alluded to, whereas the specifics or the ostensive attributes are hidden. One sees in all these works references to structures and shifts from the individual to the universal. Yet one may say that the same traits are true of the older generation. However, among the older generation, all references were to established structures (Qur'anic, calligraphy, pre- or post-Islamic historical assertions), but the new generation of artists refers to worlds that lie in shadows: the shadows of the subconscious and the shadows of concealment and dissembled identities and of a history marked by selective assimilations of information. Ultimately, in these works by Tirafkan, Alikhanzadeh, Ghazali, Ghadirian and Houshmandzadeh it is not the ostensive external that acts as the final arbiter of reality, but the gathering of infinite untold and unmeasured forces that establish a real beyond the reach of narrow interpretations and beyond the superficial intelligible. Razavipour's and Shahab Fotouhi's installation of faces in windows include human entities as faces staring into their own worlds and becoming observers and actors of the infrastructures and intrastructures of unexpected and unexplained events and lives. All these works bear the mark of a profound inquiry into the strangeness of common things and of the fantastic as ordinary. *Alice in the City* is an excellent example of how the collective body of individuals is chaos, kept at bay by the imposed frame of culture. It is an example of how the fantastic in Iran's midst is always viewed as quotidian.

In all settings, cultural and individual identities are linked. Yet, in contemporary Iran it is also the phenomenal awareness of the State-imposed identity that is significant. This is partially communicated by the absence of facial identity and partly through various juxtapositions that communicate a sort of confusion regarding the idea of Self. Contemporary Iranian art treats identity through those cultural tracts that yield uncertainty and, to put it succinctly, communicates that the real identity has been placed under erasure by either the State or its ideology. Identity is a matter of difference, and this difference is often erased by the demands of the State and its institutions. In the artwork of Mohsen Yazdipour (b. 1980) and Rozita Sharafjahan (b. 1962), identity is communicated through the State and governmental agencies. These pathways of expressing identity entail a deeper sense of the individual's inability to assert one's own ontic and signal the individual's enslavement by the system. In these works, the State is not only the recorder of the facticity, but also the imposer of the psychology of being. The State seems to have a corrosive power that robs everyone of one's will, dictates to the individual and molds one's fate. The *we* of the State often buries the unique character of the *I*. Here I think of Friedrich Nietzsche's Zarathustra when he loudly claims, "Only where the state ends, there begins the human being who is not superfluous: there begins song of necessity, the unique and inimitable tune. Where the state ends – look there, my brothers! Do you not see it, the rainbow and the bridges of the overman?"[79]

One thing is certain; that there is a fierce struggle in contemporary Iranian art to seek, understand and establish identity. Most of these works are about a confrontation with a world whose poetics are fraught with fear and brutality as they dictate roles based on ideology. The platonic bent of grace in modern philosophy showed that they believed in some fundamental essence, an incontrovertible origin. But the younger generation, to quote Sartre, believes that existence precedes essence. Thus, responsibility, action and search are the traits of this group, undoubtedly contributing factors to the ubiquitous presence of mystery and doubt in these works. To look at a few other artists one realizes that these traits are almost universal. In *Choral Singing Group* (2008) by Ali Zanjani (b. 1986), the images and thus their identities are obscured with stains, water damage, veils and many more such insidious and subversive powers of time and history. In his *Iranian Women and Basketball* (2009) series, what stands out are the abstract game and the broad idea of the act, and the individuals are masked by their submission to tasks and to plans. The preeminence of ideas rather than the individual character and identity is seen in most of the paintings of Amir Hosein Zanjani (b. 1980), which are mostly a romantic *tour de force* of characters caught in a sea of cold industrial sites and ruins of human technological wonder.

Notes and References

1 Tehran's five biennials (1958–66) are a good measure of the rapid transformations on the Iranian art scene. The first biennial presented the works of 49 artists and by the fourth Biennial the number of artists had grown to 113. The fifth included 38 Iranian artists and 37 from Turkey and Pakistan. Pahlavi dynasty encouraged modernism and sought to integrate Iranian

art into the mainstream of European and American modernisms. See *Encyclopedia Iranica*, s.v. "Post-Qajar (Painting);" and Hamid Keshmirshekan, "Textual Elements in Modern and Contemporary Iranian Art," *Art Tomorrow* 5 (Summer 2011): 154n14.

2 The reader should know that there are distinct differences between Iranian and European and American modernisms. Some of the attributes of European and American modernisms (c. 1840–1917) cited below will readily make apparent how vastly different Iranian modernism is in comparison. These attributes are wholly absent in the Iranian modern movement except in the works of artists such as Yektai and Sadr, who, of course, had fully adopted the European styles. Staci Gem Scheiwiller has argued that Iranian modernism flowered in the nineteenth century and was, more or less, a part of the global shifts of aesthetical perspectives. See Scheiwiller, "Reframing the Rise of Modernism in Iran," in *Modernism beyond the West: A History of Art from Emerging Markets*, ed. Majella Munro (forthcoming 2012). The article is highly noteworthy as it illuminates a path by which Iran joined the modern world. I, however, believe that Iranian modernism during the Qajar and early Pahlavi periods was a rather unsuccessful adaptation or mimetic pursuit of European art. The following is a summary of my forthcoming article on "Modernism in Iran and Europe." Herewith I cite a few European attributes of modernism that will exemplify the vast differences between the two contexts and their productions.

1. History is an anachronism (God is dead)

Examples of this outlook may be found in Yeats' "I spent the close of the last century trying to get out of form, now I have a strange desire to create new form"; Nietzsche's "God is dead"; Marx's "Religion is the opiate of the masses"; Darwin's theory of evolution; Fraser's anthropology; Poe's obsession with death as the final state; Melville's Ahab despising the inscrutabilities of a world no longer meaningful; Manet's transformations of mythic structures into contemporary and quotidian allusions; Monet's dissolution of the objective, consensual and well-defined forms into subjective, ambiguous and open-ended sensations; and the Futurist's hatred of history and its monuments.

Iranian modernism, however, never abandons its own cherished historical center and reverts to its earlier traditional standards, as evidenced in the hybrid stylistic forms of the modern and religious-inspired styles of the Saqqa-khaneh.

2. Subjective and solipsistic expressions (author as god)

With the dissolution of collective and consensual realities the creative individual assumed the role of creator. Modernism promises a new center: the individual and his individuated language to express the integrity and the essence of personal experience. Signs of subjective and individuated perspectives are evident in Melville's *Bartelby the Scrivener* (1853), in which the protagonist's individuation is a retreat from the demands of society and eventually his castigation by a conventional society; Cezanne, Matisse, Gauguin, Van Gogh and Picasso's insistence on a personal optic; Kandinsky, Malevich and Mondrian's abstractions to express subjective-solipsistic metaphysical sensations and truths; Lautréamont, Mallarmé and Kafka's personal nonepistemic literary structures and syntaxes; Gauguin's arbitrary colors; Conrad's ambiguity and Joyce's stream of consciousness – also a retreat into the vernacular (*Finnegans Wake*, 1939); and Kandinsky, Schoenberg and Stravinsky's chance constructions (improvisations) are all examples of subjective-solipsistic expressions in modernism. Baudelaire's transitory reality in "De l'héroisme de la vie modern" matches Einstein's restless universe (no absolute state of rest in his space-time frame of reference), Planck's chaotic world of probabilities and Heisenberg's uncertainty principle. All remind one of the implications of Nietzsche's nihilism.

3. Purifications and primal visions

Originality is only possible if the artist can purge himself from memory and return to the primal (to see the world anew as a child). Monet's distrust of memory's eye (he wished he had been born blind and gain his eyesight in his mid-30s to see the world without any preconceived notions); the romantics' primal, historically purged visions of Rousseau and de Nerval; Freud's purifications of Viennese society from sexual repression; Rimbaud's childlike screams of rage; Conrad, Melville, Poe and Mann's descent into the darkness of the unknown; Mallarmé's erasure of memory (see his "Tombeau d'Edgar Poe"); Edgar Rice Burrough's primal retreats into his Tarzan stories; Henri Rousseau's primitivism; Picasso's child-like visions; Klimt's decadent sensuality to cleanse his moribund visions of history; and Freud's forays into the subconscious and de Chirico's explorations of dreams and the dream world were attempts to eradicate historical memory and discover the fundamental truth of being in nature and man.

4. Reconstructions (structuralism)

Reconstructing the world from its primordial chaos and structuring new epistemologies to define reality were central preoccupations of modernism. The many attempts to ameliorate the negative implications and sometimes devastating connotations of a world without God appears in the new epistemic orders of Freud, Marx, Saussure, Levi-Strauss, Wittgenstein and many others. Kandinsky's theosophy and Malevich's Suprematism sought to establish metaphysical spaces where the senses served as a guide to knowledge. Likewise, the American Visionaries (Inness, Vedder) with their Swedenborgian gravitations and spiritual-naturalism found nature to be a guide to truth. Hitler's fascism, Marx's anti-Semitic diatribe and Nordau, Munch, Strindberg and Weininger's misogynistic stances were also attempts to bring structure to a world that appeared unbounded and chaotic. To many, such as Toynbee and Spengler, the modern world was a place of apocalyptic reckoning and a state of limbo.

3 See Ruyin Pakbaz, *Contemporary Iranian Painting and Sculpture* (Tehran: High Council of Culture and Art, Center for Research and Cultural Coordination, 1974); Ruyin Pakbaz, *Naqqashi Iran: Az Dirbaz ta Emrooz* [Iranian painting from its inception until now] (Tehran: Nashr-e Naristan, 1379/2000); also for a brief summary of Pakbaz's history of this period, see Rose Issa, Ruyin Pakbaz and Daryush Shayegan, *Iranian Contemporary Art* (London, Booth Cliburn Editions, 2001), 14–27.

4 For the Saqqa-khaneh, see Karim Emami, "Negahi Dobareh beh Maktab-e Saqqa-Khaneh [The Saqqa-khaneh School revisited]," in *Saqqakhaneh*, ed. Karim Emami and Peter Lamborn Wilson (Tehran: Tehran Museum of Contemporary Art, 1977); Peter Lamborn Wilson, "The Saqqakhaneh," in *Saqqakhaneh*, ed. Karim Emami and Peter Lamborn Wilson (Tehran: Tehran Museum of Contemporary Art, 1977). The best article on this movement is by Hamid Keshmirshekan, "Neo-Traditionalism and Modern Iranian Painting: The Saqqa-Khaneh School in the 1960s," *Iranian Studies* 36, no. 4 (2005): 607–30.

5 See note 47.

6 Hamid Keshmirshekan, "The Question of Identity vis-à-vis Exoticism in Contemporary Iranian Art," *Iranian Studies* 43, no. 4 (2010): 489. I mean by style both the vocabulary and syntax of expression that constitute the forms of representation (per Wölfflin these traits are: linear versus painterly, plane versus recessional, closed versus open, multiplicity versus unity and absolute clarity versus relative clarity).

7 The earlier works of Behkalam were rather political, and his later works became more and more abstract. See for his earlier works, Abbas Daneshvari, *Akbar Behkalam, Movement and Change: Paintings and Sketches, 1977–1988* (Costa Mesa: Mazda 1989); and Mathias Flügge, *Akbar Behkalam, Grenzen überschreiten* [Crossing borders] (Berlin: E. A. Seemann Verlag, 2004).

8 Armajani was initially influenced by the calligraphic arts of his contemporaries, but his later developments classify him as an American artist. If one were to classify him as an Iranian artist, it would be easier to include him among the new generation of Iran's contemporary artists.

9 Shishegaran, like Armajani, was originally influenced by the school of Naqqashi-khatt; however, as I wrote in this regard, "The skeletal motifs of Koorosh Shishegaran's abstractions may be traced back to calligraphy. However, if calligraphy is the originary cause, then he has

given that calligraphy so much momentum and energy that the images have assumed wholly new identities and have severed their ties from any recognizable past." See Abbas Daneshvari, "Dionysian Energies," *Art Tomorrow* 3 (Winter 2011): 167.

10 I am grateful to Staci Gem Scheiwiller for having allowed me access to her forthcoming article on the role of the Qajars in the rise of Iranian modernism: "Reframing the Rise of Modernism in Iran."

11 See note 2, attribute #3 on the concept of purification in Western modernism.

12 The Honarkadeh was established in 1940, two months after Kamal ol-Mulk's death. The institution was first located by the order of Reza Shah Pahlavi (r. 1925–41) on the grounds of the Marvi Seminary. After Reza Shah was forced to abdicate in 1941, the mullas petitioned Mohammad Reza Shah Pahlavi (r. 1941–79) and reclaimed their building. The Honarkadeh was then moved to the basement of the engineering building at the University of Tehran. See Abbas Milani, *Eminent Persians, The Men and Women who Made Modern Iran, 1941–1971* (Syracuse: Syracuse State University, 2008), 187. Fereshteh Daftari points out, based on communication with Yektai, that the original site of the Honarkadeh was at the Marvi Mosque. "Another Modernism: An Iranian Perspective," in *Picturing Iran: Art Society and Revolution*, ed. Shiva Balaghi and Lynn Gumpert (London, I. B. Taurus, 2002), 45n21.

13 Yektai studied at the Amédee Ozenfant studio (in operation in New York from 1939 to 1955) and later that year with cubist André Lhote (1885–1962). In the late 1940s, after he had returned to New York, he attended Robert Hale's classes at the Art Students League of New York.

14 John Ashbery, who well understood the nature of abstract expressionism as both heroic and romantic, referred to Yektai's "heroism" in his paintings. See note 11.

15 John Ashbery, "Manuchehr Yektai," *Aujourd'hui: Art et Architecture* [Today: Art and architecture] (May 1961): 5–6.

16 For some excellent examples of his paintings see, *Manuchehr Yektai, Paintings: 1951–1997* (New York: Guild Hall Museum, 1998).

17 Sadr studied at the Accademia di Belle Arti in both Rome and Florence and returned to Iran in 1957.

18 Daftari, "Another Modernism," 80.

19 Pezeshknia studied at the Leopold Levy studio in Istanbul.

20 See below my discussion of Grigorian and the Saqqa-khaneh.

21 There were five Tehran Biennials. For a brief but informative descriptions of these biennials, see *Encyclopedia Iranica*, s.v. "Post-Qajar (Painting)."

22 See Marcos Grigorian, accessed September 1, 2012, www.en.wikipedia.org/wiki/Marcos_Grigorian

23 Daftari, "Another Modernism," 47.

24 Ibid.

25 Ziapour was the first graduate of the Honarkadeh. He and the architect Houshang Seyhoun were the recipients of a scholarship to study in France. Both were selected by a committee headed by the legendary art historian André Godard. See Milani, *Eminent Persians*, 186–7.

26 The first five issues bore the name of *Khorous-e Jangi* (1948–49), the sixth and seven bore the name of *Kavir* [Desert] and four more followed during 1950–51, bearing the name of *Panjeh-ye Khorous* [The cock's claw].

27 Daftari, 74.

28 Robert Hughes, *The Shock of the New* (New York: Alfred A. Knopf, 1991). Keshmirshekan has pointed out that exoticism can alter the content and the style of a work when one aims to be meretricious or acts "purely for the interest of others." Of course, his comment is directed at contemporary artists, but the idea may be somewhat fitting for *Khorous-e Jangi*, as well. See Keshmirshekan, "The Question of Identity vis-à-vis Exoticism in Contemporary Iranian Art," 490.

29 An interesting interview with Esfandiari regarding his style and sources of influence is by Farivar Hamzeyi, online, accessed September 1, 2012, www.Youtube.com/watch?v=bGSmEooXLRk

30 *Encyclopedia Iranica*, s.v. "Post-Qajar (Painting)."

31 Daftari mentions that most of Tabatabai's sculptures expressed his fear of war and violence. See Daftari, "Another Modernism," 74.

32 For Emami's reference to these criticisms, see *Encyclopedia Iranica*, s.v. "Post-Qajar (Painting)."

33 Daftari, "Another Modernism," 67–74. Also Cyrus Zoka, "Review of the Tehran Biennial," *Sokhan* 13 (1/1962): 118. See also Mehrzad Boroujerdi, *Iranian Intellectuals and the West: The Tormented triumph of Nativism* (Syracuse: Syracuse University Press, 1996). Jalal Al-e Ahmad in the 1940s coined the term *gharbzadegi* (Western affectations – often translated as Westoxication, Occidentosis and Westitis, among others) for those who found their identity by emulating the West. His book on this subject, *Gharbzadegi*, was first published underground in 1962. For a translation see, Jalal-e Al-e Ahmad, *Occidentosis: A Plague from the West*, trans. R. Campbell, annotated and with an introduction by Hamid Algar (Berkeley: Mizan Press, 1984).

34 Akbar Tadjvidi, Introduction to *Exhibition of Iranian Contemporary Painting* (Tehran: Fine Arts Administration of Iran, 1962). See also Shiva Balaghi, "Iranian Visual Arts in 'The Century of Machinery, Speed, and the Atom': Rethinking Modernity," in *Picturing Iran: Art Society and Revolution*, ed. Shiva Balaghi and Lynn Gumpert (London: I. B. Taurus, 2002), 22.

35 Daftari, "Another Modernism," 67. See below a discussion of Mohammad Modabber and Hossein Ghollar Aghassi.

36 Monir Shahroudy Farmanfarmaian and Zara Houshmand, *A Mirror Garden, A Memoir* (New York: Alfred A. Knopf, 2007), 160–63.

37 Abbas Daneshvari, "Parviz Tanavoli, of Existential Purity and Sophistication," *Art Tomorrow* 5 (Summer 2011): 179–87.

38 Farmanfarmaian and Houshmand, *A Mirror Garden*, 163.

39 Ibid., 161–3.

40 Ibid., 171.

41 Ibid., 171–7.

42 It is not known to me how many of the paintings at the Negarestan Museum are from Farmanfarmaian's collection.

43 Her memoirs do not provide a date of Morris' visit; however, all calculations point to early 1970s.

44 Farmanfarmaian and Houshmand, *A Mirror Garden*, 186.

45 Ibid., 186–93.

46 Kamran Diba, "Iran," in *Contemporary Art from the Islamic World*, ed. Wijdan Ali (London: Scorpion Publishers, 1989), 153–8.

47 Even Tanavoli, who often used the mundane and the quotidian, could not help but to elevate them by processing them through the historical narratives of the Iranian world.

48 *Encyclopedia Iranica*, s.v. "Post-Qajar (Painting)"; Keshmirshekan, "Neo-Traditionalism and Modern Iranian Painting," 2; also see Daftari, "Another Modernism," 73, which cites a conversation with Emami regarding the coinage of the term "Saqqa-khaneh" at the Tehran Biennial of 1962; and Karim Emami, "A New Iranian School," *Keyhan International* (June 5, 1963): 6.

49 Daftari, "Another Modernism," 73–4.

50 The stylistic features of the Saqqa-khaneh are European, and in this sense they appeal to modernism and its progenitors as did the modernists. The gestural expressions of Afjei, Ehsai, Pilaram and later, Zenderoudi are a few examples to mention.

51 Daftari, "Another Modernism," 67.

52 For an excellent article on Naqqashi-khatt, see Hamid Keshmirshekan, "Textual Elements in Modern and Contemporary Iranian Art," *Art Tomorrow* 5 (Summer 2011): 152–67.

53 Ibid.

54 Ibid.

55 Wijdan Ali, *Modern Islamic Art: Development and Continuity* (Gainesville: University Press of Florida, 1997), 165–7.

56 Ibid.

57 It is interesting that the art critic Michel Tapié (de Céleyran, 1909–87) in his catalogue essay of the exhibition of Zenderoudi's paintings at the Galerie Stadler of Paris in 1971 referred to his works as "epistemological aesthetic." Quoted in Balaghi, "Iranian Visual Arts in 'The Century of Machinery, Speed, and the Atom,'" 28n24.

58 Keshmirshekan, "Textual Elements in Modern and Contemporary Iranian Art," 154.

59 Mohammad Ehsai, "Modernist Explorations in Calligraphic Form and Content," *Art Tomorrow* 6 (Autumn 2011): 166.

60 For a discussion of these points, see John D. Caputo, *Radical Hermeneutics: Repetition, Deconstruction and the Hermeneutic Project* (Bloomington: Indiana University Press, 1987), 116, 154, 234 and 288. Derrida writes in that philosophy is the "metaphysics of presence." Jacques Derrida, *L'Ecriture et la différence* [Writing and difference] (Paris: Seuil, 1967), 411.

61 The first *Heech* was exhibited at the Borghese Gallery of Tehran in 1965. On Tanavoli's "Heech," see Balaghi, "Iranian Visual Arts in 'The Century of Machinery, Speed, and the Atom,'" 28; David Galloway, "The Global Vision of Parviz Tanavoli," *Art Tomorrow* 5 (Winter 2011): 175; and Daneshvari, "Of Existential Purity and Sophistication," 179.

62 Martin Heidegger, *Being and Time*, trans. J. Robinson and E. MacQuarrie (New York: Harper San Francisco, 1962), 370–71.

63 The term is Heinrich Wölflin's, and I used it in an article on Tanavoli's works. See Daneshvari, "Of Existential Purity and Sophistication," 179.

64 Ibid.

65 For an excellent article on this topic see, A. R. Sami-Azar, "Elegy of Annihilation: An Investigation into Different Series of Works by Aydin Aghdashloo," *Art Tomorrow* 2 (Summer 2010): 163–75.

66 Ibid., 163.

67 Erik Nakjavani, "Nature as the Master Artist in Kiarostami's Photography," *Art Tomorrow* 4 (Spring 2011): 184.

68 Ibid., 185.

69 For the role of the Qajars in contemporary Iranian art, see Staci Gem Scheiwiller, *Mirrors with Memories: Nineteenth-Century Imagery in Contemporary Iranian Photography* (Saarbrücken: Lambert Academic Press, 2011), 1–44, 45–71 and 101–35, which offers valuable information and references that are too lengthy to mention here, as well as Scheiwiller, "Reframing the Rise of Modernism in Iran." Also see Carmen Pérez González, "Khatereh, Takhayul va Akasi: Tasvir-e Khial" (Memory, imagination and photography: Images of imagination), trans. Helia Darabi, *Aksnameh* 7, no. 30 (1388/2010): 25–8.

70 Actually Bahman Jalali in an interview with Staci Gem Scheiwiller points out that Iran is neither regressive nor modern ("*Iran na modern ast na aqab mandeh*"). See Scheiwiller, "Khiaban-e Dotarafeh: Safar ba Tarikh dar Aksha-ye Jalali" [A two-way street: Traveling with history in Bahman Jalali's photographs], trans. Ahmad Reza Taqa', *Aksnameh* 7, no. 30 (1388/2010): 33.

71 Daryush Shayegan speaks of the wistfulness of the Iranian spirit in regard to Jalali's fascination with the Qajars (and by extension, all other contemporary artists that use Qajar imagery). Apparently, Jalali is reifying this deeply seated sentiment of wistfulness in his photographs. See Shayegan, "Haleh-ye Baz Yafteh" (The halo to know), *Aksnameh* 7, no. 30 (1388/2010): 47–50.

72 For Shadi Ghadirian, also see Marta Weiss, foreword to *Shadi Ghadirian, Iranian Photographer*, ed. Rose Issa (London: Saqi, 2008), 4–5; Rose Issa, "Like This" in *Shadi Ghadirian, Iranian Photographer*, ed. Rose Issa (London: Saqi, 2008), 8–13; Scheiwiller, *Mirrors with Memories*, 101–59; and a recent article by Melissa Heer for a diachronic performative meaning in Ghadirian's works,

Heer, "Restaging Time: Photography, Performance and Anachronism in Shadi Ghadirian's Qajar Series," *Iranian Studies* 45/4 (2012): 507–48.

73 Abbas Daneshvari, "Sadegh Tirafkan: The Pales and Forts of Mystery," *0611* (Dubai: Exhibition at Etemad Gallery, 2011), unpaginated.

74 Jean Baudrillard, "Simulacra and Simulations," in *Selected Writings*, ed. Mark Poster (Stanford: Stanford University Press, 1988), 166–84.

75 Jean-Paul Sartre, *Mallarmé or the Poet of Nothingness*, trans. Ernest Sturm (Philadelphia: The Pennsylvania State University Press, 1991).

76 Hamid Keshmirshekan, "Reproducing Modernity: Post-Revolutionary Art in Iran since the Late 1990s," in *Amidst Shadow and Light: Contemporary Iranian Art and Artists*, ed. Hamid Keshmirshekan (Hong Kong: Liaoning Creative Press, 2011), 61.

77 Jacques Derrida, *Glas* (Paris: Galilee, 1974), 189.

78 Jacques Derrida, *Positions* (Paris: Minuit, 1972), 64, 86.

79 Friedrich Nietzsche, *Thus Spoke Zarathustra*, trans. with a preface by Walter Kaufmann (New York: Penguin Books, 1966), 51.

III

THE ISLAMIC REPUBLIC: 1979–PRESENT

8

PERFORMATIVITY AND RITUAL SPACE IN POSTREVOLUTIONARY TEHRAN

David Simonowitz

When one speaks of performing the State and of performativity, what is being performed, by whom, where and how? If performativity can be understood in terms of bodily practices – of conformity, alterity or resistance – would not the State seek to inform or control performativity, or at least foster its own form of it? A full examination of the question would need to consider, among other things, the means, the materiality and the spatiality of a practice. Furthermore, if the modern subject may perform the State in countermanded terms, would not the State, in turn, seek to thwart such strategies? More accurately, perhaps, the default or prevailing mode of performativity may be the State's, which enjoins and (re)enacts the State itself, as well as enjoining the subject or citizen.[1] Especially in polities that are premised nominally and constitutionally on faith and that associate concepts of citizenship within the practice of a faith, ritual spaces may function as forums for, and perhaps instruments of, civic performativity.

The individual subject may perform the State, whether in conformity or alterity, at what may be called a microlevel. Accordingly, the State, for its part, may inculcate its performance in the citizenry in countless individual instances at a more pervasive meso- or intermediate level. Finally, it is conceivable that the State may seek to rally, induce or compel a collective citizenry – and in some instances, non-citizens and other actors – to perform the State as a strategy of alterity of its own at a macrolevel. In so doing, the polity may integrate into a larger community despite doctrines, principles, practices or statuses that in some circumstances might exclude it.

This essay considers possible answers to some of the foregoing questions by examining specific ritual spaces in the Islamic Republic of Iran (1979–present). It is grounded in a formal – and to some degree formalist – analysis of two mosques completed in Iran since the Iranian Revolution of 1978–79. The study examines the Masjid-e Hazrat-e Ibrahim (Mosque of the Prophet Abraham, c. 1991) – hereafter referred to as the Ibrahim Mosque – a State-sanctioned mosque built in postrevolutionary Iran. I analyze the location of the mosque at the center of a major commercial and civic space and consider some of the political and historical contexts at the time the structure was laid out and built. Then the study compares and contrasts the Ibrahim Mosque with another contemporary ritual space in a nearby area of the city, the Masjid al-Ghadir (al-Ghadir

Mosque, c. 1987). One objective is to determine how factors such as structure, location, audience and historical context inform the intended function of these two structures (and vice versa), whereas the other objective is to speculate on the reception. The comparison of these two buildings makes the State-sponsored nature and purposes of the Ibrahim Mosque more apparent. The Ibrahim Mosque not only serves cultic purposes, but also complements and magnifies certain official and quasi-official positions regarding foreign and domestic policy, as well as State priorities for citizens of the Islamic Republic of Iran. In a more apparent manner than the al-Ghadir Mosque, the Ibrahim Mosque *channels* patrons into a scripted performativity that sanctions the State – or so its design suggests. Both mosques, however, are noteworthy as spaces of civic and spiritual rituals.

The Ibrahim Mosque and the al-Ghadir Mosque merit comparison for a number of other important reasons: both buildings are located in northern Tehran, both were completed after the revolution and within a decade of each other and both constitute monumental enunciations of Shiʿi doctrine. In equally monumental manner, they also commemorate pious exemplars important in Shiʿi Islam. Furthermore, both structures are formally didactic. Of special interest, the Ibrahim Mosque and the al-Ghadir Mosque reflect in exceptionally clear terms two closely related variants of a technique or strategy for imbuing ritual with polyvalent meaning and greater power, namely, transposition – in particular, through processes of miniaturization. To draw on the work in comparative religion of Jonathan Z. Smith, the first variant entails reproducing a ritual space or an element of it in varying dimensions in another place or space, especially when the primary site is distant or inaccessible. The second variant, a continuation of the former process, entails recapitulation and miniaturization of a space and the ritual itself in textual form.[2] Most remarkably, both the Ibrahim Mosque and the al-Ghadir Mosque recreate sites located in polities that have contentious relations with the Islamic Republic of Iran.

Meanwhile, contrasting the locations of the two mosques helps to explain their different programs of design and ornamentation and to clarify how emplacement informs reception. While they are located in relative proximity in northern Tehran, the Ibrahim Mosque sits at the center of an official State complex (the international fairgrounds), and the al-Ghadir Mosque is situated in a semiresidential neighborhood.

Last, the two mosques are examined together precisely because they differ formally and textu(r)ally and because they occupy distant positions on a spectrum of expressions of Shiʿi Islamic doctrine in ritual space in contemporary Iran. The study suggests that the Ibrahim Mosque is an element grounding a larger urban mechanism designed to shape domestic, and to a lesser extent, foreign apprehensions of the Islamic Republic of Iran. Furthermore, it is intended to inform understandings of inclusivity and citizenship for the individual subject in Iran and for the Iranian State itself in a hypothetical, conjecturally framed concert of nations.

Officially sanctioned performances of the State may foster both individual and collective sentiments of inclusion. Paradoxically or not, participants in an "official" performance of the State in a society underpinned nominally by religious principles, such as the Islamic Republic of Iran, may be witting or unwitting. And whether enacted pervasively, locally, discursively or materially, the performance may be more effective in specific spaces. Tine Damsholt suggests that civic rituals enacted in either religious or government locales are important means of "materializing citizenship," which make the rites more meaningful. The current trend in nominally secular Western societies, she contends, is to imbue such ceremonies and rites with more ritual (and) formality. Part of the objective is to create a sense of inclusivity, whereby citizens of diverse origins, backgrounds, creeds and experiences are incorporated into the body politic.[3] Damsholt's arguments are not only relevant for Western societies; one may also postulate that such rites, including comparable practices in Iran as is the case, contribute to a sense of (an idealized) civility. In the context of certain spaces, in which such rites may be enacted, including a mosque, for example, the personal, the mundane, the routine and the everyday are made a public practice of civility and citizenship. James Holston contends that such perceptions of inclusiveness and idealized civility are partly illusory or imprecise, and that the premise that civility as a positive good is the exclusive purview of Western democratic societies is flawed. Indeed, he argues, "all citizenships have their civility, including inegalitarian ones," and "all regimes of citizenship reproduce themselves through citizen performances fostering standards of behavior that confirm their specific modes of incorporation and distribution."[4] Thus, in examining ritual and urban spaces in postrevolutionary Tehran, the purpose of this essay is not so much to emphasize qualitative disparities of equality between Western societies and Middle Eastern ones; rather, it highlights locally specific material, spatial and discursive practices that facilitate the performance of citizenship and civility and the creation of space, as is done in many, if not most, States. Nevertheless, it is implicitly understood that the experiences and quality of life of citizens and non-citizens may vary drastically from one modern society to another.

The Ibrahim Mosque: External Ambiguity, Internal Clarity

The Ibrahim Mosque is a contemporary ritual space built at a focal point in the Tehran Permanent Fairgrounds, which are off the Shahid Chamran Expressway in the northern part of the capital. The primary patron was the Markaz-e Tawsi'eh-yi Sadarat-e Iran (Export Promotion Center of Iran). The project director was Muhammad Hashem Rokn, the head designer Muhammad 'Ali Najafi and the site foreman Jamshid Rahmaniyan. The architect was Shahram Alba.[5] It sits facing a large, round, fountain-filled basin, from which streets and paths radiate out to other parts of the fairgrounds.

The mosque combines structural and epigraphic references to Iranian culture, history and faith, although these allusions may not necessarily be apparent at first glance from the outside. In their external appearances, two of the largest elements of the complex, the prayer hall and the minaret, also evoke spaces or structures beyond Iran, however. A third major element of the exterior, the dome of the prayer hall, references a structure in Iran proper, yet that is pregnant with complex allusions and significance. A number of the structural and ornamental references in this edifice would appear recognizable to someone familiar with the major material cultural vestiges and sites of the Middle East (Figure 8.1).

Other elements are less apparent. Lest the observer miss these, the Export Promotion Center of Iran later saw to the publication of a 99-page commemorative volume for the mosque.[6] The full-color photographic volume provides a detailed list and interpretation of many of the structural elements and ornamental motifs. Nevertheless, the printed text does not explain all the design principles and purposes of the building. As I shall illustrate, the Ibrahim Mosque appears to be conceived according to important dimensions of Shi'i doctrine, namely *taqiyya* (Ar. precautionary dissimulation) and the dialectic of *al-zahir wa'l-batin* (Ar. the exoteric and the esoteric). Of further relevance, the commemorative volume is an interpretive tool that facilitates the effort of the State to create an intertextual link between printed text and building in order to delineate a prescriptive discursive space. The initial preface of the printed Persian text sets a curious tone. It consists of an address, a one-sided dialogue with, and in part a lament to, Abraham and Ishmael, in which the preface author, Mohammad Taqi Ikhtiyari, describes the state of the Ka'ba, the holy house that the two prophets constructed millennia earlier.[7] Later, the text discusses the monuments and examples of art after which many parts of the mosque were patterned.

The minaret is the tallest structure on the fairgrounds and actually visible from well beyond the premises. The lower portion of the prominent white minaret of the Ibrahim Mosque rises in a square or rectangular spiral above the surrounding fairgrounds (Figure 8.2). Paradoxically, the ziggurat-like minaret does not resemble any readily identifiable minaret of Iranian origin; rather, it initially appears similar to a famous Iraqi minaret, namely the *malwiyya* (Ar. snail shell, spiral) of the Great Mosque of the Abbasid Caliph al-Mutawakkil at Samarra (c. 851 CE). In fact, the commemorative publication for the mosque explicitly states that the minaret is based on that of Samarra.[8] Nevertheless, the minaret does closely resemble a pre-Islamic Iranian structure: the Zoroastrian fire temple at the Sasanian city of Firuzabad, the tower of which also spirals rectangularly, although in the opposite direction of the minaret of the Ibrahim Mosque. This pre-Islamic building may have also been one possible inspiration for the minaret of the Great Mosque of Samarra.[9] Names of prophets adorn the shaft of the minaret in Tehran. The upper reaches are emblazoned with the emblem of the Islamic Republic of Iran, which consists of a highly abstracted, symmetrical rendition of the name of Allah in tulip-like form.

Contrasting with the white minaret, the black granite prayer hall of the Ibrahim Mosque emulates the Ka'ba in Mecca draped with a *kiswa* (Ar. clothing, covering). Muslims all over the world face the Ka'ba in their daily prayers, and ideally every Muslim should make a pilgrimage to circumambulate it at least once in life. How this structure, currently under the custody of Saudi Arabia, plays into Iranian visual culture is a subject worthy of an entire study, and the prayer hall of the Ibrahim Mosque is not merely a simple formal homage to the holiest site and structure in Islam.

In the period immediately after the Iranian Revolution, official rhetoric contributed to the State's image as attempting to export the revolution to surrounding countries.[10] During the Iran–Iraq War (1980–88), Iranian relations with the countries of the Gulf Cooperation Council (GCC) and other Arab States deteriorated dramatically. Whereas the United States and Israel were – and continue to be – objects of revolutionary Iranian vilification, neighboring Arab countries, especially Iraq and Saudi Arabia, were also condemned in the media, propaganda and art after the revolution. Images of the Dome of the Rock (c. 691 CE) in Jerusalem were deployed to represent the struggle to liberate Palestine from Israel. Yet, alongside these representations of Jerusalem, images of the

Ka'ba in Mecca were used by Iran to portray the Saudis as unworthy custodians of the Holy House.[11] Both the Dome of the Rock and the Ka'ba appeared on Iranian currency, apparently as objectives to be liberated by Islamic revolutionary movements, whether local or global. Finally, images of the shrines of 'Ali and Hossein in Najaf and Karbala (in modern-day Iraq) often appeared alongside renditions of the Ka'ba and Dome of the Rock, especially in political murals in Tehran from the 1980s to the 1990s.

Although formal, if not close, relations were eventually reestablished with Saudi Arabia in 1991 – the year the Ibrahim Mosque was built – the GCC States continued to suspect Iran of subversion: "Thus, the challenge for Iran was to convince its neighbors that it was not in the business of exporting revolution."[12] Therefore, the utilization of forms inspired by structures in Iraq and Saudi Arabia around the time of nominal reconciliation with the latter creates ambiguous, polyvalent connotations.

The name and epigraphy of the Ibrahim Mosque express the broad theme of a genealogical chain of monotheistic prophecy. Various names and formal elements reference individuals, structures and places meaningful to all Muslims and, in some instances, to adherents of other Abrahamic traditions, including Judaism and Christianity. Thus, the names of Noah, Abraham, Moses, Jesus and Muhammad figure prominently on the minaret in the cursive *thuluth* calligraphic script. The white external protrusion of the mihrab, the niche indicating the *qibla* or direction of prayer, creates a visual link between the minaret and the prayer hall, and it is here that two more names extend the chain: *Qa'im Al Muhammad* (Ar. He who rises from the family of Muhammad (i.e., the imam) and *Zahra'* (i.e., Fatemeh)).

Though not apparent, the name "'Ali" is etched into the white travertine as a semivisible background pattern in the so-called square kufic script, otherwise known as *ma'qili* (squared, rationalized) script or *banna'i* (builder's) script. Sura 14, the name "Ibrahim" and epithets of God adorn the Ka'ba-like prayer hall. Externally, the mosque appears to enunciate a transnational Islam in its forms and an almost transcommunal prophetic theme in its epigraphy. In much subtler terms, it alludes to the continuation of the prophetic chain through the *Ahl al-Bayt* (Ar. people of the house), the immediate family of the Prophet Muhammad and his grandsons Hasan and Hossein through his daughter Fatemeh and his cousin and son-in-law 'Ali, who are all revered in Shi'i Islam. The progeny of Hossein and their descendants are also understood by the Shi'a as included in the term Ahl al-Bayt by extension. Internally, this genealogical continuation is articulated much less subtly. It is hardly surprising that a mosque in an Ithna'ashari (Twelver) Shi'i society should include references to the Ahl al-Bayt and the 12 imams. Ayatollah Ruhollah Khomeini (1902–89) himself had stated that any Muslim who expressed hostility or ambivalence toward the 12 imams was ritually unclean and an infidel.[13]

In the commemorative volume, multiple photographs show the complete sura 14 rendered in a narrow band of ocher ceramic wrapping around the black prayer hall. The ceramic band evokes the *tiraz*-like inscriptions in gold brocade that gird the black kiswa covering the Ka'ba in Mecca. However, of the 52 verses in the sura and the inscription, only one section is reproduced in the book – under the image of the corresponding section of the wall – as it would appear in a printed copy of the Qur'an, namely, verses 11 and 12. The central fragment of verse 11 reads, "*wa ma kana lana an na'tiyakum bi-sultanin illa bi-'idhni'llah.*" (And it [is] not for us to bring to you an authority but with the permission of God.) The word for authority used in this case is *sultan*, but this is, of course, the same word that eventually came to be used for holders of temporal power in certain pre-modern Islamic societies and, explicitly, at least one of the modern GCC states (Oman). Whereas verse 11 may have been emphasized to suggest divine sanction for the Iranian State, it is also conceivable that the passage was selected for potential double-entendre as an admonition to monarchs, princes and their kind.[14]

Viewed from the outside, the dome of the mosque is a white pyramid of modular blocks, which could evoke external *muqarnas* (Ar. stalactites, honeycombs, alveoles). The dome and its forms are actually intended to reference the tomb of the biblical Daniel at Susa in western Iran.[15] Yet the actual tomb of Daniel is crowned by a conical muqarnas dome rather than a pyramidal one.[16] Thus, if the forms of this mosque deliberately reference structures to the south or west of the country (Firuzabad, Susa) or beyond (Samarra, Iraq; Mecca, Saudi Arabia), they have all been "squared," so to speak.

A faience mosaic entrance portal opens a passage into the black cube of the prayer hall. Preceded by a rectangular reflective pool, this tile mosaic entrance is the clearest reference on the exterior to the Iranian Islamic heritage. Its proportions and turquoise cable moldings were inspired by the portal of the Shaykh Lutfallah Mosque (c. 1619) in Isfahan. The names of the family of the Prophet are discreetly carved into wooden panels over the door. The almost didactic symbolism of the external forms seems to suggest not only that Iran provides access to the interior of this Ka'ba-like structure, but also that Shi'ism gives access to the inner meaning of Islam itself, which is consistent with the exoteric–esoteric dialectic so important in Shi'ism.

Inside and straight in line with the entrance portal, a tiled mihrab visually echoes the portal. The background pattern inside the mihrab consists of the names Allah, Muhammad and 'Ali, and a cursive inscription of the Qur'anic sura 107 (*al-Ma'un*) frames the mihrab. The short sura enjoins sincerity, compassion and generosity, appropriate values in a business environment, such as the fairgrounds (Figure 8.3).

One of the other rare elements of faience within the prayer hall is directly opposite the mihrab, on a second-floor balcony facing the qibla. This tile frieze consists of an angular inscription of Surat Al 'Imran 3: 193, which evokes the reply of the faithful to the call of prophecy. The modern Shi'i exegete 'Allama Sayyid Mohammad Hossein Tabataba'i interprets this verse as specifically referring to the Prophet Muhammad as the caller and links it to the subsequent verse in the Qur'an, which would thereby situate Muhammad as carrying on (and completing) the mission of previous prophets.[17] Aside from the material link between the portal and the mihrab, the interior of the Ibrahim Mosque is very different from its exterior.

The most pervasive and significant elements inside the mosque are inscriptions in pink and white stucco. The format and content of these stucco epigraphic ornaments are remarkable: if the exterior forms of the building constitute a fragmented architectural map of Islam, the interior showcases partial facsimiles of famous works of Iranian Shi'i Islamic art. One stucco ornament is a modified low-relief reproduction of a votive mihrab donated by the Il-Khanid Sultan Uljaytu to the Friday Mosque of Isfahan

(c. 1310). That donation is believed to commemorate Uljaytu's conversion from Sunni Islam to Shi'i Islam. Unlike in the original however, the sultan's name does not figure into this reproduction; rather, along with other significant modifications to the text, the name of Khomeini, one of the key figures of the Iranian Revolution, and, for the last ten years of his life, Supreme Leader of the Islamic Republic of Iran, appears on the flatter facsimile mihrab. The removal of the name and title of the sultan could complement the previously suggested interpretations of sura 14:11 as alluding to the ephemeral nature of temporal rulers' authority and power granted at God's will. Simultaneously, it would emphasize the greater authority and legitimacy of the *faqih* (jurisprudent) as exemplified by Khomeini.

Another stucco panel reproduces an Iranian mihrab-form tombstone bearing *akhbar* (traditions) of Muhammad al-Baqir and Ja'far al-Sadiq, the fifth and sixth imams.[18] An angled square kufic inscription spirals from repetitions of the name Muhammad inward to repetitions of the name 'Ali as it moves toward the name Allah at the center of the panel. This reproduction clearly illustrates the Shi'i conceptual ethos of the mosque. According to the commemorative volume of the mosque, the original tombstone of Taj al-Din Mahmud is no longer in Iran but in "a museum in America."[19] In contrast, another panel partially reproduces a mihrab from the shrine of the Eighth Imam Reza at Mashhad.

In his discussion of miniaturization, Smith cites reproductions in medieval Europe of the Church of the Holy Sepulchre in Jerusalem. Depending on their dimensions, these were intended to evoke or permit recreation of sacred processes – in the Christian case, resurrection – in a new context; in some cases, they were intended to stand in for the site and the journey to it.[20] At the Ibrahim Mosque in Tehran, these types of strategies have been multiplied exponentially with the construction of external architectural elements modeled after buildings in other Islamicate countries or in distant Iranian provinces and through the deployment inside the building of countless miniature reproductions of different historic examples of Iranian Islamic art.

Not all panels replicate works of architecture. Some convey and contextualize meaning through ornamentation or stylistic choices. A panel bearing the opening sura of the Qur'an becomes an exercise in Iranian national aesthetics by virtue of its rendering – not in a calligraphic hand traditionally used for copying scripture, but in that uniquely Iranian script, *shekasteh*. Likewise, one large panel features an elaborate inscription in another characteristically Iranian script, *nasta'liq*. This panel consists of a succession of salutations to the heirs of previous prophets, descending in a chain from the heirs of Adam to the sons of the imams. There are also brief series of condemnations of the enemies and oppressors of their revered descendants. If the external forms of the building and the inscriptions appear to proclaim a more universal Abrahamic, or at least Islamic, tradition, some of the interior epigraphy would not appeal to all Muslim visitors, and the last panel mentioned could be interpreted as categorically communal in tenor. Thus, the Ibrahim Mosque is not precisely or only what it appears to be from the outside and does not merely convey what it initially appears to do.

Considering the location of the mosque in the Tehran Fairgrounds, the name and external epigraphic program hardly seem fortuitous. At the twenty-fourth International

Trade Fair in 1998, the exhibitors from Islamicate countries renting the most halls were from Sunni Muslim Turkey and Saudi Arabia.[21] In this pivotal, highly visible location, from which many of the primary axes of the grounds radiate, it would appear that the Iranian State has attempted to create a ritual space that is sufficiently polyvalent to have meaning – or to at least be tolerable – to other Muslim visitors and exhibitors who do not espouse Shi'i Islam. Yet, inside the building, the designers have incorporated pervasive reaffirmations of Shi'i Islam and of its vital inner or *batin* dimension. Regardless of whether Sunni Muslim visitors would actually pray in the mosque, their patronage of the spaces immediately surrounding the mosque and of the fairgrounds could be construed by some as tacitly validating and endorsing the Islamic Republic of Iran.

It is worth emphasizing that the emblem of the Islamic Republic of Iran appears higher on the minaret than all the names of prophets. Were that to raise eyebrows, it could be noted that the emblem consists of a stylized, symmetrical rendition of the name Allah. Nevertheless, it is an explicit fusion of the political and the religious in ritual space. In the shadow of the mosque and under the auspices of the Islamic Republic, commerce, patronage and movement throughout the fairgrounds by both aware and unaware patrons would serve the interests of the State.

It is telling that a picture of the mosque and its minaret figures on the cover of informational brochures published by the Export Promotion Center of Iran. In addition, the aforementioned 99-page photographic volume of the mosque was printed in 3,000 copies and available at the fairgrounds. Regardless of the interpretation of specific elements of the building, it appears that the official patrons intended the edifice to serve as more than a place of prayer, but as an image of the fairgrounds and of the State as well.

The concept and location of the mosque would complement Iran's efforts to stabilize its place at the broader international level and among the community of Muslim nations in the 1990s, even as Sunni Muslim polities such as Egypt, for example, continued to engage in campaigns to purge the country of supposed Shi'i provocateurs and Iranian sympathizers. The Islamic Republic of Iran had been perceived by some of its neighbors as a threat from its very foundation, with Saddam Hussein committing Iraq to an eight-year war as of 1980. Iran's relations with Saudi Arabia hardly fared better, and after over 400 Iranians making the hajj were killed – in a stampede, according to some sources or by security forces, according to others – in Mecca in the summer of 1987, the situation grew more vitriolic. To wit, in 1988 the Embassy of the Islamic Republic of Iran in Beirut, Lebanon, published a 480-page Arabic-language polemic directed at the Saudi State entitled *Majzarat Makka* (The massacre of Mecca). The first Qur'anic citation in the book is Surat al-Mumtahana 60:4, in which Abraham declares, "*inna bura'u minkum wa mimma ta'abudun min dunna Allah.*" (Lo, we are guiltless of you and all that ye worship beside Allah.)[22] A direct connection between the text published by the Iranian Embassy in Lebanon in 1988, the construction of the Ibrahim Mosque in 1991 and the publication of its commemorative volume in Tehran in 1998 is highly improbable; however, it is not improbable to suggest that the topos of Abraham as the rightful custodian of Mecca and the Ka'ba similarly informed both the built and written texts. Nor is it too much to suggest that after shaky diplomatic relations had been restored between Saudi Arabia and Iran in 1991, the mosque was presented as an ecumenical, vaguely diplomatic ritual space – one that nevertheless doubled as a partially concealed memorial and polemic.

In informal discussions about the mosque, a number of Iranians found the structure unusual and remarked that the references to Mecca could be interpreted ambivalently. The message in the architecture of the Ibrahim Mosque seems to be polyvalent and deliberately vaguer than the explicitly critical intent of images of ritual sites in Iraq, Saudi Arabia and Israel deployed by the Iranian government in certain other forms of public visual culture, such as murals, posters, stamps and currency.[23] With that said, the ultimate objective seems to have been establishing the image of an internationally validated State for domestic consumption, which may imbue the commercial, political and religious ritual(s) with greater civic meaning and power.

Such political circumstances seem to explain partly the conceptual and doctrinal ethos of this particular Shiʿi Islamic ritual space. Rather than prominently deploying names, forms or epigraphic texts that explicitly enunciate Shiʿi doctrines, such as *walaya* (Ar. devotion to the imams), it is conceived according to other Shiʿi tenets which affirm the place of the imams in a chain of succession and as the internal, immutable truth(s) revealed through the exoteric–esoteric dialectic of *al-zahir wa'l-batin*. Not all mosques in the Islamic Republic outwardly espouse such ecumenicalism among the various branches of Islam. Nor are all mosques designed to emphasize communal difference, either.

More discreetly, the Ibrahim Mosque may also embody an architectural and ritual praxis of *taqiyya*. The subtler articulation of Shiʿi texts and more restrained symbolism allow this ritual space to function as the conceptual anchor of a major public and commercial locus that encourages and relies on international attendance, sanction, validation and activation. The participation in trade under the names of the prophets, the imams and the Islamic Republic of Iran creates a space of endorsement. In certain regards, the movement through or even around the mosque engages and legitimizes the larger civic and national spaces – at least perhaps for some Iranians and for the State.

Although prayer and other religious obligations and bodily practices need not be intentionally political and may be mobile, in seeking to counter alterative implications of performativity in them, a State may politicize them in its own terms and locate them – frequently in mosques or other spaces of ritual. When those bodily practices are already intentionally political, the stakes for the State may be considerably greater. As a point of comparison in a European context, one may consider the controversial laws of 1905 and 1907 governing, among other things, religious practices, symbols and sites in France. The French government has more recently sought to extend such laws to apply not only to churches but also to other ritual spaces and especially mosques. In the case of another Muslim society, Saba Mahmood observes, "different understandings of performative behavior and ritual observance among contemporary Egyptian Muslims enfold contrasting conceptions of individual and collective freedom – conceptions that have radically different implications for the organization of political life within public and personal domains."[24] Thus, some architectural and urban planning projects may also be understood as complements of official strategies to inform ritual performativity and respond to personal tactics of alterity in any number of societies.

The al-Ghadir Mosque: External and Internal Continuity

To emphasize the exceptional character of the Ibrahim Mosque, the study now turns to a discussion of another formally remarkable mosque completed in Tehran since the Iranian Revolution: the al-Ghadir Mosque. The building is located on Mir Damad Boulevard, a major semiresidential thoroughfare in the northern part of the city. The architect was Jahangir Mazlum. Since its completion in 1987, this critically acclaimed structure has been discussed in a number of surveys in European languages of contemporary Islamic architecture and has been the subject of a number of monographs.[25] None of these studies has extensively examined the doctrinal dimensions of its forms, epigraphy or name. Nor have they attempted to extensively interpret the structure in relation to its specific neighborhood location.

The very name of the al-Ghadir Mosque evokes a pivotal event in the Shi'i tradition. On the return to Medina from his final pilgrimage to Mecca, the Prophet Muhammad stopped at a pond known as Ghadir al-Khumm and before a crowd of followers, raised the hand of his cousin and son-in-law 'Ali ibn Abi Talib, proclaiming "For whomever I was master, 'Ali is his master."[26] This utterance is understood by Shi'i Muslims as Muhammad's explicit *nass* (Ar. text, designation) of 'Ali as his successor in temporal and spiritual leadership of the Muslim community as the first imam. The hadith is *mutawattir*, the classification of the highest degree of authenticity.[27] Various sources assert that perhaps as many as 120,000 Muslims were present. Of those present, some 120 transmitted accounts that have been preserved.[28] The authenticity of this oral tradition is not disputed by Sunni Muslims. Indeed, it is included in many important Sunni hadith collections, such as *Musnad Ibn Hanbal*; however, Sunnis do categorically refute the Shi'i interpretation of the event, arguing that it has been taken out of context. Employing al-Ghadir as a name therefore charges the space with explicit communal connotations.

The most striking visible feature of the al-Ghadir Mosque is the unusual 12-sided prayer hall, which advances forward from the line of buildings on Mir Damad Boulevard (Figure 8.4). This dodecagonal form is a portentous reference to the number of imams revered in Twelver Shi'ism, the largest branch of Shi'i Islam. As there is no minaret to draw attention away from the prayer hall, the 12-sided form of the mosque appears all the more monumental against the surrounding urban fabric. The brick surface of the structure consists of dense inscriptions in the labyrinthine square kufic script. The creation of the kufic script in general is popularly attributed to 'Ali ibn Abi Talib, which may add another Shi'i dimension to the significance of the ornamentation and the texts.[29] (While the name of 'Ali rendered in square kufic script appears repeatedly on the minaret of the Ibrahim Mosque, it is an almost imperceptible background pattern, which, as I argue, is consistent with the outwardly discreet ornamental program of that structure; here, at the al-Ghadir Mosque, the square kufic script is the primary ornamental element.) Endless repetitions of the names Allah, Muhammad, 'Ali, Zahra', Hasan and Hossein adorn the cornice of the walls. Thus, the *panj-tan* (Pers. five individuals) or *ahl al-kisa'* (Ar. people of the cloak), the immediate family of the Prophet, which is particularly revered in Shi'ism, appears just below the name of God.

A practical aspect of the 12-sided prayer hall is that the architect was able to situate the mihrab on an oblique facet of the polygon, while fitting the rest of the complex between the flanking buildings on a north–south axis. The attributes of God, the names of the family of the Prophet and the names of the subsequent imams cascade down the external protrusion of the mihrab. The names of the members of the family of the Prophet and the names of the imams constitute the *chahardah maʿsum* (Pers. 14 infallibles or pure souls), which are revered in Twelver Shiʿism. Many other combinations of these names figure on the exterior, and pious invocations and formulae, ranging from the Shiʿi form of the *shahada* (Ar. witnessing or profession of faith) to Qurʾanic verses, adorn the tiered dome.

This is hardly the earliest use in architecture of the names of the 12 imams and of other figures revered in Shiʿism. Dating from the fourteenth century, the square kufic inscription in stucco on the east interior wall of the Pir-e Bakran Mausoleum in Linjan, Iran, includes the 14 names mentioned above and that of Khadija al-Kubra as well.[30] Nevertheless, the al-Ghadir Mosque displays the names externally, and they constitute the primary ornamentation due to their abundance, material and articulation.

The prayer hall of the al-Ghadir Mosque does not bear a round dome as found on many older and more recent mosques in Iran; rather, the building rises above its walls to an apex formed by offsetting successive trabeate forms one over the other. The architect designed this angular pyramidal "dome" as a response to unanticipated space and cost constraints. Later, this creative solution was met with criticism from some traditional circles on the grounds that the result was too innovative and unconventional. The technique, however, is merely a modern adaptation of one of the most traditional Iranian vaulting systems, used for centuries and perhaps millennia in monumental, and especially vernacular, architecture. (It is still used for the construction of some traditional Tajik homes.) Paradoxically, the profile of the dome of the later Ibrahim Mosque is not very different from that of the al-Ghadir Mosque. Both appear angular, stepped and quasi-pyramidal. When members of the al-Ghadir congregation later set a rotating, three-sided billboard with the name of the mosque around another sign bearing the name of Allah atop the stepped dome, it only emphasized the pyramidal effect.

Inside the dodecagonal prayer hall, endless repetitions of the name of one different imam cover each wall, explicitly articulating the formal allusion to the 12 imams on the exterior. This thematic application of epigraphy on each wall further emphasizes the solemn enunciation of *walaya*, a key tenet of Imami Shiʿism.

However, other epigraphs inside are highly varied, and inscriptions in one part reference texts elsewhere in the building. A most telling inscription, which appears once over the entrance and multiple times inside, is Qurʾanic sura 5, al-Maʾida, verse 3: "This day have I perfected your religion for you and completed my favor unto you, and have chosen for you as religion al-Islam." In his *Al-Tibyan fi Tafsir al-Qurʾan*, the medieval Shiʿi exegete Shaykh al-Tusi (d. 1067) cites a tradition of Imam Jaʿfar al-Sadiq, who explains that it was immediately after ʿAli's designation at Ghadir al-Khumm that this verse was revealed to Muhammad, and that it was the very last verse of the Qurʾan to be revealed.[31] The modern Shiʿi scholar ʿAllama Sayyid Mohammad Hossein Tabatabaʾi states that verse 67 of the same sura was revealed *before* the designation, and that it was God's express command to Muhammad to carry out the appointment.[32] In the Shi'i tradition, therefore, Muhammad's revelatory mission was not complete until this act of designation. A pattern of causal relation is thus affirmed in the mosque between the proclamation at Ghadir al-Khumm and the Qur'anic revelation.

Surat al-Qadr is among the largest inscribed inside the tiered dome (Figure 8.5). Although Muhammad received revelation progressively, he is also understood to have received it *in toto* on the "Night of Destiny" or "Night of Power," *laylat al-qadr*. The Imami traditionist Kulayni (d. 940) devotes a chapter in *Al-Usul min al-Kafi* to this sura and includes a report of Imam al-Baqir, declaring, "No prophet dies without his knowledge [entrusted] in the heart of his plenipotentiary, [when] the angels and the spirit descend on *laylat al-qadr* with the order by which He judges his servants."[33] Thus, the inclusion of Surat al-Qadr intertextually sustains the Shi'i understanding of Surat al-Ma'ida that revelation and imamate are inextricably linked.

Khomeini also stated in regard to this verse, "Full benefit can be drawn from the Qur'an only by the man to whom it was addressed – the messenger of God. All others are deprived of such complete benefit, *unless they attain it by means of instruction from him, as was the case with the awliya*" (emphasis added).[34] His statement implies that the imams inherit the inner knowledge of the revelation. Here and in other writings, he specifically interprets the verse as defining the essence of the Ahl al-Bayt. There is no obvious evidence that the designers of the mosque chose the epigraphy with Khomeini's remarks in mind; however, at the time the mosque was built, the dissemination of his comments would almost certainly inform the popular reception of any verse. When preliminary field research for this study was carried out in 1999, a large hand-painted sign in the prayer hall proclaimed a link from Khomeini to the Mahdi sustained by Ayatollah Khamenei (the current Supreme Leader since 1989). The mosque is a monument to the genealogical chain of *nass* (designation) begun at Ghadir al-Khumm and embodied in the corpus of *nass* (text), constituting the fabric of the walls. Regardless of the architect's intent however, through subsequent interventions of the congregants in the space, the building also serves to telescope the genealogy.

In the ablutions hall in the back of the building is a series of six hadiths or oral traditions of the Prophet Muhammad that are cited together to emphasize further the principle of *walaya*. Among the more salient are the aforementioned Hadith al-Ghadir and the celebrated Hadith al-Thaqalayn.[35] Transmitted in a number of slightly different variants, it is presented in one of its Shi'i forms: "*Qala Rasul Allah, sala Allah 'alayhi wa alihi, inni tarik fikum al-thaqalayn, Kitab Allah wa 'itrati, ahl bayti. Lan yaftariqa hatta yarida 'ala al-hawd. Ma in tamassaktum bihima lan tadilu abadan.*" (The Messenger of God – may God bless him and his progeny and grant them salvation – said, "Verily, I am leaving you two weighty matters: the Book of God and my Kindred, my Household. The two shall never diverge until they return to the pond [of paradise]. If you adhere to them you shall never wander astray.") This epigraph of Hadith al-Thaqalayn serves as an intertextual link between the terrestrial pool of Ghadir al-Khumm, embodied in the mosque's name, and the celestial pool of abundance evoked in Surat al-Kawthar, which is one of the other verses inscribed most prominently in the ceiling of the dome and also charged with references to the progeny of Muhammad, according to exegetical sources.[36] These hadiths are the only major inscriptions of the building not executed in either square-kufic or another angular script. They were exceptionally rendered in faience mosaic in the cursive *thuluth* script due to a shortage of funds to continue producing inscriptions in the brick or glazed-brick square kufic script.[37]

If the inscriptions are intended to be systematically read, as evidence suggests, an explanation for the use of the angular brick and faience scripts seems in order. For if the mosque was intended as an explicit expression of *walaya*, *nass* and Shiʿi victory, why not employ the more legible cursive *thuluth* used for the polychrome faience on mosques of the first national Shiʿi dynasty of early modern Iran, the Safavids (1501–c.1736)? Although the mosque and its fabric have been compared by many scholars to early Islamic tomb towers, Renata Holod and Hassan-Uddin Khan state, "The epigraphic program here has been rendered within the visual culture of its own time: posters, banners and massive revolutionary inscriptions."[38] It is tempting, for a number of reasons, to trace an answer to the ideas of the popular lay ideologue of the prerevolutionary period, ʿAli Shariʿati (1933–77). In Shariʿati's view, the Safavids had divested Shiʿism of its essence by institutionalizing and co-opting it for political purposes.[39] "Safavid Shiʿism" was Shariʿati's term for the State religion of the Pahlavi dynasty (1925–79).[40] In opposition to the religion co-opted by the two Pahlavi shahs, he advocated what he termed "Alid Shiʿism," inspired by the principles and actions of the early partisans of ʿAli ibn Abi Talib.[41] (And again, in popular belief the "kufic" script was developed by ʿAli.) Any direct link between the ideas of Shariʿati, or of Khomeini for that matter, and the inspiration for the design of the al-Ghadir Mosque is purely hypothetical. Yet, it is also highly improbable that the architect Jahangir Mazlum could have been unfamiliar with their ideas. Although the mosque was completed circa 1987, its planning actually began in the period leading up to the revolution in 1977, the very year that Shariʿati passed away. Furthermore, barely a few blocks away at the end of Mir Damad Boulevard and just around the corner, one encounters a mausoleum and lecture hall, the Hosseiniyeh-yeh Ershad, founded by Ayatollah Mutahhari (1920–79) and Shariʿati himself, and where Shariʿati delivered his lectures. The street itself is named ʿAli Shariʿati Boulevard. Finally, a younger congregant interviewed at the al-Ghadir Mosque brought up the site unprompted and suggested the location to the author. As compelling as such an explanation for the use of this script and material may seem, it is entirely speculative at best – not to mention a reification – without confirmation from the designers. Holod and Khan also note that in this period a number of buildings in Iran were constructed in brick, using minimalist forms and angular scripts.[42]

A further word about the predominant script is nevertheless appropriate; rather than discouraging reading, as has occasionally been the effect of its use in some contexts, the labyrinthine square kufic script in which the inscriptions are rendered actually compels the observer to ponder the epigraphy. A few of the larger Qurʾanic verses high up inside the dome of the prayer hall are actually executed in what could be called a quasi-square kufic script, for it is essentially proportioned like *thuluth*, the most legible cursive script. There are even diacritical dots, a feature not typical of square kufic. Yet the vast majority of the inscriptions are more traditional variants of angular scripts and square kufic in particular. In 1999 congregants informed the author that scholars often sat with the faithful in the prayer hall, explicating the epigraphy in this three-dimensional exegesis or *tafsir*. Thus, this building-cum-book is ritually read.[43]

The pervasive square kufic script draws the reader further into the text, magnifying the very details that create focus and ritual meaning. Furthermore, the brick inscriptions materialize (the names of) the *awliya'* (friends of God, saints), i.e., the 14 infallibles, *in three dimensions*. Although writ large in the epigraphy, the figures are reduced from giant imagined abstracts to human scale (Figure 8.6). The audience, too, is transposed into the ritual and built text outside and inside the mosque.

Broadly speaking, Smith's second rubric of miniaturization may be described as a movement from a more permanent sacred emplacement to a less permanent one.[44] He illustrates it by recounting the domestication of late antique temple rites and, eventually, the ritual transcription/inscription of domestic sacred rites into manuscript form, a process that I would describe as entextualization. Rather than trace the process as beginning at the space of ritual and resulting in a portable entextualized space, one may view a ritual space itself as the entextualized result of miniaturization and displacement from distant broader locales. And if the original ritual as performed in its more elemental emplacement, even in a nondescript, unseen natural topos, was/is already centered on "text," coincidentally, the effect of entextualization will be all the more organic, complete and potentially dramatic. In the case of the al-Ghadir Mosque, the process of inscription and entextualization has been monumentalized, ostensibly the opposite of miniaturization, except that the volume of the epigraphy deployed inside and outside is so massive that the scale of the actual edifice is proportionately reduced.

As the Ibrahim Mosque transposes distant ritual spaces, most notably in (Saudi) Arabia, so the al-Ghadir Mosque evokes and replaces a distant "lost" place of indeterminate expanse, again in (Saudi) Arabia (although it is no longer called Ghadir al-Khumm), wherein, according to Shi'i tradition, the first instance of the foremost ritual act in Shi'i Islam was performed. That performance was a verbal speech act: the specific designation or *nass* (lit. text) of the successor in spiritual authority, the imam. The al-Ghadir Mosque therefore transposes and miniaturizes an entire reimagined geographic locus, as well as an (almost) unique ritual performed there one time in the distant past, and materially spatializes and entextualizes these in an immediate tangible locale. Exceptionally however, the ritual that is miniaturized (to invoke Smith) and entextualized in this Iranian mosque was already a "text" at its origin. Inscribed in architecture as epigraphy and symbolic, formal references, rather than transcribed in a manuscript, those entextualized rites are perpetuated through ritual reading by the congregation.

To be sure, this is not the only example of a modern mosque in Iran to bear the name al-Ghadir or to bear inscriptions with clear Shi'i connotations – of the latter, there are many pre-modern and modern examples. That there are other similarly inspired ritual spaces in Iran speaks to the theological significance of the place which they reference, and this is again in keeping with Smith's evocation of the multiple replicas of the Church of the Holy Sepulchre in varying sizes throughout medieval Christian Europe. However, considering the name and inscriptions in conjunction with the exceptional forms and particular aesthetics of the al-Ghadir Mosque in Tehran provides an instructive point of comparison and contrast to the contemporary Ibrahim Mosque. The two mosques sit at nearly opposite poles of a doctrinal–conceptual spectrum. Nevertheless, some of the techniques employed by the designers to create greater ritual meaning in the two spaces are closely related, coincidentally or not.

Comparative Considerations

It is often claimed that little, if anything, distinguishes the ritual spaces of Shi'i Muslims from those of Sunni Muslims. This contention stems from calls for communal unity by some Muslims, and it is also implicitly supported by some scholars attempting to present a normative position of the *umma* (Ar. the greater Muslim community). The study of these two mosques suggests that this contention is an oversimplification. Furthermore, the conceptual programs of these two structures suggest that social and political contexts may prompt or inform the emphasis of different nuances of (Shi'i) doctrine within a given society. Drawing on different doctrines in the delineation of ritual spaces, without denying their authenticity or genuine spiritual value, may facilitate the emphasis of principles that foster enactment of a performativity that endorses the State, at microlevels (individual and collective), mesolevels (urban and national) and macrolevels (international), and contributes to a nationally sanctioned civility and sense of citizenship, in this case in Iran.

The Ibrahim Mosque is a civic and political space, as well as a religious one, situated at the core of a commercial forum. One may describe the mosque as a "dormant" mechanism that, when activated by patrons, directs them to perform rites that also inscribe the citizen within the State. However, the mosque also draws on the sanction, both conscious and unconscious, of foreign nationals. It thereby serves to inscribe the Iranian State into a concert of nations, validating the Islamic Republic at the international level. The mosque would seem intended to function outwardly as a symbol of a token effort at reconciliation with polities that had heretofore felt threatened by the Islamic Republic's attempts to export the revolution. It is hard to quantify or evaluate the extent to which it validates the republic at international levels; it may even be negligible. However, an inestimable benefit for the State lies in the fact that some Iranians may see or *believe* that it does that and endorse that function via prayer in it or through recognition of a validating dimension. In this regard, the value of the site is domestic, even though – or rather precisely because – its planners designed it to have an ostensibly international dimension.

Paradoxically, it is the al-Ghadir Mosque which has come to the attention of international audiences, especially scholarly and professional circles in Europe and the United States. It was nevertheless designed to fulfill the needs of a local community, although it is possible that some members of the congregation may have hoped their ritual space would serve broader interests. Despite planning during a period of political transition, the architects and patrons were apparently less constrained by communitarian tensions in a more residential quarter. The designers of the al-Ghadir Mosque intertextually enunciated in form and epigraphy the most overt proclamation of faith in Shi'i Islam. Although their solution – dispensing with a minaret and a true dome – was not without controversy, it had little to do with the clearly communal content of this hybrid text and more to do with traditional attitudes toward the perceived requirements of a mosque.[45] From a doctrinal perspective, the al-Ghadir Mosque in Tehran is a *zahir* (evident) articulation of the principle of *walaya*, for its message is consistent within and without. Given the primarily local audience, this is an unassuming, mainstream expression of faith. The building enshrines doctrines embraced nationally but eschewed by many foreign audiences. Yet the architect's creative response to constraints of the site nevertheless drew the attention of observers abroad.

In contrast, the Ibrahim Mosque initially appears to celebrate the polyphony of international commerce among the Abrahamic traditions and especially of pan-Islamic brotherhood. Upon closer and deeper inspection, it becomes apparent that, in its culturally ambiguous architectural forms, polyvalent external epigraphy and exclusivist and politicized internal inscriptions, the Ibrahim Mosque is a potentially communitarian ritual text-space. To describe the ethos of its conceptual imperatives in doctrinal terms, the Ibrahim Mosque is a *batin*, or esoterically inspired space. It constitutes a presentation of doctrinal principles as forcefully as the more immediately legible al-Ghadir Mosque, and with equally powerful political resonance. It could, however, be described as quasi-"cloaked," in line with the concept of *taqiyya* (precautionary dissimulation), which, although it is a practice of self-preservation and one synonymous with piety for Shi'i Muslims, nevertheless incites mistrust in some. For an international, public forum it could strike many as somewhat more audacious, radical, even "revolutionary," given the high profile of its external appearance, its urban placement and its reproduction on official publicity aimed at courting international patronage.

It is quite possible that the outward concealment of the intent, as suggested here, is a feigned conceit. In all likelihood, the formal references to the Ka'ba in Mecca and to the Malwiyya minaret at Samarra, but perhaps less so to the tomb of Daniel in Susa, would have appeared rather obvious to many Iranians, and all the more so given the then recent Iran–Iraq War and the incident in Mecca, in which many Iranian pilgrims had perished.[46] Some of the paradoxical forms of the mosque would not have been lost on observers from other Muslim countries either. Seen in this light, the Ibrahim Mosque may serve multiple purposes simultaneously, some of them diplomatic and conciliatory, some politically provocative or communally reassertive. Given the dramatic precedent of the nearby al-Ghadir Mosque, it is revealing that the sponsors of the Ibrahim Mosque did not opt for a comparably clear, communitarian design to represent the State's export forum.

Images of the shrines at Najaf and Karbala in Iraq and the Ka'ba in Saudi Arabia continued to be used alongside renditions of the Dome of the Rock in Israel/Palestine in political murals to excoriate Iran's enemies. How then should one interpret the significance of a contemporary mosque consisting of reproductions of an Iraqi minaret, a Saudi ritual space and a western Iranian monument to a Jewish biblical figure (i.e., Daniel), its unifying Abrahamic themes notwithstanding? Lest one argue that the image of the Dome of the Rock is required for a clear reference to the third of three sacred cities "held hostage" by Iran's enemies, the round esplanade and fountain where the Ibrahim Mosque sits in the fairgrounds is (now, at least) identified as Maydan-e Qods (Jerusalem Plaza) in some online maps.[47] Of course, to assume that all official or quasi-official policy positions should be consistent would be to ignore the internal, faction-driven complexity of the Islamic Republic of Iran. States are rarely, if ever, uniformly monolithic, despite the best efforts of some interests. Nevertheless, the real audience for these ambiguously polemical messages is the Iranian public, whose interests the State must present itself as defending and whose sentiments its representatives may seek to stir to foster loyalty. For it is the domestic audience that, in praying in the Ibrahim Mosque, in conducting business in its shadow or in recognizing it as an official sign of the Islamic Republic of Iran and its allegedly international, Abrahamic and pan-Islamic sanction, constitutes the vital participant in the performance and validation of the State.[48]

Conclusion

By comparing the Ibrahim Mosque and the al-Ghadir Mosque and their respective urban locations, I have sought to uncover clues that may explain some of the ancillary objectives of the mosques' sponsors and designers and additional meanings of the spaces; a corollary objective has been to consider the extent to which location potentially informs subsequent reception and interpretation of the space, whether by primary users, passersby or outside observers, regardless of the designers' intent. The site intertextually frames and informs the reading of the ritual space as effectively as placing two verses of scripture side-by-side. Mahmood has argued in her study of the politics of bodily practices (in Egypt), "what is at stake in these debates are different imaginaries of personal and collective freedom, presupposing different relations to forms of social authority (whether enshrined in scripture, national citizenship, or exemplary models)."[49] To different degrees, both buildings studied here create spaces that materially enshrine such authority, and in all three forms cited by Mahmood, to channel the potential of performativity.

Taking Jonathan Z. Smith's theories on transposition and miniaturization into consideration also permits a better understanding of how these mosques function as spaces of enhanced ritual meaning. The political performative dimensions of these spaces rely in part on related strategies or techniques, despite the sharply different appearances of the buildings. These meanings are not only more complex but more powerful as well, because of the intentional, if unequal, inscription of State and national symbols within the canonical signs and motifs of Twelver Shi'ism that govern the conceptual ethos of each structure. Smith does not lack critics, to be sure.[50] Nevertheless, his work does facilitate a better understanding of the potential power and dynamics of a range of performativities. What happens, one must ask, when spatial and material elements of ritual are reinscribed to make the State the primary guide of religious activity?

As a final consideration, it bears recalling that mosques in particular served as physical nodes of ephemeral and shifting activist networks during the Iranian Revolution.[51] There does remain some debate about the impact of such mosque networks.[52] Yet it should hardly come as a surprise that the Iranian State may maintain interest in the cultivation of spaces that ground so much latent discursive, social and political potential. Kurzman and Schayegh alike allude to the risk of reifying by treating semi-abstract, humanly constituted systems, such as networks in the former case and the State in the latter, as things or entities separate from society.[53] A descriptive, formal(ist) discussion of a

State-sponsored mosque runs an even greater risk. A ritual space, such as the Ibrahim Mosque, can nevertheless be studied profitably as a didactic materialization of institutional structures that the State (as a network of actors) has attempted to establish to delineate a certain scripted performativity. The preliminary glimpse of the structure presented here has not thoroughly evaluated the reception of this space or its effectiveness, however. A more systematic examination of the reactions of patrons and passersby to these mosques would be a fruitful research priority for future study.

Formal and aesthetic qualities need not *necessarily* inform or identify the function or use of a space. However, a striking difference in function of the two mosques – or, perhaps more accurately, an enhanced political function in one – is brought into higher relief through the comparison of their forms, epigraphy, sites and periods of construction. Indeed, both mosques – and most public ritual spaces, for that matter – can serve a range of political and religious functions to greater or lesser degrees. The intended function and reception of a space are not always stable, either. Subsequent reappropriations and modifications can radically change the use and meaning. And yet, these two mosques in particular merit comparison for the fact that they have been designed according to related cognitive strategies of miniaturization and transposition, which engender ritual focus, greater meaning and performative power. Ultimately, this study attempts to bring into focus some of the means by which the State may seek to inform public and discursive spaces and foster practices of normative civility and citizenship through the design and placement of an officially sanctioned ritual space, in this case almost incidentally, in the Islamic Republic of Iran.

Notes and References

1 Cyrus Schayegh notes that the emphasis on the State in historical studies of Pahlavi Iran tended to obscure other methods and subjects, and despite new historical approaches, this focus is still prevalent in studies of postrevolutionary Iran. Nevertheless, he continues, "[M]ethodological statism is not wrong. It is one-sided." Cyrus Schayegh, "'Seeing Like a State': An Essay on the Historiography of Modern Iran," *International Journal of Middle East Studies* 42, no. 1 (February 2010): 38.

2 As examples of the former, Smith cites churches, chapels, tombs, models and niches in European churches designed after the Church of the Holy Sepulchre in Jerusalem; for the latter, he cites the so-called "Magical Papyri" of later Greek antiquity. Jonathan Z. Smith, *To Take Place: Toward Theory in Ritual* (Chicago: Univ. of Chicago Press, 1987), 87; and Jonathan Z. Smith, "Constructing a Small Place," in *Sacred Space: Shrine, City, Land*, ed. Benjamin Z. Kedar and R. J. Zwi Werblowsky (New York: New York University Press, 1998), 18–31.

3 Tine Damsholt, "Ritualizing and Materializing Citizenship," *Journal of Ritual Studies* 23, no. 2 (2009): 17–29.

4 James Holston, "The Civility of Inegalitarian Citizenships," in *The Fundamentalist City? Religiosity and the Remaking of Urban Space*, ed. Nezar Al-Sayyad and Mejgan Massoumi (London: Routledge, 2011), 51, 56.

5 *Masjid-e Hazrat-e Ibrahim* [The mosque of the prophet Ibrahim] (Tehran: Sharikat-e Entesharat-e Miqat, 1999), 99.

6 Ibid., ii.

7 Mohammad Taqi Ikhtiyari, preface to *Masjid-e Hazrat-e Ibrahim* [The mosque of the prophet Ibrahim] (Tehran: Sharikat-e Entesharat-e Miqat, 1999), iv–v.

8 Ibid., xix–xx.

9 Robert Hillenbrand, *Islamic Architecture: Form, Function, and Meaning* (New York: Columbia University Press, 1994), 144–5.

10 Eric Hooglund, "Iran and the Persian Gulf," in *Twenty Years of Islamic Revolution: Political and Social Transition in Iran since 1979*, ed. Eric Hooglund (Syracuse: Syracuse University Press, 2002), 156–75.

11 The form of Sunni Islam officially espoused in Saudi Arabia, so-called "Wahhabism," draws inspiration from the teachings of Muhammad ibn 'Abd al-Wahhab (1703–91) who regarded the Shi'a – and many other Muslims who did not follow his teachings – as infidels. Many religious tracts and studies published in Saudi Arabia condemn Shi'ism in general, and in particular, the majoritarian Ithna'ashari or Twelver form practiced in Iran, Iraq, Lebanon and elsewhere.

12 Hooglund, "Iran and the Persian Gulf," 165.

13 Hazrat-e Ayatollah al-'Uzma Imam Khomeini, *Resaleh-ye Towzih-e al-Masa'il* [A clarification of questions] (Tehran: Entesharat-e Fekr-e Bartar, 2010), 22.

14 Oman in particular is one of the GCC states that has maintained good relations with Iran, however.

15 *Masjid-e Hazrat-e Ibrahim*, 22. Daniel is called a *nabi* [prophet] in the commemorative volume. Although a prophet in Christianity, he is technically not considered a prophet in Judaism. His status in Islam is not clear. See *Encyclopedia of Islam*, 2nd edition, s.v. "Daniyal."

16 There are other locales in the Middle East that claim a tomb of Daniel.

17 Muhammad Husayn al-Tabataba'i, *Al-Mizan fi Tafsir al-Qur'an* [The balanced method for the interpretation of the Qur'an] (Beirut: Mu'assasat al-'Alami li'l-Matbu'at, 1970), 4, 88. I have privileged Tabataba'i's *tafsir* [interpretation], as it is a modern exegesis still popular in Iran, before and after the revolution.

18 *Akhbar*, s. *khabar*, literally "news" or "bits of information," is the term for the oral traditions or sayings of the Shi'i imams. Cf. *ahadith*, s. hadith, the Arabic terms for the traditions of the Prophet Muhammad.

19 "Dar Yaki az Muzeha-ye Amrika […]," in *Masjid-e Hazrat-e Ibrahim*, 67. Ascribed to Taj al-Din Mahmud, the tombstone resembles one of the small terra cotta mihrabs in the collections of the Metropolitan Museum of Art, New York, or of the Los Angeles County Museum of Art.

20 Smith, "Constructing a Small Place," 20–24.

21 Export Promotion Center of Iran, *25 Tehran International Trade Fair*, October 2–9, 1999 (small brochure).

22 Al-Qism al-i'lami fi sifarat al-Jumhuriyya al-Islamiyya al-Iraniyya, Bayrut [The Information Section of the Embassy of the Islamic Republic of Iran, Beirut], *Majzarat Makka: al-dawafi' wa'l-waqa'i' wa'l-ahdaf* [The massacre of Mecca: The impetuses, the facts and the objectives] (Beirut: al-Qism al-i'lami fi sifarat al-Jumhuriyya al-Islamiyya al-Iraniyya, Beirut, 1988), vii.

23 Peter Chelkowski and Hamid Dabashi, *Staging a Revolution: The Art of Persuasion in the Islamic Republic of Iran* (New York: New York University Press, 1999), 205–6, 250, contend that the image was used on currency and postage stamps as a symbol to unify Muslims regardless of sectarian differences, however.

24 Saba Mahmood, *Politics of Piety: the Islamic Revival and the Feminist Subject* (Princeton: Princeton University Press, 2005), 122.

25 One of the earliest articles is M. Falamaki, "al-Ghadir Mosque, Tehran," *Mimar* 29 (September 1988): 24; one of the more recent is Alisa Eimen, "Negotiating Cultural Identity at Tehran's Al-Ghadir Mosque," in *Architecture and Identity*, ed. Peter Herrle and Erik Wegerhoff (Berlin: Lit Verlag, 2008), 435–49.

26 Abu Ja'far Muhammad Ishaq al-Kulayni, *Al-Usul min al-Kafi* [The principles from the sufficient] (Tehran: Mu'assasat Dar al-Kutub al-Islamiyya, n.d.), I: 287; Abu Ja'far Muhammad ibn al-Hasan al-Tusi, *Al-Tibyan fi Tafsir Al-Qur'an* [The elucidation in Qur'anic explanation] (Najaf: Maktabat al-Amin, n.d.), 3: 435; and Muhammad Husayn al-Tabataba'i, *Al-Mizan fi Tafsir al-Qur'an* 5: 196.

27 Muhammad Husayn al-Tabataba'i, *Al-Mizan fi Tafsir al-Qur'an,* 5: 196.

28 'Abd al-'Aziz al-Tabataba'i, *Al-Ghadir fi'l-Turath al-Islami* [Al-Ghadir in Islamic heritage] (Beirut: Dar al-Mu'arikh al-'Arabi, 1993), 7–8.

29 Annemarie Schimmel, *Calligraphy and Islamic Culture* (New York: New York University Press, 1984), 3.

30 Giovanni Oman, "Il 'Cufico Quadrato': Tentativo Di Definizione Delle Tre Varieta Sinora Riscontrate," *Quaderni Di Studi Arabi* 16 (1998): 69–88, 81. This article discusses, among other things, the multitude of names for the geometric form of the kufic script.

31 Abu Ja'far Muhammad ibn al-Hasan al-Tusi, *Tafsir al-Tibyan,* 3: 435.

32 Muhammad Husayn al-Tabataba'i, *Al-Mizan fi Tafsir al-Qur'an,* 5: 196.

33 Abu Ja'far Muhammad Ishaq al-Kulayni, *Al-Usul min al-Kafi,* I: 252.

34 Ruhollah Khomeini, *Islam and Revolution: Writings and Declarations of Imam Khomeini,* trans. Hamid Algar (Berkeley: Mizan Press, 1981), 392.

35 My thanks to Noushin Lavasani for supplying a photograph of the hadith al-thaqalayn inscription when I was initially studying the edifice.

36 Muhammad Husayn al-Tabataba'i, *Al-Mizan fi Tafsir al-Qur'an,* 20: 369–73.

37 Mosque staff, in discussion with the author, summer 1999.

38 Renata Holod and Hasan-Uddin Khan, *The Contemporary Mosque* (New York: Rizzoli, 1997), 210.

39 Abdulaziz Sachedina, "Ali Shariati: Ideologue of the Iranian Revolution," in *Voices of Resurgent Islam,* ed. John L.Esposito (Oxford: Oxford University Press, 1983), 207–8.

40 Shahrough Akhavi, *Religion and Politics in Contemporary Iran* (Albany: State University Press, 1980), 149.

41 Nikki Keddie, *Roots of Revolution* (New Haven: Yale University Press, 1981), 217–18.

42 Holod and Khan, *The Contemporary Mosque,* 169–70.

43 The rate of literacy in Tehran is high, and the average reached 87.9 percent in 1991. Rates in the northern half of the city, where Mir Damad Boulevard and the al-Ghadir mosque are located, were markedly higher, surpassing 90 percent of the population. Ali Madanipour, *Tehran: The Making of a Metropolis* (New York: John Wiley & Sons, 1998), 86–111.

44 Smith, "Constructing a Small Place," 24–9.

45 Eimen, "Negotiating Cultural Identity at Tehran's Al-Ghadir Mosque," 445.

46 For most Twelver Shi'a, any reference to Samarra, however oblique, would also evoke the residence of the tenth and eleventh imams and where the twelfth went into *ghayba* (occultation) in 874.

47 See, for example, www.emap.ir, accessed December 30, 2011.

48 The most ambitious State-sponsored ritual space in postrevolutionary Tehran may be the Imam Khomeini Musalla, which was begun in the mid-1990s and was still under construction as of this writing. Reversing the spatial logic of the International Fairgrounds with the Ibrahim Mosque at the center, the Musalla consists of a mosque so massive that it contains a complex of civic and cultural institutions in its perimeter, including the premises of the International Book Fair, and surrounds a vast esplanade for congregational prayer and public rallies. Its lofty prayer hall is flanked by two of the tallest minarets in the world.

49 Mahmood, *Politics of Piety,* 122.

50 "It seems to me that [Smith's] larger project is compromised by excessive reliance on spatial metaphors, which have historically served locative interests, and by his choice of long-standing temple rites rather than more utopian examples, which is to say, more recent, 'invented' rites." Ronald L. Grimes, *Rite out of Place* (Oxford: Oxford University Press, 2006), 113.

51 In the two years from 1977 to 1979 leading up to the revolution, mosques throughout Iran functioned as nerve centers for the propagation of resistance to the Pahlavi government, according to Masoud Kheirabadi, *Iranian Cities: Formation and Development* (Austin: University of Texas Press, 1993), 66. In contrast, Kurzman argues that "*[d]uring* the Iranian Revolution,

for example, the presumption that Khomeini commanded widespread allegiance through the mosque network led Iranians of various political persuasions to see him as the only viable alternative to the Shah and therefore to give him their support" (emphasis added). Charles Kurzman, "The Network Metaphor and the Mosque Network in Iran, 1978–1979," in *Muslim Networks from Hajj to Hip Hop*, ed. Miriam Cooke and Bruce B. Lawrence (Chapel Hill: University of North Carolina Press, 2005), 82–3. The intent of Kurzman's enlightening article is to refute the contention that the strength of mosque networks contributed to the outcome of the revolution. However this, his concluding example could just as easily serve as evidence to support the argument that mosque networks did contribute to the outcome. Regardless of whether it was an inadvertent reification of the mosque network by the Iranian public that led to greater support for Khomeini – as Kurzman suggests and problematizes – or whether the majority of the constituents in that network were the (ostensibly-weaker-than-believed) pro-Khomeini clerics and their partisans, the network served and fulfilled its purpose and the objectives of its members. Kurzman's observation suggests that the network was actually more powerful than commonly believed, albeit for reasons perhaps unanticipated by the members of that network.

52 Kurzman, "The Network Metaphor and the Mosque Network in Iran, 1978–1979," 69–83; and Ervand Abrahamian, "The Crowd in the Iranian Revolution," *Radical History Review* 105 (Fall 2009): 32.

53 Kurzman, "The Network Metaphor and the Mosque Network in Iran, 1978–1979," 71, 82; Schayegh, "'Seeing Like a State," 38.

9

RECLAIMING CULTURAL SPACE: THE ARTIST'S PERFORMATIVITY VERSUS THE STATE'S EXPECTATIONS IN CONTEMPORARY IRAN

Hamid Keshmirshekan

This essay deals with discourses of identity politics, their association with the State's cultural strategy, and the artist's aesthetic rebellion versus its expectations, while examining visual culture in postrevolutionary Iran.[1] I will explore the ways in which the artists' focal beliefs about social relations and cultural essentialism find expression in their artwork. This study will examine strategies employed by Iranian artists and art activists concerned with rethinking notions of embodiment and performativity in tension with the political contexts of the country. I attempt to explore what is emerging and how different subject positions are being transformed or produced in the course of unfolding new dialectics of global culture in contemporary Iran. I should also attempt in this essay to identify what has happened in the course of contemporary Iranian cultural politics during the postrevolutionary period (after 1979), which has made the current power relations between the State's formulation and the artists to reclaim their cultural spaces.

Perhaps most of the sociological theories have agreed on the inert perception of the individual agent against structure and the subject against power. Social subjects, they maintain, internalize the demands of the dominant ideology. However, cultural studies theories, such as those presented by Michel Foucault, Michel De Certeau and John Fiske, put aside the notion of the passive subject, considering it to have an active role in countering the dominant ideology. This group emphasizes the notion of resistance against the ideological representation of power. This essay agrees with this latter idea.

In his essay "The Subject and Power" (1982), Foucault chooses the forms of resistance as his starting point. He maintains that one can identify the power relations through resistance and strategic challenge.[2] He also suggests that resistance is implicit in all power relations and this allows the possibility of change. He does not see the main goal of political campaigning in the current era to be an attack on the power institutes (e.g., government, economy or an elite circle or stratum) but an attack on the technique or the form of power, which transforms individuals into subjects. This form of power imposes itself on the immediate routine life that grants the individual one's identity and imposes laws on the individual, which should be approved by oneself and recognized by others.[3] The campaign that Foucault remarks on is a campaign against becoming subject, which would be different in each society and historical period, hence different forms of resistance.

In contemporary Iranian cultural life, including artistic activities, one can discern the continual presence of the State and its role in standardizing the conventional patterns and paradigms in all cultural and artistic moods. Shireen Hunter rightly argues that in addition to Islamicizing Iran's cultural life, the State sought to install a revolutionary spirit into the country's cultural and artistic life. Indeed, a principal tenet of the Islamic Republic's cultural philosophy was that art must be in the service of Islam and the revolution. In other words, artistic expression had merit only insofar as it advanced the goals of the revolution, meaning instilling an Islamic and revolutionary spirit into the people.[4]

What the State has attempted to do is formulate a definition of an "authentic" identity based on an essential idea to present itself as a homogeneous entity. Popularization of Iranian identity, too, has taken a direction toward surfacing fundamentalist values in the postrevolutionary period. As Mostafa Vaziri remarks, "[T]he reinforcement of historical national identity by the Islamic regime was bound to a common code of culture that was centred on Islam as opposed to the secularism of the Pahlavis."[5] Mehrdad Mashayekhi also believes that the Islamic universalist tendency in the early postrevolutionary period contributed to the Islamicists' susceptibility regarding patriotic values.[6] Nevertheless, the experiences of running a complex modern State and coming to terms with a wide range of domestic and foreign issues, especially the eight-year war against Iraq (1980–88), reinforced the government's other coexisting political tendencies, specifically, its nationalism mixed with Shi'i enthusiasm; the Islamic Republic increasingly adapted its Islamic universalist ideology to the national context.[7] The State has further tried to fuse Shi'i culture and politics into a single integrated political culture,[8] which was set out systematically to be institutionalized. Mashayekhi, however, points out that "among the political leaders and the intellectual architects of the Islamic Republic one can even identify major prerevolutionary writings and speeches that had a strong nationalistic echo. It is no surprise, then, that the majority of Islamic thinkers speak of an 'Islamo-Iranian' culture and identity; they find a symbiotic relation between Islam and Iran."[9] Hunter, too, maintains, "The most important change for the Islamic regime has been to accept and legitimize the concept of Iran and Iranianism as a coequal focus with Islam of national loyalty and a component of Iranian cultural identity. The regime has now accepted the notion of an 'Iranian nation,' and it has also concluded that the nature of the Iranian culture is 'Iranian Islamic.' Of course, even now, the Islamic element is emphasized more."[10] This overcentralized, monopolistic and ideological nature of the postrevolutionary State forces any alternative reaction to be similarly and simultaneously "political–cultural" in nature.[11] Therefore, the Islamic Republic, assuming a hegemonic position in control of the State, took cultural transformation very seriously. It sought to institutionalize an Islamic political culture. It resulted in an Islamicization process to be instituted in accordance with the clerical Islamic culture – the Islamic Republic's way to rehabilitate an Islamically ill society.[12] The State has then been in direct control and exerted a strong influence over all artistic production. The Vizarat-e Farhang va Ershad-e Islami (Ministry of Culture and Islamic Guidance) developed overall control over cultural production. Based on the State's ideologically structured views, the ministry created regulations that governed exhibitions, movies and other forms of the arts. According to the ideologues of the State, ideology is used to remedy social, psychological and cultural maladjustments, such as moral and political strains.[13]

A few years after 1979 the postrevolutionary State and its cultural and artistic institutions, mainly the Ministry of Culture and Islamic Guidance (formerly Ministry of Islamic Guidance), began to encourage an approach to traditional, Islamic and so-called Eastern art in opposition to the Pahlavi's modernization and Euro-American-oriented cultural and artistic directions. The issue which was highlighted as key in these gatherings was that of cultural and artistic "identity." In the major art exhibitions, the artistic administrators suggested that more attention be paid to Islamic and national arts as a solution to the crisis over artistic identity caused mainly by the infinite Euro-Americanization of Iranian culture and art by the previous government. The State-run cultural institutions eagerly proposed traditional cultural values and the achievements of a kind of "Irano–Islamic" art, which had to gain its own characteristics different from "Western" art.[14] Then in the search for a so-called cultural and artistic identity, reference to traditional heritage and the presence of Islamic and Shi'i identity could be observed. It was suggested that it is the integral part of Iranian cultural psyche and materiality.

So it was not surprising that what could be discerned, directly or indirectly, during the 1980s and early 1990s was the evident impacts of the revolution and Islamic Republic's ideological paradigms on the artistic atmosphere of this period. It was clearer in the most important official postrevolutionary artistic events such as national exhibitions and paralleled conferences. For example, in the introduction to the First National Painting Biennial in 1991 one can see similar statements, remarking, "Revision of values and authenticities is neither an artistic and mental reaction nor is it weakness towards modernism. It is rather a strong attempt to achieve an artistic identity which is appropriated and understood based on visual and subjective frameworks originating from our cultural authenticity."[15] But, as Ramin Jahanbegloo maintains, the very notion of "ideology" gradually lost much of its coherence in the later years among the new generation of Iranian intellectuals and art activists and accompanied the crisis of political legitimacy in Iran.[16] Thus, from the majority of the artists of the new generation, this formulation of culture does not seem, in an increasingly globalized world, to be plausible any longer. One then witnesses an artistic and intellectual reaction against these stereotypes and ideas of particularism in the sense of imposing a "monolithic" or "one-view" formula. Jahanbegloo argues, "[T]oday, a democratic notion of identity, emphasizing the formation of a pluralistic civil society in Iran, is more welcomed among the new generation of Iranian elites than romantic or traditionalist notions of Iranian identity."[17]

However, what the State is still attempting to attain by institutionalizing a cultural collective identity is principally what Suman Gupta in her essay "Identity-based Political Position" (2007) calls the overdetermination of what one may think of as individual identity markers. She further maintains that each individual has a unique combination of identity markers: physiognomic features, linguistic abilities, sexual proclivities, gendered experiences, educational backgrounds, socializations, professional abilities, histories of locations and memories, cultural habits and religious beliefs. So, it is a unique combination of identity markers that constitutes one individual identity.[18] According to Gupta, "[S]uch over-determination of identity markers could be thought of as the reduction of individual identity to an aspect (or some aspects) of itself – to become an identifiable member of the identity-based collective – for political purposes."[19] These and other kinds of arguments suggest that those definitions of collective identities are basically ideological fictions, imposed from above and used to divide and control populations. Both political and cultural critics claim that one should be working to eliminate the silence of identity in everyday life, not institutionalize it.[20] It is now understood that the instabilities of collective identity reveal more about the processes and power relations in identity constructions than apparent stabilities and emphasize the social constructionist rather than essentialist character of collective identities.[21] This supposition is now evidently understood in Iranian cultural life and artists are performing against these essentialist political proscriptions while reclaiming their own cultural spaces and self-defined identities (Figure 9.1). Their main credence agrees with the theory, maintaining that identity is widely understood as lived and imagined in ways that break down its contiguousness with a geographically bounded locality (Figure 9.2).[22]

In attempting to introduce thinking about collective identities, such as cultural ones, Stuart Hall observers a similar implication: "Identities are never unified and, in late modern times, increasingly fragmented and fractured; never singular but multiply constructed across different, often intersecting and antagonistic discourses, practices and positions. They are subject to radical historicization, and are constantly in the process of change and transformation."[23] In addition, I would agree with Vikki Bell's statement, which suggests that "one does not simply or ontologically 'belong' to the world or to any group within it,"[24] and then concludes that belonging is an achievement on several levels of abstraction. Here, an emphasis should be put on the importance of more or less performative processes, including elaboration, construction, work and play, with respect to experience and identity. Performativity somehow equals relativists' ideas of (de)constructive identities and stands in opposition to essentialist views of identity, which the State ultimately promotes.

Hall's definition of identification suggests a similar connotation: "In common sense language, identification is constructed on the back of a recognition of some common origin or shared characteristics with another person or group, or with an ideal, and with the natural closure of solidarity and alliance established on this foundation. In contrast with the 'naturalism' of this definition, the discursive approach sees identification as a construction, a process never completed – always 'in process.' It is not determined in the sense that it can always be 'won' or 'lost', sustained or abandoned."[25] Indeed, taking the temporal performative nature of identities as a theoretical premise means that more than ever one needs to question how identities continue to be produced, embodied and performed, effectively, passionately and with social and political consequences.[26] It is then stated that identity is the effect of performance and not vice versa.[27] This notion of performativity has encouraged many Iranian cultural activists and artists to ponder the constitutive moments and modes of identity more seriously. This assertion coincides with Judith Butler's idea that performative acts include "legal sentences, baptisms, inaugurations" and other forms of "statements which not only perform an action, but confer a binding power on the action performed."[28] Viewing identity as performative, then, means that identities are constructed by the "very 'expressions' that are said to be (their) results."[29]

Identity is not just what defines a person or a larger collective. It also insists on the experiences of the subject, especially one's experiences of oppression and the possibility of a shared alternative, an alternative which may not necessarily be compatible with what the State is trying to frame. Hall's idea about identity deployed here is therefore not an essentialist but a strategic and positional one. According to Hall:

> [D]irectly contrary to what appears to be its settled semantic career, this concept of identity does *not* signal that stable core of the self, unfolding from beginning to the end through all the vicissitudes of history without change; the bit of the self which remains always-already "the same," identical to itself across time. Nor – if we translate this essentializing conception to the stage of cultural identity – is it that "collective or true self hiding inside the many other, more superficial or artificially imposed 'selves' which a people with shared history and ancestry hold in common" (Hall, 1990) and which can stabilize, fix or guarantee an unchanging "oneness" or cultural belongingness underlying all the other superficial differences. [30]

Hall continues exploring the same idea by saying:

> [T]hough those so-called cultural belongings seem to invoke an origin in a historical past with which they continue to correspond, actually identities are about questions of using the resources of history, language and culture in the process of becoming rather than being: not "who we are" or "where we come from," so much as what we might become, how we have been represented and how that bears on how we might represent ourselves. Identities [...] are constituted within, not outside representation. They relate to the invention of tradition as much as to tradition itself, which they oblige us to read not as an endless reiteration but as "the changing same" (Gilroy, 1994): not the so-called return to roots but a coming-to-terms-with our "routes."[31]

So he concludes, "[T]here is the *production* of self as an object in the world, the practices of self-constitution, recognition and reflection, the relation to the rule, alongside the scrupulous attention to normative regulation, and the constraints of the rules without which no 'subjectification' is produced."[32] These questions of identity are clearly in contrast with those of the Iranian State. The emphasis on being or becoming rather than the framed fixity of identity, the subject position of identity and the construction rather than the institutionalization are the main challenges here.

Based on Homi Bhabha's idea of narrating a nation, one should also draw attention to these easily obscured but highly significant recesses of the national culture, from which alternative constituencies of peoples and oppositional analytic capacities may emerge – the youth, the everyday, nostalgia, new "ethnicities," new social movements and "the politics of difference." Bhabha maintains that these alternative constituencies "assign new meanings and different directions to the process of historical change."[33] Bearing this in mind, one can detect the new interpretations of national culture and counternarratives of the State's hegemonic narrative, particularly in artistic strategies and representations in Iran. These new interpretations show strategies of representation to be reformulated in the competing claims of communities, in which, in the words of Bhabha, "[D]espite shared histories of deprivation and discrimination, the exchange of values, meanings and priorities may not always be collaborative and dialogical, but may be profoundly antagonist, conflictual and even incommensurable."[34] This claim shows that like many other similar cases elsewhere why in Iranian society the very concepts of homogeneous national culture, the consensual or contiguous transmission of historical traditions "or 'organic' ethnic communities – *as the grounds of cultural comparativism* – are in a profound process of redefinition."[35]

This very subject brings about the issue of contemporary positions of culture and identity in today's globalizing world. Stuart Hall in "The Local and the Global: Globalization and Ethnicity" (1991) points out:

> [W]hen one looks at the global post-modern, one sees that it can go in both an expansive and a defensive way, in the same sense one sees that local, the marginal, can also go in two different ways. When the movements of the margins are so profoundly threatened by the global forces of postmodernity, they can themselves retreat into their own exclusivist and defensive enclaves. And at that point, local ethnicities become as dangerous as national ones. We have seen that happen: the refusal of modernity which takes the form of a return, a rediscovery of identity which constitutes a form of fundamentalism.[36]

This statement sounds as if this situation mirrors what the Iranian State has tried to articulate and to base its cultural policies on. The formulated interests of the State clearly promote particular values as a resistance against the secular cultural norms of cultural globalization, or as the authorities put it, "Westernization." This general cultural attitude explains why it has been perfectly clear in official cultural and artistic events that encouragement is given to taking refuge in clichés of cultural authenticity, historical specificities and traditional "values," particularly Islamic or the so-called Iranian–Islamic Shi'i traditions as an integral part of the "authentic" culture. It has been then clear that any other kinds of approaches against this framework would formally be sentenced to marginalization. However, it is said that the sense of being marginalized or threatened, through which identity-based political positions consolidate themselves, naturally pulls in contrary directions. An identity-based political position that is consolidated through marginalization pits itself against the dominant establishment wherein marginalization occurs. As Gupta argues, "[W]orking against marginalization is an emancipative step, equivalent to striving for an egalitarian prospect."[37] So the artists' positions against the State's prioritization would normally be requesting their own cultural spaces and alternatives. They variously create meanings particularly through presentations of the human body as a cultural medium in their artistic practices, which make them ideological and political in an Iranian context; hence, addressing critically the actual problems and issues in society becomes an approach for artists in rebelling against the State's ideological goals (Figure 9.3). This ironic and sometimes humorous language has also become a common method to react metaphorically against supposedly united sacred values defined by the State (Figure 9.4). These artists have celebrated negotiable identities and self-definitions, which rise to the foreground, while hegemonic identities recede into the background.

The foundational importance of the body, which introduces it as site of exchange between the Self and the world, has attracted many artists who are acting against cultural limitations and formulated stereotypes, sometimes by the artist's own self-reiterations (Figure 9.5). In this sense, the body acts as a site, across which artists and interpreters engage each other in acts of making meaning.[38] This interaction can also be seen in many two-dimensional works, such as in paintings and photographs in particular (Figure 9.6). As Amelia Jones has argued, because the photographic portrait documents the embodied trace of the Self (with the mind made visible only through its body-sign), it highlights both its visible-corporeal-form, which the artist wants to serve as a guarantor of the body. She further maintains, "[T]he photographic portrait seems to reaffirm the body's never-ending 'thereness,' its refusal to disappear, its infinite capacity to render up the self in some incontrovertibly 'real' way."[39] In light of Maurice Merleau-Ponty's phenomenological theories of embodiment, which scrutinize the specificity of the body's relationship to the mind or Self and to other objects in the world, one could also observe the obsession of how artists engage with images of body, either in portraits or figures in their works. For Merleau-Ponty, the body is never simply an object but "a grouping of lived-through meanings."[40] The body is never simply a sign, either: "[T]he body does not constantly express the modalities of existence in the way that stripes indicate rank, or a house-number a house: the sign here does not only convey its significance, it is filed with it"[41] At one point Merleau-Ponty argues suggestively that the body is "to be compared, not to a physical object, but rather to a work of art," in its coextensivity with its appearance (with both, "the expression is indistinguishable from the thing expressed") and its nature as a "focal point of living meanings," rather than a fixed and static "function" of stable terms.[42] Along these lines, one realizes that it is through the body that one challenges representations, and the artists' reclaims of cultural space reveal themselves.

Parallel to the State's insisting on the formulation of a specific cultural life, another challenge in general is with the so-called "given identity" connoted by foreign expectations. In order to find some kind of uniqueness, artists are usually expected to represent their given identities as safe havens. It has now developed into a discourse. However, a group of artists has reacted against it, believing that practicing art that ensures their uniqueness and differentiates them from their Western counterparts has, in many cases, resulted in some sort of artistic blockage, making them produce monolithic art. The artists detect that institutions are accomplishing their institutional needs by relying on limited analytic templates shaped by stereotyping and ethnocentrism, the need to distinguish between Western and other art based on visual difference.[43] This dilemma is a major challenge relating to the politics of visuality, which focus on the way that certain identities become visible. Incidentally, this expectation is not in many occasions widely dissimilar from the State's own formulations. According to Khaled Ramadan, the strategy of "cultural difference" corresponds almost literally to the problem of the "representational" role of non-Western artists. As for the dominant discourse, it is so obsessed with cultural difference and identity to the extent that it too is suffering from an intellectual blockage. In addition, the obsession with cultural difference is now being institutionally legitimized through the construction of the "postcolonial other" that is allowed to express itself only as long as it speaks of its own Otherness.[44]

Many artists in Iran believe that the continued intentions to the ways that they are stereotyped and the persistent elisions of power relations that produce such stereotypes deny these artists' artistic personhoods. The major mania for many artists is that they have never considered what is "Islamic" or even particularly "Iranian" in their artwork, in the sense that these labels have been formulated or stereotyped, even if these artists deal with those issues in their work. In other words, when the disapproval against the idea of stereotypification arises, the immediate aim of the artist is to respond to the formulated demands rather than tracing the lived-experience and self-expression in any way possible, whether or not those features are indicated.

Among artists mainly from the new generation (born from the 1980s onward) who acquire an avant-garde status – precisely at the juncture when it goes outside the institution of art – and critics active in major Iranian private art scenes and journals, some have been wary of this Perso–Islamic stereotypical label, alleging that it may perpetuate stereotypes about Iranian cultural production and art in particular, invoking similar politics of representation as in Orientalist works of art. Their criticism is based on the idea that whereas Orientalism is based on how the West constructs the East, this Neo-Orientalism is grounded on how the cultural East comes to terms with an orientalized East.[45] The term "self-exoticisation" is used to explain this situation. In a radical sense, it could direct the work's internal rationale and what even governs the aesthetic choices of an artist toward an unrealistic and derivative product, which has been purely shaped by global hegemonic powers for the so-called best interests of the "Other."

Even when in the recent works of Iranian artists created in various media and presented in the dramatically more auctions or overseas exhibitions, cultural confrontations and contemporary social issues could be based on formulae and even on coded typical indigenous elements. These issues and objects have been based on a subjective exotic view of what is expected to be shown as "Iranian" and as "contemporary." Although one could argue that there cannot be an objective view either, it can be argued that they may only be based on a part of realities that can be found in contemporary Iran, such as themes of gender relations and the situation of Islamic women, the Third World and feminist elements, and have inevitably become stereotypes.

In this criticism, it is argued that the dominant discourse in the cultural domain has been "deeply affected by the relation between art from black or non-European artist and the Western art system – its historiography, market, aesthetic, and critical values – where the greater the work's visibility in terms of radical or ethnic context, the less it is able to speak as an individual utterance."[46] The galleries and museums have responded to the demands to end cultural marginality by basically exhibiting more non-European artists, although on a selective and representative basis, provided that they reveal the appropriate signs of cultural difference.

As Farideh Farhi rightly addresses, it seems that efforts to forge, almost mechanically, a formulated indigenous identity, similarly by the State and foreign agencies, as children of both Cyrus the Great *and* the Prophet Mohammad, had already seen more platitudes than possibilities to the new generation.[47] One can currently detect a variety of voices that are accompanied and valued in contrast to the existing models introduced by the State, in which the social arena is dominated by a single worldview. Many artists have explored traditions and the changing modes of social life as expressed in the visual culture of the country or the depth of personal expression. Through their artistic representations, artists play with the contradictory sacred or iconic and commercial imaginary, often symbolized by a combination of folk cultural elements with global contemporary items. This variety in contemporary Iranian art reflects the diversity and complexity of Iranian society, its multiple and varied facets, its expressions and outward manifestations and its nuanced responses to political repressions, instabilities and pervasive crises among artists in particular.

Notes and References

1 This essay was written during my fellowship at the KRC, Oxford University, in 2011–12, funded by the Barakat Trust. I am then very grateful to their generous support throughout this fellowship.
2 Michel Foucault, "The Subject and Power," in *Michel Foucault: Beyond Structuralism and Hermeneutics*, ed. Hubert L. Dreyfus (Chicago: University of Chicago Press, 1982), 346.
3 Ibid., 348.
4 See Shireen T. Hunter, *Iran After Khomeini* (New York: Praeger, 1992), 92.
5 Mostafa Vaziri, *Iran as Imagined Nation: The Construction of National Identity* (New York: Paragon House Publishers, 1993), 199.
6 Pan-Islamism is echoed in themes, such as the export of the revolution and denunciation of secular nationalism.
7 Mehrdad Mashayekhi, "The Politics of Nationalism and Political Culture," in *Iran: Political Culture in the Islamic Republic*, ed. Samih K. Farsoun and Mehrdad Mashayekhi (London: Routledge, 1992), 111.
8 According to Samih K. Farsoun and Mehrdad Mashayekhi, the Islamic political culture derived its legitimacy from 13 centuries of Shi'i history and tradition with its affinity for political protest and oppositional values. Samih K. Farsoun and Mehrdad Mashayekhi, introduction to *Iran: Political Culture in the Islamic Republic*, ed. Samih K. Farsoun and Mehrdad Mashayekhi (London: Routledge, 1992), 9.
9 Ibid.
10 Hunter, *Iran After Khomeini*, 94–5.
11 Farsoun and Mashayekhi, introduction to *Iran*, 4.
12 Ibid., 21.
13 See Rasool Najafi, "Education and the Culture of Politics in the Islamic Republic of Iran," *Iran: Political Culture in the Islamic Republic*, ed. Samih K. Farsoun and Mehrdad Mashayekhi (London: Routledge, 1992), 161.
14 See Abdolhamid [Hamid] Keshmirshekan, "Discourses on Postrevolutionary Iranian Art: Neotraditionalism during the 1990s," *Muqarnas* 23 (2006): 131–57.
15 *Tehran, guzideh-ye az asar-e avvalin nimayishgah-e biyenal-e naqqashan-e Iran* [Tehran: Selected works from the first Biennial of Iranian painters] (Tehran: Markaz-e Honar-ha-ye Tajassumi, 1371/1992), 3.

16 Ramin Jahanbegloo, introduction to *Iran Between Tradition and Modernity*, ed. Ramin Jahanbegloo (Oxford: Lexington Books, 2004), xx.

17 Ibid., xxii.

18 It goes without saying that in the last two decades. identity issues and identity politics have been subjected to not only theorizing, but also social and political organizing. As Gupta argues, identity-based political positions are taken in regard to specific groups and are exercised by or for their particular memberships and sometimes, through concordant institutions; in other words, these are positions taken in regard to, for, on behalf of and by specific identity-based groups. The practice of politics in regard to specific group identities – such as national, ethnic, religious, class, race and gender – obviously precede their being brought together under the umbrella term "identity politics." Suman Gupta, *Social Constructionist Identity Politics and Literary Studies* (New York: Palgrave Macmillan, 2007), 7.

19 Gupta, *Social Constructionist Identity Politics and Literary Studies*, 8.

20 See Linda Martín Alcoff and Satya P. Mohanty, introduction to *Identity Politics Reconsidered* , ed. Linda Martín Alcoff et al. (New York: Palgrave Macmillan, 2006), 3.

21 Gupta, *Social Constructionist Identity Politics and Literary Studies*, 12.

22 Anne-Marie Fortier, "Re-Membering Places and the Performance of Belonging(s)," in *Performativity and Belonging*, ed. Vikki Bell (London: Sage Publications, 1999), 41. Paula M. L. Moya argues that the other aspect of the dialectical concept of identity is called the subjective identity or simply "subjectivity." Subjectivity refers to one's individual sense of Self, interior existence and lived experience of being a more-or-less coherent Self across time. The term also implies one's various acts of self-identification and thus necessarily incorporates one's understanding of oneself in relation to others. Paula M. L. Moya, "What's Identity Got to Do with It?" in *Identity Politics Reconsidered*, ed. Linda Martín Alcoff et al. (New York: Palgrave Macmillan, 2006), 98.

23 Stuart Hall, introduction to *Questions of Cultural Identity*, ed. Stuart Hall and Paul du Gay (London: Sage Publications, 1996), 4.

24 Vikki Bell, introduction to *Performativity and Belonging*, ed. Vikki Bell (London: Sage Publications, 1999), 3.

25 Hall, introduction to *Questions of Cultural Identity*, 2.

26 See Bell, introduction to *Performativity and Belonging*, 2.

27 Ibid., 3.

28 Judith Butler, *Bodies That Matter: On the Discursive Limits of "Sex"* (London: Routledge, 1993), 234.

29 Ibid., 45. See also Fortier, "Re-Membering Places and the Performance of Belonging(s)," 43.

30 Hall, introduction to *Questions of Cultural Identity*, 3–4.

31 Ibid., 4.

32 Ibid., 13.

33 Homi K Bhabha, introduction to *Nation and Narration*, ed. Homi K Bhabha (London: Routledge, 1994), 3.

34 See ibid., 1–2.

35 Ibid., 5.

36 Stuart Hall, "The Local and the Global: Globalization and Ethnicity," in *Culture, Globalization and the World-System: Contemporary Conditions for the Representation of Identity*, ed. Anthony D. King (Basingstoke: Macmillan Education, 1991), 36.

37 Gupta, *Social Constructionist Identity Politics and Literary Studies*, 18.

38 See Amelia Jones, "Body," in *Critical Terms for Art History*, ed. Robert S. Nelson and Richard Shiff (Chicago: University of Chicago Press, 2003), 255.

39 Ibid., 257.

40 Maurice Merleau-Ponty, *La Nature: Notes – Cours au Collège de France* [Nature: Course notes from the College de France] (Paris: Editions du Seuil, 1995), 153.

41 Ibid., 161.

42 Ibid., 150.

43 See Khaled D. Ramadan, introduction to *Peripheral Insider: Perspectives on Contemporary Internationalism in Visual Culture*, ed. Khaled D. Ramadan (Copenhagen: Museum Tusculanum Press, 2007), 27; and Hamid Keshmirshekan, "The Question of Identity vis-à-vis Exoticism in Contemporary Iranian Art," *Iranian Studies* 43 (2010): 489–512, and "Contemporary or Specific: the Dichotomous Desires in the Art of Early 21st Century Iran," *Middle East Journal of Culture and Communication* 4 (2011): 44–71.

44 Khaled D. Ramadan, introduction to *Peripheral Insider*, 27.

45 See Keshmirshekan, "The Question of Identity vis-à-vis Exoticism in Contemporary Iranian Art."

46 Jean Fisher, "The Syncretic Turn, Cross-cultural Practices in the Age of Multiculturalism," in *Theory in Contemporary Art since 1985*, ed. Zoya Kocur and Simon Leung (Oxford: Blackwell Publishing, 2005), 234.

47 See Farideh Farhi, "Crafting A National Identity: Amidst Contentious Politics in Contemporary Iran," in *Iran in the 21st Century: Politics, Economics and Confrontation*, ed. Homa Katouzian and Hossein Shahidi (London: Routledge, 2007), 13.

10

FEMALE TROUBLE: MELANCHOLIA AND ALLEGORY IN CONTEMPORARY IRANIAN ART

Andrea D. Fitzpatrick

How can Iranian artists create meaningful art in troubled times? Can allegory be a mode to express the melancholia of a generation's losses, which include those dead individuals who cannot be publicly named and mourned, as well as ideals and aspirations that cannot be publicly spoken? What expressive strategies can be used when the expressions themselves are in question? Judith Butler theorizes melancholia in terms of its productive potential as a voice of conscience opposed to oppressive State power.[1] With Butler's views in mind, this essay will analyze artworks created by three female Iranian artists who exhibited them in Tehran, using allegorical strategies to express the melancholia and anger that ensues from the loss of social and political ideals. The installation of Parastou Forouhar (b. 1962) at the Azad Art Gallery in November 2009, entitled *I Surrender*, consisted of dozens of white helium balloons imprinted with digital drawings of female figures inflicting torture or being tortured. The exhibition *Self Service* by Neda Razavipour (b. 1969), also staged at the Azad Gallery in the autumn of 2009, offered visitors opportunities to cut pieces of hand-knotted Persian carpets and take them away in envelopes printed with a phrase from Plato's *Republic*. The exhibition of Amitis Motevalli (b. 1969) at Aaran Gallery in June 2010 consisted of black velvet banners entitled *Here/There, Then/Now*, which are symbolic to Shi'a traditional views of martyrdom and are embroidered with images of the Civil Rights Movement that took place in the United States in the early 1960s. Ambivalent, ironic, melancholic and multifaceted messages are conveyed within all these artworks, by choice as well as by necessity. All the while speaking obliquely, these three exhibitions represent instances of active collective engagement by gallerists, artists and gallery visitors who become entangled, imbricated or physically involved with the art objects in ways that are implicated by broader social and political context(s), both local and international. The artists use a strategic language of gestures, culturally sacred or symbolic objects and an insistence on the traces that reference or reconfigure those dead and wounded subjects whose names cannot always be uttered or written, but who will nonetheless be remembered and mourned. It is in this light that I read the subtlety and layered complexity of the artworks of Forouhar, Razavipour and Motevalli as melancholy allegories.

Allegorical strategies in contemporary art have been theorized by Craig Owens as the presentation of one "story" (a visual-textual framework involving decipherable objects and icons) to narrate another, which is historically different and distinct.[2] In other words, one symbolic paradigm is presented to reference, articulate and extend the meaning of another. According to Owens's classic essay, "Allegorical imagery is appropriated imagery; the allegorist does not invent images but confiscates them. He lays claim to the culturally significant, poses as its interpreter. And in his hands the image becomes something other (*allos* = other + *agoreuei* = to speak). He does not restore the original meaning that may have been lost or obscured; allegory is not hermeneutics. Rather, he adds another meaning to the image. If he adds, however, he does so only to replace: the allegorical meaning supplants an antecedent one; it is a supplement."[3] Rather than presenting a cultural text to plumb its depths for meaning (in the hermeneutic mode), the allegorist re-presents imagery to allow a variety texts to speak to and *through* each other, and thus new meanings emerge.[4] Yet, in distinction from occasions of allegory in American art of the 1980s mentioned by Owens, such as by Sherrie Levine and Robert Longo, in which the allegorist's manipulations of the "original" images may "empty them of their resonance, their significance, their authoritative claim to meaning," the Iranian artists here do, in fact, retain a strong sense of their imagery's "original" meanings to subvert them, transgress them or to suggest a state of hypocrisy and cultural tragedy surrounding them.[5] Postrevolutionary Iranian artists are, of course, not necessarily grappling with the same cultural issues that postmodern North American artists are. The situation of Iranian artists seems rather more fundamental: it is not so much the possibility of revealing new or unintended meanings, but the very possibility of meaning being revealed that is at stake, especially within an environment of ubiquitous surveillance involving potentially dire consequences for those who refuse to comply. I am not the first to perceive allegorical strategies in the work of Iranian artists. Iftikar Dadi reads the *Women of Allah* series (1990s) by Shirin Neshat (b. 1957) as "postcolonial allegories."[6] The difference is that Neshat's photographic collages were created, exhibited and circulated outside Iran (with certain creative freedoms but ultimately also a heavy price paid by the artist and her work, as this particular series is not allowed to be shown in Iran). The artworks discussed here have been exhibited in Iran and are thus subject to different, although equally complex interpretations. What I perceive as the allegorical turn in recent Iranian art is a method for artists to "speak" about polemical issues in Iran in ways that allow more safety but equally poetic, multifaceted and far-reaching results.

While the artworks to be discussed in the following pages may be understood as instances of mourning, they involve, more precisely, a melancholic aesthetic tone; in other words, the painful obsessions of the melancholic that transpire when public grief or the mourner's identification with the dead is socially prohibited. Sigmund Freud offers a pivotal distinction between mourning and melancholia in his 1917 essay,[7] which describes the former as the healthy process of turning away from the lost or dead love object, accepting the loss and turning to a new, replacement object. Melancholia, on the other hand, is at stake when the subject cannot fully identify, articulate or circumscribe what or who is lost or the extent of the losses, which may be layered or cumulative. Yet, the melancholic persists in self-beratement, incorporating the loss(es) into the ambivalent ego, again and again.

For the melancholic, the lost object or ideal cannot be precisely identified, so psychic displacements and frustration constitute a new sociality. Thus, as Judith Butler points out, ambivalence is at the core of melancholia.[8] According to Butler, the melancholic's ambivalence is evident as a form of conflicted subjectivity, suspended between the agency of self-expression and the social prohibition on certain modes of speech. Butler's work is important because she emphasizes the way social power preexists the melancholic subject, thus preempting the possible voicing of individual expressions of oppositional conscience. With melancholia, the power of the State and the various personal or social losses that have been accrued (due the State's abuses of power) are internalized by the subject in forms of psychic tension, mania, ambivalence and anger. The losses and lost ideals, however, are not forgotten but persist painfully in the melancholic's psychic landscape as a latent but silenced source of political, oppositional consciousness. This consciousness unfortunately has trouble making itself visible and audible. Butler writes:

> Indeed, the "other" may be an ideal, a country, a concept of liberty, in which the loss of such ideals is compensated by the interiorized ideality of conscience. An other or an ideal may be "lost" by being rendered unspeakable, impossible to declare, but emerging in the indirection of complaint and the heightened judgments of conscience. Contained within the psychic topography of ambivalence, the faded social text requires a different sort of genealogy in the formation of the subject, one which takes into account how what remains unspeakably absent inhabits the psychic voice of the one who remains. The violence of the loss is redoubled and refracted in a violence of the psychic agency that threatens death; the social is "turned back" into the psychic, only to leave its trace in the voice of conscience.[9]

The melancholic's voicing of dissent cannot, however, be fully prohibited. Melancholia's refracted expressions – speaking through negation or disavowals (i.e., "I have never loved X") – still comprise a manner of acknowledgment and a form of classically interpellated subjectivity for the lost "other" in a social context of oppressive power. Such modes of inversion allow the articulation, repetition and incorporation of prohibited love objects in a social manner that at once acquiesces to the mandates of State power while simultaneously turning over and against its oppressive demands.

Part of my goal is to analyze some important Iranian artworks not only in their own right and within the context of Iranian political life, but also in relationship to pivotal figures in international contemporary art. What is lacking in the current literature on contemporary Iranian art are comparative studies that contextualize Iranian artists within and against broader cultural contexts; in other words, studies that attempt to bridge differences of language, historical era, gender and even political circumstance. This is not the same as pluralism, universalism or facile multiculturalism (whose limits are well known). The rapid rise of critically important Iranian artists in tension with the ever-expanding global art markets, including museum and gallery networks, have produced an impressive number of group exhibitions of Iranian art, as well as sales (both private and institutional).[10] While this flowering of exhibitions and publications has been essential in giving international art audiences an awareness of Iranian art beyond such famous Diasporic names such as Neshat, a certain pigeonholing will (or has already) set in, which disallows the same artists their due recognition beyond the primary category of their "Iranianness" (with the other key categories being, of course, disputed terms such as "Islamic" and "Middle Eastern"). Forouhar articulates this situation as follows: "When I arrived in Germany seventeen years ago, I was Parastou Forouhar. Somehow, over the years, collaborating with Western colleagues and delineating my own artistic territory, I have become 'Iranian.' [...] The field of intercultural communication is ploughed by clichés, which cover up the 'blind spots' that threaten to grow rampant. Each effort of intercultural interaction is endangered by its own abuse."[11] Forouhar's ironic qualification of the international reputations of Iranian artists, as well as her reservations toward the aspirations of intercultural research, is particularly instructive for those like myself who approach the study of Iranian art from the position of a relative outsider.[12] Nonetheless, calls for the dual mandate to recognize in Iranian art both cultural specificity and international significance are made by theorists such as Hamid Keshmirshekan, who notes how this concern is felt strongly by the artists themselves and is evident in "the ever-present obsession with cultural and frequently social concerns with which Iranian artists are engaged, both within the country and across the diaspora."[13] Along these lines, Keshmirshekan emphasizes how "[C]ontemporary debate on Iranian art reveals deep-rooted anxieties about national and cultural identity. It raises an important question: Is it possible to open up an art practice and discourse that is both contemporary and global, but also indigenous and specific?"[14] This essay attempts to answer Keshmirshekan's question in the affirmative, providing analyses of the work of Iranian artists who are achieving this double-edged position, the simultaneity of symbolic local meanings and internationally resonant metaphors. Yet, there remains a problem with published scholarship on Iranian art, at least for those scholars who live in or want to travel to Iran. This involves how to speak without saying too much. The context of the English language, which strives for clarity and precision in scholarly writing, must be renegotiated. This is a process that engenders a substantial degree of melancholia, because one is in the position of being trapped in an echo chamber of ideas and information that is known but cannot be written. Melancholia, as Butler points out, is resistant to representation.[15]

At the Azad Gallery in November of 2009, Forouhar exhibited a magnificent canopy of helium balloons whose strings hang down into the gallery space (Figure 10.1). While the balloons covered the ceiling of the gallery, clustering like shifting clouds, visitors became playfully entangled by their delicate hanging strings, which eventually became knotted into webs (Figure 10.2). Just as important as the helium balloons are the images printed on the balloons: digital drawings of sinuous, black-outlined, cream-colored female figures (if the dresses are significant) torturing other female figures whose hands and feet are bound and tied with ropes. An earlier incarnation of *I Surrender* in which the balloons had pink rather than cream-colored figures and hovered at different heights rather than uniformly on the ceiling was held at the Martin-Gropius Bau in Berlin in 2007. In Vienna at the Belvedere Gallery in 2009, *I Surrender* was installed in a glass-walled space with such high ceilings that the balloons appeared ready to float away into the blue sky, like so many clouds swept into the atmosphere. The date and location of the exhibition at the Azad Gallery establish a political statement as local and specific, but the abstraction and stylization of the figures – with voids in place of facial features – allow the imagery to achieve a universal statement denouncing torture. As Lutz Becker writes, "[Forouhar's] response to the horrors of our times gives her work purpose and energy, living in Germany has made her aware of the burden of memory prevalent in that society for crimes committed during the Nazi period. Seeing historical and psychological parallels with the Iranian trauma, she invests her art with a sense of personal responsibility that clearly implies a collective dimension."[16] The helium balloons were mass-produced and sold for approximately $30 US at the Tehran exhibition. They may thus be seen to reference the utopic commodity fetishism of late modernity's industrial era (with its assembly lines and, as Marx would point out, disenfranchised laborers), as well as (in the Vienna and Berlin exhibitions) the pernicious genocidal misappropriation of such industrial technologies in the creation of Nazi death camps. The balloons – the takeaway, the multiple, the souvenir, the relic, the collectible – become fetishized objects of memory and memorial. With a streak of the blackest, bleakest irony, Forouhar's scathing indictment of barbaric violence perpetrated by authorities against their own citizens is delivered in a medium that is both carnivalesque and melancholic.

Forouhar's work is also compelling in terms of the connections it suggests with other contemporary artists who also address social trauma and political violence in their work. Helium balloons were previously deployed in an installation by General Idea, the Canadian art collective (comprised of Jorge Zontal, Felix Partz and AA Bronson) that produced pop-inflected conceptual art for 25 years (1967–94) until two of its members (Zontal and Partz) died of AIDS-related illnesses. General Idea's *Magi© Bullet* installation of 1992, held at the Stux Gallery in New York, consisted of 1,500 custom-fabricated silver helium balloons clustered densely on the gallery ceiling like storm clouds ready to burst into showers (Figure 10.3). General Idea's inspiration was Andy Warhol's *Silver Clouds* of 1966, a gallery installation of pillow-shaped helium balloons sparsely floating at different heights. But Warhol's light-hearted, ambivalent comment on the vacuity of the art world is transformed with General Idea into a poetic but caustic political statement. The General Idea balloons are shaped like AZT capsules, part of the medical miracle or "drug cocktail" being developed at the time to slow the progression of HIV. In a statement, the artists explain that "The term 'Magic Bullet' now commonly refers to a medicine designed to attack a virus without attacking healthy cells, a conceptual miracle cure, and now generally applied to the curative quest. 'Magic' has reappeared in mass consciousness."[17] However, due to the lack of political and economic support for advanced research and development in this area (reflecting the virulent homophobia afflicting many levels of government in the United States), the promise for remission and survival for many individuals affected by HIV and AIDS was held up in drug trials and legislation seemingly impervious to the calls from medical professionals and activists to make the medications more readily available. While inspiring news of this health salvation spread throughout the gay communities in North America and Europe, only a privileged few were able to access it. Thus during the AIDS crisis of the late 1980s and early 1990s, thousands of individuals died needlessly.

One may link General Idea's balloons to those of Forouhar on a number of levels. One is confronted with the floating, celebratory qualities of the helium balloons, which convey dystopian and utopian feelings, a perplexing sense of levity in a time of incendiary social crisis. There is also the analogy of the virus and its technologies of reproduction, which are mimicked by the mass-produced art objects themselves. Let us consider General Idea's allegorical conception of elusive hope and the cruelties of fate conveyed by the *Magi© Bullet* balloons: "Like putti, they defied gravity angelically. They formed a celestial ceiling of limited duration: due to their nature some stayed aloft while others fell by the wayside, cocoons for collectors. Thus the installations gradually dematerialized."[18] Like General Idea's *Magi© Bullets*, Forouhar's *I Surrender* presents a time-based opportunity for viewers to contemplate hope, the unpredictable twists of chance and mortality. Forouhar's installation lasted about a week, approximately the same duration of helium balloons' ability to resist gravity. After about four or five days, helium balloons wither, shrink and eventually drop to the ground. The movement of the balloons is a cipher in a microcosm for the trajectory of political protests everywhere: the festive atmosphere of mass gatherings of communities, the deflation of collective dreams, the withering of aspirations, the familiarity of profound disappointment and grief over the dead.

Elegant calligraphic arabesques (common to sacred Qur'anic and other scripts, as well as to traditional Iranian handicrafts) that outline torture techniques become Forouhar's means of communication (Figure 10.4). The lines are digital traces of the hand and form an outline of the body that is both figurative and abstract, descriptive and evasive, handcrafted and mechanical. As Becker writes, "In her [Forouhar's] depiction of everyday mental and physical brutality, she creates images of aesthetic appeal but disturbing ambiguity. References to the tradition of Persian miniatures are forever present and are fused by computer techniques into a complex imagery of both modern and traditional meaning."[19] The invocation by contemporary artists of such traditional, culturally significant art forms and their manipulation and transformation using digital imaging technologies are part of a broad matrix of strategies identified by Homi Bhabha (writing about Diasporic artists from the Middle East and South Asia) that present new and expansive notions of art-historical temporality: "The mediation of the slower, time-lagged aesthetic forms into the digitalized forms of contemporary media practices produces a form of disjunction that enables these artists to reinvent tradition while revising the cultural history of the present moment."[20] Rather than insisting on the contemporaneity of the art created by Diasporic Middle Eastern or South Asian artists who make use of traditional art forms in their work (as does Bhabha), I would like to emphasize how Forouhar's combination of the graceful, ornamental beauty of line with horrific subject matter gives her work an age-old momentum and internal conflict, precisely that which challenged so many of the masters of European art faced with representing, for example, the Crucifixion of Christ, as well as other atrocious scenes of martyrdom, with beauty and dignity. The task is to transform a scene of suffering into one that inscribes a lasting sense of shame, mourning or reverence in the viewer. The forms must be adequately compelling to achieve in the viewer a sense of philosophic or ethical meditation on instances of violence, criminality and injustice when it is not entirely clear with whom goodness or criminality lies.[21]

The confusion between victim and aggressor figures in Forouhar's balloons is as old as the issue of martyrdom and one of its central representational dilemmas.[22]

In an exhibition catalogue for a thoughtful and ambitious survey of contemporary Iranian art, Shaheen Merali writes of Forouhar's work: "Her monochromatic compositions are normally repetitions of acts of atrocious torture in medieval garb. Here, the simple anonymous human forms are twisted, deformed and altered by controlling anonyms. Her basic premise remains in questioning the wider ideology as it penetrates the psyche of its citizens resulting in a bellicose cosmos that makes the tortured into a potential torturer in a systematic use of violence, coercion and distrust that makes us all culprits to acts of evil."[23] Thus, what emerges from Forouhar's work is the unfortunate, all-too-familiar image paradigm (of shocking revenge fantasies and conflicting ideological positions) that has saturated international news media in the years after September 11, the Abu Ghraib military prison crimes and now the Arab spring, which make it difficult, if not impossible, as Susan Sontag eloquently argues, to discern what a visual ethic could possibly mean in representations of war punctuated by traumatic representations of the gruesome, humiliating deaths of "others."[24] In *The Abu Ghraib Effect* (2007), Stephen F. Eisenman discusses the artistic compulsion to depict scenes of horror in order to oppose and expose the barbaric practices of those in power.[25] Eisenman sees this as a leitmotif of critical streams of modern art, which finds its European origins in post-Enlightenment artists, such as Francisco de Goya (in his *Inquisition Album* etchings of 1810–14) and even Pablo Picasso (1881–1973) in his monumental painting *Guernica* (1937). If one examines the career of Forouhar, which demonstrates continued artistic experimentation in various media and with ever-novel imagery simultaneously with an unrelenting focus on issues of violence, it would not at all be hyperbole to claim that her name belongs within the canon of celebrated politically motivated artists discussed by Eisenman.

Also staged the Azad Gallery in the autumn months of 2009 was a "happening," created by Razavipour, called *Self Service*, which involved ten traditional, hand-knotted Iranian carpets (of Qashaqai or Tabrizi origin) in different sizes laid out on the gallery's floor, with box cutters available for guests to carve out pieces of these revered cultural treasures to take away with them (Figures 10.5, 10.6).[26] Tehran-based writer Lili Golestan outlines the cultural iconicity of the Persian carpet and why its destruction – which she considers a profanation of the sacred – is so significant: "In the traditional society that is Iran, two things are sacrosanct: bread and carpets. If you find a piece of bread on the ground, you pick it up and put it in a safe place so that it cannot be trampled underfoot by the ignorant. Carpets are given the same kind of respect. Everyone knows how much care and attention goes into making them [...]. Carpets, remember, are seen as an inseparable whole, with their *toranji* (central part), their bunches of flowers and arabesques, and their delicate, slender edges."[27]

Razavipour's work is most certainly an allegory inspired by the political events of the previous summer. Comments in the Azad Gallery guest book, transcribed by Golestan in her review, suggest as much: "The Razavipour exhibition mirrors our times. I am deeply sad for our age and for us; I do not believe it, I do not want to believe it, but whatever we say or do, this reflects the wretchedness of our times."[28] Ali Ettehad's detailed description of the *Self Service* exhibition, published in the Tehran-based journal *Art Tomorrow* (which must, like all other Iranian publications, scrupulously self-censor itself to avoid becoming yet another casualty), offers another clue: "Then the artist would take the torn piece of the carpet and put it in an envelope on which part of the fourth book of Plato's *Republic*, where Lantheus has a struggle within himself whether to see the bodies of executed people in Piraeus port, has been printed. He finally cries, 'My poor eyes! Enjoy this striking scene as much as you can.'"[29] What is decisive in terms of the meaning of Razavipour's work *Self Service* is its date and cultural context, as Ettehad discreetly writes: "The time and social conditions within which *Self Service* was performed were certainly key element[s] of the idea embodied in the work."[30] This was a time and place when the fabric of Iranian society was torn apart to a degree that was previously unthinkable.

The Persian carpet is an important leitmotif in the work of other contemporary Iranian artists, such as Jalal Sepehr's *Kish* and *Yazd* series of photographs from 2004 and 2010, respectively; Samira Eskandarfar, with her short experimental videos *Rugs & Men* and *Miss Shamsi and Her Carpet*, both 2006; and Sadegh Tirafkan's *Human Tapestry* series of digital photographic collages from 2008–10. Yet, nowhere in contemporary Iranian art does a sense of chaotic, senseless violence permeate – in such a physical and material way – the cultural iconicity of the beloved Persian carpet the way it does with Razavipour's interactive installation. The installation presented both an opportunity and an ethical dilemma: one can contribute to the success of an interactive art installation but in the process also destroy one's cultural heritage (Figure 10.7). This work allegorizes the violence perpetrated on Iran's true cultural legacy and heritage: its citizens. Ettehad notes that it took great effort to cut pieces of the carpet. Does this suggest the unbreakable spirit of the Iranian people? The blades and the struggle of the gallery participants (who had difficulty cutting through the knots of carpets that were woven to endure centuries) actualize the violence of and resistance to useless destruction (of physical and other bodies of work) for personal, political or commercial gain. Ettehad interprets the work as "therapeutic," involving a sense of catharsis but also profound loss: "A repressed surge of violence was released to make the audience cut the carpets into pieces, so that in two days what was left on the gallery floor was only dust."[31] I see this installation even more as a pessimistic, despairing view of the social situation in contemporary Iran, a fragmentation to the point of decimation and disintegration, dissemination without the promise of taking root or regrowth, exile without repatriation or return. The pieces of carpet are, after all, taken by viewers to unknown destinations, and one can never repair a carpet incised to such a destructive degree, leaving only "dust," as Ettehad calls the remains. In Razavipour's *Self-Service*, I see dark shades of malice: rapacious materialistic greed, antagonism directed at artists and artisans, irreverence toward the preservation of artistic heritage and an unthinking mob mentality (under the hideous euphemism "collective will") that discourages individual ethical responses. These are all, I believe, suggested with Razavipour's shocking work.

Razavipour's offer to gallery visitors to carve up precious carpets in order to take a piece of the artwork away suggests a connection to the work of the late Cuban American artist Félix González-Torres (1957–96). In the early 1990s, amid the AIDS crisis that eventually claimed his own life, González-Torres created a number of untitled installations comprising machine-made "objects" that could be taken away – and in many cases also consumed – by gallery visitors: candies, chocolates or large photolithographs stacked neatly in minimalist blocks. His *Untitled (USA Today)*, exhibited at the Whitney Biennial of 1991, consists of hundreds of commercially manufactured hard candies wrapped in red, silver and blue, piled high in a triangle in a gallery corner. As the visitors remove pieces of candy and, one assumes, decide whether to enjoy their tastes in a few ephemeral moments of sweetness or preserve them as relics, the pile will diminish. One of the important aspects of these installations, essentially offering his work as small gifts to individual viewers, is their never-ending quality. If the piles go down, the museums must add more to replenish the supply. The losses of the AIDS crisis are allegorized in the work: a dwindling of the body's weight in illness, the loss of individual community members, a perpetual sense of mourning and the difficulty of remembrance. But there is also miraculous regeneration. Razavipour's *Self Service*, on the other hand, is decidedly finite, and thus a sense of tragic materialism rather than beneficence ensues. The loss of the carpet's integrity seems decidedly more significant than the gain embodied by any individual fragment. While each of González-Torres's mementos is equal and nearly identical, Razavipour's pieces of carpet are unique, handmade fetishes that attempt to but cannot compensate for a greater loss. In both cases however, being able to take a small piece of an artwork home (and quite possibly also to preserve or memorialize it with thoughtful recollection) seems like minor compensation when compared to the greater cultural crises that are suggested.

According to Butler, "Melancholia is a rebellion that has been put down, crushed. Yet it is not a static affair; it continues as a kind of 'work' that takes place by deflection. Figured within the workings of the psyche is the power of the State to preempt an insurrectionary rage. The 'critical agency' of the melancholic is at once a social and psychic instrument."[32] In this light, in June of 2010, on the one-year anniversary of the demonstrations and the deaths of the protestors in the streets during the Green Revolution, Aaran Gallery exhibited the work of Los Angeles-based Iranian artist Motevalli, who illustrates the critical consciousness of a melancholic. In the main gallery space was an installation entitled *Here/There, Then/Now*, which consists of seven black velvet, triangular banners on which are embroidered in brightly colored threads the outlines of famous documentary photographs from the American Civil Rights protests of 1963 when African Americans were violently attacked by civil servants in Birmingham, Alabama. These heraldic flags – suggesting protest and mourning – reference the African American struggle for voting rights and the Shi'a commemoration of the martyrdom of Imam Hossein (who died at the battle of Karbala in 680), which occurs annually during nationwide public *'Ashura'* ceremonies (Figures 10.8, 10.9). The artist's referents are thus deftly intercultural. Many of the images appropriated by Motevalli that were embroidered on the heraldic banners are iconic in American visual culture. The celebrated documentary photographer Charles Moore's view of policemen attacking a man whose trousers are being torn by a vicious German shepherd will be familiar to those who know the history of American photography or Andy Warhol's *Death and Disaster* silkscreen painting series of 1962–64, which appropriates the same image for a number of related works entitled *Race Riot*. Many of Moore's photographs capturing demonstrators being assaulted with water shot from fire hoses were reproduced in *LIFE* magazine shortly after the events themselves occurred (Figure 10.10).

The related issues of martyrdom and mourning are fiercely polemicized in contemporary Iranian political life, a situation that was made evident by the conflicting identities that circulated in the media concerning those who were killed in the streets of Tehran during the summer of 2009 and those who perpetrated the violence. As Motevalli states in the exhibition catalogue published by the gallery, "In these works, there is an allegory for injustice that has continued throughout time and place. The flags symbolize the people's struggle to gain their freedom from under oppressive and inhumane conditions." By referencing civil rights violations committed by American authorities in the name of the law and public safety, Motevalli uses a method of transference to articulate a voice of conscience. With the black velvet, fringe-edged banners, her installation appropriates the religious motif of martyrdom (sacrifice to defend one's faith) all the while subverting its message by alluding to politically motivated – rather than spiritual – bases for such choices.

On the enormous glass window that separates the Aaran Gallery's main space from the courtyard, Motevalli affixed a Persian translation of a famous speech delivered at the 1964 Democratic National Convention in the United States by the African American activist Fannie Lou Hamer who describes the violence that she experienced when she attempted to register to vote (Figure 10.11). The sensuality of Motevalli's installation, augmented by the delicacy of the calligraphy affixed to the glass, as well as by the endearing, handcrafted quality of the media images embroidered on the dark velvet, buffers the stridency of its message. The fact that photograph-based images have been translated onto textile surfaces through the labor-intensive process of embroidery (which under modern academic determinations was downgraded as "women's work" and "craft" within the exalted masculinist hierarchy of the "fine" arts) is a contemporary feminist artistic strategy. The flag format, draped in a way that their gold-fringed triangular points rest on the gallery floor, entices viewers to become seduced by the soft, sweeping or enfolding potential of the velvet.

The combined formal choices made by the artist to deliver her sophisticated statement of protest also have ethical potential. Mieke Bal's theory of "enfolding feminism" suggests ways in which feminist aesthetics offer the extended temporality necessary to respect and mourn those who have died or been murdered: "Beyond the everyday bombardments of fleeting images, art seems a suitable place for us to stop and invest these deaths with cultural duration."[33] By closely considering Michelangelo Caravaggio's painting *Death of the Virgin* (1606) in the Louvre, Paris, Bal concludes that it is through the dynamic metaphor of the baroque fold (which is seen as a huge diagonal curtain sweeping over the prone, dead body of the saint) that a contemporary feminist viewer may be welcomed into the centuries-old painting and overcome the untenable dichotomy of the scene. This dichotomy is gendered: the mind-body split that is hierarchized is *always already* one that involves gender, such that the female is mute, spoken for and objectified, in short dead, whether literally or figuratively. According to Bal, the enveloping metaphor of the fold bridges a gap in time and space, mends rifts in feminist discourses (between essentialists and constructivists) and helps overcome binary thinking (which would pit epistemology against ontology), because the viewer must take time and attention to perceive the artwork in an embodied way. By "actualizing attention," many binary oppositions may be reconfigured.[34]

Also according to Bal, writing about the sculptural work of the Colombian artist Doris Salcedo (whose pieces of domestic furniture have been embedded with a delicate, almost imperceptible fur of individual human hairs painstakingly implanted into their wooden surfaces one by one), the extended temporality of certain artistic processes, as well as the duration it takes for viewers to fully appreciate its metaphors and nuances, fosters a contemplative recognition of dead or murdered political victims whose identities are embedded into the materiality of the work in a way that cannot soon be forgotten: "In a mode and mood that points most emphatically to a politics of embodied, enfolded vision, Salcedo's sculptures work on the basis of the performance of duration."[35] Likewise, there is duration of creation involved with Motevalli's embroidered velvet banners, *Here/There, Then/Now* (a title whose punctuation suggests a bringing together or bridging of different spaces and times). The feminist implications of Motevalli's embroidery onto the black velvet banners offsets the overbearing masculinity associated with the 'Ashura' ceremonies, which are dominated by traditional gestures of male participants who beat their chests and call out in mourning. The banners drape onto the gallery floor and point into the viewer's space, thus presenting voluptuous folds that break up the distinction between two- and three-dimensional artworks, between the mechanically reproduced and the uniquely made or auratic, the solid and the fluid, the masculinist/patriarchal and the feminist, the space of the viewer and the space of the art and, if we follow Bal's thinking, the spaces of the living and the dead.

Motevalli's banners seem to unfurl themselves toward the viewer, and in so doing, transport, by just a few inches, the viewer's attention into a transhistorical commemoration of those who have sacrificed their lives for the sake of civil and human rights. Motevalli's layered transference can be understood as a melancholic but also empowering gesture; the artwork is an allegory whose denunciation occurs by a cathexis of political references. As Butler points out, "The revolt in melancholia can be distilled in marshaling aggression in the service of mourning, but also necessarily, of life."[36] The needlework in *Here/There, Then/Now* offers only outlines of figures and traces of bodies but not a sense of depth or dimension. Thus, the time-intensive work of embroidery on Motevalli's banners could be seen as memorial labor; equally a working-through of grief, as in mourning's therapeutic qualities; or an inscription and preservation of grief, as in melancholia, which persists to haunt the melancholic and offer the agency of critical conscience against the injustices perpetrated by State power.

In conclusion, comparisons have been made between the work of these female Iranian artists – Forouhar, Razavipour and Motevalli – and other artists working in North American and European contexts. Strategies of pop art, the appropriation of iconic imagery from the mass media or from cultural traditions, and embodied audience participation are ways in which these artists convey the acute political and social concerns of their specific times and places. The community bridging or collective effort that is fostered by the artworks among the viewers – in addition to connections forged with international communities – occurs in friction with the local context of political agendas that have so aggressively threatened the cohesion and fundamental dignities of life in Iran, among the Iranian Diaspora and in other international communities. Allegories of political and social violence but also opportunities for ethical engagement and enfolding (the embrace of the dead within cultural memory) are offered by Forouhar, Razavipour and Motevalli, whose work presents cross-cultural and transhistorical instances of injustice, melancholia and – appropriate to the crises that have been witnessed – glints of resistance.

Notes and References

1 Judith Butler, *The Psychic Life of Power: Theories in Subjection* (Stanford: Stanford University Press, 1997), 167–98.

2 Craig Owens, "The Allegorical Impulse: Toward a Theory of Postmodernism," *October* 12 (1980): 67–86.

3 Owens, "The Allegorical Impulse," 69.

4 Owens's view of allegory as intertextuality against hermeneutic meaning-seeking recalls classic definitions of modernist versus postmodernist approaches in cultural theory, and in this regard it is worth citing Frederic Jameson's memorable comparison of Vincent van Gogh's *Peasant Shoes* with Andy Warhol's *Diamond Dust Shoes* to exemplify "the waning of affect" in postmodern subjectivity. See Frederic Jameson, "Postmodernism, or The Cultural Logic of Late Capitalism," *New Left Review* 146 (1984): 61–2.

5 Owens, "The Allegorical Impulse," 69.

6 Iftikar Dadi, "Shirin Neshat's Photographs as Postcolonial Allegories," *Signs: Journal of Women in Culture and Society* 34, no. 1 (2008): 125–50.

7 Sigmund Freud, *A General Selection from the Works of Sigmund Freud*, ed. John Rickman (New York: Anchor-Doubleday, 1957), 124–40.

8 Butler, *The Psychic Life of Power*, 167–98.

9 Ibid., 196.

10 See "Iran Unveiled," *ArtPress* 2, no. 17 (2010) devoted to visual art and music in Iran; Sabine Le Stum, "Middle East: a Little Less Business, a Little More Art," *ArtPress* 361 (2009): 53–6; and Fiametta Rocco and Sarah Thornton, "A Whole New World," *Economist: A Special Report on the Art Market*, November 28, 2009: 15–16.

11 Parastou Forouhar, Artist Statement, *Iranian Photography Now*, ed. Rose Issa (Ostfildern: Hatje Cantz Verlag, 2008), 44.

12 As a feminist scholar trained during the heady decades of postcolonial research in the 1990s, I am aware that the theoretical risks of a colonizing or paternalistic approach are always unfortunately there, as are (equally I am convinced) opportunities for new insights and approaches to be brought to the discourse.

13 Hamid Keshmirshekan, "Contemporary or Specific: The Dichotomous Desires in the Art of Early Twenty-First Century Iran," *Middle East Journal of Culture and Communication* 4 (2011): 44.

14 Ibid.

15 Butler, *The Psychic Life of Power*, 186.

16 Lutz Becker, "Art, Death and Language," in *Parastou Forouhar: Art, Life, and Death in Iran*, ed. Rose Issa (London: Saqi, 2010), 16.

17 General Idea, "General Idea's Pharma©opia," in *General Idea Pharma©opia* (Barcelona: Centre d'Art Santa Monica-Departament de Cultura, 1992), 62.

18 Ibid.

19 Becker, "Art, Death and Language," 19.

20 Homi Bhabha, "Another Country," in *Without Boundary: Seventeen Ways of Looking*, ed. Fereshteh Daftari (New York: Museum of Modern Art, 2006), 31.

21 John Drury, "Michelangelo and Rembrandt: The Crucifixion," *Word & Image: A Journal of Verbal/Visual Inquiry* 24, no. 4 (2008): 349–66.

22 For more on the issue of martyrdom in contemporary art in relation to Abu Ghraib and what W. J. T. Mitchell calls the "war of images," see my chapter, "AA Bronson's *Hanged Man*: Martyrdom, Ambiguity, and Abu Ghraib," in *Gravity in Art*, ed. Mary D. Edwards and Elizabeth Bailey (Jefferson: McFarland, 2012), 315–25.

23 Shaheen Merali, "The Promise of Loss," in *The Promise of Loss: A Contemporary Index of Iran* (Vienna: Galerie Hilger-BROT Kunsthalle, 2009), 16.

24 Susan Sontag, *Regarding the Pain of Others* (New York: Picador-Farrar, 2003).

25 Stephen F. Eisenman, "Freudian Slip," in *The Abu Ghraib Effect* (London: Reaktion, 2008), 18–41.
26 Ali Ettehad, "Therapeutic Effect and Experimental Interaction: Neda Razavipour," *Art Tomorrow* 2 (2010): 76.
27 Lili Golestan, "Neda Razavipour: Disfiguring the Carpet," *ArtPress* 2, no. 17 (2010): 71.
28 Ibid.
29 Ettehad, "Therapeutic Effect," 76.
30 Ibid.
31 Ibid.
32 Butler, *The Psychic Life of Power*, 190–91.
33 Mieke Bal, "Enfolding Feminism," in *Feminist Consequences: Theory for the New Century*, ed. Elisabeth Bronfen and Misha Kavka (New York: Columbia University Press, 2001), 340.
34 Ibid., 338.
35 Ibid., 344.
36 Butler, *The Psychic Life of Power*, 191.

IV

THE IRANIAN DIASPORA

11

PERFORMING VISUAL STRATEGIES: REPRESENTATIONAL CONCEPTS OF FEMALE IRANIAN IDENTITY IN CONTEMPORARY PHOTOGRAPHY AND VIDEO ART

Julia Allerstorfer

Iran's internal dispute with national identity found a new culminating point in the course of the Green Movement after the 2009 Iranian presidential elections. Supporting the campaigns of Mir Hossein Mousavi (b. 1942) and protesting against a renewed presidency of Mahmoud Ahmadinejad (elected 2005–present), a younger generation of Iranians spread these contested election results to the countries of the global Iranian Diaspora. This political struggle for a redefinition of national identity chiefly aimed at, among other things, reforms of the existing constitution of the Islamic Republic Iran. It is interesting to observe how these controversies over "Iranian" identity in a transnational context and in light of the age of globalization find their special and multifaceted expressions in the visual arts. Since the last decade, and especially after September 11, 2001, a remarkable shift of global interest in emerging contemporary Iranian art on the international art scene and art market has been noticeable.

During his State of Union address in 2002, former United States president George W. Bush (contestingly elected 2000–2008) labeled Iran, Iraq and North Korea as the "Axis of evil," accusing these governments of supporting terrorism, as well as seeking weapons of mass destruction. Soon thereafter, Iran became the focus of renewed international attention and criticism since the Iranian Revolution (1978–79) and the Iran–Iraq War (1980–88). In dealing with ostensible political, religious and social factors of Islam during the period after 9/11, an intensified awareness was also given to the respective countries' specific art scenes, especially the Iranian. Following the arguments of Mahmood Mamdani,[1] Salah M. Hassan characterizes this phenomenon of renewed interest in contemporary art from Islamicate countries as a "culturalistic approach Islam,"[2] which is not only practiced in the political arena, but has also captured the field of "Islamic" art and is exploited by museums and curators to demonstrate the positive aspects of a "moderate" Islam. Hassan is describing a specific North American perspective on the "Islamic world," which strengthened after the terrorist attacks of 9/11 and established qualitative differences between "bad"/"terroristic" and "good"/"modern"/"secular" Muslims within the United States. The fascinating, yet paradoxical, result is an increased interest in the "West" for art from Islamicate countries,[3] while simultaneously demonizing those countries.[4] Jessica Winegar and Finbarr Barry Flood are of the opinion that recent American and European cultural discourses on "Islamic" art have to be considered as consequences of the "war on terror," public diplomacy and measures against a rising Islamophobia in the wake of 9/11.[5] According to them, the intensified continued interest in contemporary Iranian art during the last decade can be regarded in light of this reasoning, as well as more recent political events in Iran, such as the Green Movement.

This spotlight on Iran due to these political events has created the need to examine performativity in Iran and the diaspora, and in particular, how that performativity is expressed in representation. Using the term "performative" in accordance with the theme of this volume, I address the visual strategies used by Iranian women artists, living both in Iran and in the Iranian Diaspora, who perform various issues concerning gendered identities in the context of Iranian politics, society and State. As identity finds its expression in the display of the human body, I focus on female bodies that serve as the media on which identity issues are performed in the visual arts. I discuss the articulations and visualizations of female Iranian identity – that is, gender constitutions, constructions and roles and how they are performed in Iran and in the diaspora. I concentrate on images of the body, self-portraiture and self-display, which are relevant and particularly worthwhile for a debate on the perceptions of performance, gender and identity, and in this case, in relation to Iran.

In the analysis of various concepts and strategies of gendered State identities (or contested ones), artistic production in Iran and the Iranian Diaspora should be taken into account. It is important to consider the global impact of these representations, because Iranian contemporary visual culture consists of artistic production both inside and outside Iran. As Anthony Downey states, "the Iranian Diaspora, like all migrant communities, looks both westward and eastward, to the present and the past, to the legacy of tradition and the ever-pressing immediacy and, ultimately, relates back to national practices within Iran itself."[6] Put another way, Iranian Diaspora artists are in a close dialogue with their homeland, while they likewise grapple with local conditions of their host countries. At the same time, cultural production in Iran both informs the diaspora and international art practices and is equally informed by diaspora and global artistic movements.[7] In view of these performative strategies in visual articulation, it is interesting to analyze this correlation between the artwork of female Iranians living in Iran with those in the Iranian Diaspora. Therefore, I suggest that addressing approaches and perspectives from both inside and outside Iran are significant for an in-depth analysis of a gendered Iranian performativity.

I frame my discussion of Iranian women artists working in Iran and in the diaspora by comparing and contrasting three women artists who demonstrate these nuanced differences. Iranian women are more focused on due to the Orientalist fascination with the veil, and since the European Enlightenment of the eighteenth century, women have become a litmus test of progress in the global community. The artists living in Iran are Shadafarin Ghadirian (b. 1974) and Simin Keramati (b. 1970). Later, these artistic positions will be compared and contrasted with that of an Iranian-born artist in diaspora, Parastou Forouhar (b. 1962), who now lives in Germany. It is worth noting that all these women were born before the Iranian Revolution of 1978–79 and therefore experienced a period of substantial and radical change in Iran's history of the twentieth century. The identities they are subverting and performing have to be considered in this sociopolitical context and, at the same time, as still rather "new." In relation to the field of identity as a main issue in the mentioned artistic positions and in contemporary Iranian art in general, it is essential to cite a crucial essay by art historian Hamid Keshmirshekan.[8] According to him, there are two primary concerns in the artistic practice, namely "identity" and "exoticism."[9] With respect to themes of gender relations, the situation of Iranian Islamic women and feminism in representations that form part of contemporary Iran's realities, Keshmirshekan alerts the reader to the danger that they become stereotypes: "Even when in the recent works of Iranian artists created in various media and presented in the dramatically more numerous auctions or overseas exhibitions, cultural confrontations and contemporary social issues could be based on formulae and even coded forms of typical indigenous elements. These issues and objects have been based on a subjective exotic view of what is expected to be shown as Iranian' and as contemporary.'"[10] Among others, he alternatively references several female artists, such as Jinoos Taghizadeh (b. 1971), Nazgol Ansarinia (b. 1979) and Shirin Aliabadi (b. 1973), who are concerned with the depictions of the younger generation in the wave of change pervading contemporary Iran. With a need for self-representation and working with various artistic practices, their rather critical, satirical, ironic and sometimes humorous artistic language "has also become a common method to criticize exoticism and as a metaphorical reaction against united sacred values defined by officials."[11] Their crucial interest in social and political realities, as well as their immense contribution to the process of "inventing a new politics of identity for the twenty-first century,"[12] is also true for the selected artistic positions in this essay. Here, the controversy of female identity and the visual depiction of women are linked to skeptical self-reflection and a critique of the politics of representation and gender relations, both of which, I suggest, do not always degenerate into stereotypes or exoticism.

These photographers and video artists share an explicit interest in the female figure in general and reveal the constructions and perceptions of specific feminine "Iranian identities" in very critical and ironic ways. Here, it is interesting to take a closer look at the performative visual strategies and concepts of representation of "Iranian" womanhood in the different social contexts of Iran and the Iranian Diaspora, specifically in the European States. Special aspects which concern female "Iranian" identity structures and become manifest in these artistic positions, are issues of censorship, which are fought on the battlegrounds of women's bodies (Ghadirian), intimate surveys of personal conditions, which also reflect social and political realities (Keramati) and the ironic *mis-en-scènes* of the chador in a German public space (Forouhar).[13] Each of these works is framing alterity and can be interpreted as a serious consideration of the Self as an image of the Other, whereas Forouhar maybe addresses the perpetual European debates on veiling, too.[14] In light of these artistic positions, which address gender or gender identity, the following aspects are of particular relevance: images of Self and Other, strategies of visualization, representational methods, constructions of identity, authorship, (inter-) cultural codings and decodings and social aspects of artistic autonomy and restriction, all of which contribute to gender-related performances of the Iranian State, both in and outside the country. In view of these three female positions, it is interesting to analyze the artists' different approaches and visual strategies in the depiction of veiling and covering the female body. These approaches incorporate the thematization of the chador and censorship by means of overpainting and the deployment of black color over the female body.

Why Photography and Video?

I draw from the media of photography and video because these media are widespread, popular among a younger generation of Iranian artists and frequently intertwined with various topics in relation to self-expression, identity and gender. The abundant creative work with these media may be explainable due to their international popularity, as they are rather easy, affordable and available, as well as they can be distributed quite rapidly. Historically, as a medium, photography has been closely related to and used for constructing identity in Iran. Due to its indexical constitution "to capture" and fix rays of objects on a photosensitive surface, photography has turned into a prominent and staged medium for displays of Self and Other, however false or problematic those displays may be, since the second half of the nineteenth century. Moreover, the photograph has become the identity card.[15] Roland Barthes explains: "[P]hotography, moreover, began historically as an art of the Person, of civil status, of what we may call, in all senses of the term, the body's formality."[16] Photography began to spread in Iran in the 1840s, a few years after its announcement in 1839 in France, and was largely promoted by the initiatives of the Qajar court, especially by the ruler Nasir al-Din Shah Qajar (r. 1848–96). Equally, cinema was introduced in Iran some years after Nasir al-Din Shah's son, Mozaffar al-Din Shah, became aware of it during his visit to Europe at the beginning of the twentieth century. In 1904 the first public cinema was opened in Tehran.[17] In this way, the histories of photography and cinema in Iran more or less proceeded simultaneously with European developments. Harking back to a long and rich visual past, the heterogeneous and complex "nature" of Iranian photography can be characterized by its incipient foreign (European) influences, as well as its prominent local traditions. From the outset, portrait photography and the depiction of the individual ranked among the common categories and practices in the country, much like in Europe and the United States. Therefore, photography in Iran, as in other places, has been a historical and suitable medium for dealing with the constructions of identity.

As opposed to cinema, which has an older history in Iran, video art is a relatively young medium in the Iranian art scene; its history goes back only to the mid-1990s. Since the last decade, an increasing popularity is observable among younger artists who have started their artistic careers primarily through video only.[18] Intervening "at an ideological level by deconstructing and disrupting dominant modes of representation,"[19] video art can be instrumental in delineating contemporary performative strategies which are practiced multifariously by women artists from diverse cultural contexts on a global scale.

To name but a few, video has a number of certain qualities: its expanded range of expressive possibilities, its position as an antistatic, shifting and hybrid medium, its instantaneity and intimacy and its remarkable impact on the viewer. Therefore, video art is an appropriate medium for visual strategies, which aim at the deconstruction and transformation of previously fixed cultural notions of gender, race and class. Hence, it becomes clear why this relatively new medium is popular among women artists in Iran.[20]

With reference to the situation of American and European feminist artists during the 1970s and 1990s, it may be argued that this attraction to video art results from "its lack of a history as an art medium free from the male-dominated precedence of the traditional mediums of painting and sculpture."[21] It is necessary, however, to remark that video art coincides with performance art and can be traced back as early as the 1960s by artists in general. According to Jean Fisher, women "found [that] video and time-based media could provide a method of re-presenting subjectivity and transforming a sense of self-hood from previously fixed notions," and "women's art practice (and that of other marginalized groups) rejected a fascination with the static and autonomous art object, recognizing that it was inadequate as a model of subjectivity in a world of ever-shifting-identities."[22] This aspect of video, which opens new possibilities to express and outline the "ever-shifting identities" of the artist's subjectivity and self, permits a relevant and germinal nexus between the term "performativity" and the works by women Iranian artists discussed in this analysis.

Contemporary Iranian photography and video art are distinguished by their high quality, dynamism, multifaceted richness and complexity and play significant cultural roles inside the country. Michket Krifa describes this phenomenon as a literal explosion of pictures that testifies to the necessity of artistic expression, as well as defines individual identity and confirms the current predominant discourses within the Iranian populace, which manifests its desires for open-mindedness, opening up borders and progressive changes.[23] Galleries, exhibitions and events with their foci on photography and video are continually growing, and different universities with courses in photography have numerous students each year, many of whom are women.

Krifa explains several facets of postrevolutionary Iranian photography that are also partly applicable to video art. According to her analysis, the existential or private perspectives in examples of plastic photography would, by no means, suggest an avoidance of social and political concerns, even though plastic photography does not always express these concerns as blatantly as documentary photography can. In this regard, the careful suggestion and outlining of contours of sociopolitical issues serve as the artists' subtle forms of resistance to the still-prevalent restrictions and censorship that are present not only in the cultural sector but also in society as a whole. As an example of these subtle forms of resistance, she mentions the reversal of reality into metaphor.[24] This artistic strategy of metaphor has established itself increasingly as a prominent feature in the field of Iranian pictorial art. "Metaphors" are achieved lyrically and poetically, allowing the works to transform into subversive art by referring to a mythic or distant past. Such a perspective of diversions and inversions has been formed and stylized by constantly changing cultural codes and is to be understood as a form of transgression and even violation of the arbitrary limits and restrictions imposed on everyday life. In the intimacy of their pictures, Iranian photographers and video artists illustrate their individual perspectives, lives, impressions, sensations and spiritual moments.[25] In these highly creative and imaginative visual representations, the total control of the private is configured by the public.[26]

Although Krifa is certainly correct when she states that the private realm is shaped by the overall surveillance of the public and State, her claim can also be rephrased in another way. Due to several constraints and restrictions imposed by the Iranian government, critical messages in artistic expression often find their articulation less obvious or ambiguous. Thus, many Iranian artists relate their subtexts to topics which concern questions of individual biography, identity and everyday life. In letting the private speak of the public, various possibilities and multifaceted ways are opened for subtle commentaries on society and politics. In other words, the public and official realms of the Iranian State are configured and also subverted through performative strategies that are located in the artist's private and personal scope. Consequently, the State and personal identity are in a continuum of fluid interchanges and have a great impact on each other.

Rosa Issa mentions another important aspect which is distinctive for a younger generation of indigenous Iranian artists. The use of irony and dry humor illustrates the paradoxes with which Iranian women are confronted and in conflict with in a society torn between tradition and modernity, as so many societies are in a moment of globalization.[27] Great talent among Iranian artists is to be found among the younger generation whose works are gaining increasing international attention. Of interest in this context are also the activities of artists of the Iranian Diaspora. Many art students who had lived outside Iran for various reasons during the outbreak of the revolution and war remain abroad. Even now, a wide range of young art students have left or attempted to leave their homeland to study at American or European universities. Beyond that, many Iranian artists are forced to leave Iran due to political reasons or voluntarily emigrate in the hope of finding freer artistic expression.

Performativity

In analyzing women artists' works, I rely on Judith Butler's writings, in which she addresses gender performativity. In her groundbreaking work *Gender Trouble* (1990), she characterizes the notion of gender identity as being performative and an effect of reiterated performative acts and processes of discursive productions that establish the illusionary category of a static, normal and true gender, as well as the constructed binary matrix of normative heterosexuality.[28] In my analysis of the artistic positions of female Iranian photographers and video artists, I take a closer look at the performative subversions and parodic practices, which Butler proposed to deconstruct normative categories of body, sex, gender and sexuality.

The concept of "performance" in general generates from linguistic philosophy of the 1950s when the term was regarded as an antonym to "competence." "Performance" – the applied and embodied language – refers to the actual use of language and means the realization of expressions in a particular situation by an individual speaker. "Competence" is interpreted as a speaker's idealistic notion of being able to form an unlimited number of utterances with a limited number of linguistic elements. The concept of "performance" negates this implicit metalevel of "competence." According to John L. Austin's speech act theory in the posthumously released *How to Do Things with Words* (1962), language has not only a referential but also a performative function. By inaugurating the term "performative speech acts," he opened the "paradigm of performativity" in the field of linguistic utterances.[29] With this designation he was describing speech acts that fulfill actions, "conventional procedures."[30]

A relevant assessment of performative utterances is not their values of truthfulness, but the success or failure of their intended meanings. "Performative," then, is to be understood as the constitution of an important action. Whereas the humanities and social sciences regard texts, monuments and artifacts as sole subjects and research forms in which culture finds its manifestation, anthropologists such as Milton Singer, have stated that culture also was produced by performances.[31] During the 1980s and 1990s, the term "performance" was reintroduced by Michel Foucault,[32] Jacques Derrida,[33] Judith Butler,[34] and Erika Fischer-Lichte.[35] Foucault and Derrida extended the linguistic approximation of the term toward a sociological and critical one, and Butler added the argument of a performative gender identity. Fischer-Lichte, co-founder of the research program Cultures of Performativity,[36] asked for strategies of staging as a performative element in contemporary culture.

According to Butler, the "biological" and "social" sex, as well as sexuality, are considered as performative effects of gender discourses, in which sex is repeatedly fabricated in discursive practices: "There is no gender identity behind the expressions of gender; identity is performatively constituted by the very 'expressions' that are said to be its results."[37] The performative act of embodiment is a condition for the constitution of gender identity.[38] In *Bodies That Matter* (1993), Butler distinguishes between "performativity" and "performance." The latter is understood as a consciously staged enactment and requires the existence of an acting subject that, according to Butler's notion of performativity, is established through carrying out (speech) acts. The success of these acts is dependent on performative utterances and their perceptibility and repeatability within a system of canonical conventions and norms: "[P]erformance as bounded 'act' is distinguished from performativity insofar as the latter consists in a reiteration of norms which precede, constrain and exceed the performer and in that sense cannot be taken as the fabrication of the performer's 'will' or 'choice'; further, what is 'performed' works to conceal, if not to disavow, what remains opaque, unconscious, unperformable. The reduction of performativity to performance would be a mistake."[39] The authority and subsequent impact of performativity are due to permanent ritualizing iterations of socially enforced conventions bound to the binary matrix of heterosexuality. At the same time, the performativity of sexual affiliation enables the undermining of the discursive normalization of gender identity, because the shift of a context, in which an attribution occurs, modifies its meaning. Thus, lapses and displacements and oppositions are located in the repetitive performative practices within the matrix of power that utter gender identity.[40]

In *Gender Trouble*, Butler states, "the parodic repetition of 'the original' [...] reveals the original to be nothing other than a parody of the idea of the natural and the original."[41] Beside failure, citation and recitation, which are crucial to her discussions on subversive gender performative practices, she names parody and travesty as stratagems of subversive repetition that can denaturalize and resignify bodily categories. Butler exemplifies the strategies of parody and travesty by drag performance: "In imitating gender, drag implicitly reveals the imitative structure of gender itself – as well as its contingency."[42] Moreover, she considers citationality and enacted performativity of gender as disputatious practice and political agency. In other words, drag performance attains the imitation or fake of gender through slipping into the role of the other sex, which mostly is accomplished by cross-dressing, makeup, gestures and mimicry. Through this strategic mimesis of gender, the boundaries set by the binary matrix of gender differences and heterosexuality become indistinct. With the possibilities of imitating gender, drag performance unmasks the artificial and constructed texture of gender and thus deconstructs the perception of its authenticity, naturalness, originality and contingency. Regarding the artistic positions in this essay, the concept of drag performance can be linked with the traditional variant of the Iranian dress, the chador. It is interesting to observe, how this garment is used and performed by female artists living in Iran and in the Iranian Diaspora in distinct ways. The issues of drag performance and chador in contemporary Iranian photography and video art can be considered in relation to the artistic positions in this essay.

I also want to bring in the Persian term *naqsh*, which can be associated with performance and performativity and therefore, with the aforementioned subversive artistic strategies. Naqsh has several meanings,[43] yet concerning my discussion here, I use it in terms of copy, model and role. I refer to the exhibition *Naqsh: An Insight into Gender and Role Models in Iran*, held in Berlin in 2008, in which naqsh was associated with traditional and present-day images of gender identities, role models and behavioral patterns in Iran.[44] On one hand, the signification of naqsh is related to artistic portrayals of Self and Other, and on the other hand, it can be referred to as role models that are integral to the social organization and regulation of gender. These role models, constituted by political, social and religious conditions of everyday life, are not static but discussed, criticized and unsettled via subversive artistic strategies: "In affirming, reproducing, questioning or resisting gender categorization in Iranian society."[45] A performative involvement with naqsh at last provides the means to unmask its projection for perceived cultural norms and to unveil it as a powerful social construction. This assessment directly leads to my selected artists' positions. Embarking on performative strategies, the female artists' complex access to categories, such as body/gender/identity, provides fragmentary insights into inter- and transcultural processes in the terrain of contemporary Iranian art and establishes new perspectives in the course of discussing contemporary art from the Middle East.

Two Female Artists from Tehran and One from the Iranian Diaspora in Europe

In the selected works by female Iranian artists, performativity, parody and irony are employed as subversive artistic strategies to challenge gender-specific and sociopolitical conventions and norms. It goes without saying that the artists operate within the "matrix of authority/power" (i.e., the Iranian State) that trespasses its cartographical national borders into the diaspora.[46]

Two photographs by Shadafarin Ghadirian, taken from two different series – *Real Ones* and *West by East* (both 2004) – deal with social and political restrictions and conventions in Iran that are usually fought on the battlegrounds of women's bodies (Figures 11.1, 11.2). Both pictures frankly illustrate the extent of censorship imposed by the current Iranian government. Political laws control mass media and private communication to suppress unwanted content that is contrary to these laws. As Ghadirian's photographs show, such trends are also common in the fields of education and fashion. In *Real Ones*, Ghadirian scanned several books she had read during the 1990s while attending the Azad University and used them as the basis of the series. One sees a depiction from a book about European art history, which shows a painting of Agnès Sorel (1421–50), a favorite mistress of King Charles VII of France (r. 1422–61), produced by the French artist Jean Fouquet (c. 1420–81). In the original painting, Sorel wears a contemporary dress and is veiled with a long and transparent cloth. The visibility of her left breast is the most exciting detail and recalls her status as a mistress at the royal court of King Charles VII. At the same time, this iconography recalls the motif of the Madonna *lactans*, in which Mary is nursing the baby Jesus Christ.

In the course of Ghadirian's act of appropriation, she chose this already repainted image from a book about European art history. It is necessary to know that censored volumes with repainted naked bodily parts are quite common course books at Iranian art universities. In the case of Agnès Sorel, it was not the artist who undertook the overpaintings of her cleavage and breast with a black marker; rather, some government officials had edited the image. Ghadirian only scanned the image and re-presented it as a rather exact and detailed copy of the repainted image in the book.

The artist's active interventions relate to the isolation of a censured image out of the context (i.e., the book). Through this act, possible manipulation in terms of size, color, material and medium may be some of the factors that modify the encountered image in the book. Yet, her act of "copying" follows deliberate and strategic considerations. At this juncture, it is necessary to remind the readers of the wide extent of governmental censorship within the Islamic Republic. Among others, these regularities affect the dress code for Iranian women in the public space, as well as female depictions in general (e.g., those in magazines or books). By her act of appropriation, Ghadirian therefore reiterates a common and official praxis of editorial control, which is emphasized through the image's isolation and ironized through its presentation as an "artwork."

In *West by East*, Ghadirian again thematizes censorship, but applies a slightly different strategy. Here, different posing models are staged in the style of "Western" fashion magazines in her studio. Before taking the photographs, Ghadirian placed a glass between her and the protagonists and painted those parts with a black color, where naked body parts were visible. In a statement by Ghadirian, she expresses her views on censorship: "You know, first we censor ourselves. It is very hard for us, we should tell a story in a way we can and in a way it is possible, and that's because we work much stronger I think […] I prefer to show reality and work for myself, so I have my freedom."[47] According to Ghadirian, a certain kind of self-censorship is usual for artists living and working in Iran. Consequently, this stressful balance between the artist's personal intentions and fulfilling societal norms has immediate effects on the artistic process and the artwork itself. This inevitably developed tactic behind the artistic production demands elaborate and sophisticated preliminary considerations, rather than spontaneous creativity. Ghadirian is working with these given tensions and considers them as an artistic potential rather than solely a hindrance. Her focus on subjects with a strong degree of reality, as well as her decision to work autonomously, would make it possible to gain some liberty within the confines of the State apparatus.

One may link Ghadirian's attitude toward censorship to the concept of the "triple bind," which Trinh T. Minh-ha presented in "Commitment from the Mirror-Writing Box" (1989).[48] Here, Trinh describes the conflicted situation of female writers of color being Third World members. "Triple bind" shows their dilemma of choosing from among three conflicting identities: "Writer of color? Woman writer? Or woman of color?"[49] In the introduction to the German translation of Trinh's *Woman, Native, Other*, Anna Babka also refers to the political perspective of "triple bind" in terms of a "triple discrimination" based on race, class and gender.[50] In addressing censorship in the artistic process, Ghadirian simultaneously thematizes the three issues of gender, ethnicity and profession that reflect Trinh's concept of the "triple bind," Ghadirian's status as a woman, an Iranian and an artist. Currently, she is one of the most famous Iranian photographers in Europe and the United States, making the onus of representation quite enormous on her as an Iranian woman artist. Being in this situation of triple self-censorship and adopting the expurgation of the official requirements of the Iranian government in her appropriations and overpaintings, she only seemingly operates within the predefined guidelines of political policies. At the same time, she also addresses societal topics and restrictions which exist in Iranian everyday life, especially those that affect Iranian women. Consequently, this applied artistic strategy of using a "language or method" similar to that of the official State may also serve as a way to level latent criticism against its limitations and editorial controls.

In titling these works rather cynically with *West by East* or *Real Ones*, Ghadirian's critical review of not only Iranian conventions of censorship, but also of European and American cultural hegemonies, is noticeable. Through Ghadirian's application and appropriation of repainted source material out of European art history, as well as her censuring reenactment of "Western" fashion photography through the bodies of Iranian women, she places her works in between different cultural spheres of Iran and Europe/the United States, thereby leveling criticism at both the "East" and "West." Her parodic approach is also perceptible in the titling of the two photographic series. *Real Ones* ironically alludes to the notion of the "genuine" and "authentic" artwork that generated in European art history. At the same time, in view of the black censoring color, the term "real" refers to sociopolitical realities and representational politics of the Iranian State that form a distinctive contrast to European conventions. In the title *West by East,* these cultural dichotomies are addressed in a very direct manner: bound to the clothing regulations of the Iranian State, "Eastern women" are representing "Western" fashionable trends. Therefore, both titles reflect Ghadirian's skeptical attitude toward

European hegemonies and the cultural and social conventions of the Iranian State. This critical transcultural approach is accompanied by the concept of the "triple bind," which addresses her status being a woman, an Iranian and an artist in the context of (self-) censorship. Additionally, she could also be seen as an artist who carries the heavy burden of speaking for the Iranian State outside Iran.[51]

In the video *Self-Portrait* (7 mins 19 secs, 2007–2008), Simin Keramati deals with her own female identity (Figures 11.3, 11.4). Stylistically, she acts with a successful combination of text and image. According to alphabetic conventions, written texts in both Persian and English appear from right to left and vice versa on the dark screen and seem to reflect Keramati's personal handwriting. These seemingly diary entries make visible her personal thoughts and emotional states to the viewer: "I do walk a lot these days; I just want to get rid of my thoughts."[52] Later, one can read that she poetically puts her mind under her feet while walking, and listen to the sound of footsteps and breathing. Behrang Samadzadegan has correctly stated that Keramati's focus on the "self" happens in the audio-visual context of her internal and external worlds in a narrative, blunt and simplistic style.[53] In the video, the two layers of her outer and inner lives coincide with the activities of walking and the artist's personal wish to break away from her thoughts. It is interesting that only the sound suggests that she is located outdoors; one can listen to the rustling of leaves, which is eventually caused by her footsteps.

In using both the Persian and English languages, the artist anticipates a local as well as an international audience, although she is based in Iran. After one minute, Keramati herself appears in the middle of the dark screen, and her countenance is serious and motionless. A threatening black liquid begins to spread over her left eye and quickly occupies the whole face. Therefore, under pressure, her writings seem to come out faster and more hectic, and several words are erased again, although the canceling of expressions is a defining feature of this video. It is the rapidly expanding dark fluid that hinders and undermines her recordings. So, the impression is created that the artist, who obviously is threatened in her existence, is writing against time. Before the black color has finally wiped out Keramati's face completely, leaving only her scarf visible, the spectator can read the artist's final notes: "There is always this portrait of myself, melting, while walking I feel drops of my face, running over each other and fall into nowhere, and at last, I find myself walking on the streets of this city while I am faceless."[54] In the light of these last comments and Keramati's effaced countenance, there are various possible meanings and implications. The drops of her face can be interpreted as her tears and be identified with the black liquid. The latter can be exposed as a metaphorical emblem of personal depressive thoughts and sociopolitical conditions in the context of the Iranian State.

Keramati dramatically addresses the process of losing her own face – that is identity; the "surviving" element is only the heavily symbolic veil, demonstrated by the black ink. Thus, the artist is performing the interrelation and interaction between the visual items of the face, veil and personal handwriting and the rather abstract idea of "identity." Together, these factors construct an image which can be defined or identified as a self-portrait of the artist. The displayed elements, such as Keramati's face and handwriting, are deeply associated with her personal identity. The veil, beside the artist's handwriting, finally remains as the only visible icon in the video and functions as a general emblematic indicator of cultural conventions in Islamicate societies, such as Iran, where women are obliged to wear the veil. In regard to Keramati's work, the veil reflects uniformity, which, together with the ominous black liquid, seems to conflict with the other signs, such as the face and handwriting that represent the artist's self and personal identity. The ink as a strong visual icon can be related to writing and expression and signify censorship in a metaphorical way, which can be connected to Ghadirian's works. Even though Keramati appears faceless at the end of the video, her handwriting and, by association, her personal and underlying messages, keep on proceeding before the screen finally obscures. Beyond that, the viewer can still listen to the sound of her breathing and footsteps. Therefore, Keramati challenges several normative characteristics that are closely linked to the allocation and determination of identity. In addition to the sounds in the video, it is her writing that suggests that she has not been silenced. The script as the carrier of messages can also be interpreted as a sign of resistance and agency. In the context of the State of Iran, it is interesting that both Keramati and Ghadirian are addressing censorship in relation to the veil. In this regard, the black liquid or color, together with the veil, is a metaphor for censorship and concealment of female identities, whereas perhaps female Iranian artists in the diaspora would not employ the veil in a similar manner.

At this juncture, it is interesting to compare these two visual strategies of depicting female Iranian identity by an artist who lives and works in a European country. Hamid Naficy has strikingly described the Iranian Diaspora artists' situation, in which they are among an ever-growing group of intellectual artists in Europe whose creations transcend boundaries of style, genre, gender, race, nationality, ethnicity, language and culture. Many of them are exiles, émigrés and casualties of the diaspora who live in an oppressive space of cultural difference. They are situated in a position in which "home" is neither here nor there and this status of being "in between" may also form their authority. According to Naficy, these exiles move in between the crevices of various social collectives and artistic approaches. Thus, they are also in a position to criticize accepted values and practices, both in their homeland and their adopted countries. As this criticism lends to certain accents in their work, he describes the work of filmmakers, such as that of Shirin Neshat (b. 1957), as a "cinema of accents," giving expression to a sense of rootlessness, while simultaneously embodying it.[55] In focusing on representations of women in general, and more specifically on self-displays, various female Iranian artists living in the diaspora reveal this embodiment or reflections of it. In dealing with artists of the Iranian Diaspora, however, it is important to consider the different motifs and reasons why they left or had to leave their homeland. In this respect, one has to differentiate between the various generations of emigrating artists. Rose Issa has described some of the geographical and cultural paths that Iranian artists may follow: some have left their country permanently, some return regularly to their country of origin for inspiration, some live outside Iran but are inspired by events within it, while others live abroad and challenge global concepts by navigating between Iran and their adopted country.[56] Parastou Forouhar is assigned to the latter group.[57]

Based in Germany since 1991, Forouhar is an artist who travels from Europe to Tehran nearly every year. Her artistic work is closely associated with the 1998 murder of her parents, Dariush and Parvaneh Forouhar, who were oppositional politicians in Iran.

In the course of this discussion, if there are differences or parallels in the aesthetic and artistic language among the artists living in Iran and those in the diaspora, it may be helpful to consider aspects of performative identity in Forouhar's work.

Parastou Forouhar primarily concentrates on the political context of Iran and subverts constructs of the Other. As shown daily in international mass media, the chador, veil, beard and turban are all visual signs of Arabs (who are often conflated with Iranians), regardless if those mediated images hold truths or not. Forouhar only seemingly meets these expectations, playing with what is intrinsically one's own Self and the foreign Other and between tradition and modernity, as well as other dialectical categories, such as male and female.[58] In respect to one of Forouhar's artistic concerns, her following statement seems useful: "Which space will be granted to art in the new world order, and what significance will be lent art from foreign regions? Western society's interest in art and culture from the Oriental–Islamic world has increased rapidly. Perhaps this is a well-meant attempt to find out more about these societies. But how open are Western societies and how many Oriental–Islamic features must this art contain in order to be recognized as such?"[59] The artist's critical interrogations recall the notion of "exoticism," which Keshmirshekan has identified as one of the main concerns and features in Iranian contemporary art.[60] Forouhar also problematizes the rising international – mostly "Western" in terms of American or European – concern in arts from Islamic-coined cultural spheres. In still pursuing sentiments of Orientalism[61] – which may happen consciously or unconsciously – this "Western" interest is often accompanied by expectations of the character and texture of artworks produced in the Middle East. These artworks should display "exotic" or "Oriental" traits to be discernible and identifiable and therefore live up to these expectations. Certainly, these requirements may affect the artistic work in negative ways. As a female Iranian artist living in Germany, Forouhar is fully aware of these difficulties. In her artwork, she has developed certain strategic interventions to challenge and dismantle those monolithic beliefs, conceptions and perspectives concerning "Islam"/"Islamic" or "Iran"/"Iranian."

A photograph in Forouhar's series *Swanrider II* (2004) may illustrate her strategy of an ironic play of differences (Figure 11.5). A woman, who is recognizably the artist herself dressed in a black chador, is riding along a river on a huge white swan. The contrast between black and white, which dominates the scene, refers to the way fairy tales are structured by opposites, such as good and evil, fortune and misfortune and beautiful and ugly. According to Alexandra Karentzos, there are also echoes of Hans Christian Andersen's tale of the ugly duckling (1843) that becomes a beautiful swan: "It is the tale of the outsider who becomes the radiant focus of attention – for the supposed duck is rejected because it is different and has dark feathers. Such references to miraculous transformations are an ironic take on the role of the woman in the dark chador."[62] In the course of the association with a common European fairy tale, it becomes clear that the dark garment, representing the duckling's dark feathers, suggest alterity, Otherness and (cultural) difference. Being "different" in terms of having another physical appearance, which would not conform to the norms of a particular society, would, for the most part, result in prejudice, refusal and discrimination. Considering Forouhar's work, it may be asked whether the woman in the black chador would experience a similar "miraculous transformation" as the ugly duckling, how she would look like afterward and if she may be exempted from her role as an outsider. Taken together, the artist cynically reflects perceptual processes related to cultural conventions peculiar to Western Europe, where she is now living.

Karentzos also points out that the image reminds one of other metamorphoses in European culture, such as Richard Wagner's opera *Lohengrin* (1850). On the condition of keeping his identity a secret, Lohengrin appears to defend Princess Elsa of Brabant from the false accusation of killing her younger brother Gottfried. Lohengrin is then appointed leader of the duchy of Brabant and, despite intrigues, marries Elsa. Because his spouse is asking for his name and origins, Lohengrin, Parzival's son and delegate of the circle of the Holy Grail, finally has to leave. The knight in shining armour, the epitome of the German ur-myth, is carried on a boat drawn by a swan who later turns out to be Gottfried. For her own performance, Forouhar has chosen the town of Bad Ems on the river Lahn in Germany. In her photograph, however, the swan is an ordinary paddleboat, and the veiled woman is marked out as foreign and "Other."

Finally, in accordance with Karentzos, there is also a reference to the myth of Leda and the swan, in which the god Zeus seduces the beautiful virgin Leda in the guise of a swan. In the photograph, it is not Zeus who covers the woman, but the chador that spreads out ornamentally over the swan. Seemingly dominating the scenery, it is the woman in the black chador who is sitting on the swan that is the figurative version of god Zeus. Considering the image in this way, the act of the rape is virtually reverted. In addition to this aspect, there is also the classical interpretative possibility to read the Zeus metaphor in Forouhar's photograph. In this case, "[T]he woman [...] is introduced to us as a character obscured by her chador which is covering and protecting her against men."[63] At the same, the chador can also fail to function as an icon of protection or deterrent against male intentions, which is another option to reading the image.

In adopting significations, by which European societies construct and define their identities, "[T]his work by Forouhar is clearly aimed at a Western audience, or at viewers familiar with Western cultural traditions, whereas in Iran, the different cultural context would stand in the way of these interpretative associations."[64] Based on a European approach, at first sight, the depiction of a woman in a chador sitting on a swan-like paddleboat evokes tension and incoherence. These perceptions are predominantly grounded in the heavily symbolic veil and its stereotypical connotations, for instance, repression and passivity. In combining the protagonist with a paddleboat in the form of a swan, the situation escalates in scurrility, while at the same time, associations with those fairy tales and myths out of a European cultural context become possible. It is interesting that both the artists in Iran and diaspora, Ghadirian and Forouhar are quoting old European culture. In the case of Forouhar, the whole staging is chiefly constructed and performed for a European adoption. Nevertheless, it is possible that some of these associations, such as Leda and the swan, are also to the common knowledge in Iran due to Iran's own ancient classical heritage. Hence, even a different cultural context must not always act as a stumbling block to the interpretative approaches of an artwork. In terms of the work's affiliation to the Iranian State, it is noticeable that it is the chador which is performed as a metaphor for censorship, as well as its index for alterity in a European State.

The selected artistic positions demonstrated the different visual strategies of articulation, visualization and performance of female Iranian identity. The link between the discussed artists is their attempts to deconstruct stereotypes of traditional European perceptions of gender roles in the context of an Islamic Iranian structure of society. At the same time, clichéd Iranian perspectives are addressed, especially the State mandate to wear *hejab* (Islamic dress). In an act of appropriation, Ghadirian employs female depictions from European art history with overpainted nude body parts and represents them as autonomous masterpieces, ironically entitled *Real Ones*. Alternatively, she stages models in the manner of fashion magazines in her studio and "censors" parts of their bodies with black color. Beside Trinh T. Minh-ha's concept of the triple bind, the performance of the censured women in the photographs reflects the artist's application of a strategy of parodic iterations and imitations of social conventions and norms, which reveal the powerful processes involved in gender constructions.

Keramati also dramatically addresses the seeming loss of her identity with the *mise-en-scène* of her own person, the visualization of her handwriting and the scoring of her breath, all of which serve as indicators of self-reference. She performs and stages her own body both calmly and motionlessly as the target of black liquid. Although her face is wiped out in the end of the work, she still possesses her beliefs and thoughts that she expresses in terms of her handwriting. Through these conflicting semiotic signs, Keramati challenges several normative features that are ostensibly closely linked with the assignment and determination of "identity."

In relation to diasporic artists, Parastou Forouhar's critical play, with the expectations of how an "Iranian" woman should be, confronts the European gaze with different, unusual perspectives and compels the viewer to differentiate between these various perspectives. The viewer's own image of the strange is further estranged, further turning it into an alien image itself.[65]

One of the most complex issues is that of the differences in the visual languages between the artists living and working in Tehran and those of the European diaspora. Here, it rather seems impossible to allege absolute and generalizing criteria, but as already pointed out, it is necessary to reflect on the different generations of emigrating artists and their respective circumstances in leaving their homeland. In the case of Forouhar, she retains strong associations with her native country through her continued travels to Tehran, as well as her contact and dialogue with Tehran's art scene. The situation of being "in between" different cultures has led her to an artistic approach of combining and bringing together the distinct features and particularities of Iranian culture with her host country's culture. Here, it is interesting to note that Forouhar focuses on the articulation and staging of the black chador in public spaces, as opposed to Ghadirian's and Keramati's feelings of Otherness that are conceptualized quite differently. In their works, they almost imply that it is a private or an inner space, which can be seen as a censorship of the mind.

While imbedding the chador – a visual icon with close references to Iranian culture and society – in their artworks, Iranian women artists simultaneously introduce other semiotic levels that are entangled with cultural conventions and the viewing patterns of their host countries. In reference to European art history or through the integration of English translations of the Persian language, both Ghadirian and Keramati obviously address an international audience and therefore seem to operate from another kind of "in between" situation, which has developed in their country itself. This condition seems somehow to result from the transcultural exchanges and also the internal tensions between the private and the public and the local and the global (i.e., cultural heritage, indigenous imagery, globalization and international art). Ghadirian and Keramati focus on sociopolitical or personal subjects taken from their lives that are interwoven into Iranian culture. At the same time, they bring in international references or topics that address and affect human beings in general.

In conclusion, I suggest that in the selected three artistic positions, we can identify more common than distinctive characteristics. One of these linking points is the ambiguity or negation of a distinct geographical localization. The settings given in the photographs or video stills could have occurred any place in the world and are not bound to a specific culture. A next point is the usage of the chador. Whereas the chador is clearly detectable in Forouhar's work, Ghadirian applies censorship in terms of overpaintings of body parts with a black color, and Keramati uses the black backdrop and the diffusing liquid over her face. As pointed out in these artworks, the articulations and depictions of female "Iranian" identity are intensely associated with several performative concepts of representation. These strategic and subversive approaches encompass irony, parody, metaphor and symbolic ideas that are related to female bodies in the private or public realm. Both in Iran and the Iranian Diaspora in Europe, female artists provide insight into personal examinations of the concepts of the self, gender and perception. As a result, images are created, which address issues of the social place of the body and the complexity of gender relations and their interactions with sociopolitical power relations. At the least, these artistic positions stage and expose the constructed nature of gender and power relations, as well as their sedimentary processes and stabilizations, both inside and outside Iran. These performative and destabilizing strategies applied in contemporary art find their inscriptions from the patterns of Iranian society and State and form part of the wave of sociopolitical transformation and change.

Notes and References

1 Mahmoud M. Mamdani, *Good Muslim, Bad Muslim: America, the Cold War, and the Roots of Terror* (New York: Pantheon, 2004), 18.

2 Salah M. Hassan, "Contemporary 'Islamic' Art: Western Curatorial Politics of Representation in Post 9/11," in *The Future of Tradition – The Tradition of Future: 100 Years after the Exhibition Masterpieces of Muhammadan Art in Munich*, ed. Chris Dercon et al. (Munich: Prestel, 2010), 34–5.

3 The utilization of the colonial and quite blank term "Western" needs to be problematized here. If Said's argument that the Orient is a political representation and fantasy of the Occident, so are "Eastern" and "Western." Truly, these terms tell us nothing about geographical locations or their cultures. See Edward W. Said, *Orientalism* (New York: Vintage, 1979).

4 Hassan, "Contemporary 'Islamic' Art," 35.

5 Jessica Winegar, "The Humanity Game: Art, Islam, and the War on Terror," *Anthropological Quarterly* 81 (2008): 651–81; Finbarr Barry Flood, "From the Prophet to Postmodernism? New World Orders and the End of Islamic Art," in *Making Art History: A Changing Discipline and its Institutions*, ed. Elizabeth Mansfield (London: Routledge, 2007), 31–53.

6 Anthony Downey, "Centralizing Margins and Marginalizing Centers: Diasporas and Contemporary Iranian Art," in *Iran Inside Out: Influences of Homeland and Diaspora on the Artistic Language of Contemporary Iranian Artists*, ed. Sam Bardaouil and Till Fellrath (New York: Chelsea Art Museum, 2009), unpaginated.

7 Ibid.

8 Hamid Keshmirshekan, "The Question of Identity vis-à-vis Exoticism in Contemporary Iranian Art," *Iranian Studies* 43, no. 4 (September 2010): 489–512.

9 First, Keshmirshekan defines a local, historical, imagined and collective identity and also self-identity, thereby addressing how artists have interpreted contemporary aesthetics in light of national and indigenous ideologies. The second issue is related to the ever-present obsession with cultural and indigenous ideologies and can be seen as an outcome of the first. Both of them involve challenges relating to the conception of "Self" and "Other," as well as the issue of "expectation." Ibid., 489.

10 Ibid., 498–9.

11 Ibid., 506–7.

12 Ibid., 512.

13 The chador is a loose female garment covering the body, sometimes also the face. For an extensive explanation of this piece of clothing and its historical context in Iran, see *Encyclopaedia Iranica*, s.v. "Čādor (2)."

14 Here, I address the headscarf bans for teaching staff in schools and universities in several German federal states and the French parliamentary order of a headscarf ban in public facilities in 2004, as well as the more recent prohibition against wearing the burqa in official French departments and administrative bodies.

15 Kerstin Brandes, *Fotografie und "Identität": Visuelle Repräsentationspolitiken in künstlerischen Arbeiten der 1980er und 1990er Jahre* [Photography and identity: The visual politics of representation in artwork of the 1980s and 1990s) (Bielefeld: transcript Verlag, 2010), 18.

16 Roland Barthes, *Camera Lucida: Reflections on Photography*, trans. Richard Howard (New York: Hill and Wang, 1981), 79.

17 Hamid Reza Sadr, *Iranian Cinema: A Political History* (London: I.B. Tauris, 2006), 9.

18 Susan Habib and Helia Darabi, "Video Art as a Rising Medium in Iranian Contemporary Art" (paper presented at the International Congress of Aesthetics: "Aesthetics Bridging Cultures," Ankara, Turkey, July 9–13, 2007).

19 Ibid.

20 In contrast to film, there are almost no essays or books on video art in Iran. Beside this lack of basic literature, it would make for a future study to analyze the impact of past and present approaches to video art by female Iranian artists who took up this medium in the mid-1990s.

21 Chris Meigh-Andrews, *A History of Video Art: The Development of Form and Function* (Oxford: Berg Publishers, 2006), 236.

22 Jean Fisher, "Reflections on Echo: Sound by Women Artists in Britain," in *Signs of the Times: A Decade of Video, Film and Slide-Tape Installation in Britain 1980–1990*, ed. Chrissie Iles (Oxford: Museum of Modern Art, 1990), 62.

23 Michket Krifa, "Iran, une révolution photographique [Iran, a photographic revolution]," in *Regards persans: Iran une révolution photographique* [Persian gazes: Iran, a photographic revolution], ed. Michket Krifa (Paris: Paris Musées, 2001), 20.

24 In dealing with metaphor as one of the characteristics of contemporary art, see Craig Owens, "The Allegorical Impulse: Toward a Theory of Postmodernism," *October* 13 (1980): 58–80.

25 Krifa, "Iran, une révolution photographique," 21.

26 Michket Krifa, "La photographie plasticienne ou les interrogations du Moi," in *Regards persans: Iran une révolution photographique* [Persian gazes: Iran, a photographic revolution], ed. Michket Krifa (Paris: Paris Musées, 2001), 32–3.

27 Rose Issa specifically addresses the works of the female artists Bita Fayyazi, Shadi Ghadirian and Ghazel in "Borrowed Ware," in *Contemporary Iranian Art*, ed. Rose Issa et al. (London: Booth-Clibborn Editions, 2001), 26–7.

28 Judith Butler, *Gender Trouble: Feminism and the Subversion of Identity*, rev. ed. (1990; repr., New York: Routledge, 2007).

29 John L. Austin, *Zur Theorie der Sprechakte* [How to do things with words], ed. Eike von Savigny (Stuttgart: Reclam, 1979), 35, 45–6. Compare also with Walburga Hülk, "Paradigma Performativität" [Paradigm of performativity] in *Avantgarde-Medien-Performativität: Inszenierungs- und Wahrnehmungsmuster zu Beginn des 20. Jahrhunderts* [Avantgarde-media-performativity: Stagings and perceptions at the beginning of the twentieth century], ed. Marijana Erstic and Gregor Schuhen (Bielefeld: transcript Verlag, 2005), 2–3.

30 John L. Austin, *Zur Theorie der Sprechakte*, 35, 45–6.

31 Milton Singer shaped the term "cultural performance" at the end of the 1950s and used it to describe the "particular instances of cultural organization, e.g., weddings, temple festivals, recitations, plays, dances, musical concerts etc." Milton Singer, *Traditional India: Structure and Change* (Philadelphia: American Folklore Society, 1959), xii–xiii.

32 Foucault problematizes the iteration and repeatability of language utterances and emphasizes the consequent difficulties to determine identity. Beyond that, he undertakes the monumentalization and materialization of the notion of performance. According to him, the materiality of a language utterance is constitutive of the utterance itself, because it requires substance, a carrier, a place and a date; if these situational indices change, the utterance modifies its identity, too. Michel Foucault, *Die Archäologie des Wissens* [The archeology of knowledge] (Frankfurt: Suhrkamp Verlag, 1969), 147. Uwe Wirth, "Der Performanzbegriff im Spannungsfeld von Illokution, Iteration und Indexikalität" [The concept of performance in the field of tension between illocution, iteration and indexicality], in *Performanz: Zwischen Sprachphilosophie und Kulturwissenschaften* [Performance: Between linguistics and cultural studies], ed. Uwe Wirth (Frankfurt: Suhrkamp Verlag, 2002), 42–3.

33 In the course of his deconstructionist critique of the speech act theory, Derrida introduces the categories of success and failure of speech acts and confronts the speech act theory, as Foucault does, with the problem of iteration as recitation. Therefore, he brings together the notion of performance with that of script: the functionality of language generally is linked with that of script in Derrida's sense. Jacques Derrida, "Signatur Ereignis Kontext" [Signature event context], in *Limited Inc*, trans. Werner Rappl (Vienna: Passagen Verlag, 2001), 38–9; Wirth, "Der Performanzbegriff im Spannungsfeld von Illokution, Iteration und Indexikalität," 19.

34 Butler, *Gender Trouble.*

35 Central to Fischer-Lichte's theatrical concept of performance, which is placed in a mutual dependency between the terms staginess and enactment, are corporeal aspects. She links staginess and performativity and distinguishes four different aspects: performance, enactment, corporality and perception. Performance is defined as a process of representation through the body and voice in front of physically attendant spectators. Erika Fischer-Lichte, "Grenzgänge und Tauschhandel: Auf dem Weg zu einer performativen Kultur" [Bordercrossings and negotiations: Toward a performative culture], in *Performanz: Zwischen Sprachphilosophie und Kulturwissenschaften* [Performance: Between linguistics and cultural studies], ed. Uwe Wirth (Frankfurt: Suhrkamp Verlag, 2002), 299.

36 Erika Fischer-Lichte, "List of All Projects: Aesthetic of the Performative," October 25, 2008, accessed November 2, 2012, http://www.sfb-performativ.de/seiten/b1_vorhaben_engl.html.

37 Butler, *Gender Trouble*, 34.

38 Judith Butler, "Performative Acts and Gender Constitution: An Essay in Phenomenology and Feminist Theory," in *Writing on the Body: Female Embodiment and Feminist Theory*, ed. Katie Conboy et al. (New York: Columbia University Press, 1997), 402.

39 Judith Butler, *Bodies That Matter: On the Discursive Limits of "Sex,"* (London/ New York: Routledge, 1993), 234.

40 Based on Butler's books *Gender Trouble*, *Bodies That Matter* and *The Psychic Life of Power*, Hannelore Bublitz provides a useful synopsis on Butler's notion of "gender performativity." Hannelore Bublitz, *Judith Butler zur Einführung* [Introduction of Judith Butler] (Hamburg: Junius Verlag, 2007), 70–74.

41 Butler, *Gender Trouble*, 43.

42 Ibid., 187.

43 B. N. Goswamy mentions the following meanings of the term *naqsh*: painting, printing, staining of two or more colors, embroidering, carving and engraving. Additionally, he brings up the association of the word with the rituals of an order among the Sufis, the *naqshband*. He translates the term "naqshband" as pattern-drawer in "Pattern-drawers of Benares," *The Tribune*, October 5, 2003, accessed November 2, 2012, http://www.tribuneindia.com/2003/20031005/spectrum/art.htm.

44 Melanie Nazmy-Gandchi, *Naqsh: An Insight into Gender and Role Models in Iran* (Berlin: Museum für islamische Kunst, Pergamonmuseum, 2008), 4–5.

45 Ibid., 4.

46 Here, I adopt Bublitz's term, which can be identified with Butler's notion of the binary matrix of heterosexuality or the matrix of intelligibility. Bublitz, *Judith Butler zur Einführung*, 75.

47 Julia Allerstorfer, "Shadafarin Ghadirian: An Iranian Artist in the Field of Tension between Tradition and Modernity" (MA thesis, University of Vienna, 2004), 123.

48 Trinh T. Minh-ha, "Commitment from the Mirror-Writing Box," in Trinh T. Minh-ha, *Woman, Native, Other: Writing Postcoloniality and Feminism* (Bloomington: Indiana University Press, 1989), 5–44.

49 Ibid., 6.

50 Anna Babka, introduction to Trinh T. Minh-ha, *Woman, Native, Other. Postkolonialität und Feminismus schreiben* [Woman, native, other: Writing postcoloniality and feminism], ed. Anna Babka, trans. Kathrina Menke (Vienna: Turia & Kant Verlag, 2010), 12.

51 In this regard, it is interesting to quote another statement by Ghadirian that reflects her skepticism about diasporic artists speaking for an Iranian identity. When I asked her about her opinion of Shirin Neshat's photographical series *Women of Allah* (1990s), Ghadirian answered: "I like her photos very much; unfortunately I had never the possibility to meet her. More than her photos, I like her videos, in my opinion they are stronger. But there's a problem I have with Shirin Neshat, she does not live in Iran, so I think she isn't really in touch with our problems here. She is in another country, America, and wants to tell about the problems of Iranian women. I have to think about that when I look at her photos and her imagination about the veil." Allerstorfer, "Shadafarin Ghadirian," 126.

52 Video-stills with excerpts from Simin Keramati's handwriting can be found on her official website, accessed November 2, 2012, http://www.siminkeramati.com/gallery_17.html#

53 Behrang Samadzadegan, "The Judge of Other's Judgement: A Glance at the Works of Simin Keramati," *Art Tomorrow* 3 (Winter 2011): 83.

54 Keramti, official website, accessed November 2, 2012, http://www.siminkeramati.com/gallery_17.html#

55 Hamid Naficy, "Parallele Welten, Über die Videoarbeiten Shirin Neshats" [Parallel worlds], in *Shirin Neshat*, ed. Gerald Matt and Julia Peyton-Jones (Vienna: Kunsthalle, 2000), 42–4.

56 Rose Issa, "The Fabric of Life and Art: the Emergence of A New Aesthetic Language," in *Amidst Shadow and Light: Contemporary Iranian Art and Artists*, ed. Hamid Keshmirshekan (Hong Kong: Liaoning Creative Press, 2011), 169–70.

57 Ibid.

58 Alexandra Karentzos, "The Location of Art: Parastou Forouhar's Displacements," in *Intersections–Reading the Space* (Melbourne: Jewish Museum of Australia, 2005), 54–67, accessed November 2, 2012, http://www.parastou-forouhar.de/english/texts/The-Location-of-Art.html

59 Parastou Forouhar, "Andersdenkende" [Protestors], in *Der Orient, Die Fremde: Positionen zeitgenössischer Kunst und Literatur* [The Orient, the hinterland: Positions in contemporary art and literature], ed. Regina Göckede and Alexandra Karentzos (Bielefeld: transcript Verlag, 2006), 125–6.

60 Keshmirshekan, "The Question of Identity vis-à-vis Exoticism in Contemporary Iranian Art," 489.

61 In *Orientalism,* Said has developed the concept of Orientalism, which he exposed as a comprehensive, interdisciplinary discussion of an entire epoch. The publication serves as a key document in postcolonial theory and describes how Other (Eastern or Oriental) cultures are represented and therefore created by dominant (Western or Occidental) cultures. This discourse has been used to expand European colonial domination: the supposed knowledge of the Orient has served for a direct exercise of power but also for the legitimacy of violence.

62 Alexandra Karentzos, "Unterscheiden des Unterscheidens: Ironische Techniken in der Kunst Parastou Forouhars" [Other of the other: Ironic techniques in the art of Parastou Forouhar], in *Der Orient, die Fremde. Positionen zeitgenössischer Kunst und Literatur* [The Orient, the hinterland: Positions in contemporary art and literature], ed. Regina Göckede and Alexandra Karentzos (Bielefeld: transcript Verlag, 2006), 134.

63 Hamid Jalili, "Iraj Mirza: Blowing Our Cover, Beware of People's Various Facades, Be It a Chador or…," *The Iranian,* October 2, 1998, accessed November 2, 2012, http://www.iranian.com/Features/Oct98/Irajm/index.html

64 Karentzos, "Unterscheiden des Unterscheidens: Ironische Techniken in der Kunst Parastou Forouhars," 135.

65 Karentzos, "The Location of Art," accessed November 2, 2012, http://www.parastou-forouhar.de/english/texts/The-Location-of-Art.html

12

PAINTED AND ANIMATED METAPHORS: AN INTERVIEW WITH ARTIST ALIREZA DARVISH

Mina Zand Siegel and Carmen Pérez González

The most striking aspect of the paintings of artist Alireza Darvish (b. 1968) is the use of symbolism, although the "symbolism" itself is subject to change and redefinition in his works. Whereas in his earlier illustrations, images and recurring elements are used as symbols and representatives of something "forbidden" or even "impossible" (Figures 12.1, 12.2), they gradually turn into subject matter in their own right in his later works (Figure 12.3). Darvish, starting his artistic career at the dawn of the Islamic Republic (after 1979) with its unwelcome restrictions forcefully imposed on society and felt painfully by all those who had a calling for expressing themselves, had to take refuge like others in a world of the permissible to express the nonpermissible. The symbol "fish" became a substitute for women, sensuality and female productivity (Figure 12.4), elephants for resilience, steadfastness and looking for a way to survive, and books for the essence of life – knowledge and information (Figures 12.5, 12.7).

Time and again, Darvish has used his own symbols to express not only the forbidden, but also to challenge and criticize the act of forbidding. Whereas certain books are not allowed to be published and read, and thus ideas remain unexpressed, his images set forth to challenge this silence. Lips are sewn, and book covers bear stitches. Whereas movements are controlled, mobility and travelling are restricted and particular gatherings are considered to crimes, the desire to move and flee creeps under the scales of fishes to slip out of sight to the depth of freedom – swift and fast.

Mina Zand Siegel and Carmen Pérez González: When did you start your career and how did it begin?

Alireza Darvish: I was only 14 [in 1982] when I left home in Rasht and went to the capital city Tehran to continue my education in painting in the country's only art academy [School of Visual Arts]. Tehran, with a population of 10 million in those days, was a wild city, burning with war fever [during the Iran–Iraq War, 1980–88], where the march of death was the only melody of the time. But our academy of art was a safe island of calm and quiet in the middle of all this chaos and insecurity.

There, my art historian teacher Mr Samii, a poet and a literary critic, played an important role in the development of my thought and contributed to my transformation into whom I became. He was the first one who taught me and encouraged me to free myself from the dogmas I had picked up in the early years of the [Iranian] Revolution [1978–79] and taught me to be a freethinker. He introduced me to contemporary, as well as classic, Iranian and world culture and literature. He coached me to return to books with a new perspective, albeit more vivid and more creative.

Shortly after graduating, I had an exhibit in the famous Noor Gallery in Tehran, which happened to be successful, and led me to more exhibits in very famous and upscale galleries, such as Seyhoon and Sabz. I was only 19 and still too young to attract the attention of the giants of the field, such as [artists] Massoumeh Seyhoon [1934–2010] and ʻAli Akbar Sadeghi [b. 1937], as I later did.

Of course, I did have my own share of failure during those years, as well. I had an exhibit in the Sabz Gallery in which I sold almost all my works. Walking home with a bag full of money, as was customary in the revolution's early years, a motorcycle ran by and grabbed my bag and disappeared into the crowded traffic of Tehran. The first policeman who could have reached the guy refused to help: "This is not within the range of my activity," he said very casually. I wound up paying the gallery fee and commission out of [my own] pocket!

My professional artistic career as an illustrator started at the age of 20 when I started working in the prestigious literary magazine *Donya-ye Sokhan* (The world of speech). This magazine was one of the two rare literary and cultural publications that had survived [the revolution] and continued to survive with much effort. There, not only did I find the opportunity to meet many of the great names in art and literature, but I also stumbled on a subject which is still the main "persona" in my works, the book. Making a design for an article about book burning, something that [had] happened quite so often before the Islamic Revolution during the last years of previous regime [Pahlavi dynasty, 1925–79], was quite shocking to me and opened a new era in my life. It involved me in a subject that I had felt with all my heart and mind – a subject so close to me emotionally that it became the subject of my works to this very day, as you can see. I used the book as the subject of my work and as a building block of my paintings. I used it both as a symbol and as a real object of my interest.

I continued working in this magazine, as well as in *Naqsh-e Qalam* (The role of the pen) magazine in Rasht out of my love and admiration for both of them. I also taught in the School of Visual Arts in Tehran, the same school I had graduated from, and also holding workshops in the Cubic Studio until I left the county.

MZS & CPG: In Iran, you had a distinct visual language. Were you able to use the same language in Europe, too? Do you think that the social, political or artistic atmosphere has any effect on the visual language characterizes your work?

AD: The imagery in my early paintings and illustrations in Iran was actually a reflection of our experiences, our worries and concerns, as well as our ideals of those times; though, like many other artists of our time, I chose to present those realities in the form of symbols. When citizens are barred form using a clear straight talk, when censorship rules, not only does this domination itself become a subject of the artist's discourse, but it forces him to employ the language of metaphors, similes and symbols. But whereas this media makes arts more colorful and has aesthetic value, it reduces or even eliminates the human values in arts: directness, clarity and transparency.

In my early works in Iran, I used symbolism quite abundantly, but after living a few years in Germany, very surprisingly, I noticed that I had no use for it. I did not need to use a symbol for every fact of life. Indeed, all those symbols were the products of the complicated and difficult conditions of life in Iran, where my audience was used to receiving a message through a labyrinth of signs and symbols. I found that my audience here in Germany is not used to this – this kind of indirect communication was unknown to them. I found that the language I had learned and was familiar with was of no use to me in the West and I'd better learn the language of my host society. Gradually, I even learned different ways to see things, something I had not learned before. This may explain my "noncreative" first few years in Germany when I mostly imitated modern art. They were not good works; they didn't come from my inner soul. It took me a few years to regain my self-confidence and my artistic balance.

This does not mean I abandoned the use of symbols, but I used them in a different way. Wherein my earlier works in Iran, symbols were used to explain and show what was forbidden, in my latter works, symbols became the subject matter of my paintings in their own right (Figure 12.8).

MZS & CPG: Did these symbols have any other function besides being symbols, such as being cultural references? And do they play the same roles in your works now? Are they still useful to you now?

AD: I was among the very young artists after the revolution. The previous generation of artists [such as the artistic group Saqqa-khaneh] who had developed before the Islamic Revolution was interested in developing techniques and styles to present modern art along with native and historical values. But our generation was more concerned with finding a window to let in the fresh air, fresh air to breathe among all the burned ashes created by our predecessors. Never mind that they themselves were trapped in what their older brothers had fed them about the Utopia that must be created; and now failing, they were tasting the fruit of their labors and paid back for acting immaturely to build that Utopia, something that never found a chance to materialize.

Of course, I do not disagree with artists seeing these symbols from various perspectives, but I believe this kind of creativity is always sheltered and hidden; it is unhealthy and could hurt.

It is true that sometimes, without force or restriction, I mischievously sought some aesthetics in my vision and language. I still have a bit of the old system in my head that is going to stay with me forever, but in any case, I will not try to clean up my mind.

MZS & CPG: Why do the signs of desert and water have such an undeniable presence in your illustrations?

AD: Yes, it is true that the two elements of water and desert are never absent in my works. Whereas water seems to be a natural ingredient of the mindset of a child born and raised by the seaside, the desert seems quite out of character. I think it is the migrating bird in my soul, who thirsts to break the shell, to leave and to cross borders, as I did so early in my life when I ran away from a provincial city to the capital city Tehran to study in the art academy at the age of 14 – when I left my homeland for good, as a refugee to live in Europe. Movement, leaving and crossing borders as textures of my life appear in my paintings and animations, not only as a movement or a figure but also as the textures of my paintings and animations.

It is my habit of mind that is able to juxtapose desert and parched, cracked land with water in my paintings, as well as my animations. I use both as symbols for opposite pairs of deprivation/wealth, lacking/abundance, forbidden/freedom and impossibility/possibility. I also use the desert and dryness to show the desire for the Other, as a motivating force to struggle to reach the Other, whereas dry land is associated with the thirst for water and censorship and awakens the desire for knowledge, and the lack of freedom calls forth a desire for free expression. I think I share this desire for excellence and achievement with many of the artists of my generation who were deprived of a proper environment for growth and perfection. It has been exactly in that dry atmosphere that a dream is conceived and born, and it is in the cradle of the same dry land that a dream is nurtured to a mature thirst for water to immerse in saturation.

MZS & CPG: Is the idea of migration in your work a reflection of your own experience?

AD: I travelled when I was 14 and moved from the city of Rasht to the capital, Tehran. This was the beginning of many moves in my life, inner as well as outer, from one city to another and then from one country to another. A trip for some is a just a concept, goal, habit or luxury. The same could be said of being in one place, one body or geographical location.

I think it is fair to say that just as my monologues and philosophical thoughts find their real place in my work, so do the concepts of "trip" or "going," which are among my philosophical dialogues that naturally manifest themselves well within my works. Diaspora is always the other side of this "going"; it is a long rope that drags me to the future. It will appear in my work consciously and unconsciously as long as it follows me, visibly or not.

However, diaspora has never had that sense of melancholy or nostalgia that many of us experienced when leaving our homeland. For me, it is like an individual who is going through a tunnel of time to find his destiny somewhere bigger and better, just as in my paintings and even more so in my animations. I do not hesitate to drag my characters from one frame through some passage to another frame in a happier setting, much freer and happier than the original frame.

For me, moving and migration are not intellectual choices or political forces, but are calls for something that I have to respond to in a positive and favorable way. These borders we cross are not merely geographical, but also separate one clan from the others and keep them from becoming parts of the larger global life. Of course, this does not diminish the importance of being individuals who appears quite often in the closeups of global life. It is these closeups that manifest themselves within the frames, though they all are connected to the universalism encapsulating them. It is my sense of movement and my call for trips that create such dimensions in my works, as I move back and forth between these closeups, to their peripheries and the larger world.

MZS & CPG: What is the relationship between your paintings/illustrations and your animations?

AD: If there are any borders between them, they are only various aspects of my thoughts and life. They are the borders that I have to cross, one after the other, to reach my final destination, a global life.

I started my illustrations with the subject matter of books some 20 years ago. This period started by a design I had to make about burning books, an epidemic of life under censorship. The article I was designing for was shocking. It was by a writer narrating his bitter and painful experiences and those of his generation in a book. Reading it while my work progressed, I came to a very familiar sense of walking into some realm of affinity. The story brought back the memories of my childhood and the book burnings I had seen and participated in. The repetition of the same act by two generations penetrated me so strongly that I could not detach myself from it. Actually, it was a turning point in my life. I knew that it would be the subject matter of my work, but there was something else, too, a permanent union of the books and us human beings. It seems we all share the same destiny. We are the books, and the books are us; we are the components of the books and its words, though some never find a chance to be written, some are written but never read and some are read but read very badly! This series of works changed in various situations of my life, and their language changed accordingly. In these series, I have mingled and united the human being with the books.

But this is not my viewpoint in my paintings anymore when I pay more attention to these aspects of books that have become part of me, and in a way, are parts of my mind and perceptional building blocks. These shifts in my viewpoint are quite noticeable in my collections of papers and collages (Figure 12.9). The vulnerability of paper made me use it not as a texture, but as a subject to present time, memory and what is written or said on the canvas.

Now, when we are on the verge of transforming all our knowledge from material form into the digital world, my ideal is to be able to register and immortalize our memories in painting, too. I think my attraction to animation is motivated by such an ideal. Animation, because of its organic connection with modern technology, is the best medium to connect me and my language to modern contemporary life. Actually, all my concerns as a globalist and a citizen of the world are what link my paintings, illustrations and animations together. More precisely, my paintings and illustrations become objectified in my animations. All my learning and knowledge manifested in my paintings and illustrations find a dynamic vividness in my animations, even though I try to carry my experience and my learning from animation to my painting techniques, too.

MZS & CPG: What is the effect of life in the diaspora on your identity?

AD: I try to talk about this word "identity" with great care. Sometimes I ask myself when I started to think about my identity. As I have mentioned before, every shred of my life is woven with moving, leaving, crossing, going and migrating. The modern world we live in is becoming more and more united. An Iranian who has been far from his birthplace for such a long time and has never returned to it finds himself in the middle of all this change that has taken place to bring this huge world together.

To answer this question, I have to ask first what the original identity we are talking about is. If by identity you mean the usage of calligraphy, miniature, arabesque or objects, such as the veil, which in the West we consider native cultural representations, I should say that since the beginning of my artistic career I have tried to stay away from them. I avoid using any sort of cliché, because I think as a human being, I had a right to choose my place in life, and from this unique place belonging to me alone, I have no intention to form this place, consciously and willingly, according to what has become habit and custom. But I have said a lot about diaspora.

MZS & CPG: And what about performing identity?

AD: Of course, the Islamic Republic has, since its dawn, aimed at a true cultural revolution just to create a new identity for Iranians, and even enforced it vehemently. Iranian artists responded to this wave of identity change in various ways. Some [artists] complied with it by returning to calligraphy, adorned borders and even depicting Islamic narratives. Some tried to give a sense of nostalgia to it by mixing it with naïve folkloric depictions of images. Some incorporated these into their modern styles. And some looked at it critically by targeting the paradoxes it created. As far as my personal reaction to this phenomenon, as far as I am aware, I think I stayed unaffected by this wave, even though my viewers may find a trace of each in my work. Actually, as far as I recollect, I very stubbornly resisted these fads, partly because I do not believe in changing identity. I consider identity something formed in the most inner part of the human being in the course of history, and it develops accordingly and so gradually we will not be able to point at its various stages. I think the emergence of instances of these sharp signs here and there do not possess enough strength to find a way to represent our identity.

13

IN THE HOUSE OF FATEMEH: REVISITING SHIRIN NESHAT'S PHOTOGRAPHIC SERIES *WOMEN OF ALLAH*

Staci Gem Scheiwiller

Many scholars have already written on the 1990s photographic series *Women of Allah* by artist Shirin Neshat (b. 1957), but the series' relationship to its written texts has not been fully explored or explained, such as in her photograph *Rebellious Silence* of 1994 (Figure 13.1).[1] This paper seeks to address this need by examining the importance of the written words inscribed on the images and texts that have created the ideal revolutionary woman in Iran during the Iranian Revolution (1978–79). In accomplishing this task, I argue two major points: first, one must read the Persian texts inscribed on these photographs or find their translations, as understanding what these texts say results in a more nuanced exegesis of the images. Neshat's appearance becomes subversive only when one reads the texts, thus dislodging prototypical representations of postrevolutionary Iranian women. Neshat's photographs offer more psychologically complex representations of Iranian women than the global mass media has projected.

My second point is that through the mixture of texts, both written and visual in Neshat's photographs, the representations of her body become metaphors for feminized spaces of sacred empowerment by reencoding signs that transform the female body into a house of Fatemeh. Hazrat-e (Her Holiness) Fatemeh Zahra' (c. after 605–32 CE) was the daughter of the Prophet Muhammad (c. 570–632) and the mother of Imams Hasan (625–69) and Hossein (626–80), Hazrat-e Zaynab and Umm Kulthum, making her a locus of religious feminine authority in Shi'a Islam. Moreover, the writing inscribed on Neshat's images of women's voices has a similar aesthetic form as that on the literal house of Fatemeh – the mosque. This comparison between Neshat's photographs of the female body as a sacred site through texts with actual sacred sites inscribed with texts, such as the mosque, allots women a more privileged space in the theocratic State of the Islamic Republic of Iran and Shi'a Islam than politically, socially or consciously accorded to them.

To Read or Not to Read?

The main tension in the *Woman of Allah* series has to be the Persian texts inscribed by Neshat herself on the photographs after other photographers had taken them. The texts are originally by four modern Iranian women writers: Forugh Farrokhzad (1935–67), Tahereh Saffarzadeh (1936–2008), Simin Behbahani (b. 1927) and Moniru Ravanipur (b. 1954). There has been much debate on whether one should read the texts written on the photographs, whether it is possible and if the act of reading these texts is important. In line with Carly Butler and Nina Cichocki, I insist that one must read or attempt to understand the texts in order to interpret the many layers of interpretation that this series suggests.[2] Amelia King-Kostelac has also emphasized the importance of the texts: "Even without understanding the text, one can understand the text as having descriptive authority over the subject. The inscribed poem is both a textual and a physical intervention upon the photograph as a subject as well as upon the subject of the photograph."[3] After all, the text is the first layer that makes contact with the viewer – then the photograph and finally the woman – becoming a visual metaphor for Jacques Derrida's concept of writing as "the signifier of the signifier" by making the speaking subject literally removed from the inscriptions through the interface of the photograph.[4]

Part of the problem that makes interpretation an issue is that Neshat produced the series in New York City and exhibited it to audiences outside the Persianate world who would mostly not have the capability to read the Persian texts. Neshat has commented that she does not expect non-Iranian viewers to read the photographs, as their understanding of them would be limited: "I don't think it matters that the writing can't be understood in the West. So much of it is written within the context of Islamic religion, politics and the history of feminism in Iran that it would not have the same meaning for someone who was not from Iran as it would for an Iranian."[5] In a 2004 interview with film scholar Scott MacDonald, she stated, "Iranians could not only read and understand the meaning of the poetry, but are also very familiar with the history and place of the writers in relation to Iranian society – something that would be impossible to translate to Westerners."[6] Furthermore, Neshat sets up a dichotomy within her audience: those who cannot read Persian and those who can, indicating that the written texts can and will be read by some but not by most, thus creating multiple interpretations depending on the viewer's background.[7]

Many viewers who cannot read Persian have invoked either a Qur'anic reading of the texts or summon their own biographies, instead of making an effort to listen to the voices speaking from the photographs. When Rachel Bailey Jones saw Neshat's photographs at the Museum of Modern Art in New York in 2006, she noticed that most viewers quickly viewed the photographs and then walked away without even reading the posted translations.[8] Misconceptions brought about the viewer's disinterest in researching the images have included calling the texts "love poems,"[9] which they are not, or "militant,"[10] a label that carries negative associations and implies a challenge to the status quo. In "Women in Black" (2001), curator Igor Zabel revisits his first impressions of Neshat's work: "When I first saw Neshat's photographs […] I immediately thought that I recognized the represented person: I 'knew' I was looking at an Islamic terrorist."[11] Later, he absorbs his reaction: "I was able to […] recognize in them a mixture of old and more recent stereotypes and preconstructed ideas about the 'Orient,' the Middle East, and the Muslim world."[12] Actually, he argues that these particular photographs mimic European Orientalist fantasies and mediated images to deconstruct them. There is a natural inclination for Europeans and North Americans to believe that Neshat has tailored these images for them to question themselves, because these photographs are shown primarily in their own cultural venues. Therefore, the refusal to read Persian on the part of the viewer or the denial of its importance collapses the images into Eurocentric readings. In this analysis, the nonrecognizable writing is reduced to being secondary, ornamental or almost meaningless.

If one does care about hearing global voices, voices of the Other and voices from the margins, then one should be concerned with what these written voices on Neshat's photographs have to say. To further my point, I refer to Maria Lugones and Elizabeth Spelman's feminist essay "Have We Got a Theory for You!" (1983), which begins in Spanish and then converts to English. The point of this particular essay is that one must learn to speak the Other's language, instead of women of color always having to speak in English to white women. Actually, the essay begins in Spanish specifically as a test to the reader. Will one attempt to read the text or find its translation? Is the feminist interested in learning the text that is not in English? "We cannot talk to you in our language because you do not understand it. You are ill at ease in our world [...]. You must [...] accept that you must learn the text [...]. So you need to learn to become unintrusive, unimportant [...]. You will also have to come to terms with the sense of alienation, of not belonging."[13] Hence, one must read the texts inscribed onto Neshat's photographs to push the boundaries of one's own biography, experience and comfort zone and to understand Neshat's work in multiple ways. Stopping short of trying to find the text's translations is a refusal to engage in dialogue with someone different from the Self. Actually, I am curious how these images would become dissident at all without reading the writing.

What makes Neshat's photographs powerful and still a topic of discussion is that they have a tendency to make global audiences uncomfortable, and the texts become a challenge, because normally, they are not read. This moment of tension however should be, as Gayatri Spivak has called it, the "unlearning of one's privilege,"[14] during which the viewer must leave the space of security and become alienated, just as the portrayals of Iranian women intimate an alienation that is not uttered. When one is center, especially English speakers, one does not feel burdened to traverse the margins and can stop reading the photographs whenever it suits oneself; however, if the viewer wants to have an intelligible grasp of these images, then a bit of footwork and discomfort must be undertaken. The viewer's resistance to reading could also be viewed metaphorically in relation to current events, as proposed in art historian Iftikhar Dadi's "Shirin Neshat's Photographs as Postcolonial Allegories" (2008). The catastrophes of 9/11, Gulf War II (2003–11?) and the Afghanistan War (2001–present) are, in part, due to the refusal of American politicians to communicate on equal terms with the governments of the Middle East and Southern Asia.

Despite Neshat's expressed confidence in those who can read the Persian written onto her photographs, the texts are fragmented. The texts are not complete, because the demarcations of Neshat's skin and clothing interrupt them; hence, the voice is fractured, making effective communication hindered. There are also mistakes in the texts shown on the photographs. For example, in Neshat's photograph *Guardians of Revolution* (1994), there is a mistake in a text by Ravanipur, in addition to the verses being interrupted (Figure 13.2). The text reads on the top of the right hand, "زنها طبل می میزدند" (*zanha tabl mee meezadand*), meaning "Women were drumming." The error is the repeated use of the continuous marker "می" (*mee*). Most likely, this error will not alter the reading or understanding the sentence, but it does show, nonetheless, that these inscribed texts are fallible and imperfect. In another instance, in the fifth line down, moving into the sixth line, it reads, "و مرد از/و از روی آب‌انبار"(*va mard az/va az ruye ab-anbar*), meaning "and the man from/and from on the reservoir," which demonstrates a disrupted transition. The verses stop and start, creating breaks that are not fluid or do not communicate in the most efficient manner.

I do not think, though, that the texts are simply ornamental or not meant to be read due to these mistakes and fractures.[15] On the contrary, I argue their imperfections are meant as a dialogue between the viewer and a fragmented subject or voice, because Neshat has always agreed that Iranians can read and identify the texts inscribed. The texts are actually extremely legible and written in very clear handwriting.[16] Dadi has also made the point that Neshat's inscriptions are very carefully done and do not possess the intricacies of Arabic or Persian calligraphy or henna work;[17] hence, the texts are not altogether calligraphic, meaning they are not simply aesthetically pleasing.[18] If the texts are not solely calligraphic, then they must be transmitting a message that seeks to be heard and communicated. So the interruptions may be demonstrative of subaltern voices of women in Iran, as Neshat has mentioned, "the woman, forced to hide behind the veil, has no way of expressing her thoughts and feelings."[19] Through the written word, then, the woman and the photograph come alive, activated by Neshat's hand, but her speech is still hindered and misunderstood. This aspect of the series would go unnoticed unless one reads the texts.

Whose Texts Are They?

This series seems to have been the psychological inner workings of Neshat whose idea of Iran had changed vastly after her 11-year hiatus (1979–90) while living and attending school in the United States.[20] She has told MacDonald about the conditions in making the series, "I had no art career; I was not thinking about the audience since I didn't have any; I was making this work [the series] for *myself*."[21] Several scholars have criticized Neshat's work as being Orientalist and replicating stereotypes, but no one seems to have analyzed these photographs through a Barthesian approach, which would posit these photographs as ones of loss and grief by a former disrupted Pahlavi subject. But in addition to redirecting this grief into the visual, she has also stated that the *Women of Allah* series is about the Iranian Revolution, its relationship to Iranian women, martyrdom,[22] and ultimately how the representations of these women have had a profound effect on Neshat's own experience as a woman returning to a changing Iran, after both the revolution and Iran–Iraq War were over.

The series has four major signs: women, texts, weapons and chadors, all of which compose the representation of the postrevolutionary woman in Iran. Neshat has explained these signs: "a few elements were repeated [...] including *the female body*, a very problematic topic in Islamic culture as it suggests ideas of shame, sin, and sexuality; *text*, I inscribed calligraphy – poetry by Iranian women writers – directly *on* the photographs; *weapons* [...] a symbol of violence; and [...] the *veil* [...] which has been considered both a symbol of repression and [...] liberation – resistance against the Western influence."[23] In an earlier interview with Anne Doran, she describes further the role of weaponry in her series: "I use guns or bullets to suggest terrorism and how that idea can raise so much fear about Arab identity in the West. Those props shatter our stereotype of the typical Muslim woman as a passive and submissive victim. Islamic women have actually always been very active in the military – in some ways that is one area in which they are equal to men."[24]

These four major signs – woman, text, weapon and veil – each have signifiers and signifieds that make them complicated signs on their own, and they have elaborate discourses behind their constructions. Although Neshat has not mentioned the specific revolutionary sources I discuss in this paper, and I am not claiming that Neshat composed her work in relation to these writers, she hints that she is very aware of revolutionary literature.[25] She has also acknowledged that the Iranian government uses the matriarchal figures of Fatemeh and Zaynab as prominent models of Iranian womanhood.[26] If one thinks of the landscape as ideological,[27] in which the ideal postrevolutionary Iranian woman is framed, that landscape is (re)drawn with texts, including those from the revolution and the Islamic Republic.[28] Hamid Dabashi has described the representation of the body in Neshat's photographs as a critical contestation of these proscribed texts: "Bodies are the signed and sealed signatures of a culture. In and of themselves bodies are already inscribed, constituted, defined, veiled beyond recognition."[29] What are the signifiers and signifieds, then, behind the signs that make the representation of the postrevolutionary Iranian woman, and how does Neshat challenge these established discourses by inscribing the written texts after the photographs have been taken?

Although discourses on the ideal revolutionary Iranian woman are vast, I focus on the contributions by two prominent scholars: ʿAli Shariʿati (1933–77) and Ayatollah Morteza Mutahhari (1920–79). Rapid modernization, accompanied by changing moral attitudes, foreign interference and the growing disparity between the wealthy and poorer classes had left many women and men confused about their roles in society and the perceived social order between men and women appeared imbalanced. The spokeswoman of Iran, Mohammad Reza Shah Pahlavi's third wife Farah Diba (b. 1938), had embodied a national prototype of an Iranian woman who sported European fashion, wore makeup and softened her public identity as a Muslim. In his major contribution *Fatima is Fatima* (1971), Shariʿati constructed a role model for Iranian women that would restore the moral fortitude that had been seemingly lost to overwhelming Euro-American mass consumption during the reign of Mohammad Reza Shah (r. 1941–79): "What creatures [women] they [the monarchy] have sent to the market place [to shop]! Creatures without sensitivities, without knowledge, without pain, without understanding, without responsibility and even without human feelings. Fresh, clean dolls, 'worthy ones.' It is obvious what their worthiness is in and for what work. Their means of support and its derivation are also obvious. This is thrown at our women and they know why. It is because of them that 'Who am I? Who should I be?' is pertinent. They want a model.

Who? Fatima."[30] Unhappy with the status of women and government affairs in general, Shari'ati fashioned a transformed identity of the Iranian woman, whom he based on the matron of Shi'a Islam, Hazrat-e Fatemeh. In the persona of Fatemeh, a woman could be strong, authoritative, moral and religious.

The Prophet's daughter Fatemeh had assisted her father in his many ordeals and endeavors, and, in return, he showed her great respect. Her devotion to her father, her husband (the first Imam 'Ali) and her children Imams Hasan, Hossein, Hazrat-e Zaynab and Umm Kulthum, as well as her rebellion against the Sunni Caliphate, transformed her into a courageous, pious and righteous figure in Shi'a Islam. Fatemeh was the heir of the Prophet, but when he died in 632, two factions split off into what would be known as the Sunni, the followers of Abu Bakr (the Prophet's father-in-law) as the first caliph, and the Shi'a, the followers of Imam 'Ali (the Prophet's cousin and son-in-law) and his family. Moreover, the discourses of the Iranian Revolution replaced the representation of Farah as the ideal Iranian woman with a more outwardly virtuous, upright one that did not compromise the basic beliefs of the Shi'a. Shari'ati repackaged the role model of Fatemeh as the image of the modern Muslim Iranian woman who did not capitulate to models based on Euro-American women.

In a set of lectures entitled *The Islamic Modest Dress* (1966), Ayatollah Morteza Mutahhari outlined proper Muslim women decorum, which included wearing *hejab* (Islamic dress). Shari'ati had also dealt with the issue of modest dress, but his views were vaguer on the issue, advising not to adopt traditional dress, but a modern, Islamic, modest dress that would encapsulate the religious revival brewing under Pahlavi rule.[31] To prove Mutahhari's discussions that a good Muslim woman must wear hejab, he also illustrated the example of Fatemeh to make his points. For example, when arguing that women's hands are acceptable to look at, he cited the tradition in which the Iranian companion of the Prophet, Salman al-Farisi, entered Fatemeh's house and saw her hands bleeding from grinding barley.[32] In another tradition narrated by the Companion Jabir ibn Abd-Allah, he went with the Prophet to the house of Fatemeh. Before entering, the Prophet asked if they could enter, but because Jabir was with her father, Fatemeh responded, '"No [...]. [W]ait until I cover my head."'[33] Then when Jabir did enter, he saw that Fatemeh's face was sallow from lack of nutrition.[34] From this tradition, Mutahhari argued that seeing a woman's face must be acceptable as well, because Fatemeh did not attempt to cover it. Finally, Imam Hasan as a child ran into the house to ask his mother, '"What things are better than any other for women?"' Fatemeh replied, '"That she sees no man and no man sees her."'[35] Mutahhari concluded that men should not look at women and vice versa; therefore, hejab was a necessity for women. Moreover, the icon of the woman of the Iranian Revolution manifested, in part, through the melding of these texts by Shari'ati and Mutahhari. Shari'ati illustrated how women could empower themselves and become model women of the State. In turn, Mutahhari fashioned the physical appearance of women with a similar goal in mind. Together, their new visions of a revamped Iranian woman challenged the current images of women, who had adapted Euro-American tastes during the Pahlavi government, which was seen as the reincarnation of the Sunni Caliphate that had murdered the Prophet's family.

Fatemeh's daughter Zaynab is also considered a revered role model for women, because Zaynab assisted her brother Imam Hossein at the Battle of Karbala (680). The prototype of the brave woman slinging a gun is based on the concept of Zaynab as the warrior sister. Yet, according to Shari'ati, Zaynab was also an extension of Fatemeh's house, from her womb and raised in her home. Zaynab's strength of character was indebted to her mother; hence, all ties lead back to Fatemeh. In *Expectations from the Muslim Woman* (1972), Shari'ati claimed:

> [I]n training and nourishing children like Hasan, Husayn and Zaynab [...] Fatima was the mother [...]. All of them were elevated symbols. All of them gathered in one family [...]. Husayn himself is a symbol of humanity, but Zaynab is more important. The image of Fatima in Zaynab is more important [...] when a woman sees such heroics from a woman [Zaynab] who belonged to Fatima's family, she understands where she must look, how she must be [...]. Fatima trained Zaynab inside her home and in her lap. The role of Zaynab in the revolution of Karbala [...] resulted from Fatima's teaching.[36]

Thus, the two role models for women promoted by the Islamic Republic are two sides of the same person, with Fatemeh being the most important, from whom all legitimacy flows, because she was the daughter of the Prophet and the (fore)mother of all the imams in Twelver Shi'a Islam, except her husband 'Ali, the first imam.

In relation to the texts by Iranian women writers that Neshat literally inscribes onto the photographs, each woman has taken a different ideological stance during and after the Pahlavi monarchy. One example is the poet Forugh Farrokhzad, possibly Iran's greatest modern poet, who revealed the tragedies of her life through her body – in both the act of writing itself, as well as her continual engagement with her body in the language of her poetry. The loneliness caused by her separation from her son through divorce and by other unhappy relationships appears quite frequently in her texts. Yet, not only does Farrokhzad's poetry express melancholy but also challenges the *hejabi 'iffat* (veil of chastity) by discussing female sexuality and atheism frankly in a society that had restricted both.[37] An example of one of her poems is "My Heart Grieves for the Garden," in which the speaker expresses sorrow for the garden – a metaphor for the speaker's body and soul: "No one is thinking about the flowers/No one is thinking about the fish/No wants to believe/that the garden is dying/that the heart of the garden has swollen under the sun/that the mind of the garden is slowly, slowly/draining of green memories/and the garden's feeling/is some abstract thing/rotting in the solitude of the garden."[38] These verses not only demonstrate the neglect by others of women's desires and bodies but also show dissatisfaction with women's limited options and life choices in Pahlavi society. Everyone is self-absorbed and in denial that major problems exist, while the woman-cum-garden continues to suffer in silence and loneliness. Although Farrokhzad had died in 1967 in a suspicious car accident before the revolution gained momentum in 1978, it was clear in her work that she saw life in Iran as suffocating and unequal for many types of social groups, such as in her film *The House is Black* (1962), which exposed the frightful conditions of an Iranian leper colony, thus propelling Queen Farah and the government to address the problem.

In comparison, the poetry of Tahereh Saffarzadeh glorified the coming revolution as both liberating and uniting her compatriots. Saffarzadeh, like Farrokhzad, also discussed her life as a woman in Iran, but there was a significant transition in her poetry before and after the revolution. Her prerevolution poetry tells of sexuality, disappointment and dissatisfaction with relationships, the Pahlavi monarchy and life in the United States, where she studied. For example, in the poem "Nostalgia" (1969), the speaker laments, "We are tired, we ought to go back and sit/Under the tree of our neighbor's hostility/And pass around the cup of mutual trust [...]/Our trip is from one Continent of blood to another/There is such chaos [...]/Why should we feel so nervous so scared/We are surrounded by men/Policemen businessmen security men."[39] By the upswing of the revolution, however, she delved into religious and revolutionary sentiments of martyrdom and sacrifice for a rebellion against the shah. For instance, in her 1980 poem "Allegiance with Wakefulness," which she presented to Ayatollah Khomeini (1900–89),[40] the speaker declares: "O, you martyr/Hold my hands/With your hands/cut from earthly means,/Hold my hands,/I am your poet,/with an inflicted body,/I've come to be with you/and on the promised day/we shall rise again."[41] This type of religiosity associated with martyrdom and *jihad* (struggle) stood in direct opposition with the Pahlavi monarchy, which had promoted secularism. Yet, not only did Saffarzadeh become a revolutionary and devout Muslim, but also insisted on preserving women's rights in the formation of the new Iranian constitution;[42] thus, her position remained complex as both an avid supporter of Islam, Khomeini and women's rights.

A novelist featured in the series is Moniru Ravanipur who began her writing career in Iran but now lives in the United States. Ravanipur comes from the city of Jofreh in southern Iran, which has its own cultural and linguistic differences associated with the Persian Gulf areas,[43] thus giving Ravanipur an Other status within mainstream Iranian culture. Literature scholar Nasrin Rahimieh argues that the southern dialect used in Ravanipur's first novel *Ahl-e Gharg* (The drowned ones, 1989) not only creates a magic realist atmosphere but also makes the characters alienated figures due to ineffective communication,[44] once again illuminating Neshat's choice to utilize this text as an appropriate one in expressing misunderstood speech. Ravanipur's text from *Ahl-e Gharg* appears in several of Neshat's photographs, including *Guardians of Revolution*: "Women were drumming [...] dancing with their arms reaching toward the skies [...] an ugly and black hand emerged, had wrapped around the moon [...] the moon was choking [...] dying before the women's eyes [...] with the sound of drums there came a sudden silence."[45] As the passage continues, the men run away frightened, and water floods the town in which they live. The brave women, however, continue to drum and dance in their magical efforts to repel the waters. The narrative is clear that the women are the heroines, whereas the men prove worthless in their fear to save anyone or anything except themselves.

Neshat's photographs, then, become the spaces and intermediaries in which diverse texts meet and congeal, thus creating a third text of intertexuality that offers more profound, complicated representations of Iranian women after the revolution. Neshat has told writer Shadi Sheybani, "Each time I inscribe a specific woman's writings on the photographs, the work takes on a new direction."[46] It seems that it was Neshat's intent to use the written texts to transform the photographs from stock mediated photographs of postrevolutionary women into documents that would attempt to convey deeper psychological dimensions of the lives of women in Iran.[47] Samar Mohammad Bush suggests that the calligraphy was added after the photographs were taken to make each photograph unique and create Benjamin's theory of the photographic aura – in other words, give each semblance of the women or personae of Neshat individual, irreproducible presences, which mass media usually denies (Iranian) women.[48] Finally, Cichocki in "Veils, Poems, Guns, and Martyrs" (2004) has also explained the role of the writing in Neshat's series, showing how it unravels the prototypical representations of these particular women: "Neshat, with […] the radically self-revelatory feminist poetry of Farrokhzad and the prorevolutionary neotraditionalist poetry of Saffarzadeh […] addresses issues that are dear to […] women who sat at two opposite positions within the spectrum of women's experiences. The poetry provides these women with a voice [ordinarily masked by the males discourses of the revolution]; and its divergent contents deny any totalizing claims on the experience of Muslim women."[49] After the inscriptions, another layer of meaning, which the initial image and writing do not share, emerges; this layer illustrates not just the voices of women writers, but also how Neshat has ingested and reinterpreted images of postrevolutionary women after her shocking return to Iran in 1990.

In the House of Fatemeh

Shi'a Islam is indebted to Fatemeh for its existence, because she was the Prophet's daughter and the matriarchal ancestor of the imams. In addition, Shari'ati declared Fatemeh as central to Iranian culture: "Our nation has created a culture around the gate and roof of Fatemeh's house."[50] On the Masjed-e Shah Mosque (1612–30) in Isfahan, built by Shah 'Abbas I (1571–1629), Fatemeh's subtle presence, in the form of her written name among the holy men of Islam, looms over this sacred space, quietly asserting her place as the mother of Shi'a Islam (Figure 13.3). Although the mosque in general is a space primarily dominated by men, the first mosque, the Prophet's Mosque in Medina, became the last residence of Fatemeh and 'Ali, and the *mihrab*, the niche that indicates the *qibla* – the direction of prayer toward the city of Mecca – is associated with Fatemeh.[51] Yet just as this written form of Fatemeh's sign softly anticipates a figural embodiment, incarnations of her appeared in the texts disseminated during the Iranian Revolution. Fatemeh is Fatemeh is Fatemeh, and the layers continue to unravel, as Neshat adds other dimensions to what it could mean to be Iranian, female, Shi'a and revolutionary. After all, Fatemeh is one of the "Women of Allah" and arguably the most important one.

The role of writing transforms both the mosque and Neshat's photographs, from mundane entities into Shi'i sites of divinely guided female authority, strength and sanctity. Female authority is inherent in Shi'a Islam through Fatemeh, Zaynab and Fatemeh Massoumeh (790–816), and just as the writing of Fatemeh's name on the Masjed-e Shah acknowledges that female authority, Neshat's photographs seek to restore some of that privilege to women in Iran and Islam. Filmmaker Shoja Azari has described the *Women of Allah* series as "Neshat's intervention" that "penetrates the sacred space and iconography of Islamic cannon, and deconstructs its mythical metalanguage by returning the distorted signification back to the semiological system."[52] The writing on both the mosque and Neshat's photographs has a transformative ability in its own right, making the spaces of the building and photographs into sites infused with feminine power. Disparate texts are attached to both the buildings and Neshat's body, creating alternate meanings for their audiences. Somehow, the attachment of verses and the names of holy figures to the actual building of the mosque transform its mundane spaces into sacred ones. The floating writings of Farrokhzad, Saffarzadeh, Behbahani and Ravanipur, which have their own contexts and meanings, become attached to these images of Iranian women in chadors with guns, producing another layer of meaning that the two do not share independently.[53] The writing creates a threshold, through which the meaning of the object changes once it goes through another signification.[54]

The body represented in Neshat's photographs takes up and creates space like an architectural site. The hejab itself becomes an architectural veil that allows women to maneuver in and out of public spaces effectively. Similar to the mobility of the texts written by Iranian women, the donning of hejab also allows for public mobility that permits the average Iranian woman to work, attend school and exist in the same space with unrelated men. The chador sanctions the woman to take a piece of her private space with her. Actually, the word hejab literally means "curtain," and chador means "tent." Inside a woman's chador is the private space of her home that she personally embodies. The chador protects what lies beneath its folds and acts as the intermediary between the woman and those in her public/private spaces.

The photograph itself has a space between four frames, and if the photograph is similar to a window of the world, then the frame shows these representations of women in the space of the Iranian State. The fact that all the photographs show women veiled implies public spaces open to unrelated men, as women do not normally veil in private spaces.[55] Moreover, the writing on the photographs creates a rupture that opens these spaces to more possibilities for women's agency. According to Begüm Özden Firat, "Neshat [...] imposes the aesthetics of calligraphic writing onto the photographic image and the very corporeality of the letters opens up an aesthetic scriptural space on the visual surface."[56] Derrida calls this creation of scriptural space a "breaching" of space through writing, a breaking through of a pathway.[57] King-Kostelac has also described the spatial qualities of Neshat's photographs, specifically through its written interventions: "The text, which appears to almost float behind the women, does not mediate the space between subject and viewer but rather comprises the physical space that the women inhabit. The calligraphic space in which the figures stand does not deemphasize the materiality of the women exactly, but it does suggest the ubiquity of not only overt, ideological content, but also the rooting of their physical actions in the discourse of the Revolution."[58]

On a tertiary level, Neshat's appearance in *Rebellious Silence*, for example, recalls the texts by Shari'ati and Mutahhari. The hejab illustrates Mutahhari's call for modest Islamic dress in revolt against the Pahlavi promotion of Euro-American products and mannerisms, exhibited by Queen Farah and other wealthy, upper- and middle-class Iranian women. In essence, the hejab signifies a Muslim identity, and according to

Mutahhari, Fatemeh's supposed wish that a Muslim woman dress modestly; its blackness emulates the appearance of Fatemeh, whom Mutahhari described as covered in black from head to toe in soot when she worked outside the house.[59] Furthermore, during the summers of 1995 and 1996, scholar Faegheh Shirazi saw the graffitied slogan on a public wall, "Veiling is a sign of her Holiness Fatima Zahra,"[60] hence making the connection between the female saint, hejab and a woman's moral character. Aside from dressing in a manner usually identified with Fatemeh and simply abiding the dress codes, Neshat acts with the resolve and vigor of Fatemeh as well. Shari'ati sanctions Fatemeh in his text, strengthening Iranian women with a positive, powerful role model. In the photograph, Neshat seemingly handles the rifle with ease, illustrating her physical prowess and skill, as well as her capability to injure and kill. Yet, at a closer glance, the gun seems to float, just as the text does when Neshat attaches it to the photograph in a collage of signs. The rifle actually splits her face into bilateral sections, creating the image of the spine of a book and her face as the leaves: "The skin becomes a book."[61] This "book" adds to the discourses on contemporary Iranian women and tells another story that differs from the texts written by men. Though the image is two-dimensional, a voice emerges from its frame and materializes. The woman may be "silent," but that "rebellious silence" becomes audible through the rifle, gaze and text.

On a second level, the actual reading of the inscriptions by Iranian women writers reveals other in-depth interpretations of these photographs, such as resistance and empowerment. Neshat informed Sheybani that she employs the texts of these women to add to the plurality of voices of Iranian women: "[T]he use of poetry is particularly apt, because literature has historically played a major part in the struggle against political repression. The poetry is the literal and symbolic voice of women whose sexuality and individualism have been obliterated by the chador."[62] For instance, Neshat inscribes the poetry of Saffarzadeh, thus giving her photographs another twist in their meanings in relation to the body as a sacred site. On *Rebellious Silence* is Saffarzadeh's poem "Allegiance with Wakefulness," which I quoted earlier. The earlier quotation illustrates the corporeal presence of both the speaker and addressee in liberating Iran through revolution. Continuing from "Allegiance," "O Guard/in the heart of night's cold/you watch as if from outside/the house of your own body/with tired eyelids/– a night nurse – /so that the wounded city can rest/from the plunder of death."[63] Saffarzadeh continues an emphasis on the physicality of martyrdom by morphing the body into a spatial site – a house. Because Persian is non-gender-specific, the guard could be either male or female, but usually, the martyr has been thought of as male; however, Iranian women have sacrificed themselves as martyrs during the revolution and Iran–Iraq War, contributing greatly to their successful conclusions.

Neshat's photograph implies that the guard is specifically female, emphasizing the commanding intensity of the women in the Islamic Republic. The woman with the gun in the uniform-like hejab watches from outside the house of her body and protects the city that has been infringed on by foreign interests and the shah's repressive measures against human rights. Later, that struggle would extend to the Iran–Iraq War. Neshat explains her juxtapositions of images of mighty women with this Saffarzadeh poem by disclosing to Sheybani the important role that women have had in jihad as martyrs of the faith: "[T]he *shaheed* or martyr stands at the intersection of love, politics, and death. She is committing a crime because she loves God and this love entails violence. The poetry [...] is by [...] Saffarzadeh, who expresses the strong conviction many Iranian women have for Islam. They feel liberated from the previous class structure and certain social constraints by the Islamic revolution."[64] As Saffarzadeh's poem continues, the word *baradar* (برادر, brother) does appear, but the gun in Neshat's image partially covers it, making it ambiguous. Yet, the theme of being silenced resonates with the motifs present in Neshat's photographs, also alluding that the martyr in question is female: "Stories of your martyrdom/like martyrdom of the people/remain unheard/they have no voice, no image, no date,/ they are unannounced."[65] These verses coincide with title of Neshat's photograph – the stories of female martyrs are usually unheard, unannounced and unappreciated, evoking a rebellious silence, because they continue to be vigilant without recognition.

In two other photographs, *Seeking Martyrdom #1* and *#2*, in which Saffarzadeh's poem also appears, show Neshat in the persona of a female martyr, her hands covered in blood in one image, while holding a rifle with a tulip inside it in the other (Figures 13.4, 13.5). In these photographs, the implication of the guard (martyr) being a woman is highly plausible, because the presence of the blood and tulip are indicative of such. The word "baradar" does appear to the left of Neshat's head in *Seeking Martyrdom #1*, but it is at the level of her forehead, perhaps suggesting equality between their sacrifices. In variation #2, the word "brother" does not show up at all. In addition, the tulip in #2 signifies martyrdom, because when blood of the martyr is spilled on the ground, a tulip will grow in its place.[66]

Yet, the spilled blood of women in Neshat's photographs has a more subversive function, as women's blood is usually considered *najesse* (Islamically unclean). Social anthropologist Azam Torab has argued that this topos of martyrs' blood traditionally refers to the spilt blood of male martyrs, whereas the blood of women is usually associated with menstruation and therefore, pollution.[67] For example, Ayatollah Khomeini declared that a woman should refrain from regular prayers while menstruating, and if her husband has vaginal sex with her, he must donate money to the poor.[68] In light of these statements, it is astonishing to see Neshat's hands doused in red, signifying blood; hence, Neshat's photographs place women's blood, contributions and sacrifices on the same par with men in the Islamic Republic, blurring any sense of inequality in relation to the quality of blood spilled in martyrdom. The body of Fatemeh itself is thought to have been pure and without pollution;[69] hence, women molded in her holiness should have their blood sacrifices honored. Ahmad T. posits that variation #1 relates to the *vozoi-e khun* (blood ablution), in which the blood of martyrs could be used for ablutions before *namaz* (prayers).[70] He bases this interpretation on the story of Zaynab who could not find water for her ablutions in Karbala and used her dead brother Imam Hossein's blood instead. This interpretation has merit, as Neshat has marked the forearms and hands with blood, which is one of the important parts of the body to wash for prayers. Despite Ahmad T.'s understanding of the photograph, the blood becomes another floating sign, because there is no dead body present in the photograph.

While Torab was in Iran in 1992–93 (around the same time Neshat was visiting Iran regularly), she documented many pious women looking to famous female figures of Islam as ways to celebrate women and their contributions to Islam, as well as diplomatically protest the patriarchal structures of the religion and State. For instance, one women's strategy to accomplish these aims is a series of rituals called the *Fatemiyeh*, which mourns Fatemeh's suspicious death by replicating "the first ten days of Muharram."[71] Muharram is the first month of the Islamic calendar, in which the Shi'a honor the *'Ashura'*, a holiday of mourning for the death of Imam Hossein at the Battle of Karbala; thus, through the rituals of the Fatemiyeh, a symbolic association between the martyrdoms of mother and son is made. Moreover, Neshat's photographs commemorate the sacrifices of Muslim women to Islam, the revolution and the war and that their commitments and sacrifices are no less than their male compatriots. Women in Iran have found ways, as Neshat has noted in her comment about women being in the military, to find empowerment and female authority in Islam and in the Islamic Republic.

In the photograph *Stories of Martyrdom #1*, the aforementioned text by Ravanipur appears from the novel *Ahl-e Gharg* (Figure 13.6). Hands are outstretched in prayer, while a rifle rests on the arms of a woman. The focus of both the photograph and the text is on the hands and arms of the women – a woman praying in the photograph, with women drumming and dancing in the text. The same women in the photograph and text are called to defend the people in a similar manner to the representations of *Seeking Martyrdom*. The men have run away, leaving the women to fend for themselves. The women are the brave ones, not the men. In addition, the women possess divine powers that will save the day. Spiritual authority is conjured through praying, drumming and dancing, thus implying that women are closer to the divine and use its forces to promote good and protection. The photograph illustrates a veiled woman praying and the text shows women drumming and dancing, displaying an almost primeval physicality that connects women to the forces of nature. Although this sort of association may seem essentialist, one could argue that it gives women a legitimacy and vigor that men do not possess. It is usually a power suppressed in women by men because it is so overwhelming and magnificent.

Neshat's visual text and Ravanipur's written one create an image of a mighty and divinely guided woman and determine the Shi'a woman as the major site of spiritual power. The implication could be made further that the revolution and war would not have been won without the spiritual powers of Shi'a women. Actually, before the revolution, Khomeini stood against women's suffrage, but changed his mind after he saw that the success of the revolution was in large part due to women's participation.[72] The implication in both these texts is that only women possess the capacity to conjure the divine and protect the State, nation and faith. When times are troubled, only the women will carry everyone through to safety.

The close-up of the hand in this particular image recalls a talisman called "the hand of Fatemeh."[73] The Hand of Fatemeh is also known as *Panjtan Paak* (The Five Pure Ones), with each finger signifying Fatemeh and her male family members: the Prophet Muhammad and Imams 'Ali, Hassan and Hossein (Figure 13.7). Through Fatemeh, the holiest figures of Shi'a Islam are connected – her body is the vital connection through which Shi'a Islam survives and thrives. These talismans usually have calligraphy inscribed on them, sometimes from the Qur'an (c. 650), and act as a protective or blessing amulet.

Talismans are common in Iran, and Neshat personally amassed them: "I collected in Tehran's bazaars small plates, good luck charms, where mythological figures of men, women, and animals are covered with inscriptions."[74] In Neshat's photograph, her hand, in the guise of a postrevolutionary Iranian woman, is also the hand of Fatemeh. Through her womb are the martyrs of the revolution and the Iran–Iraq War. Through her sacrifices, the revolution and war have been won, the Iranian people are protected and the State of Iran will continue to thrive. She wards off the evil eye and brings blessings and successes. In addition, these talismans are mobile and can be found in both the public and private spheres, having the ability to transform the space of the State and every household into the house of Fatemeh.[75]

By invoking the poetry of Farrokhzad, Neshat presents several contrasting dynamics in her photographs, especially in the play of contradictions when she inserts these insubordinate texts into authoritative master texts. As Neshat's body transforms into a site complementary to the Masjed-e Shah, the poetry of Farrokhzad inscribed on her body also reflects the body as the embodiment of space. King-Kostelac suggests that the writing mostly on the body parts in Neshat's photographs actually assist in embodying the body further.[76] On one hand, it is a matter of aesthetics that writing on black chadors may not be productive visually, but on the other hand, the writing on the body makes the body more visible and mediates between the body and the viewer.

The image *Untitled* discloses the earlier quoted Farrokhzad poem "My Heart Grieves for the Garden," in which the garden, an architectural landscape, becomes a metaphor for the decaying body and soul (Figure 13.8). The inner courtyards and the environs surrounding mosques and houses provide private, yet outdoor, areas characterized by order and stable proportions. Although women are not excluded from courtyards, they are traditionally thought of as male spaces, whereas the domestic spaces are associated with women.[77] In the poem, however, the motif of the garden is associated with the female body, which should connote fecundity and fertility. In Neshat's sacred site, the garden, which usually overflows with abundance in Iranian literature, now reflects unhappiness and dissatisfaction, because it cannot grow if it is suffocated and suffering from neglect and lack of love and appreciation. Even in the fruitful garden, things must die and decay. Curator Feresteh Daftari has noticed that the finger is placed on the lips, possibly implying internal discord by silencing herself.[78] In essence, not only do holiness, piety and righteousness live in the garden of matriarchy but also loneliness, abandonment and frustration.

The cultural sign of the hand of Fatemeh seems quite prominent in this photograph, as well as well as the feminizing of authority in Shi'a Islam. In the center of the hand Neshat has written in the most pronounced calligraphy *ya qamar-e bani hashem* – an invocation to Imam Hossein's half-brother Hazrat-e 'Abbas.[79] While on the battlefield of Karbala, the men fighting under the Umayyad caliph of Sunni Islam, Yazid (r. 680–83), refused water to Imam Hossein and Hossein's wounded men. 'Abbas attempted to obtain water from the Euphrates River for their encampment, but one of Yazid's men severed his hand. Moreover, the sign of the isolated hand in Iranian visual culture could also be a synecdoche for 'Abbas. Yet, in this case, the hand is female, and as the dying garden-cum-woman aches for (emotional) nourishment, it is now the hand of Fatemeh (or the woman's) that should be invoked or will provide the refreshing, reviving water.

With Farrokhzad, a voice of a woman that seems to differ drastically from that of Saffarzadeh's comes to light, but that voice is also placed on the prototypical postrevolutionary woman. Neshat relates to Sheybani, "[N]o other woman before her [Farrokhzad] had ever dared to speak so freely on the subjects of female emotional and sexual desires."[80] On one hand, Neshat shows another type of woman other than Fatemeh that is revolutionary. To be an Iranian woman disgruntled with the Pahlavi dynasty did not necessarily prescribe that one must follow the path of Fatemeh. On the other hand, Neshat could also be presenting another facet of a sincerely pious woman, or because all women in Iran must wear hejab regardless of their belief systems, a woman may appear religious, but is not at all. By inscribing the body with the poetry of Farrokhzad, the body of an ideal Shi'a woman becomes not only a sacred site but a melancholic and mortal one as well.

The most interesting dynamic, however, is not only Neshat's hand becoming a metaphor for Fatemeh's hand, but also this hand has the poetry of Farrokhzad, connecting the three women in one. Like Farrokhzad, Fatemeh faced many hardships that broke her spirit. She and 'Ali lived in poverty; she had lost her mother Khadijeh (555–619) at an early age, and she had to take care of her father's emotional needs soon thereafter. When the Prophet died, Abu Bakr and his followers jilted Fatemeh's family. Shari'ati detailed Fatemeh's depression, especially after Omar had attacked her and aborted her son Mohsen: "[H]er days passed with the taking of her children's hands and walking outside the city to a place called 'House of Sorrows.' There she would sit and cry. She would speak ill of the usurpers of Ali's rights. She would cry and lament for hours. She spent her short life crying and cursing her fate until she died."[81] Not only does this passage reflect the Shi'i sacrifice for the true and just path but also illustrates a devout, divinely guided woman as a normal one who feels depression and hopelessness. Fatemeh's very short life had never been easy or peaceful; hence, the placing of Farrokhzad's poetry on the women of Fatemeh presents more natural human facets of their lives and personalities. One could even argue that the voices of Farrokhzad and Saffarzadeh are not so different from each other but simply present different sides of one woman, thus making her psyche multidimensional and not a flat, mediated representation, as the photographs may *initially* represent.

Finally, in several photographs Neshat poses with her own son, demonstrating a mother–son motif that became entrenched with the image of Fatemeh after the revolution. In *My Beloved*, mother and son face the viewer, both enwrapped in a white chador and centered within the composition (Figure 13.9). She holds him close to her womb, enfolding him with her garments and thus her authority within the private "spaces" of her chador and body.[82] From the title, one may assume that the Beloved is the son, but the Beloved in classical Persian poetry can also be a lover or God (who is also a lover in Sufism). Yet the white chador is indicative of mourning, and because there is no father pictured, he might be the one for whom they mourn. A rifle is propped up, almost haphazardly, on the left side of the photograph, and again, like floating signifiers, the persons, weapon and text create a narrative within the picture plane for the viewer, despite there being no concrete connections between the three. Other photographs in the series have privileged women's status as martyrs, so there is the visual implication that the gun belongs to her and that she is willing to sacrifice her life not only for religion and country, but also for her son, because the protection of religion and country ultimately means protection for him. In addition, the grim inclusion of the white chador with the gun in the same frame may foretell of another death, but who will be the next to pass away, the mother or the son who will follow the example of his father?

The motif of a strong bond between mother and son in Iranian culture is, in general, prominent, and after the revolution and during the war, this motif was used for religious and persuasive ends. Neshat told Octavio Zaya in a 1997 interview, "[T]he Muslim woman is idealized as a mother and wife who is engaged in domesticity [...]. The Iranian government elaborates this definition by using the example of Fatemeh."[83] An example of the government's promotion of Fatemeh is a postage stamp from 1986 in which the ideal woman in chador holds her son with one side of the chador draping his back (Figure 13.10). The stamp commemorates Fatemeh's birthday, which coincides with International Woman's Day, March 8. On the boy's head is a red headband that says, "Ya Zahra'," which is another name for Fatemeh. This headband is the one worn by Iranian soldiers in battle during the war.[84] One could advocate that the battle to protect Iran is synonymous with the battle to protect the house of Fatemeh, and by extension, the women of the State who usually comprise men's honor. Much like the image of the Virgin and Child, in which the sad Virgin knows that her Son will ultimately die on the cross, the Shi'a mother stares bravely toward the future, knowing that one day her son will go to the battlefront and serve God and country. Also mentioned earlier, the rituals of the Fatemiyeh during the month of Muharram form a symbolic association between the martyrdoms of mother and son, Fatemeh and Imam Hossein. Thus, the stamp also creates a martyrology of strong women who have the integrity and love to raise their sons properly with the result of offering them up as the ultimate sacrifices for the State. Like Fatemeh, whose three sons (if one includes Mohsen) were martyrs to Shi'a Islam, Iranian women have the burden and God-ordained destiny to produce righteous men who will defend to the death.

As Neshat appropriates this mother-son-martyr motif in this photographs, the photograph shows the first verses of a Farrokhzad poem, "From you, I am dying/But you were my life."[85] Although only these two verses are clearly legible, the speaker of the poem addresses the tenderness of a particular person, yet this person is not quite sympathetic with or in touch with the speaker. The two persons have a strong bond, but a disconnect exists as well. The visual exegesis that Neshat puts forth is that the speaker is a mother, addressing her child. With this interpretation in mind, the child brings so much joy, yet he never truly understands his mother or sympathizes with her sorrows. Perhaps reflective of Farrokhzad's torture of being separated from her own son, any romanticism associated with motherhood becomes challenged through this poem. The message of the postage stamp illustrating the mother–son relationship seems straightforward, encouraging women to perform the duty of raising heroic martyrs, but with the inclusion of Farrokhzad's verses on the images with Neshat's son, motherhood becomes a condition characterized by painful, lonely moments and uneven exchanges. This nuancing of motherhood in the image of the ideal postrevolutionary Iranian woman, who is modeled after the great mother of Shi'a Islam, narrates that motherly love is both the greatest experience in life and the most sorrowful and can destroy a mother's heart, which the white chador might also insinuate. The mother is always the true martyr.

Overall, I have attempted to demonstrate two major points on Shirin Neshat's *Women of Allah* series: First, the Persian texts written on the photographs, inscribed by Neshat herself, must be "read" in some way for the subtleties of the series to unfold in front of the viewer. I have tried to deconstruct the system of signs within the series, such as the texts behind the sign of the ideal revolutionary woman and the texts by women writers, and how the melding of these many texts actually create an intertexuality that offers another dimension to the stereotypes and prototypes of these initial representations of women. Moreover, part of Neshat's performance in the photographs is an embodiment of the proposed ideas by Shari'ati and Mutahhari, but she also reveals the manipulation of the female form by demonstrating how the addition of divergent texts changes the body's signification. Second, I made the visual connection to the female body in Neshat's photographs to the inscription of Fatemeh's name on the Masjed-e Shah, because the mosque also possesses the potential for matriarchal authority, its legitimacy relying on Fatemeh. The mosque is generally not a site of gender equality, but Neshat's body transforms into a house of Fatemeh that holds the power to feminize the Iranian State and provides a sacred space by complicating authoritative texts of the revolution through their merging with texts of Iranian women writers who were also instrumental in forming another dissident consciousness. The representation of the female body in Neshat's photographs is not simply the proposed archetype of the State, but one also fashioned by other women's voices (as well as her own). Her movement in space creates an agency that, in turns, creates another text of her own that allows her to formulate commentaries based on multifaceted discursive discourses on modern Iran.

Notes and References

1 I would like to thank Michael Jerryson, David Simonowitz and Nuha Khoury for their feedback and comments on earlier drafts of this paper. I would also like to thank Julie Reuben for always going the extra mile to help me retrieve research material. Finally, I am grateful to Shirin Neshat and the Barbara Gladstone Gallery for their graciousness and kindness in their communications and permissions.

2 Carly Butler, "Ambivalence and Iranian Identity – The Work of Shirin Neshat," *Eastern Art Report* 47 (January 2002): 42; and Nina Cichocki, "Veils, Poems, Guns, and Martyrs: Four Themes of Muslim Women's Experiences in Shirin Neshat's Photographic Work," *thirdspace* 4, no. 1 (November 2004): 47–56. I used the web version, accessed August 15, 2012: http://www.thirdspace.ca/journal/article/view/cichocki/161

3 Amelia King-Kostelac, "Inscribing Meaning: Ambiguity and Agency in Shirin Neshat's Women of Allah" (master's thesis, University of California, Davis, 2008), 3.

4 Jacques Derrida, *On Grammatology*, trans. Gayatri Chakravorty Spivak (Baltimore: Johns Hopkins University Press, 1998), 7.

5 Shirin Neshat, "Women of Allah: Secret Identities," *Grand Street* 62 (Fall 1997): 145.

6 Scott MacDonald and Shirin Neshat, "Between Two Worlds: An Interview with Shirin Neshat," *Feminist Studies* 30, no. 3 (Fall 2004): 630.

7 Wendy Meryem K. Shaw has discussed "Iranian specificity" in relation to Neshat's films. "Ambiguity and Audience in the Films of Shirin Neshat," *Third Text* 15 (Winter 2001/02): 43.

8 Rachel Bailey Jones, "(Re)Envisioning Self and Other: Subverting Visual Orientalism through the Creation of Postcolonial Pedagogy," (PhD diss., University of North Carolina at Greensboro, 2007), 156.

9 Valentina Vitali, "Corporate Art and Critical Theory: On Shirin Neshat," *Women: A Cultural Review* 15, no. 1 (2004): 12.
10 Amei Wallach, "My Canvas, My Self Using Her Own Body, Shirin Neshat Turns Her Iranian Past into Art," *Newsday* (February 23, 1994): 50; and Amei Wallach, "Shirin Neshat: Islamic Counterpoints," *Art in America* 89, no. 10 (October 2001): 136.
11 Igor Zabel, "Women in Black," *Art Journal* 60, no. 4 (Winter 2001): 25.
12 Ibid.
13 Maria C. Lugones and Elizabeth V. Spelman, "Have We Got a Theory for You! Feminist Theory, Cultural Imperialism and the Demand for the 'The Women's Voice,'" in *Women and Values: Readings in Recent Feminist Philosophy*, ed. Marilyn Pearsall, 2nd ed. (Belmont: Wadsworth Publishing Company, 1992), 21, 27.
14 Gayatri Chakravorty Spivak, *The Post-Colonial Critic: Interviews, Strategies, Dialogues*, ed. Sarah Harasym (New York: Routledge, 1990), 42.
15 Richard Ettinghausen makes the argument that Arabic calligraphy on mosques or objects sometimes has mistakes and is difficult to decipher, implying that its presence is more symbolic or decorative than meant to be read. See "Arabic Epigraphy: Communication or Symbolic Affirmation" in *Near Eastern Studies Numismatics, Iconography, Epigraphy and History: Studies in Honor of George C. Miles*, ed. Dickran K. Kouymijian (Beirut: American University of Beirut, 1974): 297–317.
16 Begüm Özden Firat, "Writing over the Body, Writing with the Body: On Shirin Neshat's *Women of Allah* Series," in *Sign Here: Handwriting in the Age of New Media*, ed. Sonja Neef, José van Dijck and Eric Ketelaar (Amsterdam: Amsterdam University Press, 2006), 212.
17 Iftikhar Dadi, "Shirin Neshat's Photographs as Postcolonial Allegories," *Signs: Journal of Women in Culture and Society* 34, no. 1 (Autumn 2008): 137, 142.
18 Oleg Grabar, *The Mediation of Ornament* (Princeton: Princeton University Press, 1992), 67.
19 John Goodman, "Poetic Justice," *World Art* 16 (1998): 52.
20 Lila Azam Zanganeh, *My Sister, Guard Your Veil; My Brother, Guard Your Eyes: Uncensored Iranian Voices* (Boston: Beacon Press, 2006), 44.
21 MacDonald and Neshat, "Between Two Worlds," 629.
22 Ibid., 627–8.
23 Ibid., 628.
24 Neshat, "Women of Allah," 145.
25 Shadi Sheybani, "Women of Allah: A Conversation with Shirin Neshat," *Michigan Quarterly Review* 38, no. 2 (1999): 206–7; Marine van Hoof, "Shirin Neshat: Veils in the Wind," *ArtPress* 279 (May 2002): 37; Shirin Neshat, *Expressing the Inexpressible: Shirin Neshat* (Princeton: Films Media Group, 2000); and Neshat, "Women of Allah," 145.
26 Shirin Neshat and Octavio Zaya, "Bounds of Desire, Zones of Contention: Islam, Women, and the Veil," in *Carnal Pleasures: Desire, Public Space and Contemporary Art*, ed. Anna Novakov (San Francisco: Clamor, 1998), 160.
27 King-Kostelac mentions "ideological landscape" in relation to Neshat's photographs. See "Inscribing Meaning," 26.
28 Hamid Dabashi also comments that Neshat's images challenge hegemonic texts and language, specifically naming. See "Bordercrossings: Shirin Neshat's Body of Evidence," *Shirin Neshat* (Milan: Charta, 2000), 36.
29 Ibid., 45.
30 Ali Shariati, *Fatima is Fatima*, trans. Laleh Bakhtiar (Tehran: The Shariati Foundation, 1980), 121; 'Ali Shari'ati, *Zan: Fatemeh Fatemeh Ast* (Tehran: Chapakhsh, 1368), 112.
31 Ali Shariati, *The Modest Dress*, in *Shariati on Shariati and the Muslim Woman*, ed. Laleh Bakhtiar (Chicago: ABC International Group, 1996), 46; Shari'ati, *Zan*, 285.
32 Mutahhari, *The Islamic Modest Dress*, 55.
33 Ibid.
34 Ibid., 55–6.
35 Ibid., 78.

36 Ali Shariati, *Expectations from the Muslim Woman*, in *Shariati on Shariati and the Muslim Woman*, ed. Laleh Bakhtiar (Chicago: ABC International Group, 1996), 68–9, 71–2; Shari'ati, *Zan*, 243, 247–8.

37 Afsaneh Najmabadi, "Veiled Discourse – Unveiled Bodies," *Feminist Studies* 19, no. 3 (Fall 1993): 488.

38 Forugh Farrokhzad, *Another Birth: Selected Poems of Forugh Farrokhzad*, trans. Hasan Javadi and Susan Sallée (Emeryville: Albany Press, 1981), 79; Forugh Farrokhzad, *Majmu'eh-ye Ash'ar-e Forugh* [Collection of Forugh's poems] (Saarbrucken: Nawid-Verlag, 1992), 426.

39 Tahereh Saffarzadeh, "Nostalgia," in *The Red Umbrella* (Iowa City: Windhover Press, 1969), 10–11.

40 Farzaneh Milani, *Veils and Words: The Emerging Voices of Iranian Women Writers* (Syracuse: Syracuse University Press, 1992), 169; and Elhum Haghighat, "Quest for Solidarity, Resisting Patriarchy, and Seeking Connection: An Analysis of Persian Poetry Written by Women," *Journal for Politics, Gender and Culture* 2, no. 1 (Summer 2003): 116.

41 Shirin Neshat, *Women of Allah* (Torino: Marco Noire Editore, 1997), 7.

42 Leonard P. Alishan, "Tahereh Saffarzadeh: From the Wasteland to the Imam," *Iranian Studies* 15, nos.1–4 (1982): 203–4.

43 Nasrin Rahimieh, "Magic Realism in Moniru Ravanipur's *Ahl-e Gharg*," *Iranian Studies* 23, nos. 1–4 (1990): 61.

44 Ibid., 74.

45 Adapted English text by Moniru Ravanipur in Artspeak Gallery, *Shirin Neshat: "Women of Allah"* (Vancouver: Artspeak Gallery, 1997), 28. For original text, see Moniru Ravanipur, *Ahl-e Gharg* [The drowned ones] (Tehran: Nashr-e Gheseh, 1383), 142.

46 Sheybani, "Women of Allah," 207.

47 Neshat says that she was influenced by the dichotomizing black-and-white photographs in photojournalism. Sheybani, "Women of Allah," 205.

48 Samar Mohammad Bush, "Complicating the Veiled Iranian Woman: The Work of Shirin Neshat and Shadi Ghadirian" (master's thesis, University of Connecticut, 2008), 16–17. See also King-Kostelac, "Inscribing Meaning," 17. For a discussion of Walter Benjamin's photographic aura, see *Illuminations*, ed. Hannah Arendt, trans. Harry Zohn (New York: Schocken Books, 1968),

49 Cichocki, "Veils, Poems, Guns, and Martyrs."

50 Shari'ati, *Zan*, 23.

51 Mary F. Thurlkill, *Chosen Among Women: Mary and Fatima in Medieval Christianity and Shi'ite Islam* (Notre Dame: University of Notre Dame Press, 2007), 111–13.

52 Shoja Azari, "An Inside Look at Shirin Neshat's Art," in *Shirin Neshat*, ed. Paulette Gagnon (Montreal: Musée d'art contemporain de Montréal, 2001), 115.

53 I take this concept from Valérie Gonzalez, "The Double Ontology of Islamic Calligraphy: a Word-Image on a Folio from the Museum of Raqqada (Tunisia)," in *M. Uğur Derman armağani: altmışbeşinci yaşı münasebetiyle sunulmuş tebliğler*, ed. Irvin Cemil Schick (Istanbul: Sabancı Universitesi, 2000), 1–28.

54 Oleg Grabar's chapter 11, "The Intermediary of Writing," inspires this concept, but his argument is that writing is not necessarily meant to be read or transmit a message when it transforms an object into an aesthetic object. The writing on an object creates a relationship to its surface, thus transforming the object into a work of art through writing's calligraphic nature. Grabar, *The Mediation of Ornament* (Princeton: Princeton University Press, 1992), 47–118.

55 Hamid Naficy, "Poetics and Politics of the Veil, Voice and Vision in Iranian Post-Revolutionary Cinema," in *Veil: Veiling, Representation and Contemporary Art*, ed. David A. Bailey and Gilane Tawadros (Cambridge, MA: MIT Press, 2003), 146.

56 Firat, "Writing over the Body, Writing with the Body," 211.

57 Jacques Derrida, *Writing and Difference*, trans. Alan Bass (Chicago: University of Chicago Press, 1978), 213.

58 King-Kostelac, "Inscribing Meaning," 10.

59 Mutahhari, *The Islamic Modest Dress*, 65.
60 Faegheh Shirazi, *The Veil Unveiled: The Hijab in Modern Culture* (Gainsville: University of Florida Press, 2001), 106.
61 Nathalie Leleu, "Shirin Neshat: The Image Dispute," *Parachute* 100 (October 2000): 78.
62 Sheybani, "Women of Allah," 207.
63 Neshat, *Women of Allah*, 8.
64 Sheybani, "Women of Allah," 208.
65 Neshat, *Women of Allah*, 8.
66 The genealogy of the tulip growing from martyrs' blood has not been fully investigated. It is not clear when the motif was transferred to the Karbala paradigm. In the Iranian national epic *Shahnameh* (Book of Kings, c. 1010), a *giya* (plant) springs from the Persian prince Siavash, not a *laleh* (tulip). See Abu'l-Qasem Ferdowsi, *Shahnameh-ye Hakim Abu'l-Qasem Ferdowsi* (Tehran: Moaseseh-ye Intisharat-e Amir Kabir, 1341), 142. An example from classical poetry comes from Hafez (1325–90), who mentions a tulip growing from Farhad's blood tears, although such a scene is not in Nizami's *Khamseh* (1177–80). See Khajeh Shams al-Din Hafez-e Shirazi, *Divan-e Khajeh Shams al-Din Hafez-e Shiraz* (Tehran: Chapkhaneh-ye Farhang, 1372), 68. The modern poet Arif Qazvini (1882–1934) would invoke this motif of the tulip from the spilled blood of laypeople and nationalist revolutionaries in his poem "*Az Khun-e Javanan-e Vatan Laleh Damideh*" [Tulips have grown out of the blood of the young people of the homeland], which he wrote during the Constitutional Revolution (1906–11). See Mirza Abulqasem Arif Qazvini, *Arif-e Qazvini* (Brea: Nashre Karoonshat, 1375), 363.
67 Azam Torab, *Performing Islam: Gender and Ritual in Iran* (Leiden: Brill, 2007), 186–91.
68 Ayatollah Sayyed Ruhollah Mousavi Khomeini, *A Clarification of Questions* [Resaleh Towzih al-Masael], trans. J. Borujerdi (Boulder: Westview Press, 1984), 56–7.
69 Thurlkill, *Chosen Among Women* 43.
70 Ahmad T., untitled statement, in *Shirin Neshat: "Women of Allah"* (Vancouver: Artspeak Gallery, 1997), 23.
71 Torab, *Performing Islam*, 157.
72 Hamideh Sadghi, *Women and Politics in Iran: Veiling, Unveiling, and Reveiling* (New York: Cambridge University Press, 2007), 157.
73 Amna Malik makes the visual connection between Neshat photographs and the *hamsa* talisman in "Dialogues Between 'Orientalism' and Modernism in Shirin Neshat's '*Women of Allah*,'" in *Global and Local Art Histories*, ed. Celina Jeffery and Gregory Minissale (Cambridge: Cambridge Scholars Publishing, 2007), 162–3.
74 Feresteh Daftari, "Islamic or Not," in *Without Boundary: Seventeen Ways of Looking*, ed. Feresteh Daftari (New York: The Museum of Modern Art), 13.
75 Thurlkill, *Chosen Among Women*, 116.
76 King-Kostelac, "Inscribing Meaning," 3.
77 Thurlkill, *Chosen Among Women*, 43.
78 Daftari, "Islamic or Not,"13.
79 Sussan Babaie, "Locating the 'Modern' in 'Islamic' Arts," *Getty Research Journal* 3 (2011): 137. See also Heyam Dannawi, "Women in Black: Shirin Neshat's Images of Veiled Revolutionaries" (master's thesis, University of Arkansas at Little Rock, 2008), 32.
80 Sheybani, "Women of Allah," 208. Dabashi also points out this dichotomy of religion and sexuality in *Untitled*. See "Bordercrossings," 37.
81 Shariati, *Fatima is Fatima*, 24; Shari'ati, *Zan*, 9
82 King-Kostelac, "Inscribing Meaning," 20.
83 Shirin Neshat and Octavio Zaya, "Bounds of Desire, Zones of Contention (Islam, Women and the Veil)," in *Women of Allah* (Torino: Marco Noire Editore, 1997), unpaginated.
84 Shirazi, *The Veil Unveiled*, 130.
85 Farrokhzad, *Majmu'eh-ye Ash'ar-e Forugh*, 388.

ILLUSTRATIONS

2.8 Antoin Sevruguin, *A Persian Anderun* (Harem) (1503), 1870–90. Albumen print. Formerly in the Stuart Cary Welch Collection. Published as *Grande dame persane recevant ses amies* [A great Persian lady receiving her friends] in Henry René d'Allemagne, *Du Khorassan au pays des Backhtiaris: Trois mois de voyage en Perse* II (Paris: Hachette, 1911), 5.

2.9 Antoin Sevruguin, *A Woman of the Harem with her Daughters* (661), c. 1870s. Albumen print. Also titled *A Persian Harem* or *Aristocratic Court Women.* Formerly in the Stuart Cary Welch Collection. Another print is in the collection of the National Museum of Ethnology in Leiden, the Netherlands.

2.10 Antoin Sevruguin, *Two Women with Bouquets of Flowers*, c. 1870–90. Albumen print. Private collection, Tehran.

2.11 Antoin Sevruguin, *Harem Women*, c. 1870–90. Albumen print. Private collection, Tehran. Right half of image published in Taj al-Saltaneh, *Anguish: Memoirs of a Persian Princess form the Harem to Modernity 1884–1914*, ed. Abbas Amanat, trans. Anna Vanzan and Amin Neshati (Washington, DC: Mage Publishers, 1993), 133.

2.12 Luigi Pesce, *In the Mosque of the Damegan/The Eunuchs*, c. 1850s. Album 683, fol. 40. Reproduced by permission from the Metropolitan Museum of Art, New York, 1977.683.21. Gift of Charles Wilkinson, 1977.

3.1 Antoin Sevruguin, *Shahr-i farang*, c. 1890–1900. Gelatin silver print. Reproduced by permission from the Myron Bement Smith Collection, Freer Gallery of Art and Arthur M. Sackler Gallery Archives, Smithsonian Institution, Washington, DC. Gift of Katharine Dennis Smith, 1973–85.

3.2 Anonymous, *Shahr-e farang*, c. 1940s, repository unknown. Published in Mohamad Tavakoli-Targhi, *Refashioning Iran: Orientalism, Occidentalism, and Historiography* (New York: Palgrave, 2001), cover photograph.

3.3 Antoin Sevruguin, *Ice Cream Vendor.* Gelatin silver print, print number 58.g.9. Reproduced by permission from the Myron Bement Smith Collection, Freer Gallery of Art and Arthur M. Sackler Gallery Archives, Smithsonian Institution, Washington, DC. Gift of Katharine Dennis Smith, 1973–85.

3.4 Antoin Sevruguin, *A Boy Receiving Punishment with Small Crowd of Male Spectators.* Gelatin silver print, print number 58.g.61. Reproduced by permission from the Myron Bement Smith Collection, Freer Gallery of Art and Arthur M. Sackler Gallery Archives, Smithsonian Institution, Washington, DC. Gift of Katharine Dennis Smith, 1973–85.

4.1 Kamal al-Mulk, *Takkiyeh Dowlat: Talar Salaam*, n.d. Golestan Palace.

5.1 Judy Dater, *Farah Diba Pahlavi and Donna Stein*, 1990. Gelatin silver print. Courtesy of the artist, copyright Judy Dater.

13.5 Shirin Neshat, *Seeking Martyrdom #2*, 1995. B&W RC print and ink (photo taken by Cynthia Preston). All images are copyright Shirin Neshat. Courtesy Gladstone Gallery, New York.

13.6 Shirin Neshat, *Stories of Martyrdom #1*, 1994. B&W RC print and ink (photo taken by Cynthia Preston). All images are copyright Shirin Neshat. Courtesy Gladstone Gallery, New York.

13.7 Banner depicting the *Panjtan Paak*, 1999. Courtesy of David Simonowitz.

13.8 *Untitled*, 1996. B&W RC print and ink (photo taken by Larry Burns). All images are copyright Shirin Neshat. Courtesy Gladstone Gallery, New York.

13.9 Shirin Neshat, *My Beloved*, 1994. B&W RC print and ink (photo taken by Cynthia Preston). All images are copyright Shirin Neshat. Courtesy Gladstone Gallery, New York.

13.10 Stamp from the Islamic Republic of Iran, depicting Fatemeh's birthday and Woman's Day, March 8, 1980. Public domain; collection of the author.

Illustration 1.1

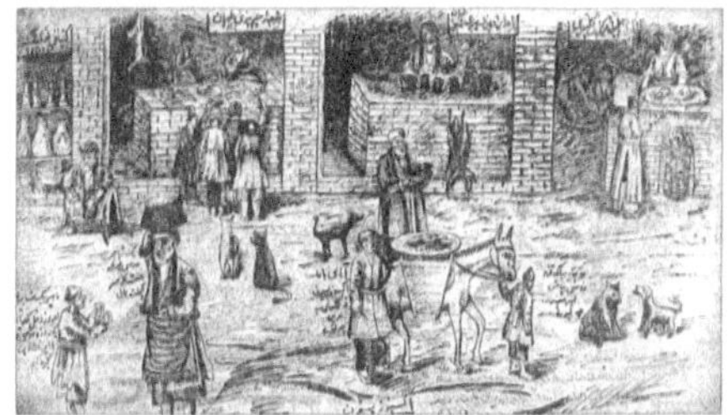

Illustration 1.2

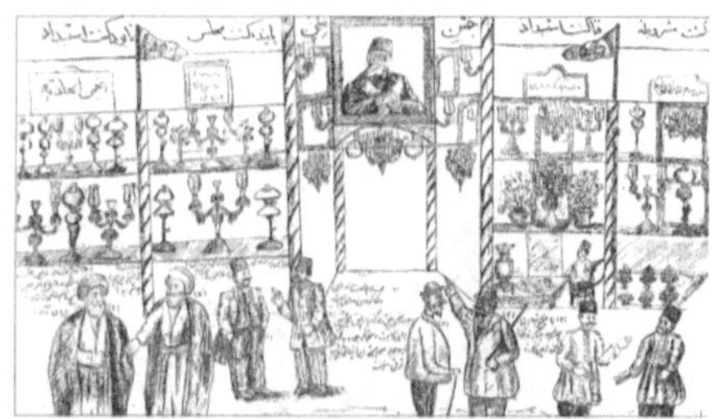

Illustration 1.3

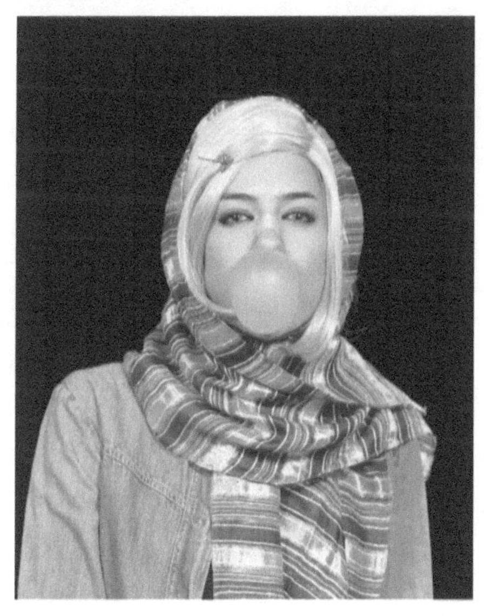

Illustration 2.1

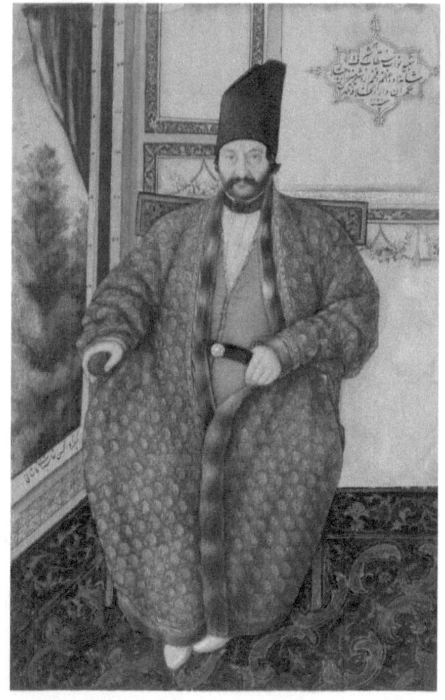

Illustration 2.2

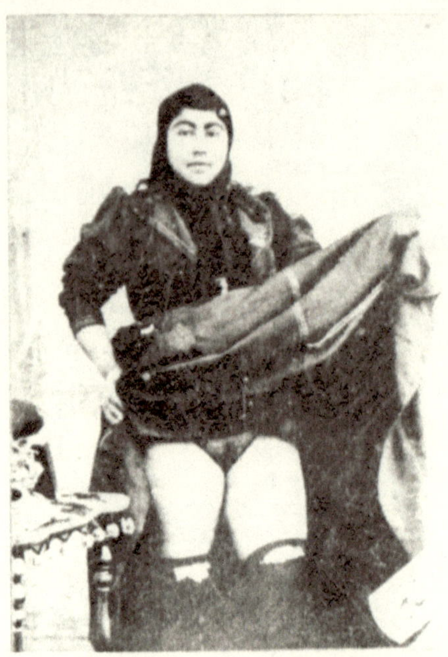

Illustration 2.3

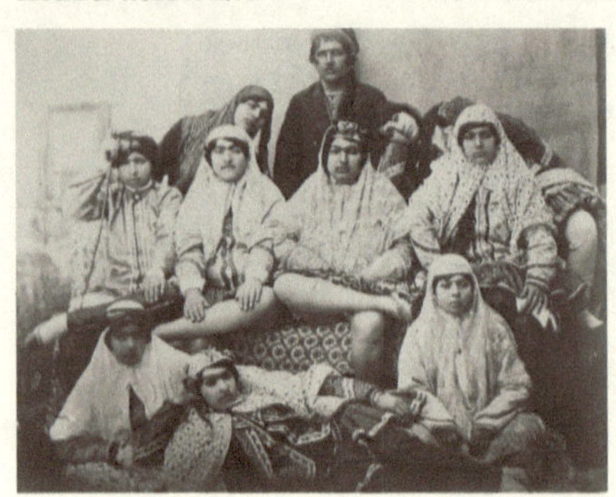

Illustration 2.4

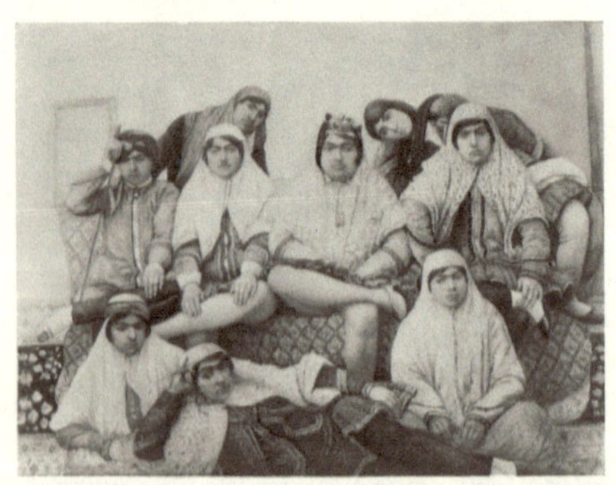

Illustration 2.5

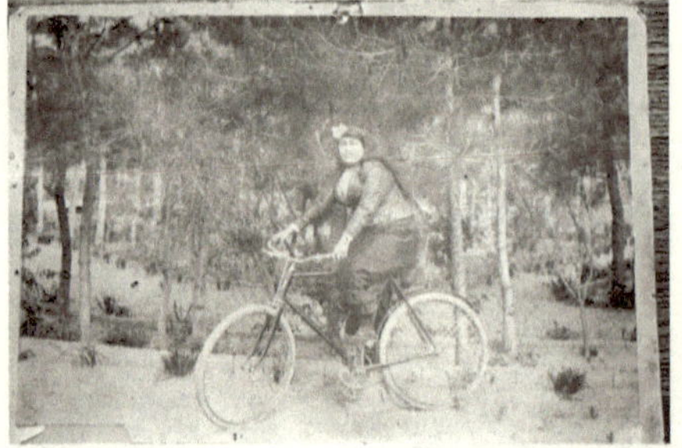

Illustration 2.6

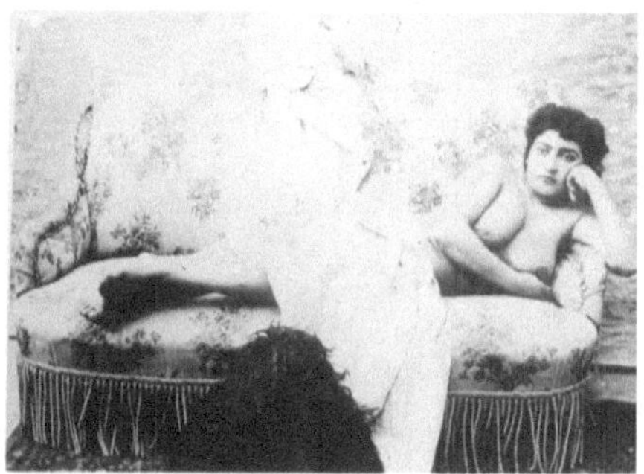

Illustration 2.7

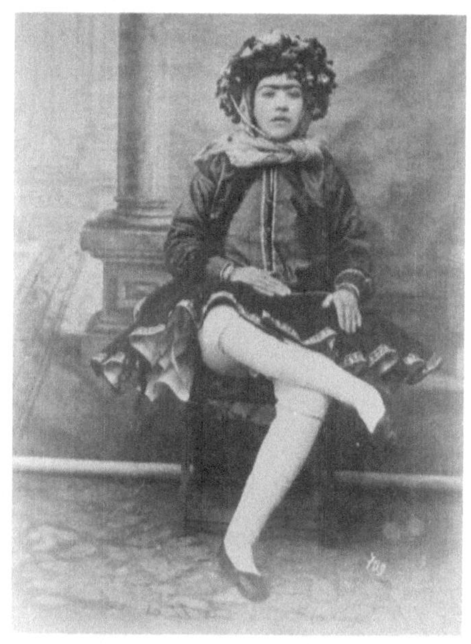

Illustration 2.8

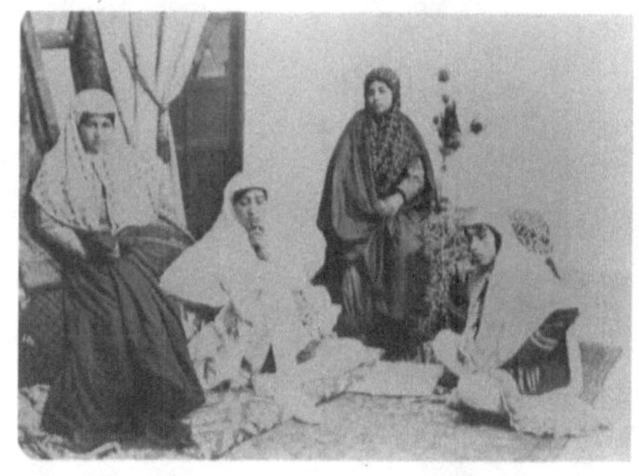

Illustration 2.9

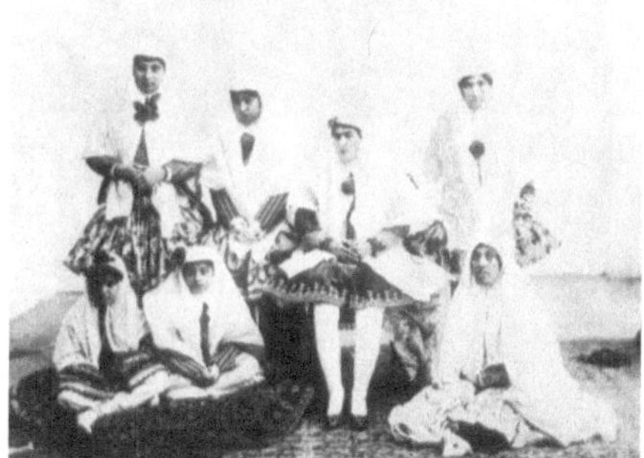

Illustration 2.10

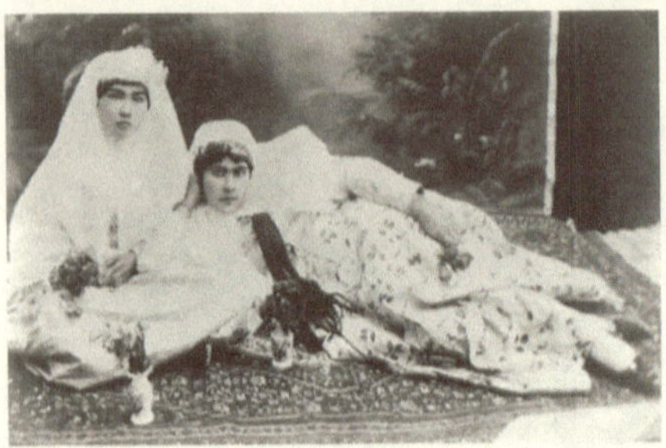

Illustration 2.11

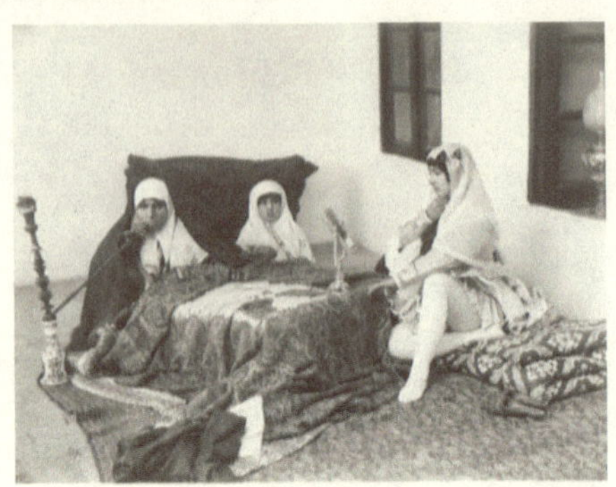

Illustration 2.12

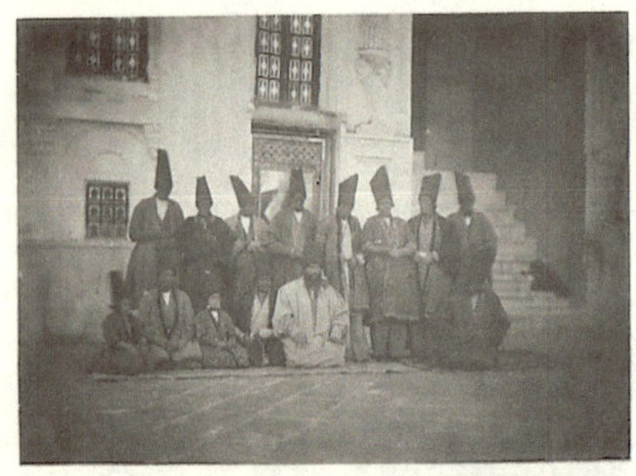

Illustration 3.1

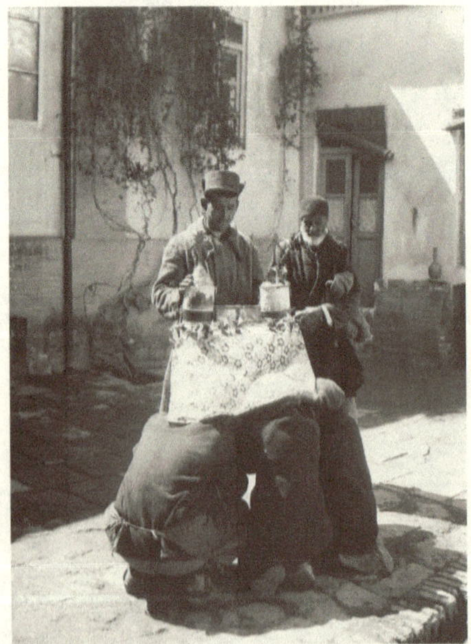

Illustration 3.2

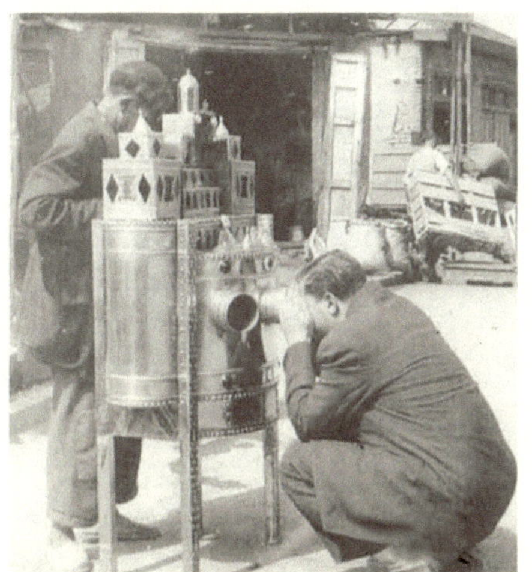

Illustration 3.3

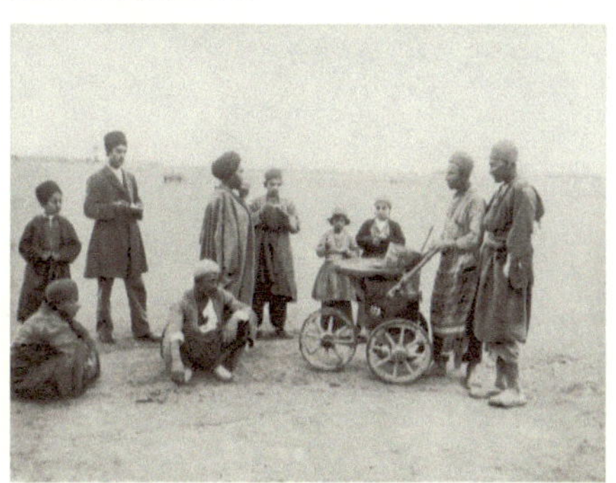

Illustration 3.4

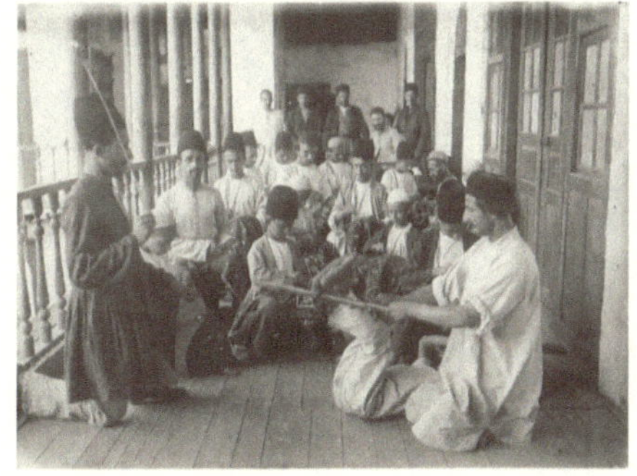

Illustration 4.1

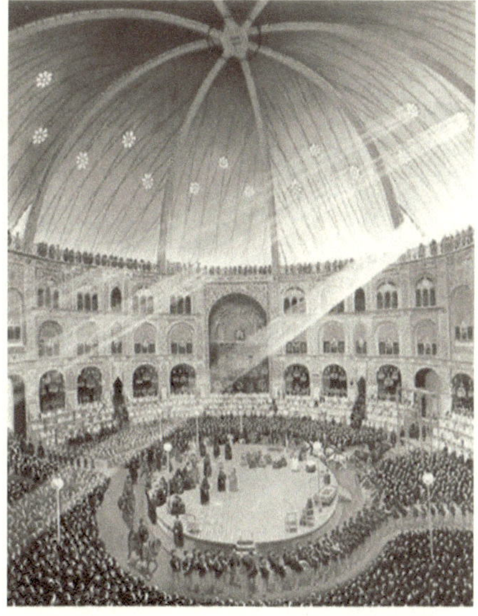

Illustration 5.1

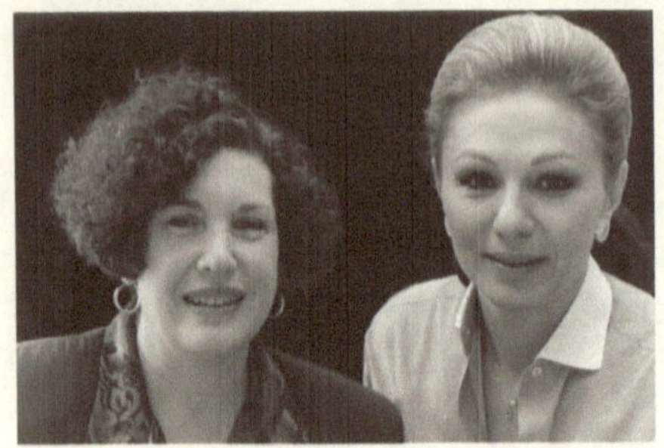

Illustration 6.1

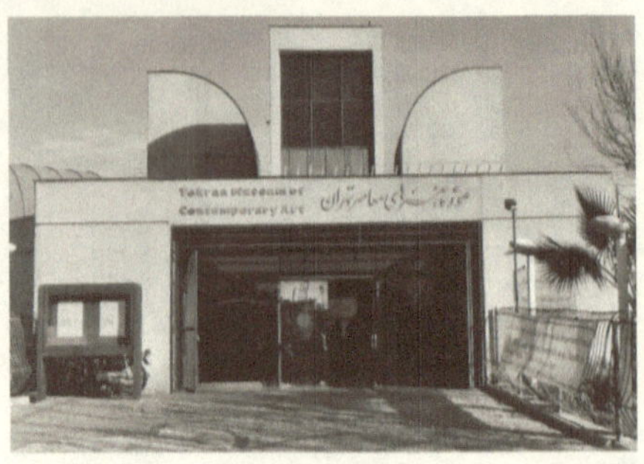

Illustration 6.2

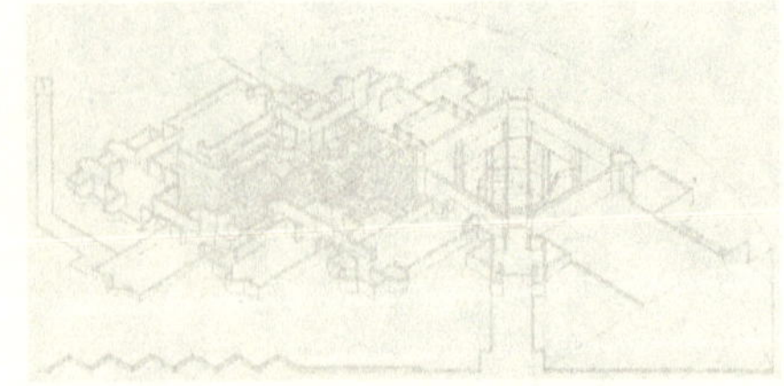

Illustration 7.1

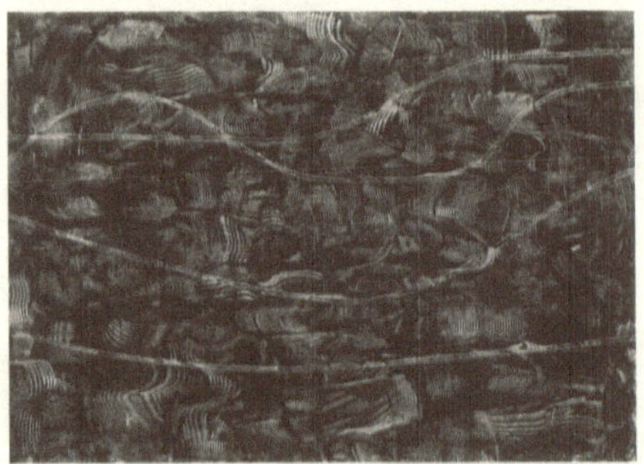

Illustration 7.2

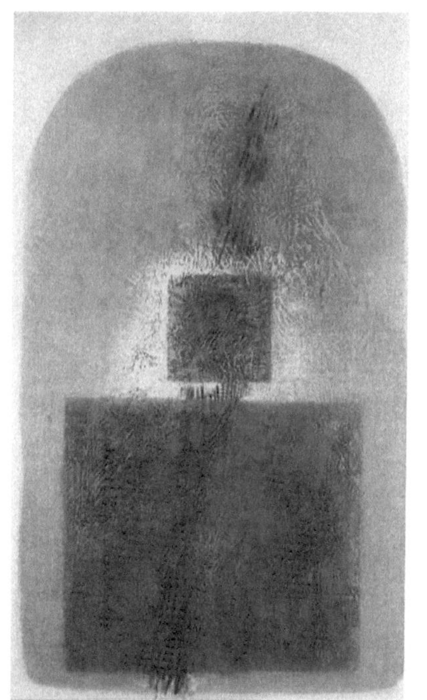

Illustration 7.3

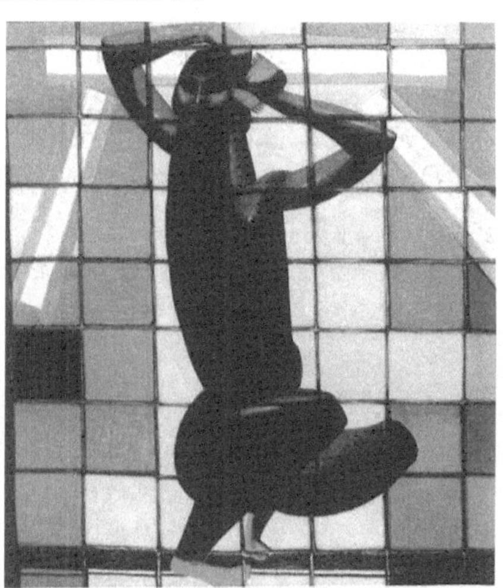

Illustration 7.4

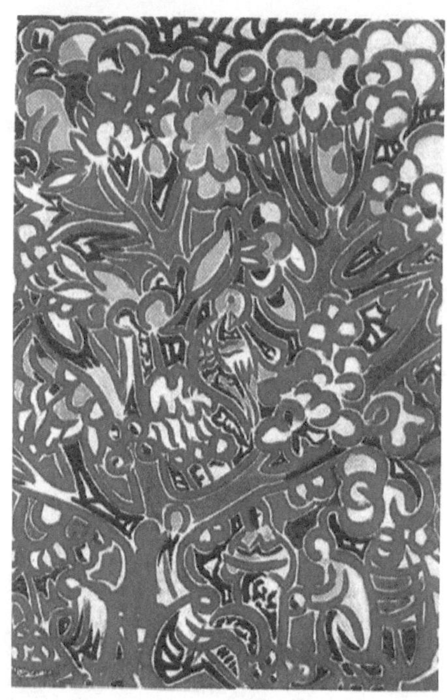

Illustration 7.5

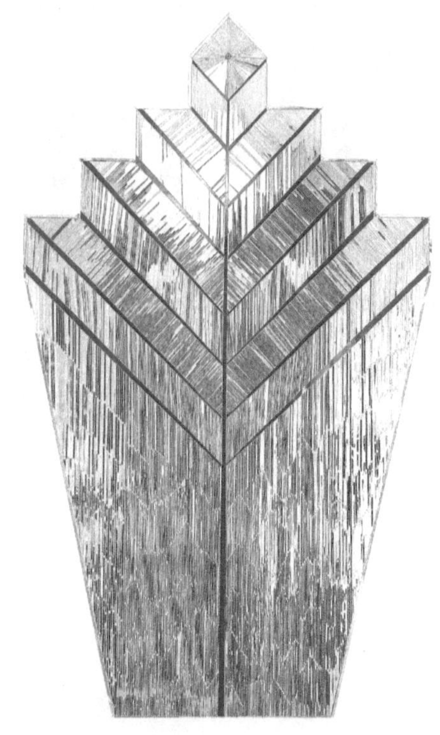

Illustration 7.6

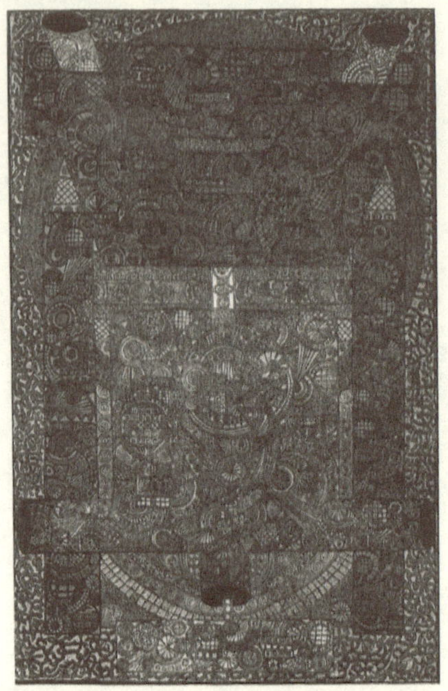

Illustration 7. 7

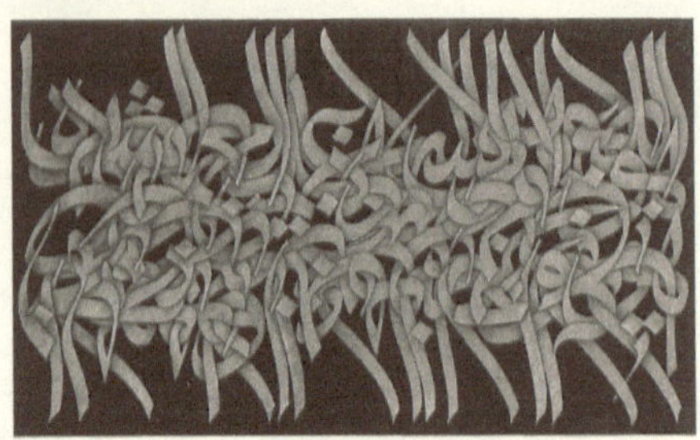

Illustration 7.8

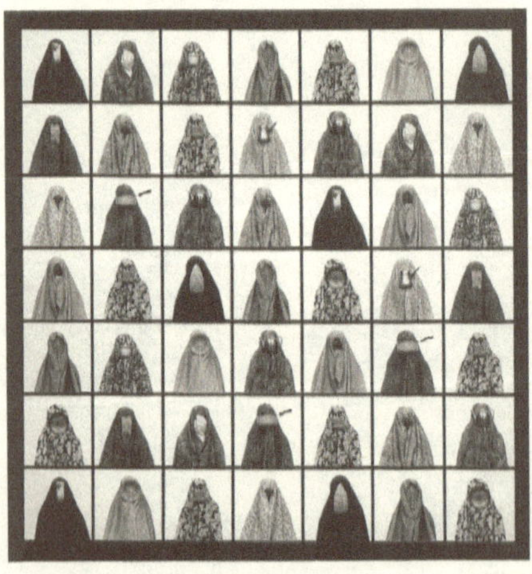

Illustration 7.9

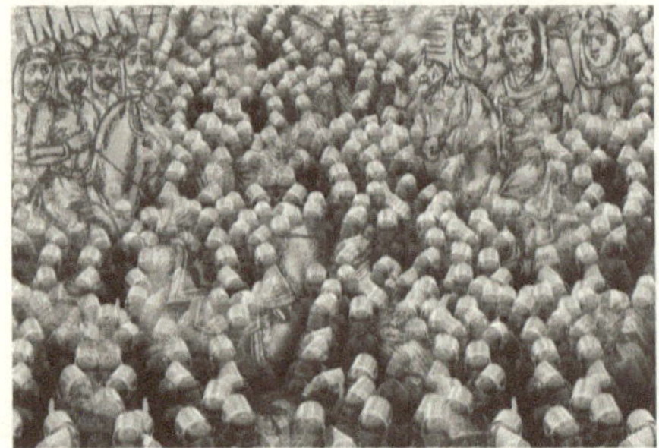

Illustration 7.10

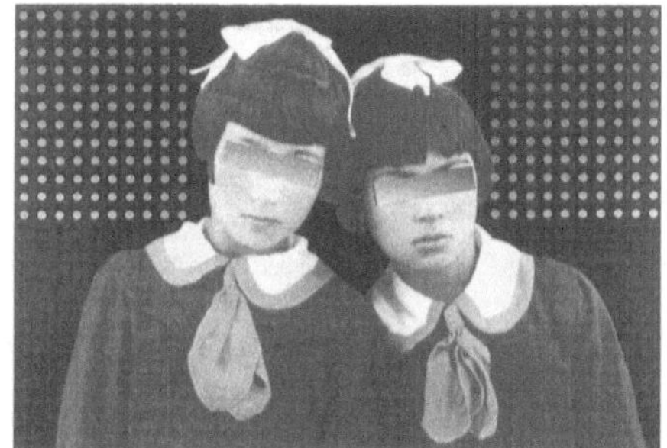

Illustration 8.1

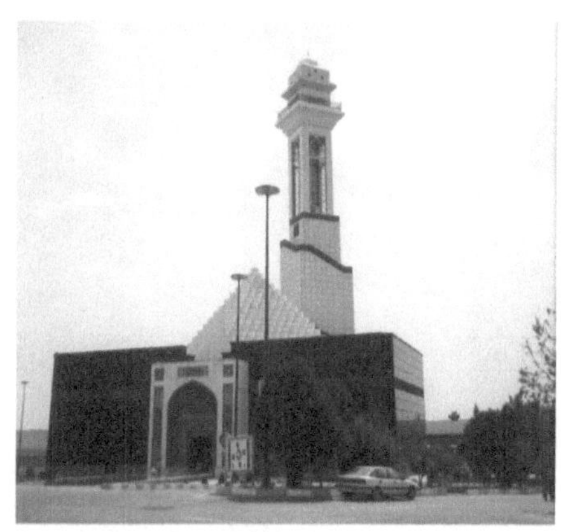

Illustration 8.2

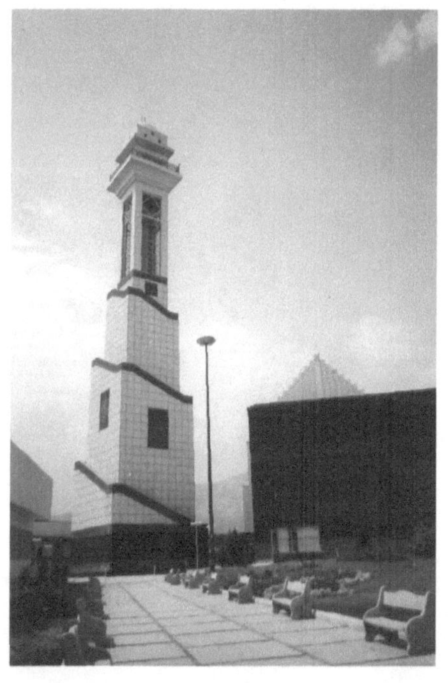

Illustration 8.3

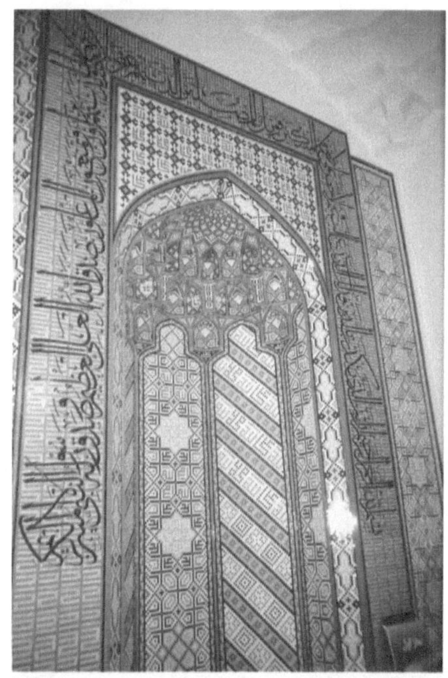

Illustration 8.4

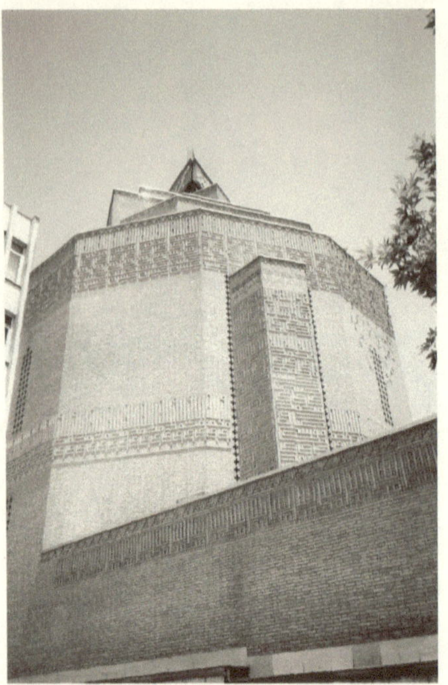

Illustration 8.5

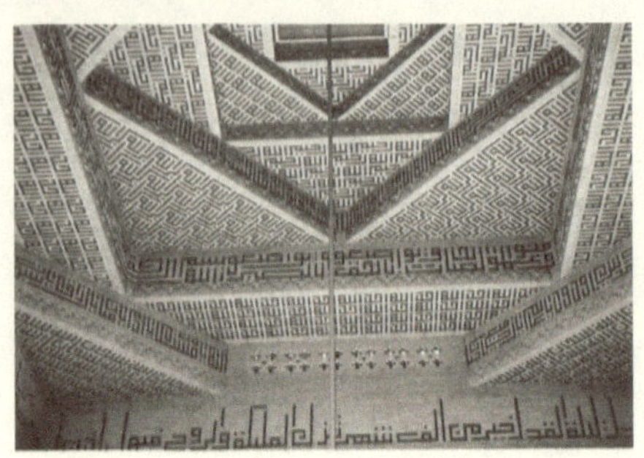

Illustration 8.6

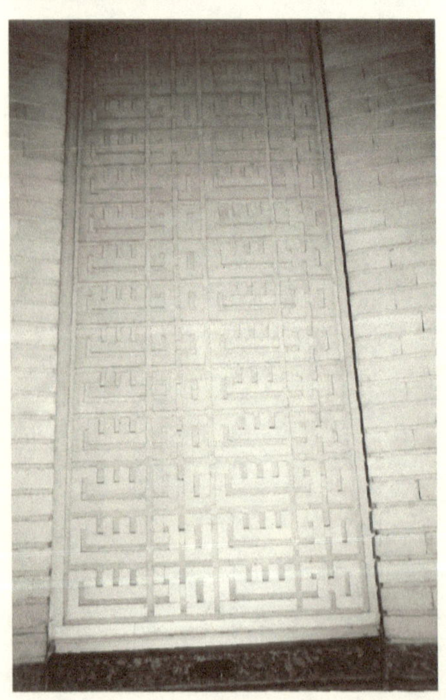

Illustration 9.1

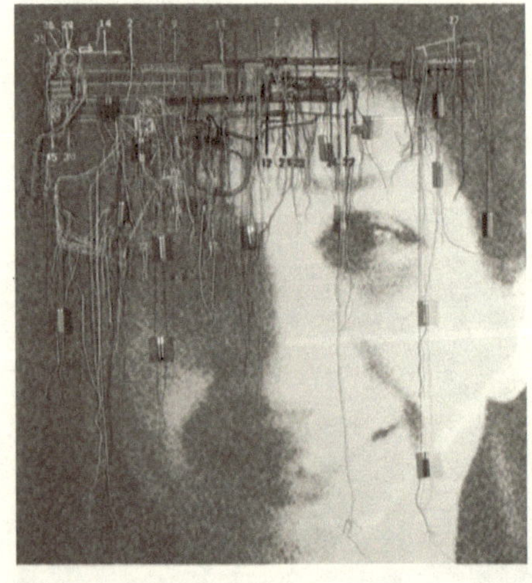

Illustration 9.2

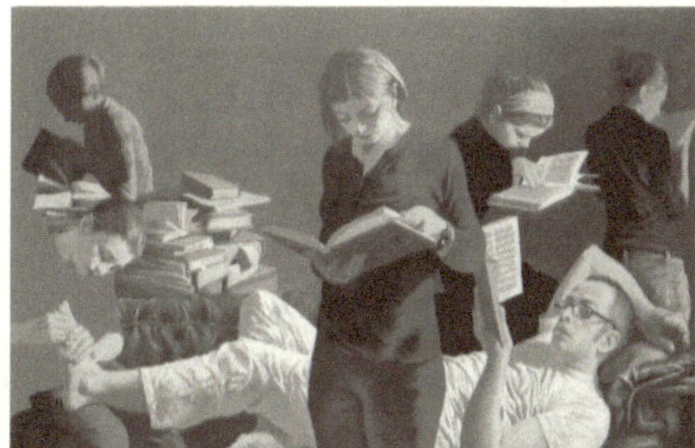

Illustration 9.3

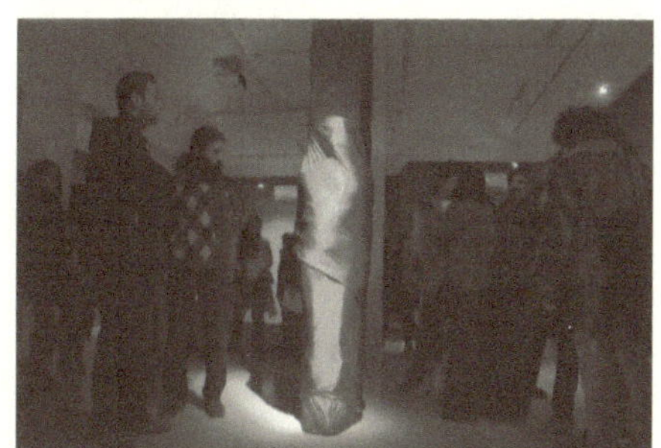

Illustration 9.4

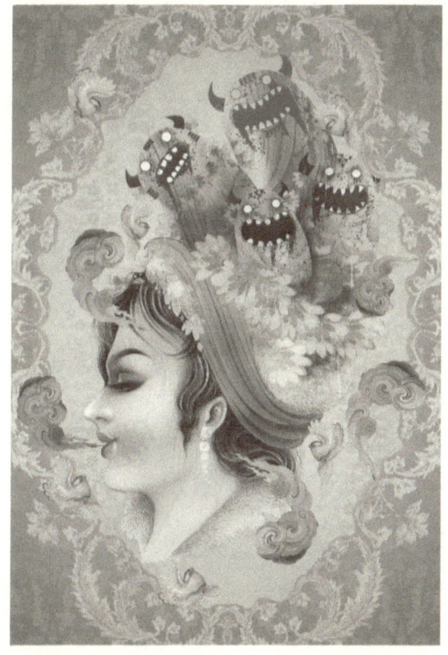

Illustration 9.5

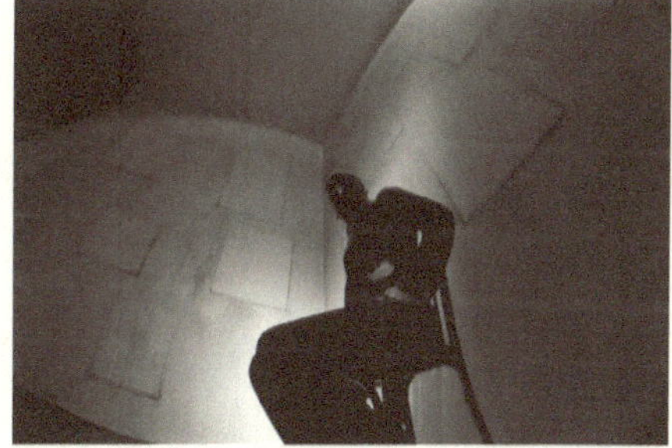

Illustration 9.6

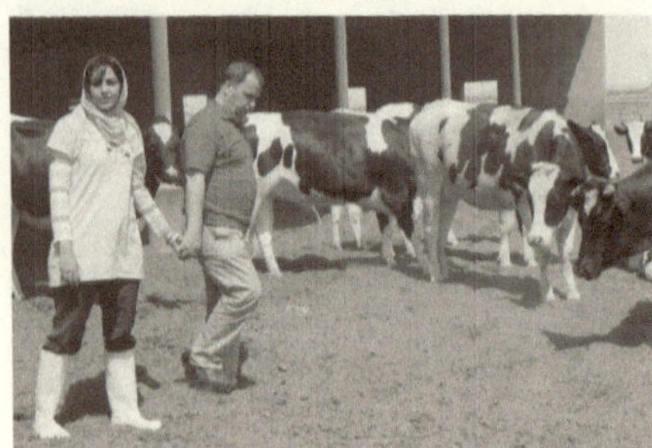

Illustration 10.1

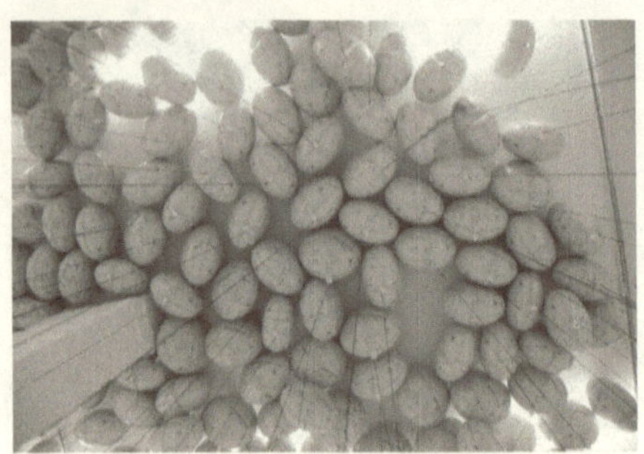

Illustration 10.2

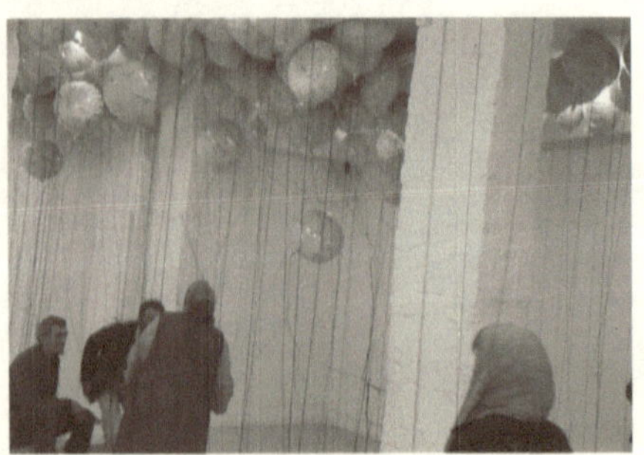

Illustration 10.3

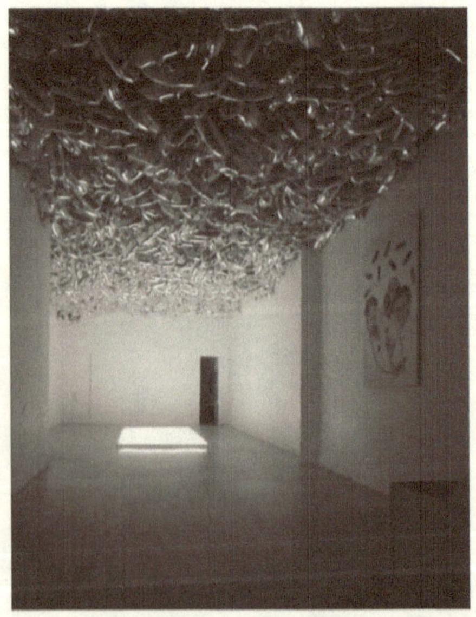

Illustration 10.4

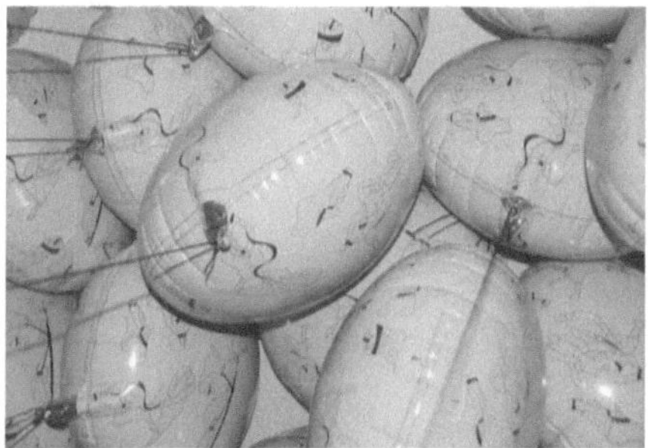

Illustration 10.5

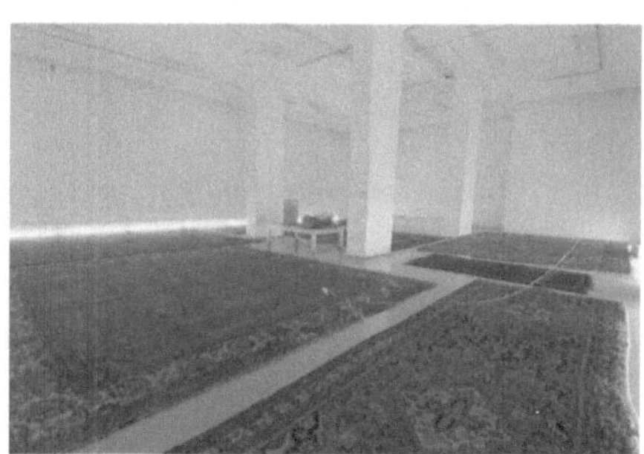

Illustration 10.6

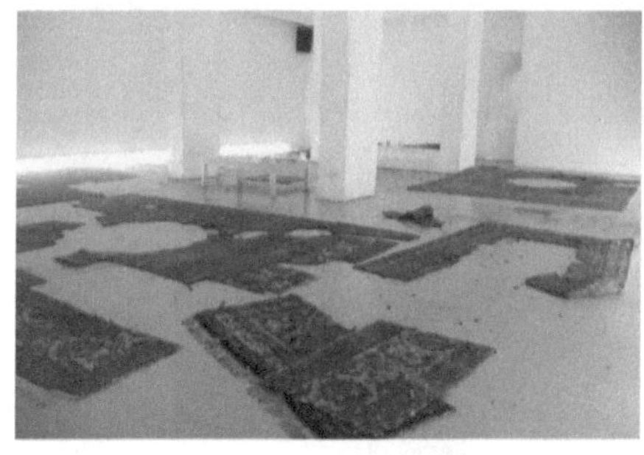

Illustration 10.7

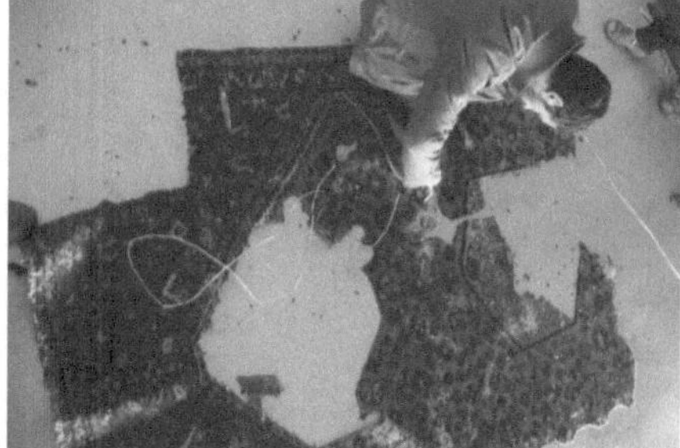

Illustration 10.8

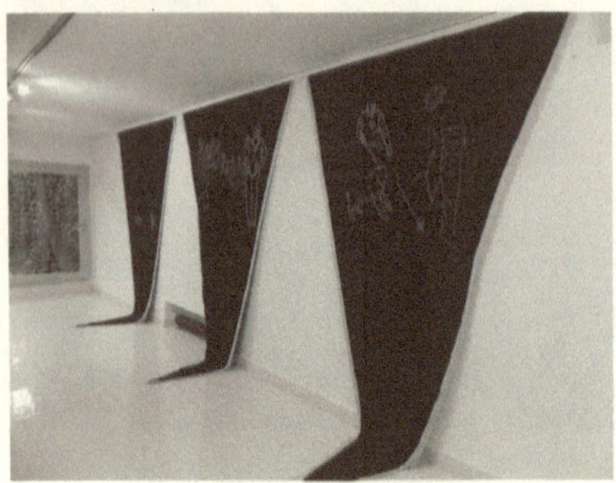

Illustration 10.9

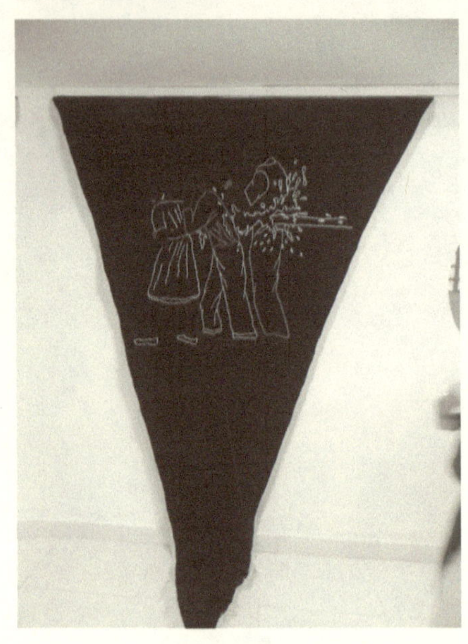

Illustration 10.10

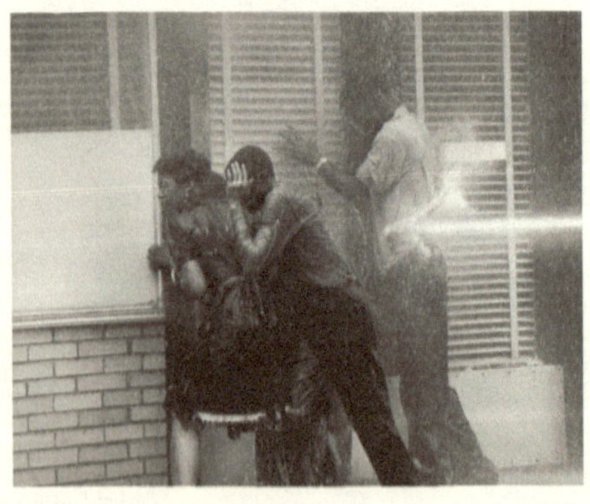

Illustration 10.11

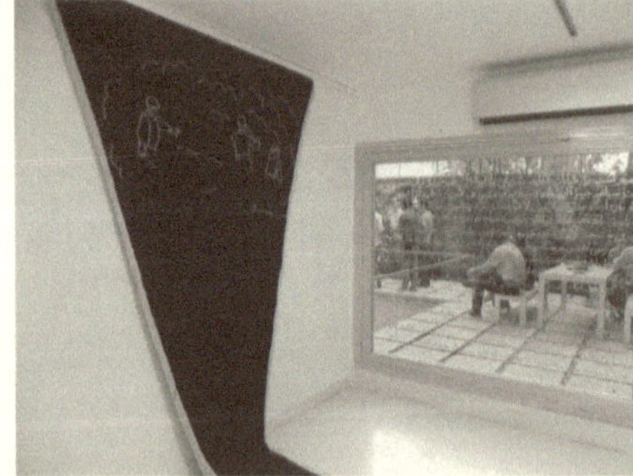

Illustration 11.1

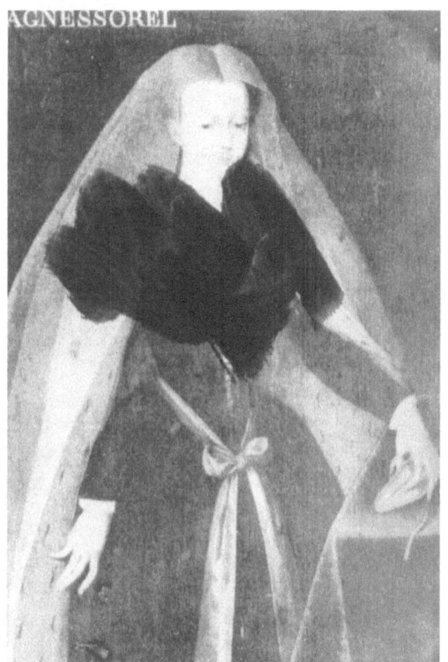

Illustration 11.2

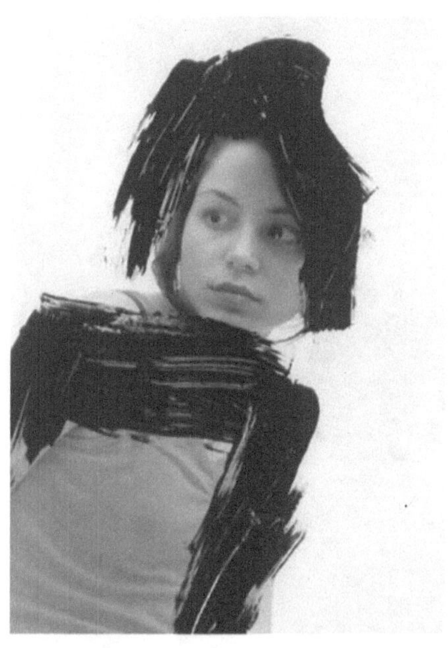

Illustration 11.3

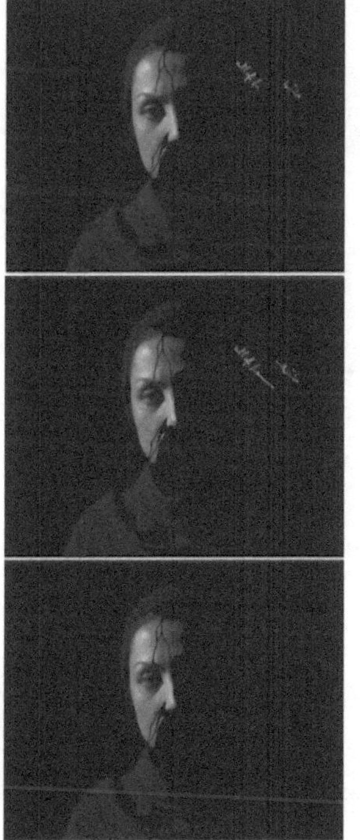

Illustration 11.4

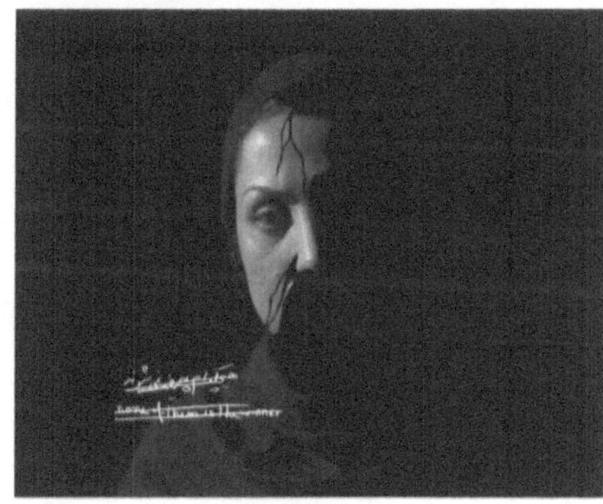

Illustration 11.5

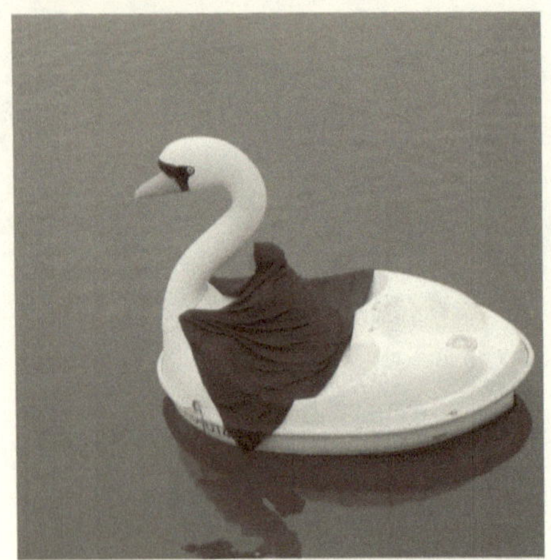

Illustration 12.1

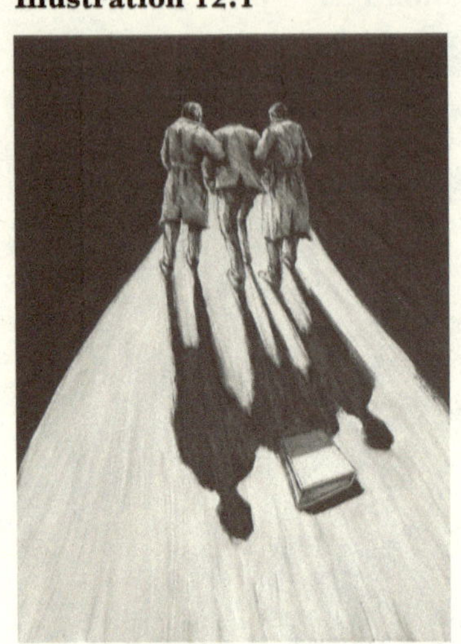

Illustration 12.2

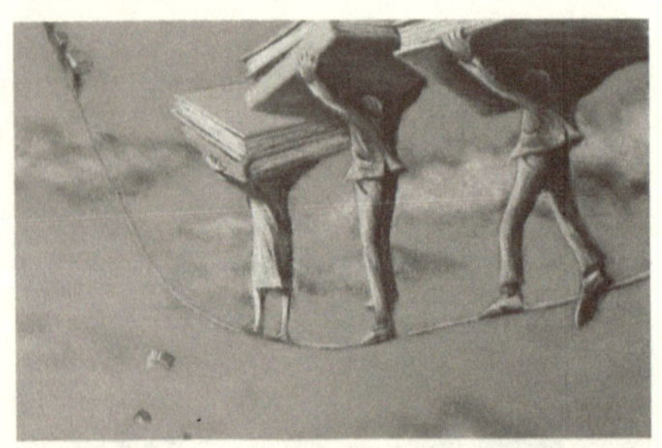

Illustration 12.3

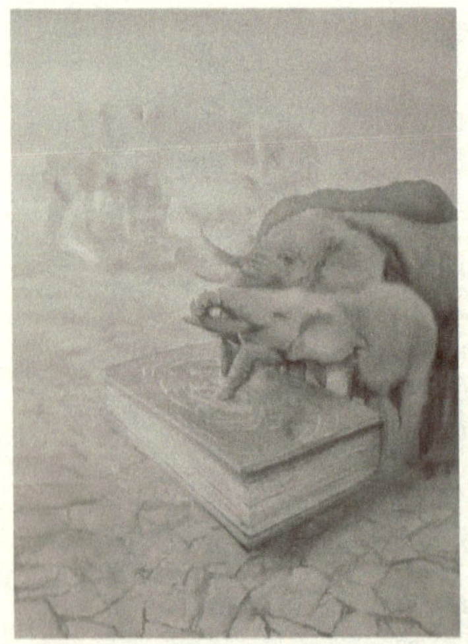

Illustration 12.4

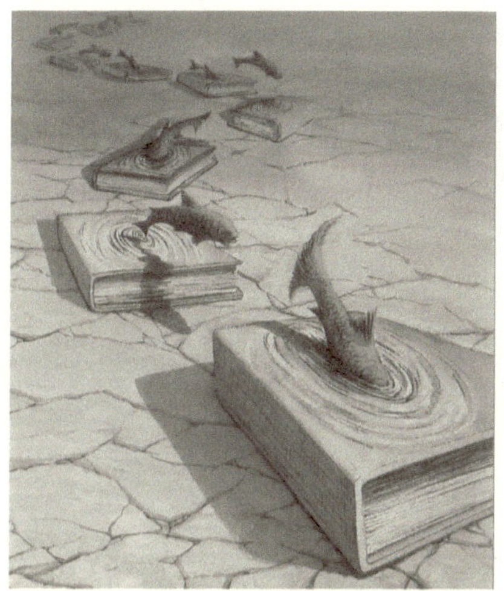

Illustration 12.5

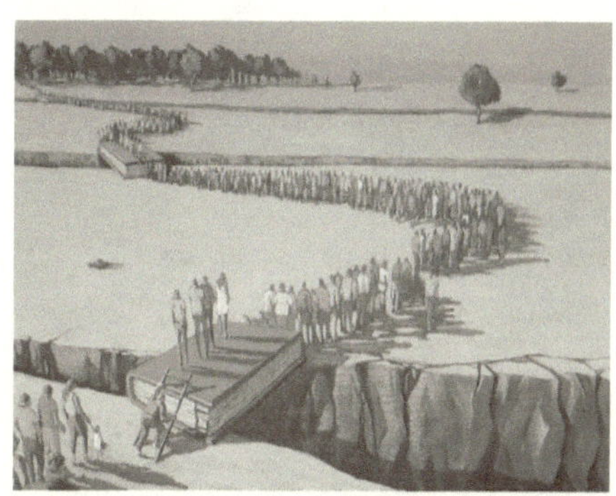

Illustration 12.6

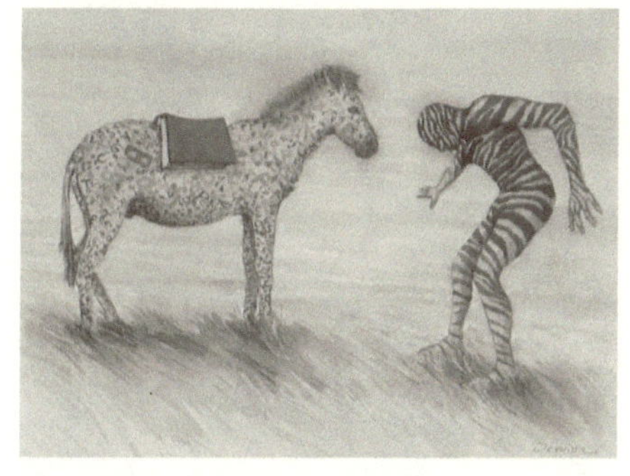

Illustration 12.7

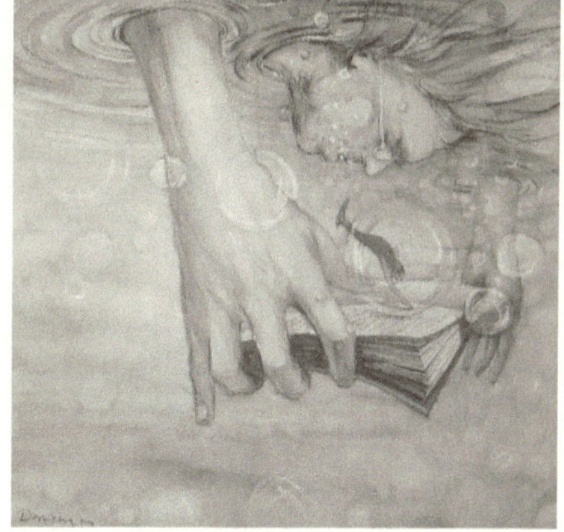

Illustration 12.8

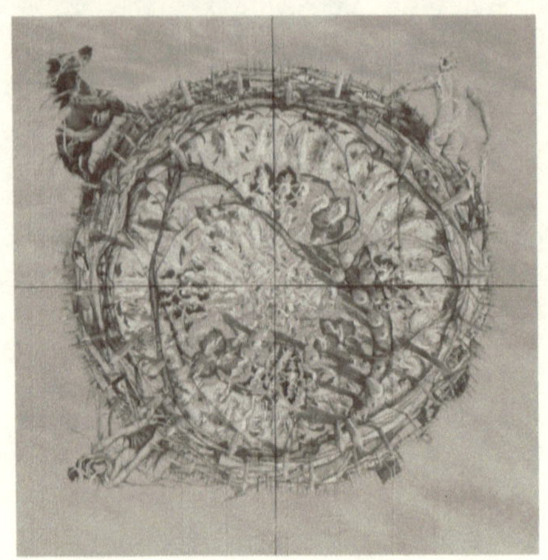

Illustration 12.9

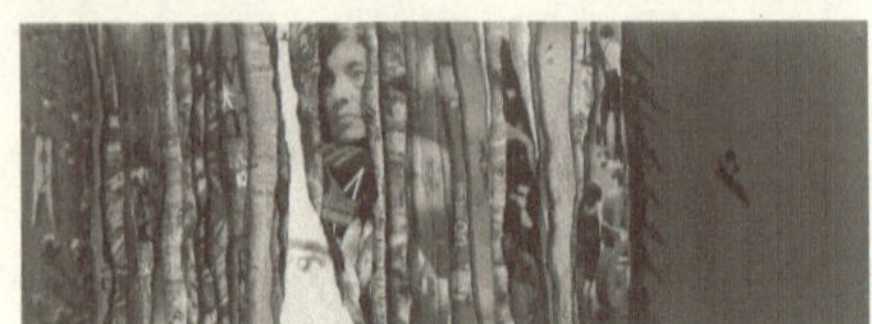

Illustration 13.1

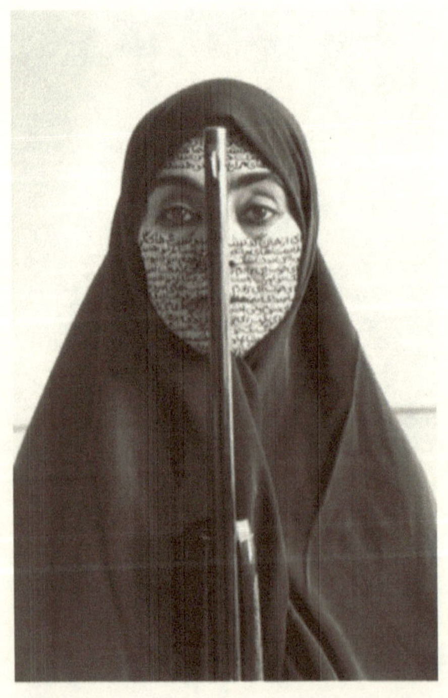

Illustration 13.2

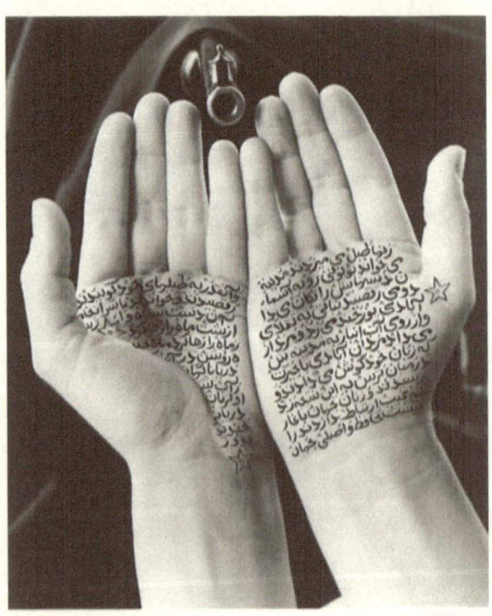

Illustration 13.3

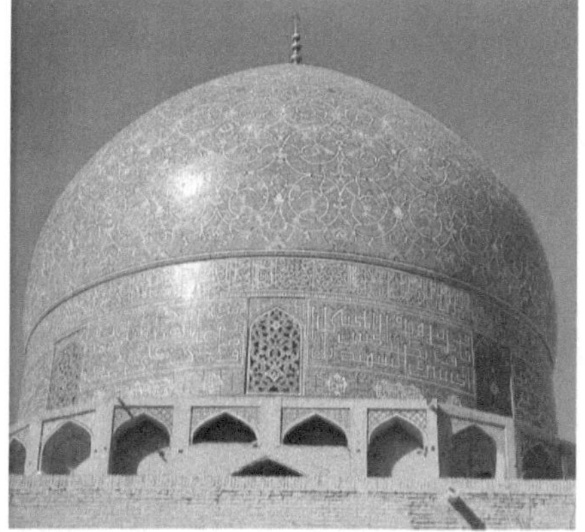

Illustration 13.4

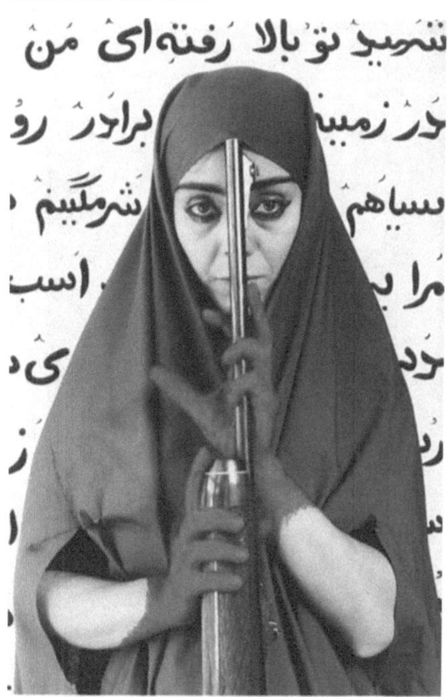

Illustration 13.5

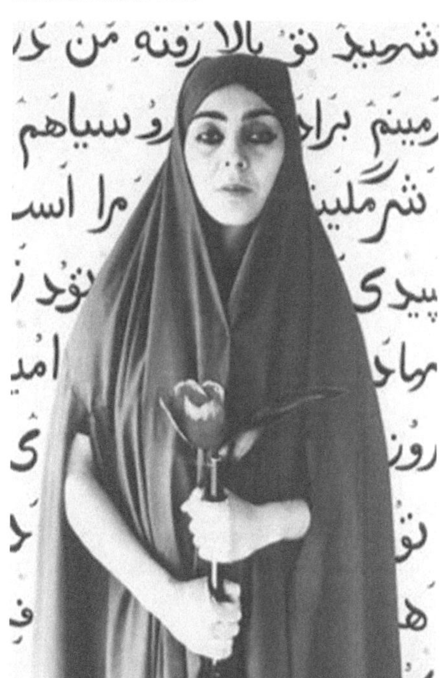

Illustration 13.6

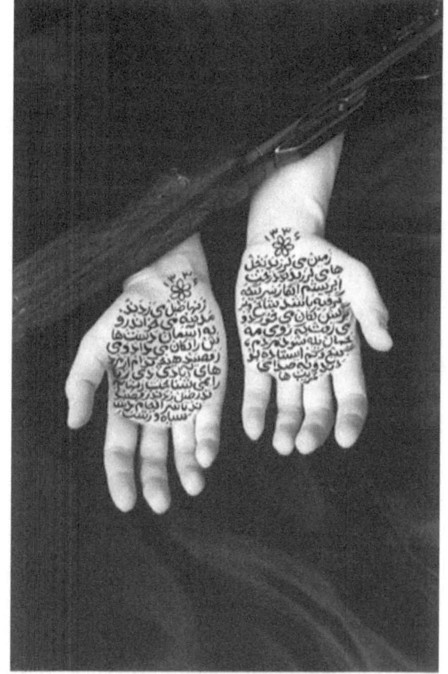

Illustration 13.7

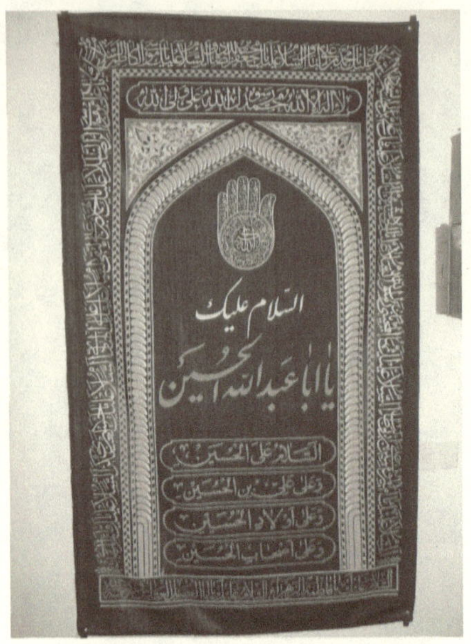

Illustration 13.8

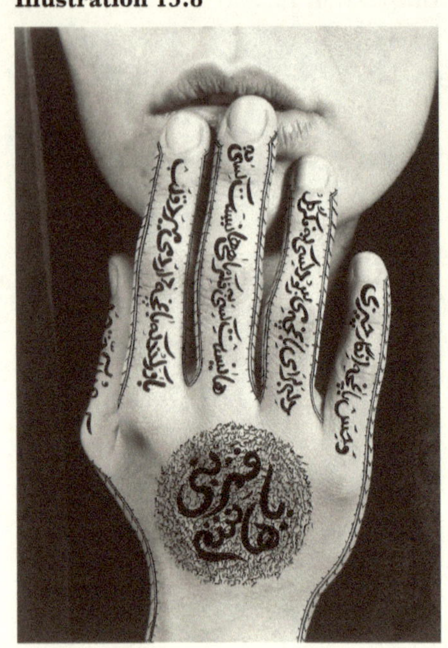

Illustration 13.9

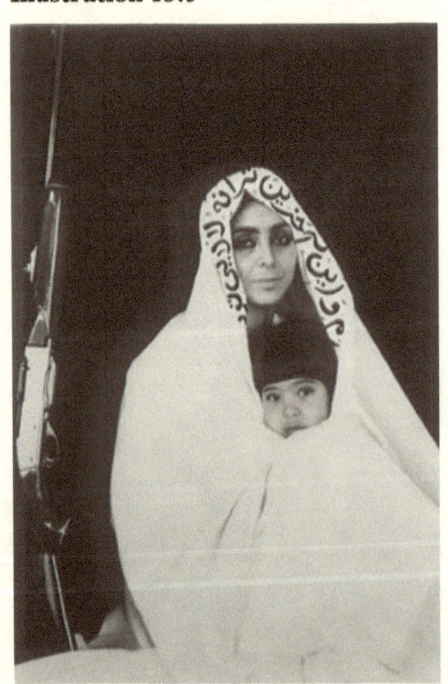

Illustration 13.10

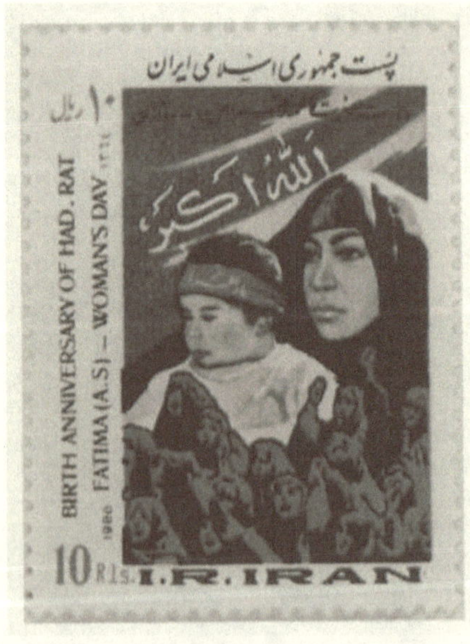

LIST OF CONTRIBUTORS

Julia Allerstorfer has been a guest curator of several exhibitions in Vienna, including *Preview of the Past: Contemporary Iranian Video Artists and Photographers* (2010) and *Crossing Boundaries – Transforming Identities? 6 Iranian Artists in Vienna* (2011). She has also published an interview with Iranian artist Shadafarin Ghadirian in *Kunst und Kirche* and co-authored "Schleier" (Veil) in *Linzer Schriften zur Frauenforschung* [The Linz compendium on Women's Studies], addressing veiling in contemporary Iranian art. She is currently a PhD candidate in the Department of Art and Philosophy at the Catholic Theological University Linz, Austria, writing on contemporary Iranian photography and video art in relation to self-representation.

Abbas Daneshvari received his PhD in art history from the University of California, Los Angeles and is presently professor of art history and chair of the Department of Art at California State University, Los Angeles. Daneshvari is the author of various books, including *Animal Symbolism in* Warqa wa Gulshah (1983), *Medieval Tomb Towers of Iran, An Iconographical Study* (1983), *Of Serpents and Dragons in Islamic Art* (2011) and *Amazingly Original: Contemporary Iranian art at Crossroads* (2012). He is also the author of numerous articles on contemporary Iranian and European art and the iconography of medieval Islamic art.

Alisa Eimen received her PhD from the University of Minnesota in 2006 and is associate professor of art history at Minnesota State University, Mankato. Her areas of research include nineteenth- and twentieth-century developments in art and architecture in Iran and South Asia as they relate to identity, ideology and debates surrounding modernism. Currently, she is extending her research to developments in contemporary mosque architecture in Germany.

Andrea D. Fitzpatrick, PhD, is a Canadian art historian, based in Ottawa. Her research explores performative strategies involving embodiment, gender and politics in contemporary international art. In 2012 she curated two exhibitions on Iranian lens-based art: "Ciphers: Tension with Tradition in Contemporary Iranian Photography" at the SAW Gallery in Ottawa and "Gender and Exposure in Contemporary Iranian Photography" held at Gallery 44 in Toronto, which was featured in the CONTACT Photography Festival. Currently, she is doing research for a book and traveling exhibition on the issues of martyrdom and mourning in contemporary Iranian art and visual culture from the 1979 Revolution to the present.

Hamid Keshmirshekan is an art historian, critic and visiting fellow at the Faculty of Oriental Studies, University of Oxford and editor-in-chief of the bilingual (English–Persian) quarterly, *Art Tomorrow*. He obtained his PhD in the history of art from SOAS, University of London and was awarded postdoctoral fellowships by the Barakat Trust in 2004–2005 and the British Academy, AHRC and ESRC in 2008, at Oxford University. He has been the organizer of several international conferences on the aspects of modern and contemporary Iranian art and contributed extensively in several publications. His latest edited book is *Amidst Shadow and Light: Contemporary Iranian Art and Artists* (2011).

Carmen Pérez González received her doctorate in art history from Leiden University, specializing in nineteenth-century local Iranian photography. She was awarded the International Convention of Asia Scholars (ICAS) Best PhD Thesis. As a photographer, Pérez González has published a catalogue of photographs of women workers in Asia, taken during a two-and-half-year journey, as well as several other portfolios. She has also organized exhibitions at the Science Museum in Barcelona and the Department of Culture of the Embassy of Spain in Prague. Since 2009 she has been working as a curatorial research fellow at the Museum of East Asian Art in Cologne and is currently preparing an exhibition and catalogue for the museum entitled *From Istanbul to Yokohama: The Camera Meets Asia, 1839–1900*. Pérez González has published several articles about nineteenth-century photography in Iran, India and Japan.

Babak Rahimi is associate professor of communication, culture and religious studies in the program for the study of religion at University of California, San Diego's Department of Literature. He received a PhD from the European University Institute, Florence, in October 2004. Rahimi has also studied at the University of Nottingham, where he obtained an MA in ancient and medieval philosophy, and the London School of Economics and Political Science, where he was a visiting fellow at the Department of Anthropology, 2000–2001. Rahimi has written many articles on culture, religion and politics, and regularly writes on contemporary Iraqi and Iranian politics. He has been the recipient of fellowships from the National Endowment for the Humanities and the Jean Monnet Fellowship at the European University Institute and was a senior fellow at the United States Institute of Peace, Washington, DC and a visiting scholar at the Internet Institute, University of Oxford. Rahimi's current research project is on the relationship between digital culture, politics and religion in postrevolutionary Iran.

Staci Gem Scheiwiller is an assistant professor of contemporary and modern art history at California State University Stanislaus. She received her PhD in the history of art and architecture from the University of California, Santa Barbara in 2009. Her field is modern and contemporary art with an emphasis in contemporary Iranian art and photography. Scheiwiller is focused on issues of modernity and modernism in Iran during the nineteenth and twentieth centuries and is currently researching constructions of gender, beauty and sexuality in nineteenth-century Iranian photography and cinema.

Mina Zand Siegel has degrees in medieval art history, medieval English literature and philosophy. She has taught at the City University of New York and New York University in the Department of Philosophy and the Department of Religion. She has been involved in the English division of the site Feminist School (www.feministschool.com) as a translator and contributor to the literary section. She also runs an English language blog, www.iranwrites.blogspot.com, which is devoted to Iranian culture and politics. She was the producer of Alireza Darvish's short animation film *What If Spring Does Not Come?* (2007), which was screened in prestigious film festivals around the world and received the Special Jury Prize at the International Film Festival in New York and at the 12th Ismailia International Festival in Cairo, both in 2008. Currently, Siegel is a writer, blogger, translator and cultural activist living in New York City. She is preparing a collection of her short stories based on the Iranian–American community.

David Simonowitz is assistant professor of Middle East studies at Pepperdine University, Malibu. He teaches visual culture of the modern Middle East, history of the Middle East and Islam, history of Islamic art and Arabic language. His research interests include architecture and urbanism, calligraphy and textual studies. He is a member of the steering committee of the Consultation on Space, Place, and Religious Meaning of the American Academy of Religion.

Donna Stein, associate director of the Wende Museum and Archive of the Cold War, has worked as an art historian, curator and essayist. In the mid-1970s, she was art advisor to the Private Secretariat of Her Majesty Queen Farah of Iran in preparation for the opening of the Tehran Museum of Contemporary Art. Stein has published articles on the history of nineteenth-century Iranian photography for the journals *History of Photography* and *Muqarnas*, as well as books and articles on contemporary Iranian artists, including Monir Farmanfarmaian, Ghasem Hajizadeh and Marco Gregorian. She has also published over 100 articles and more than 40 books and catalogues related to her curatorial interests.

www.ingramcontent.com/pod-product-compliance
Lightning Source LLC
LaVergne TN
LVHW091041080826
845145LV00002B/581

* 9 7 8 1 7 8 3 0 8 3 2 8 2 *